How Autocrats Compete

Most autocrats now hold unfair elections, yet how they compete in and manipulate them differs greatly. *How Autocrats Compete* advances a theory that explains variation in electoral authoritarian competition. Using case studies of Tanzania, Cameroon, and Kenya, along with broader comparisons from Africa, it finds that the kind of relationships autocrats foster with supporters and external actors matters greatly during elections. When autocrats can depend on credible ruling parties that provide elites with a level playing field and commit to wider constituencies, they are more certain in their own support and can compete in elections with less manipulation. Shelter from international pressure further helps autocrats deploy a wider range of coercive tools when necessary. Combining in-depth field research, within-case statistics, and cross-regional comparisons, Morse fills a gap in the literature by focusing on important variation in authoritarian institution building and international patronage. Understanding how autocrats compete sheds light on the comparative resilience and durability of modern authoritarianism.

Yonatan L. Morse is Assistant Professor of political science at the University of Connecticut. He is the author of articles on democracy, authoritarianism, and African politics that have appeared in the journals *World Politics, Comparative Politics, Democratization, Qualitative Research,* and *International Political Science Review.* His dissertation was awarded the Harold N. Glassman Award in Social Sciences from Georgetown University. He has also consulted for various government institutions and written for the *Washington Post* and the blog *Presidential Power.*

How Autocrats Compete

Parties, Patrons, and Unfair Elections in Africa

YONATAN L. MORSE

University of Connecticut

CAMBRIDGE
UNIVERSITY PRESS

University Printing House, Cambridge CB2 8BS, United Kingdom

One Liberty Plaza, 20th Floor, New York, NY 10006, USA

477 Williamstown Road, Port Melbourne, VIC 3207, Australia

314-321, 3rd Floor, Plot 3, Splendor Forum, Jasola District Centre, New Delhi - 110025, India

79 Anson Road, #06-04/06, Singapore 079906

Cambridge University Press is part of the University of Cambridge.

It furthers the University's mission by disseminating knowledge in the pursuit of education, learning and research at the highest international levels of excellence.

www.cambridge.org
Information on this title: www.cambridge.org/9781108465465
DOI: 10.1017/9781108596817

© Yonatan L. Morse 2019

First published 2019
First paperback edition 2020

A catalogue record for this publication is available from the British Library

ISBN 978-1-108-47476-4 Hardback
ISBN 978-1-108-46546-5 Paperback

Dedicated to my parents for instilling in me the love of a good debate and a sense of adventure.

Contents

Figures

Tables

Abbreviations

CND	Centre National de Documentation
CNU	Cameroon National Union
CPDM	Cameroon People's Democratic Movement
CPNC	Cameroon People's National Convention
COTU	Central Organization of Trade Unions
CHADEMA	Chama Cha Demokrasia na Maendeleo
CCM	Chama Cha Mapinduzi
CUF	Civic United Front
CUT	Cooperative Union of Tanzania
DP	Democratic Party
ELECAM	Elections Cameroon
PDCI	Democratic Party of Côte d'Ivoire
PDG	Democratic Party of Gabon
FORD	Forum for the Restortation of Democracy
FORD-A	Forum for the Restoration of Democracy-A
FORD-K	Forum for the Restoration of Democracy-K
IDEA	International Institute for Electoral Assistance
IMF	International Monetary Fund
IPPG	Inter-Parties Parliamentary Group
IRI	International Republican Institute
KADU	Kenyan African Democratic Union
KANU	Kenyan African National Union

KNDP	Kamerun National Democratic Party
KPU	Kenya People's Union
LDP	Liberal Democratic Party
MDR	Movement for the Defense of the Republic
MINAT	Ministry of Territorial Administration
FRELIMO	Mozambican Liberation Front
RENAMO	Mozambican National Resistance
NAK	National Alliance Party of Kenya
NCCR-M	National Coalition for Reconciliation and Reform
NCEC	National Convention Executive Council
NDC	National Democratic Congress
NDI	National Democratic Institute
NDP	National Democratic Party
NELDA	National Elections Across Democracy and Autocracy
FONADER	National Fund for Rural Development
NARC	National Rainbow Coalition
NUDP	National Union for Democracy and Progress
OTTU	Organization of Tanzanian Trade Unions
RPP	Peoples Rally for Progress
QED	Quality of Elections Data
RPT	Rally of Togolese People
BIR	Rapid Response Brigade
PDS	Senegalese Democratic Party
PS	Senegalese Socialist Party
SPPF	Seychelles People Progressive Front
SDF	Social Democratic Front
SCNC	South Cameroonian National Council
TAA	Tanganyika African Association
TANU	Tanganyikan African National Union
TLP	Tanzanian Labor Party
TYL	TANU Youth League
UPC	Union of Peoples of Cameroon
JUWATA	Union of Tanzanian Workers
UC	Cameroonian Union

UDC	Cameroon Democratic Union
UDP	United Democratic Party
UNIP	United National Independence Party
USAID	United States Agency for International Development
V-DEM	Varieties of Democracy
ZANU	Zimbabwe African National Union

Preface and Acknowledgments

This book is an examination of the ways by which autocrats compete in unfair elections, and the underlying factors that structure those contests. The ideas that guide it were first discussed in graduate seminars held back in 2007, at a time when terms like competitive and electoral authoritarianism were just coming into vogue. Now, over ten years later, the initial motivations for this study seem entirely justified, and perhaps more needed than ever. As an era of electoral authoritarianism continues to unfold, to understand the challenges that democracy faces we must also contend with the evolving and complex nature of authoritarian government. This is my modest attempt at shedding some light on these issues, and adding new perspectives on the intersection of authoritarian and electoral politics.

However, this book is also very much reflective of my own evolution as a scholar. I did not start out as an Africanist, nor had I even visited the continent prior to this project. I was initially inspired by my experiences living in the Middle East. In college I was an Islamic studies major, and spent a summer intensely studying Arabic in Jordan. When I entered graduate school, my initial impulse was to learn more about the challenges of democracy in the Middle East. I delved into the burgeoning literature on electoral authoritarianism and authoritarian institutions. The rise and fall of the Mexican Institutional Revolutionary Party (PRI) stood out in particular. For over seventy years the PRI dominated unfair elections without having to expend that much coercive effort. Instead, the PRI relied on a novel turn in authoritarian politics – institutionalized succession. I wondered whether there might be something like the Mexican PRI in the Middle East. It turned out that I was off by a few degrees of latitude, since it was in Tanzania and its ruling party CCM that I found the strongest parallels.

This set me off on a transformative path that reshaped the project as one that would be Africa-centric and firmly qualitative. In 2010, I left for a six-month trip to Tanzania. I spent countless hours speaking with average citizens and interviewing dozens of political elites who shared stories of living under unfair elections. My fieldwork expanded to Kenya, and in 2012 I visited the remains of the once mighty KANU party, by then relegated to a small compound behind a shopping mall. In 2015, I travelled to Cameroon and spent extensive time making inroads with regime insiders and confidants who could share stories of life in the ruling party. Many of the ideas I was discussing, such as the role of international actors, were specific to Africa and even just a select number of cases. My commitment turned to using comparative politics theory to inform our understanding of Africa, but also to using cases from a vastly diverse continent to inform comparative politics. In other words, I wanted to write a book that spoke to broader issues regarding modern authoritarianism, yet was still context driven. Interviews, thick description, and case studies became my key methodological tools.

These ten years of work in diverse and novel geographies could obviously not be accomplished without a tremendous generosity of time and spirit offered by so many. Whether it was detailed comments, help with fieldwork, or just a quick word of encouragement, I owe a true debt of gratitude to a global network. They pushed and prodded me to make the best book that I could write. I cannot say that the process was brief! But, with each additional step I learned not only about the painstaking process of generating knowledge, but also the importance of mentorship, collegiality, and friendship. The opportunity afforded me to write this book has been one of the greatest privileges of my life.

My first thanks must go out to the members of my dissertation committee. Daniel Brumberg challenged me to think about the concept of authoritarianism and the very paradigms that guide how we study the world. I was lucky to have him on my committee, and later as my boss at Georgetown's Democracy and Governance program. A draft of this research was written for Andrew Bennett's seminar on qualitative methods. He supported the project with razor sharp comments, and encouraged me to think seriously about qualitative and case-based research. Scott Taylor graciously joined my committee from Georgetown's African Studies program, and was instrumental in my conversion to "Africanist." Finally, my chair Marc Morjé Howard has been an endless supply of support and inspiration. He has been my champion and critic, and continues to serve as a role model for what it means to be a scholar, activist, and mentor.

Georgetown University is also responsible for many of the opportunities that made this project possible. The Department of Government provided funding for my first trip to Tanzania, and the African Studies Program hired me to be the field director for a study abroad program in Dar es Salaam in 2012. In 2013 I also became the associate director of Georgetown's Democracy and Governance program. Support from the affiliated Center for Democracy and Civil Society (CDACS) helped fund my 2015 fieldwork in Cameroon, and the position allowed me to make some important connections with the democracy promotion sector. I am grateful for the advocacy of my department chairs: George Shambaugh, Michael Bailey, and Charles King. Many other faculty at Georgetown have also been influential figures and deserve thanks: Harley Balzer, Matthew Carnes, David Edelstein, Desha Girod, Thane Gustafson, Steven Heydemann, Diana Kapiszweski, Stephen King, Eric Lagenbacher, Eusebio-Mujal Leon, Hans Noel, Lahra Smith, and Clyde Wilcox.

Many of these ideas first found their voice during graduate seminars populated by a tremendous group of peers. I am in awe of their professional accomplishments, and grateful for their input. My thanks go out to David Buckley, Anjali Dayal, Jennifer Raymond Dresden, Cory Julie, Paul Musgrave, Yu Ming Liu, Zaccary Ritter, and Hesham Sallam. I also thank the many students I had in seminars that I taught while faculty at Georgetown. I learned immensely from my students. They prodded me with great questions and feedback that sharpened my thinking and writing. Many of them have gone on to be inspirational new leaders in the democracy and governance sector.

Two critical platforms were fundamental for this project's success and were also sponsored by Georgetown University's Department of Government. First, Georgetown funded my participation in the Institute for Qualitative and Multi-Method Research (IQMR) at Syracuse in 2011. In classes led by David Collier, Thad Dunning, James Mahoney, and Jason Seawright I grounded myself methodologically and embraced a social science that accounts for complexity, contingency, and nuance. Second, Georgetown funded a book workshop held in April 2016. I was immensely lucky to have the participation of Daniella Donno, Sebastian Elischer, Jennifer Gandhi, Adrienne LeBas, and David Waldner. Their collective comments constitute some of the most substantial input into the contents of this book. Importantly, they taught me about the process of book writing itself. I am grateful to them for their generosity, and helping me find my voice as an author.

In 2016 I left Georgetown for my current academic home, the University of Connecticut, and I could not have asked for a more collegial and caring department. Specific thanks go to David Yaloff for his countless words of encouragement. Our coffee sessions at Atticus Books in New Haven were instrumental in working through my book writing neurosis. My colleagues Matthew Singer and Prakash Kashwan have also been kind enough to spend time with this project, and I must thank Cyrus Zirakzadeh for his very helpful title suggestions.

I have also benefitted from a circle of near and far colleagues in comparative politics, African studies, and the policy community. I am very thankful to the late Joel Barkan for his early support. Joel's ideas were a major inspiration to me, and he provided my first elite contacts in Tanzania and Kenya. I wish that he were here to see the final outcome. Leonardo Arriola, Matthijs Bogaards, Aurel Croissant, Olli Hellman, Barak Hoffman, Brendan Kendhammer, Kennedy Opalo, Lise Rakner, Rachel Beatty Riedl, Philip Roessler, Landry Signè, and Michael Wahman have all been extremely generous and commented on various parts of the project. Keith Jennings and Christopher Fumonyoh of the National Democratic Institute and Jerry Lavery of the National Endowment for Democracy were crucial resources during fieldwork. Michael Bernhard, Nic Cheeseman, Kim Yi Dionne, Henry Hale, Catherine Kelly, Steven Levitsky, Staffan Lindberg, Andreas Schedler, Dan Slater, Ben Smith, Nicolas van de Walle, and Lucan Way have all offered help and support along the way. I extend deep and sincere thanks to all of these amazing scholars.

Internationally there are countless people who shared their lives with me and offered unmatched generosity. Much gratitude goes to the departments of political science at the University of Dar as Salaam, the University of Nairobi, and the University of Yaoundé. I also thank the staff at Research and Education for Democracy in Tanzania and the faculty at the Institute for International Development in Nairobi. In Tanzania specific thanks go to Samuel Mushi (RIP), Max Mmuya, Raphael Ongagi, and Mwesiga Baregu. In Kenya thanks go to Adams Aloo, Njunga N'gethe, Ken Okoth, and Michael Chege. In Cameroon I thank Norbert Fru Suh and Veronique Ntamack. Special thanks go to my research assistants: Samuel Bille (Cameroon) and Emmanuel Segere

(Tanzania). You made my life so much easier, but you also opened up your homes to me and gave me new perspectives into your country.

The process of book writing is lengthy, and I am so lucky to have had the fantastic support of Cambridge University Press. My thanks go to Sara Doskow and her excellent team who have guided me step by step through this process. I am also thankful to the anonymous reviewers who took significant time from their schedules to write in-depth and boundlessly useful comments.

No work is possible without the encouragement and support of family. My thanks go out to all the Morses, Eisenbergs, Meonis, Meads, and Klags who have sustained me with good company, great food, and tremendous love. This book is dedicated to both of my parents: my father, Rabbi Alan Morse, for always being there to have a deep conversation about everything from politics to the Rambam, and my mother Deborah Morse for her grammatical exactitude, and for telling me a long time ago during a critical moment in my life to embrace adventure. Finally, I owe so much to my wife Erin, the bravest and kindest person I know. The journey has been thrilling and at times daunting. None of it was possible without you at my side.

I

The Puzzle of Electoral Authoritarian Competition

> No party which limits its membership to a clique can ever free itself from
> fear of overthrow from those it has excluded.
> —Julius Nyerere (*Freedom and Socialism*, 1968)

Autocracies now regularly hold multiparty elections that do not live
up to commonly held democratic standards. Persistent exclusion, censorship, fraud, and at times violence push many regimes into what is
increasingly identified as *electoral authoritarianism* (Schedler 2006a,
2013). This major global development has opened up a whole new set of
fascinating questions into the dynamics and endurance of authoritarian
rule. What benefits do elections bring autocrats? Under what conditions
do elections sustain rather than undermine authoritarian regimes? Do
electoral authoritarian regimes sow the seeds of democratization? While
these questions largely address whether electoral autocracies are likely
to withstand elections, absent is a clearer account of how such regimes
actually compete in them. Indeed, two electoral authoritarian regimes
might endure for similar periods of time, but differ greatly in terms of
how much popular support they can muster at the ballot box and what
degree of manipulation they employ. These differences in how autocrats
compete have not been properly understood, but in fact inform us greatly
about how contemporary authoritarianism functions.

In this book I argue that how autocrats compete does not depend
primarily on their manipulative skills or cleverness, but rather on the
relationships they foster over time with elites, citizens, and external
actors. With an eye toward the African experience, I contend that electoral authoritarian competition is influenced primarily by the ability of

regimes to sustain ruling institutions that foster stable and credible relationships with supporters, and secondarily by the postures of international actors toward democratic norms. It is an argument derived from a specific subset of African cases, and rooted in the role of historical legacy and variation in the investments authoritarians make in their formal ruling institutions, namely parties. It is also an argument that clarifies under what conditions and how external actors influence electoral authoritarian competition.

The following examples illustrate what I mean by differences in electoral authoritarian competition. In Tanzania, Chama Cha Mapinduzi (CCM) and its predecessor the Tanganyika African National Union (TANU) have governed the country since independence as a single-party regime. After elections were restored in 1995, CCM sailed to easy victories, at times winning upwards of 80 percent of the vote. Notably, it contested elections with relative ease. Election observers and opposition parties have noted occasional polling irregularities like missing ballots, instances of intimidation, and media bias. Likewise, the election management body and voter registration process has repeatedly come under scrutiny. However, while Tanzanian elections are not clearly democratic, they are far from the stereotype of sham elections seen elsewhere. On the mainland, fraud is not pervasive, and the opposition is not subject to draconian measures like blanket arrests or excessive state violence. This was true even in 2010 and 2015, when the regime appeared vulnerable for the first time in a decade to new opposition challengers, yet still maintained a firm grip on the legislature and won 63 and 58 percent of the presidential vote respectively. In Tanzania, elections are relatively open if one-sided affairs.

This contrasts with the multiparty experience elsewhere in Africa. Across the continent, Cameroon also transitioned to elections in 1992 after a prolonged period of single-party rule. As in Tanzania, the ruling Cameroon People's Democratic Movement (CPDM) has, in some form or another, led the country since independence. However, in this case multiparty elections clearly leveled a more serious challenge. In 1992, the CPDM temporarily lost its legislative majority, and sitting president Paul Biya could only draw victory with a simple plurality of voters. At the same time observers noted severe flaws in the electoral process, including blatant ballot stuffing, harsh media restrictions, and significant state violence. These serious issues with electoral integrity persisted in subsequent elections, but also appeared to pay off. By 2008 Biya had abolished term limits, and in 2011 he won a controversial fourth term with 78 percent of the vote. Two years later the CPDM won 85 percent of the legislative seats. Harsh manipulation has therefore consistently sustained the regime's dominating electoral performances.

Such manipulation is not, however, always a successful strategy. Just to the north of Tanzania the Kenyan African National Union (KANU) likewise made the transition from single-party rule to multiparty elections in the early 1990s. Once again, elections were comparatively more challenging, and in 1992 KANU only won 53 percent of the legislative seats while president Daniel arap Moi eked by with just 37 percent of the presidential vote. As in Cameroon, starker levels of repression accompanied elections that ranged from blatant electoral fraud, manipulation of Kenya's money supply, and shocking ethnic violence that killed and displaced thousands. However, while manipulation and violence persisted during the 1997 election, the outcome was once again very close. By 2002, the electoral process had improved slightly, but the regime could still not draw substantial electoral support and dramatically lost to an opposition coalition. Manipulation only helped KANU win razor-thin victories, but it did not secure stronger vote shares.

While all three of these cases are considered examples of electoral authoritarianism, their divergent response to the challenge of multiparty elections raises some important questions. When is an electoral authoritarian regime likely to use more manipulation to win elections? When is manipulation likely to be a successful strategy and ensure substantial vote share? If a regime can mobilize significant voter support with comparatively less manipulation, what does that tell us about the sources of authoritarian resilience and durability? Indeed, by giving more attention to the specific manner in which autocracies compete in elections, and not just simply whether they win them or not, we must also appreciate the diverse resources and capabilities autocrats bring with them to the electoral arena, as well as their relative ability to deploy those tools.

For these three cases, which are central to this book's arguments, legacies of authoritarian institution building are a critical factor. Tanzania's regime was armed with what I call a *credible ruling party*. It is a party that emerged from a specific historical juncture, but developed features that stabilized how elites and voters engaged with the regime, and consequently helped secure longer-term and more enduring commitments from them. This allowed Tanzania to contest elections with stronger assurances of support *prior* to the election, and therefore to compete with less overt manipulation. Cameroon and Kenya lacked such credible institutions, and therefore faced much higher levels of elite and voter discord prior to elections. Absent an institutional platform to interact with supporters, these regimes had to deploy harsher manipulation and find ways to coopt or coerce opponents. However, the utility of this manipulative strategy, particularly as it plays out in Africa, is constrained by international actors. The direction of *international patronage* determined the range of tools an autocrat could employ, and whether this translated electorally. In Kenya, international patronage tilted toward democracy, while in Cameroon it supported autocracy.

In the next sections of this introductory chapter I discuss the question of electoral authoritarian competition in broader terms, and in the African context specifically. I overview some of the major approaches to studying electoral authoritarian politics, and make an argument for research that looks beyond the question of regime survival, but rather approaches the specific question of electoral authoritarian competition with contextually driven and case-based analysis. I outline in more detail my own explanation and discuss how this argument contributes to the literature on authoritarian institution building and provides insights into the comparative resilience of authoritarian regimes. Finally, I discuss the book's research strategy and specify how it is situated in current thinking about qualitative and case-study methods.

DEFINING THE PUZZLE OF ELECTORAL AUTHORITARIAN COMPETITION

Electoral authoritarianism has become the modal form of nondemocratic politics in the post–Cold War era. For a significant period of time regimes that combined elements of democratic and autocratic practice merited added adjectives to their democratic credentials. Regimes were often categorized as "semi-democratic," "new democracies," "illiberal democracies," or more broadly merely as "hybrid."[1] To claim that these perspectives were completely teleological or simply suffered from a "fallacy of electoralism" is an overstatement (Karl 1990). Nonetheless, in previous work there was a much deeper concern with how remnants of authoritarianism were holding democratic progress back, rather than how little regimes had changed or how elections (and other hybrid institutions) actually benefitted autocrats. Consequently, the transition to the study of electoral authoritarianism reflects both the end of a paradigmatic way

---

[1] Space precludes a full listing of this early wave of literature, but see the work in Collier and Levitsky (1997), Zakaria (1997), Rose and Shin (2001), Brumberg (2002), and Ottaway (2003).

of thinking about regime trajectories, and the inauguration of a new set of research questions into the study of contemporary authoritarianism (Carothers 2002).

Of course elections under authoritarian conditions are not new phenomena, and the question remains whether electoral authoritarianism reflects a new regime type rather than just "Babel in democratization studies" (Armony and Schamis 2005). For instance, in Juan Linz's classic work on authoritarianism he distinguished limited pluralism and popular mobilization as defining features of autocracy (2000). Likewise, studies of single-party African states in the 1960s and 1970s often emphasized the role of controlled and uncompetitive elections as tools of authoritarian survival.[2] The literature on transitions from authoritarianism highlighted the role of elections in the process of regime liberalization. While elections were often restored in a very narrow sense – either locally or solely for legislatures – they laid the groundwork for further strides toward democratic transition (O'Donnell, Schmitter, and Whitehead 1986). But, it was not until the end of the Cold War that regular, contested, and unfair elections became a reality across such a broad swathe of previously authoritarian countries (Roessler and Howard 2009). In many ways multiparty elections have become a *fait accompli* of the modern era.

But authoritarian elections, in the words of Andreas Schedler, are also a "Janus-faced" affair (2013). Elections do more than just reveal regime weaknesses, and they are not simply façade events or window dressings to appease international donors. At times autocrats actually appear to derive strength from elections, and are able to mobilize diverse resources that help them compete (Gandhi and Lust-Okar 2009). On the other hand, elections might expose and exacerbate critical vulnerabilities that can be an autocrat's ultimate undoing. Indeed, autocrats often play a two-leveled game, whereby manipulation of the electoral process to ensure victory leads to unforeseen costs elsewhere. Step too far and an authoritarian regime risks signaling weakness rather than strength. Pull back too much, and new opposition parties might take advantage of the more even playing field. Put more succinctly, multiparty elections have a varied and not necessarily one-sided impact on authoritarian politics.

Many studies address this ambiguity by distinguishing between electoral authoritarian outcomes that are "competitive" rather than "hegemonic."

---

[2] The early studies of single-party regimes in the developing world often addressed the role of elections. See for example, Zolberg (1966), Morgenthau (1967), Coleman and Rosberg (1970), and Collier (1982). The most comprehensive early account of authoritarian elections can be found in Hermet, Rouquie, and Rose (1978).

The language used is notoriously unclear, but it is a sincere attempt to convey valid information about the phenomenon.[3] A key point of debate is over the connotation of the term "competitive." In some studies, competitive refers to the actual process of contestation, or the rules and restrictions that shape whether voters can translate their preferences into actual outcomes (Levitsky and Way 2010). According to this understanding, competitive regimes are more open and less manipulative than hegemonic regimes. On the other hand, competitive can refer to the electoral outcome, or the capacity of participants to effectively mobilize voters (Roessler and Howard 2009; Schedler 2013). This is often captured in measures of vote-share or regime longevity. In competitive regimes electoral competition is more meaningful, while hegemonic regimes correspond more with Giovanni Sartori's understanding of the term: the perception that alternation is near impossible (Sartori 1976). To borrow a sport's analogy, competition can signify the rules of the game or the player's athletic abilities.

In part because of this ambiguity, much of the scholarship does not appreciate the full range of outcomes by which electoral authoritarianism can differ. Take for example perhaps the most important volume on the subject in the past decade, Steven Levitsky and Lucan Way's *Competitive Authoritarianism* (2010). Levitsky and Way make a distinction between "stable" and "unstable" competitive authoritarianism. Stable authoritarianism refers to when an incumbent autocrat has not yet lost power at the ballot box, while an unstable regime is one that has succumbed to electoral turnover but still falls short of a democracy. Since Tanzania and Cameroon have survived elections for similar periods of time, by Levitsky and Way's definition both are considered cases of stable electoral authoritarianism even though they have contested elections by very different means in terms of processes and outcomes.

Other studies of electoral authoritarianism similarly focus on regime survival, and treat the ambiguous question of competition as the independent rather than the dependent variable. For instance, Roessler and Howard find that competitive authoritarian regimes are ephemeral and tend to tip toward minimal democracy or authoritarian retrenchment

---

[3] For instance, Beatriz Magaloni (2006) and Kenneth Greene (2007) use the terms "hegemonic" and "dominant" interchangeably to connote long-lasting electoral authoritarian regimes in Mexico. Aili Mari Tripp distinguishes between "semi-democratic" and "semi-authoritarian" regimes (2010). Axel Hadenius and Jan Teorell use the categories "dominant party multiparty" and "pure limited multiparty" to make similar distinctions (2007). Within the African context Nicolas van de Walle refers to "status quo" regimes versus "contested autocracies" (2002).

(2009). Jason Brownlee argues that competitive regimes are more likely than hegemonic regimes to be followed by democracy (2009). Likewise, Andreas Schedler shows that competitive regimes are more sensitive to factors like public protest (2013). In each of these cited examples the term competitive invokes electoral outcomes, not the process of contestation or the rules of the game. There is little discussion of why some regimes dominate election outcomes to begin with, or why electoral dominance might be sustained with more or less manipulation of the electoral process.[4]

Thinking of competition as a multi-dimensional concept is more accurate empirically and theoretically. Undoubtedly there is a relationship between uncompetitive processes of contestation and uncompetitive electoral outcomes. Indeed, there is scholarship that suggests that electoral violence, which makes the electoral process less competitive, is primarily a reaction to perceptions of electoral weakness (Hafner-Burton, Hyde, and Jablonski 2014). By contrast, one can imagine that when regimes are able to secure substantial vote share this reflects stability, and therefore reduces the need for heavy manipulation. But, as this book will demonstrate the empirical record is actually quite mixed. Only at times is heavy manipulation a losing strategy, and dwindling electoral prospects do not always inevitably lead to repression. For instance, prior to its defeat in Ghana, the National Democratic Congress (NDC) accepted more open contestation even as it was seriously challenged at the polls. Nor are all dominating regimes less coercive, as seen most clearly in the contrast between Tanzania and Cameroon.

But more importantly, differences in electoral competition reflect variation in the underlying features that sustain regimes. When an autocrat can contest and dominate elections with relatively less manipulation, this signals a fundamentally different kind of authoritarian regime than one that must manipulate heavily to achieve similar electoral results. I claim that in Tanzania this kind of electoral authoritarian outcome is possible because the regime can tap into a wider spectrum of benefits offered by ruling parties. By contrast, if a regime needs to manipulate heavily to generate vote-share, this reflects a vulnerability that might be rooted in the absence of institutional guarantees of support, or other discriminating factors. As discussed in the cases of Cameroon and Kenya, the longer-term success of more repressive electoral authoritarianism depended on whether an international actor lent a helping hand or kept regimes under

---

[4] The focus on authoritarian survival versus breakdown also permeates the literature on authoritarian institutions. See Gandhi (2008) and Geddes (1999).

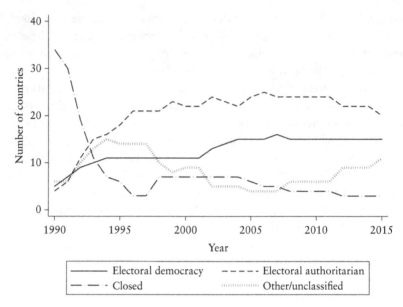

FIGURE 1.1. *Growth in African electoral authoritarian regimes (1990–2016)*
Note: Countries are considered electoral authoritarian if they hold at least two consecutive and contested elections for national executives and legislatures, and their Freedom House Political Rights score in the year prior was above 2 and their Polity IV score was below 7. A regime is democratic if their Freedom House score was below 3 or their Polity IV score was above 6. A regime is closed if it does not hold multiparty elections, and is other/unclassified if it is in a state of conflict or has not held two consecutive elections.
Sources: Freedom House (Various), Polity IV (Various)

more duress. But, only by focusing on a multifaceted notion of competition can we observe this underlying variation.

The study of electoral authoritarianism competition is particularly relevant for the context of sub-Saharan Africa. Since 1990 there has been a dramatic growth in this regime type, and notable divergence in patterns of electoral contestation. While in 1990 there were only four African countries that held regular multiparty elections – Botswana, Mauritius, Senegal, and Zimbabwe – by decade's end there were only a handful of countries that did not. Yet, while this transition to multiparty elections was meaningful in many important ways, as the new era unfolded it became evident that African party systems were evolving in diverse and often nondemocratic ways. Some literature assessed the "puzzle" of Africa's new multiparty politics through the lens of party system institutionalization (Kuenzi and Lambright 2001, 2005; Manning

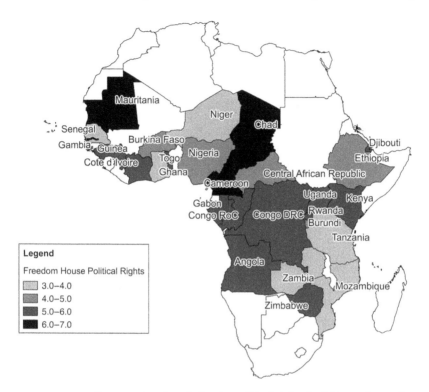

FIGURE 1.2. *Cross-national variation in political rights in African electoral authoritarian regimes (1990–2016)*
Information on each specific country can be found in Appendix A.
Source: Freedom House (Various)

2005; Mozaffar and Scarrit 2005). Recently, there has been more systematic analysis of African electoral regimes through the distinct language of electoral authoritarianism (Lynch and Crawford 2011; Bogaards 2013). Figure 1.1 summarizes this trend by depicting the growth in African electoral authoritarianism between 1990 and 2015.

Within the population of African electoral authoritarianism there are considerable differences. Figure 1.2 maps the average Freedom House Political Rights score in all African electoral authoritarian regimes identified between 1990 and 2016. While a fuller range of manipulative options is discussed in Chapter 3, the Political Rights score provides a useful initial proxy that captures the degree to which the electoral process is competitive and more open contestation is tolerated. There is clearly a spectrum of restrictions on political activity that ranges from more repressive conditions in Cameroon, Chad, and Mauritania, to more tolerable

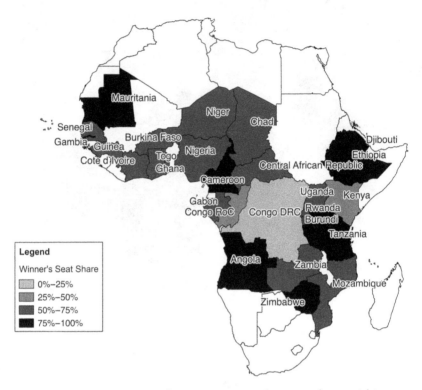

FIGURE 1.3. *Cross-national variation in incumbent seat share in African*
electoral authoritarian regimes (1990–2016)
Information on each specific country can be found in Appendix A.
Source: African Elections Database (Various)

environments in Mozambique, Senegal, and Tanzania. Figure 1.3 looks
at the average legislative seat share in African electoral authoritarian
regimes, which provides a comparable measure across presidential and
parliamentary systems of the competitiveness of outcomes. Once again,
there is variation in the ability of incumbents to generate strong and dominating vote shares. Looking at these two measures simultaneously, we get
a much more nuanced view of African electoral authoritarian competition.

The purpose of this book is to better explicate this diversity of electoral
authoritarian experience. I define electoral authoritarian competition as
a combination of the extent and severity of restrictions on free competition, and the ability of incumbents to generate large vote shares. Electoral
authoritarianism in Tanzania combines overwhelming vote shares (an
uncompetitive outcome) with lower degrees of manipulation (a competitive process). This makes it a fairly odd specimen that I term a *tolerant*

hegemony. This contrasts with the experiences of a case like Cameroon where heavier manipulation generates electoral hegemony, making it a *repressive hegemony*. There are also cases where repression does not pay electoral dividends as in Kenya's *repressive non-hegemony* between 1992 and 2002, and cases not discussed here where lower degrees of manipulation do not coincide with larger vote shares as in Ghana's *tolerant non-hegemony* between 1992 and 2000. The current literature on electoral authoritarianism and African politics does not generally address or offer a satisfying account of this variation.

EXPLAINING ELECTORAL AUTHORITARIAN OUTCOMES

In *Competitive Authoritarianism*, Steven Levitsky and Lucan Way highlight a set of international and domestic factors that allows them to distinguish between stable authoritarianism, unstable authoritarianism, and democratization. According to Levitsky and Way, electoral authoritarian stability is rooted in the ability of autocrats to wield significant organizational power to muster elite and voter support and deter emerging political opposition. Organizational power, which consists of party, state, and economic capacity, is itself influenced by the degree to which international actors hold leverage over poorer and more aid-dependent countries. Electoral authoritarianism endures when either an international actor does not stop autocrats from rebuilding their organizational basis, or when they do not use their leverage to keep autocrats from utilizing their organizational tools. Notably, international leverage is considered a structural condition, meaning it explains a balance of power between international actors and electoral authoritarian regimes.

In addition to my focus on electoral competition, my argument differs from Levitsky and Way in two other important ways. First, I more keenly examine the internal workings of ruling parties and namely how they foster credible relationships with elites and citizens. In Levitsky and Way it is unclear what aspects of organizational power matter more or less in different contexts. Rather, all dimensions of organizational power are conceptually equivalent. Electoral authoritarian regimes sustained by strong ruling parties are equated with those that are rooted in powerful states or oil wealth, simply because both might endure for similar periods of time. Similarly, individual elements of organizational power are shortchanged for the sake of broader cross-regional comparisons. This is quite evident in the discussion of ruling parties, which views them as predominantly administrative tools that help regimes coerce, coopt, and mobilize voters. While factors like elite cohesion are mentioned, there is not enough reference to the literature on ruling parties as institutions that foster credible exchange, and can deter rather than just react to opposition (Gandhi 2008; Magaloni 2008). Peering deeper into the "black box" of authoritarian institutions is precisely what is needed to understand differences in electoral authoritarian competition.

Second, I show that the motivations of international actors and their level of commitment are in fact dynamic, not static. Levitsky and Way make references to the vulnerabilities of target states and the presence of overt conflicting foreign policy goals as the essential components of international leverage. While these structural conditions undoubtedly shape international behavior, the proof is in the proverbial empirical pudding. There is now a substantial literature to draw on that addresses the mixed record of foreign aid and conditionality (Dunning 2004; Knack 2004; Brown 2005; Wright 2009), democracy assistance (Finkel, Pérez-Liñán, and Seligson 2007), election observation (Hyde 2011; Kelley 2012b), and diplomatic pressure (Donno 2013a). This literature suggests that notions of the national interest evolve, and the consequences of international engagement are often much more marginal. International actors might not always be able or willing to push decisively on questions of democratic reform, but a closer examination of their actual range of activities can shed light on how they impact electoral authoritarian competition.

My focus on credible ruling parties and international patronage therefore builds on Levitsky and Way, but provides a much more nuanced and accurate account of the specific puzzle of electoral authoritarian competition. In the next sub-sections, I review some rival approaches to the study of electoral authoritarianism: the role of opposition behavior and coordination, state capacity and patronage politics, and economic performance. I argue that while this literature is useful for studying electoral authoritarian survival, it is not a primary cause of differences in electoral competition and not always applicable in Africa. Some of these factors are further discussed in the upcoming chapters as controls or intervening variables, but they are not a part of my main explanation.

Opposition Behavior and Coordination

Some scholars attribute variation in electoral authoritarian outcomes to the decisions and actions of major opposition actors. In particular, the literature notes three factors that appear to matter: the extent to which opposition parties institutionalize, their ability to foster coalitions, and their choice of whether to participate or not in elections. Despite severe resource asymmetries, opposition parties do devise different models of party building and political action. Weak party and party system institutionalization is believed to limit democratic accountability, and therefore facilitate electoral authoritarian survival (Mainwaring and Scully 1995; Randall and Svåsand 2002a). Valerie Bunce and Sharon Wolchik argue that smart campaigning and coordination between opposition parties and civil society groups were instrumental for the success of the major color revolutions of Eastern Europe (2011). Opposition coalitions are also important factors that facilitate "liberalizing electoral outcomes," whereby an incumbent's vote share drops, or there are forced changes to the rules of contestation (Howard and Roessler 2006; Donno 2013b; Wahman 2013). The consensus on boycotts is more mixed. In the short term they have fairly negative consequences for competition, and lead to higher incumbent vote shares (Lindberg 2006b). However, as a longer-term strategy they might ultimately create legitimacy issues that force more regime liberalization (Smith 2013).

These issues are particularly relevant for electoral authoritarianism in Africa, where the weakness of opposition parties is generally seen as detrimental to democratic reform (Kuenzi and Lambright 2005). The standard lament is that African opposition parties lack physical organization, are nonexistent between elections, and are mere vehicles for expelled elites to regain access to power (Rakner and van de Walle 2009). Often African opposition parties are jokingly referred to as "briefcase" parties that fail to provide basic political functions and are narrowly ethnic (Posner 2005; Ferree 2010; Elischer 2013). Consequently, many African party systems are volatile, and opposition party fragmentation and party hopping are quite common (Kuenzi and Lambright 2001; Randall and Svåsand 2002b; Manning 2005; Mozaffar and Scarrit 2005). The record on opposition participation is also quite mixed, and it is notably difficult for elites of different ethnic backgrounds to form credible and lasting coalitions (Lindberg 2009b; Arriola 2012). Using an updated data set of African elections originally created by Staffan Lindberg, I calculate that in just 20 percent of electoral authoritarian elections do opposition parties form coalitions, and in 18 percent of elections opposition parties completely boycott the process.[5]

---

[5] This data comes from Lindberg (2006a) and has been updated by the author to range from 1990 to 2015.

The scarcity of viable opposition parties in Africa makes it difficult to use this variable to explain variation in electoral authoritarian contestation. Only on rare occasion could African opposition parties bank on historical linkages with preexisting organizational bases like unions to form more credible alternatives (LeBas 2011). Many of the stable parties and party systems are found in democratic regimes, many of which actually had authoritarian origins (Riedl 2014). But, in electoral authoritarian regimes it is tough to find institutionalized and coordinated oppositions. Most opposition parties were created *ex nihilo* and remained relatively weak. This is true in the three major cases discussed here. The initial wave of opposition parties in Tanzania, Kenya, and Cameroon were generally elite-driven and founded by former regime insiders. In each case there were major splits and rivalries, and many parties were confined to specific regions. During the electoral authoritarian period, forceful coordination across opposition parties was nearly nonexistent, with the notable exception of Kenya in 2002 and Tanzania in 2015. While there are more nuanced differences in the comparative strengths and weaknesses of opposition parties, it is hard to see this as a primary causal factor explaining differences in electoral competition.

Beyond this empirical reality, there are also challenging issues with regard to the direction of causality. Opposition party weakness is as much derivative of the competitive environment in which they compete, rather than the actual cause of it. Repressive conditions and overpowering executives limit the opportunities for opposition parties to plant deeper roots. In many instances this creates strong incentives for "competitive clientelism," and for parties to remain smaller so they can signal their loyalty to the incumbent in order to secure continued access to privileges of the state (van de Walle 2003; Lust-Okar 2009). This is evident in Kenya, where the National Rainbow Coalition (NARC) of 2002 did not really take form until a wave of elite defection severely handicapped KANU (van de Walle 2006). Likewise, it is not on the face of it clear how stronger and more coordinated opposition parties actually influence competition. A stronger opposition might incur a repressive reaction from the incumbent, but by the same token might force regime concessions.

State Capacity and Patronage Politics

Another approach to the study of electoral authoritarianism looks at the central role of state capacity. High capacity states are considered those that can marshal strong extractive, bureaucratic, and coercive institutions like tax authorities, civil administrations, and military units to stabilize autocratic rule (Gryzmala-Busse 2008; Slater 2010; Anderson, Moller, and Rorbaek 2014). This is largely because higher capacity states increase the range of carrots and sticks available to autocrats to deter opponents and maintain ruling coalitions. For instance, electoral authoritarian regimes might utilize their administrative capacity to coordinate electoral fraud across the country (Seeberg 2014), or use exclusion and violence to respond to political challenges (Levitsky and Way 2010). A state's administrative and extractive capacities can also strengthen patronage networks by increasing the amount of resources available to distribute, or by diverting them to supportive constituencies (Anderson, Moller, and Rorbaek 2014). Powerful states are often inherited or captured by autocrats, and are generally fueled by monopolies over crucial economic resources (Greene 2010; Levitsky and Way 2010). Importantly, a powerful autocratic state need not exhibit Weberian norms of bureaucratic professionalism, but be merely available to autocrats. This means that autocratic states are often fueled by public corruption, or can seem weak on certain indicators of state capacity (Darden 2008).[6]

Indeed, the remarkable endurance of electoral authoritarianism in Africa is puzzling given the low scores on state capacity the continent regularly receives. Most African states are colonial inheritances, which bequeathed fairly limited bureaucracies, disorganized militaries, and a very narrow tax base (Herbst 2000). By most standard measures of state capacity, Africa persistently rates very low. For instance, the World Bank's Statistical Capacity Index, a proxy often used to measure a state's administrative capacity, is just 57.58 in Africa while in other regions (excluding the United States and Western Europe) it is 69.4. The average military spending per capita in Africa is $37.87, while elsewhere it is closer to $270. Rates of taxation in Africa and the share of taxes as a proportion of GDP are also generally lower than in other regions (World Bank 2016).[7]

One explanation for the endurance of electoral authoritarianism despite weaker states is that it is actually the power of presidents vis-à-vis

---

[6] Another perspective on the question of state capacity looks at the differentiation between regime and state, and views state capacity as a configuration of factors that improves the transparency and regularity of state operations. This approach is generally more concerned with the role of state capacity in the process of democratic consolidation. See Linz and Stepan (1996), Rose and Shin (2001), and Bratton and Chang (2006).

[7] Within the population of Africa's electoral authoritarian regimes there appears to be no relationship between these measures of state capacity and regime longevity. State capacity in electoral authoritarian regimes with tenures of over ten years is statistically indistinguishable from regimes with tenures less than ten years (author's calculations).

other political institutions that matters, rather than the absolute power of the state. In some contexts, this is referred to as "hyper-presidentialism," but in Africa it is most often termed the "neo-patrimonial" nature of the African state (Jackson and Rosberg 1982; van de Walle 2003; Arriola 2009). The study of patronage and neo-patrimonialism has a long pedigree in the Africanist scholarship. Broadly speaking, in these systems presidents personalize power and overwhelmingly centralize access to limited state resources. These resources are then distributed selectively to accommodate elites that generally represent important social or ethnic groups (Arriola 2009; Baldwin 2015). Formal state institutions are deliberately weakened so that elites can generate wealth from their positions of prestige to maintain their own clientelistic networks (Chabal and Daloz 1999). During elections it is expected that elites will utilize their networks and mobilize supportive communities. Since African voters are largely rural, they are also fairly demobilized and cheap. For opposition parties, powerful incumbent patronage networks limit their own appeal and ability to cooperate. Therefore, when presidents are left untamed by factors like legislatures, constitutions, or term limits, they can more easily win elections (Posner and Young 2007; Barkan 2009b; Cheeseman 2010).

While Africa provides few clear examples of demonstrably powerful authoritarian states, the more limited state itself still seems to matter for electoral authoritarian outcomes. Indeed, the decline in the availability of patronage resources obtained from the state was a significant factor that led to the political opening of the early 1990s (Bratton and van de Walle 1997). Since most African countries were low-income and indebted to international lenders, they could be forced to liberalize state-led economies and reform their public sector. Many countries were able to skirt wholehearted reform, but this simply meant that the state continued to hold influence in maintaining neo-patrimonial regimes (van de Walle 2001). Similarly, while it is difficult to find an African country with an intelligence service that rivals say the KGB, there are notable differences in coercive capacity. Most obviously, former French colonies were more frequently home to presidential guards and *gendarmeries* that could later be used by regimes against civilians (Gregory 2000).

But, can the role of the state independently explain differences in the quality of contestation, and not just regime survival? This book makes two major arguments regarding this point. First, since in comparative perspective African states are weaker and more enmeshed in international relations, the real question is why were some electoral authoritarian regimes able to leverage their limited states while others were not? I contend that it is not so much the slight differences in African state capacity that mattered, but real differences in how international actors engaged with African states at the end of the Cold War. Second, state capacity cannot explain differences in the quality of contestation. In many ways the exercise of state capacity to coerce responds to dissent but does not deter it. In the language of autocratic politics, it is useful for resolving vertical rather than horizontal threats (Svolik 2012). When an electoral authoritarian regime turns repressive this reflects an actual physical ability to respond to challenges with violence, but also the absence of mechanisms that might have limited the need for violence to begin with. I argue that credible ruling parties are one of the only institutions that can serve this function. And indeed, more credible ruling parties generally mean that the power of presidents and the influence of neo-patrimonialism are less pronounced, and vice versa.

Economic Conditions and Performance

The third major argument regarding electoral authoritarian outcomes essentially reinforces a performance-based notion of nondemocratic politics (Gasiorwoski 1995; Haggard and Kaufman 1995; Magaloni 2006). Strong economies afford a twofold advantage to autocrats. First, growing economies provide incumbents with the resources necessary to maintain extensive patronage coalitions and clientelistic networks (Greene 2010). This can involve rents from state-owned enterprises, natural resource extraction, or wealth generated from the private sector that must pass through government channels. Either way, a growing economy provides incumbents with much more flexibility during elections in their management of ruling coalitions. Second, a growing economy can help preserve voter loyalty by providing more employment opportunities to citizens, raising incomes, and minimizing the impact of price inflation. In the African context, economic performance coincides with demands placed on the state for improvements in social welfare and better government provision of club goods like educational opportunities, access to healthcare, and infrastructure. Therefore, in electoral authoritarian regimes strong economic performance might be correlated with higher incumbent vote shares and a lower propensity toward heavy manipulation.

One of the issues with using economic performance as an explanatory variable of electoral authoritarian competition is the fact that the record of growth and social welfare in Africa has not been stellar since the end of the Cold War. During the past decade some countries have benefitted from a significant economic boom, which was often the result of growth in natural resource extraction and new trade ties to countries like China (Brautigam 2009; Shinn and Eisenman 2012). But, for many countries rates of real economic growth have been relatively flat. Likewise, in many countries growth has been uneven, resulting in higher levels of inequality or mixed gains on indicators of human development. A second issue is that in Africa economic performance is also tied to the actions of international actors, and their ability and willingness to enforce lending agreements that require structural adjustment. For example, in Kenya international pressure likely helped sustain the economic crisis of the early 1990s much longer than in Cameroon, where the regime received substantial French financial support (Arriola 2012).

ARGUMENTS OF THE BOOK

As Tanzania's eminent father figure suggests at the top of this chapter, autocracies are beset by uncertainty. Electoral competition increases this uncertainty, and this is manifest in the observable differences in electoral competition. My primary contention is that a central factor that helps autocrats mitigate uncertainty during elections is the presence of institutions, and especially formal ones, that foster credible exchanges with followers. A credible ruling party is generally quite large, institutionalized and autonomous, internally democratic, and has longstanding ties with broad segments of the population. As detailed in Chapter 2, the notion of a credible party is that these institutional features build expectations of regularity, voice, and even fairness. It shapes how ambitious elites vie for power and how voters assess their exchanges with the regime. Credibility produces longer time horizons from followers and reduces the incentives for defection. Regimes with credible parties can then contest elections with confidence and use manipulation more strategically rather than systematically. This is emblematic of Tanzania, where an electoral authoritarian regime could win big without cheating big.

Credible parties are rare, and in most African regimes the office of the presidency looms large as the locus of political power. In these regimes elite careers are less structured and depend more on networking, personal resources, and the strategic needs of the presidency. Likewise, there is often a distributive tilt toward narrower urban or ethnic constituencies. This is part and parcel of a strategy of elite coalition building common in Africa that produces a more zero-sum and competitive form of politics

(Bratton and van de Walle 1997; Arriola 2009). Elite and voter loyalty to the regime is much more opportunistic, and therefore also contingent. During elections, dissent is likely to be more apparent and regimes must deter defection by either buying or coercing support. In both Cameroon and Kenya elections were much more contentious than in Tanzania because regimes had no institutional mechanism for signaling the credibility of their commitments to their followers. Elites could not be assured that power would transition smoothly, and a critical mass of voters could not be confident that they would be rewarded for their support.

Without credible ruling parties, how autocrats compete in the long term is more contingent. A secondary argument this book puts forward is that in the context of African states and the post–Cold War environment, international actors were at an advantageous position to influence electoral conditions when regimes lacked credible ruling parties. When we consider the totality of actual international engagement with African electoral authoritarian regimes, there are discernible differences between democratic and autocratic patronage. Higher levels of democracy assistance, aid conditionality, and diplomatic pressure can foster political and economic reform that might fall short of ideal, but impacts how autocrats compete. While democratic patronage might not lead to regime change or entirely constrain an autocrat, it can exacerbate the inherent problems of electoral authoritarian competition without credible institutions. This was evident in Kenya, where international actors could not curtail blatant uses of violence, but did limit the use of electoral fraud and inhibited the ability of the regime to use state patronage.

On the other hand, autocratic patronage produces the opposite effect. In these cases, external actors might lend financial assistance at moments of fiscal crisis, limit their commitments to election observation and democracy assistance, and press softly on questions of economic reform. This leaves more tools in the hand of electoral authoritarian regimes, which can compensate for the absence of credible institutions. Likewise, when opposition actors are cut off from external sources of support – both material and rhetorical – it is more difficult to sustain party cohesion and active mobilization. This has been the case in Cameroon, which was initially quite sensitive to external pressure, but for political reasons enjoyed strong French support in the early 1990s. Following the terrorist attacks of September 11, 2001 the United States has also become much less vocal on questions of democracy and governance. Paul Biya has had comparatively more leeway to use state resources to commit fraud and entice elites back into his ruling coalition. Relatedly, he faced little international condemnation when he removed term limits, which likely prevented a serious crisis within the ruling party.

It is important to clarify the parameters of these arguments. First, this is an account of how the presence or absence of credible ruling parties influences unfair electoral competition, not of where credible parties come from in the first place. Indeed, the formation of credible ruling parties is a tricky proposition and rooted in specific historical processes. It obliges leaders to have a longer-term perspective on institution building at critical moments, and a set of conditions at regime inception that incentivizes that view (Smith 2005). In the context of Africa's weak states and politically mobilized ethnic groups, credible institution building was not always a realistic proposition. It is difficult to pinpoint the exact origins of authoritarian institutions, or to completely separate their emergence and subsequent impact from crucial background factors (Pepinsky 2014). Likewise, it is not always clear how these institutions replicate themselves across time. In later chapters I do try and parse out some of these factors, and argue that institution building cannot be reduced completely to prior structural conditions. However, my focus remains on how the specific institutional features of ruling parties create enduring legacies that impact elections.

Second, my argument is not directly about when electoral authoritarian regimes are more likely to lose elections, or more ambitiously democratize. Rather, it is about the factors that shape how autocrats compete – their propensity toward manipulation and ability to generate large vote shares. Coercion and manipulation are therefore outcomes to be explained rather than a causal factor. There is literature on the "menu of manipulation" (Schedler 2013) and discussions of differences between "clumsy" and "skilled" manipulation (Case 2006). And indeed, it could be that some autocrats are not bestowed with foresight or might in fact be socialized into highly coercive behavior. While this is a valid argument, I contend that autocrats generally would prefer to win elections by large margins without having to expend resources on costly manipulation (Wintrobe 1998). Likewise, the longer-term contours of electoral authoritarian contestation do not discernibly depend on the vagaries of manipulative choices (Lehoucq 2003; Calingaert 2006), but rather the underlying institutional and international contexts that drive strategies and outcomes.

Third, this is an argument about how the record of international action impacts electoral authoritarian competition, not about whether international actors can foster regime change. Whether regimes are sufficiently vulnerable and whether a formidable opposition can coalesce depends on numerous factors not straightforwardly addressed here. My suggestion is that that life becomes worse for electoral authoritarian regimes when they cannot rely on credible parties *and* when international actors take an active role. This suggests that international actors are influential, but in a much more limited sense. They might make it more difficult for regimes without credible ruling parties to employ certain forms of manipulation or offer specific forms of patronage. International action is a not a primary cause, but one that at times significantly shapes how autocrats compete.

CONTRIBUTIONS OF THE ARGUMENT

This book adds to a growing literature on authoritarian institution building and provides new insights into comparative electoral authoritarianism. Autocracies, by definition, are faced with more severe institutional and informational uncertainties than democracies (Wintrobe 1998; Schedler 2013). To manage these challenges, autocrats traditionally deploy combinations of coercion, patronage, and ideological legitimation (De Mesquita et al. 2005). Institutions, and particularly quasi-democratic institutions like legislatures, parties, and even elections, help autocrats function and deploy these tactics more efficiently (Gandhi 2008; Gandhi and Lust-Okar 2009). Yet, the reality is that institutional investments under autocracy are grossly uneven, and this has real consequences for how autocracies operate. Not all autocratic regimes create the same supportive institutions, and those very institutions are often unequally imbued with meaning. Indeed, only under certain conditions do authoritarian institutions also build credibility and foster longer-term investments from elites and citizens.

Specific discussions of ruling parties are often unclear about these uneven institutional investments. As elaborated on in Chapter 2, parties provide some basic organizational means to autocrats, but are also able to shape elite career trajectories, and at times help forge credible commitments between regimes and their followers. Yet accounts of how parties foster credibility tend to be quite functional. As Beatriz Magaloni notes in her own work on authoritarian parties, we know how credible parties potentially benefit autocrats, but we know less about the distinct factors that create that credibility (Magaloni 2008, 725). Absent greater knowledge of specific examples, or without looking more closely at the internal workings of actual ruling parties and their operation in practice, we cannot fully understand how institutions benefit autocrats.

Therefore, a major contribution of this study is that it contrasts institutional investments in ruling parties across a number of diverse cases, and demonstrates how these differences underpin variation in electoral authoritarian experiences. Prior to the end of the Cold War and the spread of electoral norms it was in fact quite difficult to observe this variation. Consider the point that in Tanzania, Cameroon, and Kenya we find three single-party regimes that all emerged in the immediate postindependence era, survived uninterrupted until the early 1990s, and then all incorporated multiparty elections at roughly the same time. For nearly thirty years, most studies simply considered these cases as examples of "single-party regimes." It was not until the inauguration of elections that the impact of different institutional investments became much more evident (Geddes 1999).[8] With new incentives for elites and voters to defect from ruling coalitions, the spread of elections in Africa revealed previously understudied differences in ruling parties.

My argument also complements accounts of regime outcomes in Africa. Building on Robert Dahl's work, Nic Cheeseman has persuasively argued that when the costs of repression are lower than the costs of reform, African regimes are more likely to repress than liberalize (Cheeseman 2015, 5–12). My argument is similar in that I account for how some forms of manipulation are constrained by international actors. However, I differ by focusing on electoral competition and providing a clearer explanation for why some regimes might need to resort to repression to begin with. For instance, in Tanzania the more open electoral process was not forced liberalization, but a sign of the regime's confidence in its ability to contest the election. Likewise, Moi and Biya might have repressed because they felt the benefits outweighed the costs, but the prior question is why were their regimes so sensitive to begin with? In another sense, my theory sets out a more limited set of factors that shapes a regime's cost-benefit calculation and impacts their propensity toward manipulation and ability to generate vote share. It is not an argument that applies to all of Africa, but to a select number of cases.

The ability of regimes to foster credibility is also a missing component from studies of African authoritarianism. As noted, the resilience of political regimes in Africa is often attributed to the use of informal institutions of patronage to sustain elite coalitions. Rachel Riedl further

---

[8] This does not mean that differences among these regimes were unnoticed by scholars, especially those of African politics (Coleman and Rosberg 1970; Collier 1982). But, from the perspective of the literature on authoritarian politics they were similar because they survived for similar periods of time.

notes that when regimes brokered with traditional elites they were more consolidated and could control the transition to democracy. By contrast, regimes that used the state to supplant traditional elites were more precarious (Riedl 2014). These regime strategies interact with formal institution building and credibility. Autocrats can cede authority to traditional elites through fairly informal means, but this does not necessarily create a credible exchange. Autocrats have to be able and bind themselves to their commitments through some official rules (Bratton 2007). Likewise, creating credible institutions might compensate for the futility of state substitutive strategies. Tanzania is the case in point – a very stable regime that circumvented traditional elites and built new systems of authority via a credible ruling party. The integrity of Tanzania's ruling party likely offset its more limited material capacities.

Finally, drawing attention to electoral authoritarian competition is ultimately about specifying when regimes are not just resilient but durable in the face of elections. There is a critical difference between the concept of resilience – the ability to recover from adversity – and the concept of durability – the ability to withstand and perhaps even deter adversity. My contention is that credible parties sustain a more durable form of electoral authoritarianism; one that is less manipulative but still electorally powerful. Indeed, this is a long-term equilibrium that should not be confused with democratic progress. It would require significant change to alter. By contrast, electoral authoritarian regimes without credible ruling parties might simply be resilient. A resilient regime can be adaptive to elections and possibly survive for extended periods of time. However, this does not necessarily reflect a regime that can consistently reproduce decisive victories from election to election. Short-term changes like an upcoming term limit or a shift in the international environment can tilt the balance.

In summary, this book contributes to ongoing and fascinating research on authoritarian institutions and authoritarian politics, with a specific focus on the sub-Saharan African experience. The evidence provided in the upcoming chapters validates that differences in electoral competition are substantial, and cannot be taken at face value as evidence for stronger democratic norms or autocratic weakness. Previous scholarship is not clear on what explains these differences in how autocrats compete. I argue that in many cases it primarily reflects under-specified differences in the ability of ruling parties to build credible exchanges with elites and voters, and secondarily due to differences in the international environment of competition.

RESEARCH DESIGN AND BOOK ORGANIZATION

In the next chapters I develop my theory of electoral authoritarian competition and discuss in greater detail the role of credible ruling parties and the postures of international patrons. Cases were selected with an eye toward scope conditions and theory development. This study is focused specifically on sub-Saharan Africa, and even more particularly on former single-party regimes that survived their transition to electoral authoritarianism. An emerging consensus from a number of studies is that electoral authoritarianism differs across both time and space (McCoy and Hartlyn 2009; Roessler and Howard 2009; Kaya and Bernhard 2013). Much of this has to do with the context in which multiparty elections were introduced. For instance, in post-Communist countries electoral authoritarianism emerged out of regime collapse. As Lucan Way notes, this led to "pluralism by default" and factors like the control of nationalist narratives or state capacity were more meaningful (Way 2002). In Latin America democratic backsliding was more important, while in Eastern Europe the proximity to the European Union made Western linkage particularly influential (Levitsky and Way 2010). In Africa, a large proportion of transitions were from previously single-party regimes to electoral authoritarian regimes.[9]

Limiting the main inquiry to former single-party regimes allows us to more easily isolate the importance of credible ruling parties. Single-party regimes had time to develop institutional features like political parties prior to elections. By contrast, military regimes like Blaise Compaoré's in Burkina Faso or Lansana Conté's in Guinea generally constructed ruling parties haphazardly just years before foundational elections. This meant that other factors besides the presence or absence of credible ruling parties likely exerted strong influence, namely the political role of the military. Likewise, there are a handful of revolutionary regimes in Africa that overthrew incumbent governments with little experience in civilian politics. This stipulation excludes fascinating electoral authoritarian experiences in Chad, Ethiopia, Rwanda, Uganda, and Zimbabwe. Limiting the study to cases that survived their foundational elections also helps focus the study on evolving patterns of electoral competition, and

---

[9] By my estimation of the forty countries that held elections in the early 1990s, 40 percent were former single-party regimes, 27 percent were military regimes, and 33 percent were ambiguous. This latter category includes transitional regimes in Benin and Mali, postcolonial and postapartheid transitions in Namibia and South Africa, monarchies in Lesotho, and acute conflict states in Comoros and Zaire.

TABLE 1.1. *Case selection criteria*

Case	Ruling party credibility	International patronage	Electoral authoritarian competition	Theoretical utility of case
Tanzania	Credible	Status Quo	Tolerant hegemony	Theory confirming
Cameroon	Non-credible	Status Quo/ Autocratic	Repressive hegemony	Counterfactual case
Kenya	Non-credible	Democratic	Repressive non-hegemony	Counterfactual/ equifinal case

Notes: All three cases are former African single-party regimes that transitioned to multi-party elections.

recognizes the unique circumstances that often shape first elections. This excludes Cape Verde, Malawi, Sao Tome and Principle, and Zambia. But, by staying attentive to cases with comparable postindependence roots and similar electoral authoritarian origins helps to isolate and contextualize the posited causal factors.

As noted in Table 1.1, the three cases of Tanzania, Cameroon, and Kenya reflect important and demonstrable variation along the major moving parts of the argument, and also serve distinct theoretical purposes.[10] The specific measurement of cases is detailed in the next chapter, but by most indicators Tanzania possesses a credible ruling party while the other two cases do not. Likewise, international patronage in Tanzania was mainly status quo oriented, while in Cameroon it tended toward authoritarian and in Kenya it was democratic. Electoral authoritarian competition in Tanzania took the form of a tolerant hegemony, while in Cameroon it was a repressive hegemony and in Kenya a repressive non-hegemony. Tanzania also acts as a theory confirming case, where the major moving parts of the theory are clearly present. Cameroon and Kenya are by contrast counterfactual cases where the absence of a credible ruling

---

[10] An electoral authoritarian period begins with the first multiparty election and ends once an incumbent loses an election, steps down, or is removed from power. Therefore, since the Kenyan ruling party KANU lost the 2002 election, the subsequent 2007 and 2013 elections are not considered in this study. This does not necessarily mean that Kenya became an electoral democracy after 2002, only that a different set of factors is likely influential after an electoral defeat. It should also be noted here that the Tanzanian case refers mainly to the mainland and not the islands of Zanzibar, which have been semi-autonomous since 1964.

party pushed them down different paths. Kenya is also an "equifinal" case, and demonstrates the contingent impact of international patronage on electoral authoritarian competition (Goertz and Mahoney 2012).

There are limitations to any case selection strategy, especially if the aim is to generate strong causal inferences by using Millian methods of comparison. Structured comparisons must cope with several background factors that cannot be completely controlled for, as well as an empirical reality that generally limits the range of cases you can choose from. Moreover, institutional analysis often has difficulty separating the impact of background structural conditions from the impact of institutions themselves (Pepinsky 2014). For instance, the colonial experience was unique in each case, and there are differences in ethnic demography. Using Dan Posner's index of Politically Relevant Ethnic Groups Tanzania scores 0.59, Cameroon 0.71, and Kenya 0.57 (Posner 2004). There are further subtle differences in the distribution and concentration of ethnic groups. These factors might have impacted whether a credible ruling party emerged, and influenced subsequent electoral authoritarian competition.

However, the goal here is not to leverage too much from the comparison of cases or to generate far beyond a select population that helped to generate theory. Rather this book elucidates different causal pathways, or types of electoral authoritarian outcomes (George and Bennett 2005).[11] This is concurrent with new insights in qualitative methodology and case-study research that stresses the role of process tracing, theoretical congruence, and causal process observations.[12] A fundamental principle here is

---

[11] There have been significant developments in qualitative methodologies and case study research since the seminal work of King, Keohane, and Verba (1994). In recent years a growing amount of literature has emerged to defend and elaborate upon qualitative methodology as a distinct research tradition, while also stressing synthesis (George and Bennett 2005; Brady and Collier 2010; Goertz and Mahoney 2012). These developments include innovations in concept formation (Goertz 2006; Gerring 2012), case selection (Gerring and Seawright 2008) process tracing (Collier 2011; Bennett and Checkel 2015), set-theory (Ragin 2008; Schneider and Wagemann 2012), and typological theorizing (Elman 2005; George and Bennett 2005).

[12] There is some disagreement over the parameters of process tracing and its distinction from the congruence method. The classic approach to process tracing developed by Alexander George is rooted in decision-making theory and asks that we clearly link individual sequences from cause to outcome (George and Bennett 2005, 205–232). But, in comparative politics research that looks at non-linear, long-term, and complex causal processes, the term process tracing is "an analytical tool for drawing descriptive and casual inferences from diagnostic pieces of evidence – often understood as part of a temporal sequence of events or phenomena" (Collier 2011, 824). David Waldner considers this latter form of process tracing inferior since it does not satisfy a "completeness standard" that clearly links cause to effect via specific mechanisms (2015). Nonetheless,

that causal process observations are pieces of evidence that "provide information about context, process or mechanism, and that contribute distinctive leverage in causal inference" (Brady and Collier 2010, 277–278). Causal process observations are not always comparable across cases and depend on the specific theoretical expectations regarding each individual case (Bennett 2008). As such it is not the quantity of evidence that necessarily matters or the comparison of cases, but the discerning quality of *individual* pieces of evidence with regard to causal processes in *individual* cases.

This approach helps with the presence of potentially confounding background factors. While Chapter 4 dedicates some space to contrasting differences in state capacity and political competition at independence, the book emphasizes how these factors manifested in different kinds of ruling parties. The empirical chapters then trace a direct link between the presence and absence of certain party institutions and electoral authoritarian outcomes. Background conditions are still relevant, but the appropriate counterfactual to ask is how might a case without a credible party had acted if it had a credible party, and vice versa? This does involve some explicit case comparison, but the pertinent controls are for more immediate factors. For instance, Chapter 5 examines the record of elite defection across the three cases while controlling for similar levels of regime vulnerability. These comparisons add to the major causal inferences, which are derived from tracing processes in each case.

The book also utilizes the tool of typological theorizing to offer some contingent generalizations regarding a wider range of former single-party African regimes that transitioned to electoral authoritarianism. Typological theorizing is similar in many ways to qualitative case analysis and is useful for research questions that are concerned with causal complexity and equifinality (Elman 2005; George and Bennett 2005, 233–263). A typological space arrays cases along a range of similar variables and looks for factors that are necessary conditions, but also emphasizes the importance of "types" rather than homogenous causal stories. In this case it validates the role of credible ruling parties in sustaining more tolerant electoral outcomes, but also indicates that there are additional factors that underlie repressive electoral authoritarian outcomes. The typological theorizing allows us to draw some broader conclusions by moving beyond possible selection bias in the initial case selection, but also maintains a commitment to explicating a complex social world.

I embrace this perspective because it corresponds better with the more limited nature of observational data when dealing with complex and historical political phenomenon.

The evidence presented in the following chapters draws on historical records, archives, elite interviews, and within-case statistical analysis to validate the posited causal processes. I implicitly subject each case to a number of critical "hoop tests" that they must pass in order to help affirm causal inference.[13] For instance, the case studies demonstrate that the presence or absence of credible ruling parties influenced how elites viewed their own career trajectories and incentives for defection. Likewise, I present evidence that demonstrates that voters interacted with ruling parties differently, and that international actors shrunk or expanded the resources available to incumbents to contest unfair elections. These data were collected across several years of fieldwork in three countries. I gathered sub-national statistical data and conducted over seventy in-depth elite interviews in each country. These interviews often lasted hours and include regime and opposition figures. At times it was important to get information from key decision-making actors or anonymous whistleblowers (Tansey 2007). At other times the aim was to derive some consensus over how elites viewed the ruling party, contestation, and international influence.

There are real challenges when conducting research in authoritarian settings and tracing historical processes to contemporary outcomes. Authoritarian parties are not always open about their inner-workings or campaign strategies, and there are issues with the quality of statistical data in these contexts. Likewise, elite interviews are not randomly sampled and some actors, especially in electoral authoritarian settings, have an incentive to overstate or obscure (Berry 2002; Mikecz 2012). As a researcher, one is left with the delicate task of parsing through what is reliable information and what is not. The extent of fieldwork and the time spent developing relationships with interview subjects helps with these assessments. While I might cite individual quotes, they represent a viewpoint that emerged from numerous in-depth conversations across extended periods of time. Moreover, while individual pieces of evidence might be challenged, I argue that the cumulative impact of evidentiary material presented sustains the main arguments.

Chapter 2 introduces my theory of electoral authoritarian competition by discussing the role of authoritarian uncertainty and introducing

---

[13] Passing a hoop test presents strong evidence in a theory's favor, but cannot on its own affirm casual inference with certainty. It is often by passing numerous hoop tests for a posited theory, and failing to pass hoop tests for rival theories that we ascertain causality. Other tests include straws in the wind, smoking guns, and doubly decisive tests, but due to the nature of political science phenomenon and data, hoop tests are most often employed (van Evera 1997).

the concepts of credible ruling parties and international patronage. I link differences in ruling parties to the divergent capacity of electoral authoritarian regimes to compete in multiparty elections, and describe the major observable implications in terms of elite and voter loyalty. Likewise, the chapter discusses in greater detail the literature on international democracy promotion, and notes some of the predicted consequences of democratic versus autocratic patronage for electoral competition. I briefly apply these concepts to the three cases, which sets up the empirical chapters to follow.

In Chapter 3 I evaluate in greater detail the dependent variable of this study: electoral authoritarian competition. I overview some of the major conceptual challenges inherent in identifying electoral authoritarianism, and provide some new criteria that can be applied to a fuller spectrum of regimes. The chapter primarily builds on data from the Varieties of Democracy project. Looking at the African continent, I demonstrate how electoral authoritarian regimes differ in the extent to which they dominate elections (hegemony vs. non-hegemony) and the degree to which they are tolerant of contestation (repression vs. toleration). These two dimensions are used to classify configurations of electoral authoritarian competition. When applied to Africa, there is indeed a diversity of experience, and some tentative relationships between credible ruling parties and competition.

Chapter 4 looks at the postindependence period in Africa as a critical juncture during which basic regime features fell into place. I discuss the divergent response rulers in Tanzania, Cameroon, and Kenya had to the governance challenges of postindependence and outline some factors that likely led to the emergence of a credible party rather than a presidential-dominant regime. While it is difficult to pinpoint one clear set of factors, I demonstrate that differences in political organization, inherited state capacity, and leadership were all influential. The other contribution of the chapter is to describe empirical differences in ruling parties that influence credibility in terms of physical size, decisional autonomy, and internal democracy. In addition, I look at divergent patterns of social incorporation under single-party rule. The majority of these ruling party features endured throughout single-party rule, leaving regimes differentially equipped at the transition to multipartyism.

Chapter 5 is the first empirical chapter of the book that looks at one of the key observable implications of ruling party credibility – the ability of the party to retain elite loyalty in the face of crisis. The chapter uses historical evidence on elite defection, several participant interviews, and structured case comparisons to examine the divergent ability of ruling parties to manage elite competition during party primaries, despite similar vulnerabilities. I trace the record of elite defection in each case, and look for evidence of how parties leveraged their institutional structures to manage elite disputes during the nomination process. Particularly, the absence of institutionalized processes for selecting legislative and presidential candidates in Kenya and Cameroon created severe resentments that fueled comparatively larger waves of defection. On the other hand, in Tanzania the ruling party repeatedly reinforced its autonomy and control over nomination rules.

The second major implication of party credibility is traced in Chapter 6 – the ability of the regimes to mobilize substantial voter support. The chapter also draws on participant interviews, but a primary source of data for this chapter also comes from sub-national data on elections, socioeconomic indicators, government provision, ethnic identity, and measures of social incorporation unique to each case. This is one of the only attempts to model patterns of electoral support using finer-grained data at the constituency and district level. Through spatial representation and within-case statistical analysis I demonstrate the impact of party organization on voter mobilization, and provide evidence that legacies of coalition-building rooted in the single-party era determine to a large degree the breadth and depth of contemporary electoral support.

Chapter 7 turns to the role of international patrons in Kenya and Cameroon by combining historical data, participant interviews, and previously classified embassy documents. The chapter uses numerous data points to establish levels of patronage in each case. I then trace differences in international patronage to a regime's ability to employ manipulation and cooptation. In Kenya strong democratic patronage, in part sparked by an activist US ambassador, led to a dramatic increase in election observation, reform of the public sector, and ultimately an empowered opposition. By contrast, in Cameroon authoritarian patronage from France and later the United States increased the coercive capacities of the ruling regime, and left opposition actors with very little material or rhetorical support.

Chapter 8 explores the boundaries of these arguments by comparing a wider range of ten former single-party African regimes using typological theorizing. Based on quantitative and qualitative data I compare each case according to their ruling party credibility, international patronage, opposition coordination, and record of economic performance. The chapter validates many of the findings from Chapter 5 through Chapter 7, and finds that party credibility is a necessary condition that distinguishes between tolerant and repressive electoral authoritarianism.

The typological space also confirms that other variables are of secondary value, but there are in fact multiple pathways of electoral authoritarian contestation where economic performance and opposition capacity might have some influence.

The conclusion discusses the book's implications for the broader study of authoritarianism, African politics, and democratization. I suggest some avenues for further research on authoritarian institutions, counter some of the pessimism regarding the ability of regimes in Africa to offer institutionalized politics, and bring forward some ideas regarding the prospects for democratization. While repeated unfair elections might improve over time, this can in fact suggest authoritarian durability rather than democratization. However, the greater institutionalization of some ruling parties might also provide the anchor for future democratic party systems.

Credible Parties, International Patrons, and Electoral Authoritarian Competition

If I could do it all again I'd be a farmer.

—Mobutu Sésé Seko

Gabon without France is like a car with no driver. France without Gabon is like a car with no fuel.

—Omar Bongo (September 18, 1996, *Le Libération*)

In this chapter I outline a theory of electoral authoritarian competition rooted in the role of credible ruling parties and international patronage. My argument, which is sketched out in Figure 2.1 is that the presence of a credible ruling party influences the degree to which incumbents can maintain elite and voter loyalty during elections, and therefore their expected vote share. Consequently, regimes with credible parties are less likely to employ high degrees of manipulation to win, but will nonetheless win elections decisively. By contrast, if a regime is not confident in their predicted vote-share it will have to manipulate more and dispense large amounts of patronage to retain support and secure electoral victory. The longer-term utility of this manipulative strategy, at least in parts of Africa, depends on the role of international actors and whether they exercise sustained and strong pressure. In addition to focusing on the distinct outcome of competition, the novelty of these arguments rests on finer-tuned understandings of what benefits ruling parties actually provide autocrats, and by noting the specific ways in which international actors limit autocratic maneuverability.

As discussed below, a credible ruling party is one that has cultivated regular and predictable exchanges with supporters. Credibility is fostered with elites when parties retain a significant physical presence, preserve

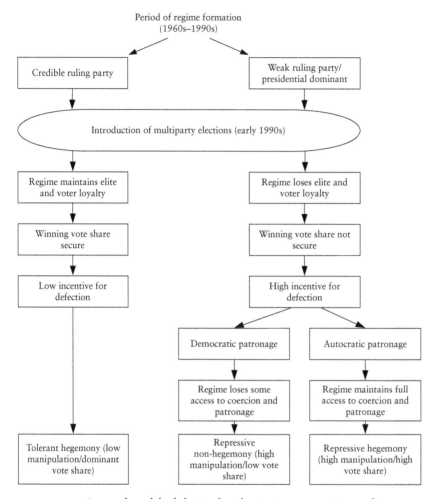

FIGURE 2.1. *A causal model of electoral authoritarian competition: ruling party credibility and international patronage*

some decisional autonomy, and provide competitive but fair avenues for advancement. This helps guarantee to elites that their career trajectories are stable. Credibility is also fostered with voters when ruling parties maintain wide distributive commitments and avoid bias that might manifest as ethnic or urban favoritism. This tells voters that they can expect consistent delivery of government-provided goods. Importantly, credibility makes elites and voters put aside immediate material opportunism, and forces them to take a longer-term perspective on loyalty to the regime based on their historical interactions. This helps mitigate a fundamental challenge for all autocracies – their uncertainty in their own level of support. Elections make that uncertainty all the more acute by providing new opportunities for opposition mobilization and defection.

This argument meshes with other work on authoritarian politics. Previous research has demonstrated that parties in general elongate authoritarian tenure (Geddes 1999). Yet, this is misleading given that opposition parties in party-based authoritarian regimes highlight very different constraints on contestation. For example, in Tanzania the Secretary General of the National Convention for Construction and Reform (NCCR-M), Samweli Ruhuza, states that, "CCM has the network, can field candidates who are not very strong, and still gets the votes."[1] This echoes sentiments heard throughout Tanzania that CCM is a party with a unique presence and historic constituency. By contrast, opposition figures in Cameroon or Kenya rarely discuss the ruling party in these terms, but rather emphasize the role of the presidency. A more nuanced look at ruling parties would demonstrate that in fact while parties provide a range of advantages to autocrats, they are distributed unevenly across contexts. Some ruling parties are more influential than others.

Recently, there has been more serious investigation of how ruling parties develop formal institutional features that enhance their ability to make credible commitments to elites and voters (Magaloni 2008). Indeed, much of what we know about the role of credibility in authoritarian politics comes from discussion of individual cases like the Mexican Institutional Revolutionary Party (PRI) (Magaloni 2006) or the Chinese Communist Party (Manion 2004). It is not always clear what institutional features foster credibility, and there has not been an attempt to link credibility to how autocrats compete. Current scholarship cannot account for why electoral authoritarian regimes might be equally hegemonic, but deploy quite different sets of manipulative tools. This chapter fills that gap by clarifying what a credible ruling party is, and linking it to how autocrats compete.

These insights also extend to the role of international actors, which I contend are most meaningful when autocrats do not have institutional means of securing support. Scholarship is often unclear under what conditions external actors will intervene in another country's politics, and whether they are actually impactful. A prevalent assumption is that international actors are unlikely to be able to use tools like democracy assistance or

---

[1] Samweli Ruhuza (Secretary-General, NCCR-M). Author Interview. Dar es Salaam. (November 22, 2010).

aid conditionality to push authoritarian regimes over the brink toward democracy. But, there is also some agreement that democracy assistance, aid conditionality, and diplomacy in fact still matter (Hyde 2011, Donno 2013a). For example, in a study of the role of foreign aid in democratization Stephen Knack finds a very weak relationship, but also notes that his finding "does not imply that none of the democracy-promoting projects sponsored by donors had any effects" (2004, 262). This is particularly relevant in Africa where international actors have been persistently involved in processes of economic and political reform (van de Walle 2001).

Missing is an account of the totality of international intervention and its impact on more limited outcomes like electoral competition. International patronage is also distributed unevenly across contexts. Only at times are major external actors democratic patrons who combine democracy assistance, aid conditionality, and diplomatic pressure to push regimes toward reform and to empower oppositions. More often, external actors use a more limited range of tools, or actually act as autocratic patrons invested in the status quo. This has consequences, perhaps not for a regime's ultimate survival, but for how they contest elections. Indeed, we do not have a satisfactory account of why two seemingly similar repressive strategies sometimes lead to hegemonic electoral outcomes and sometimes to non-hegemonic outcomes. International patronage might not fully constrain an autocrat or compel transformational change, but it can limit their range of action and the utility of their repression.

In this chapter I review some of the literature on ruling parties and international patrons that has informed my own theory of electoral authoritarian competition. I discuss the problem of authoritarian uncertainty more broadly and in the face of elections, and describe the role of credible ruling parties in mitigating that uncertainty. This provides the basis for a theory that explains when regimes are more or less likely to use manipulation to secure vote share. I then address the ambiguous role of international actors, and note how their actions might influence electoral competition. Using this framework, I explain differences in competition and briefly introduce the three cases of Tanzania, Cameroon, and Kenya.

AUTHORITARIAN UNCERTAINTY AND THE ROLE OF RULING PARTIES

Despite Mel Brooks's often-cited adage, it is not always "good to be the king." In fact, authoritarian regimes suffer from persistent institutional and informational deficits due to the absence of legitimate and established mechanisms for managing dissent or generating reliable information about their own support (Wintrobe 1998, Schedler 2013). Historically, autocrats have had to worry about numerous threats to their own survival, such as military coups, regime splits, insurgencies, and even international intervention. The presence of multiparty elections opens up a new set of regime vulnerabilities. Opposition parties can utilize new political space to defeat autocrats at the polls, or provide sound alternatives that foster regime defection (Bunce and Wolchik 2011). Incumbents also have to mobilize support to win elections, which means they need information regarding their own public standing, and some basic ability to campaign and reach voters.

Autocrats generally cope with threats to their survival through combinations of coercion, cooptation, and ideological indoctrination. For instance, during elections an incumbent might commit fraud, use vote buying, or bank on the popularity of a candidate or the historical legacy of the regime. None of these are panaceas for the dilemmas of autocratic rule, and in their barest form they incur significant costs. Coercion is risky, and can lead to declines in legitimacy or signal weakness rather than confidence. Ideologies, as famously argued by Juan Linz, are often nothing more than "mentalities," and dissipate over time (2000). Cooptation, perhaps the most pernicious and widespread facet of authoritarian rule, is also expensive and tricky absent steady streams of revenue, efficient means of distributing resources to supporters (or away from detractors), and mechanisms for ensuring compliance. Likewise, while "selectorate" theories of authoritarian rule emphasize the use of resources to carve out "minimal winning coalitions" (De Mesquita et al. 2005), they do not fundamentally answer the question at the core of what Ronald Wintrobe identifies as the "dictator's dilemma" (1998). An autocrat can never be completely assured that the resources they cede for cooperation will not be turned against them, and participants in a ruling coalition have no real assurances that an autocrat will maintain their commitments.

One of the solutions to the inherent uncertainty of autocratic rule is the use of personalism as a means of exercising power (Svolik 2012).[2] In Africa this is often associated with the utility of "neo-patrimonialism" and "Big Man" politics that supposedly permeates the continent (Chabal and Daloz 1999). Autocrats in these instances rely on fairly blatant

---

[2] There is some disagreement over the use of the terms sultanistic or personal to describe regimes. On the one hand some scholars see this as a distinct regime type (Chehabi and Linz 1998, Geddes 1999), while others see it as a style of politics that differs across cases (Snyder 2006).

authoritarian tools of coercion and patronage, and are untethered from constraining political institutions. This gives them the leeway they need to manage ruling coalitions. Personal regimes also frequently fall back on the apparent stability of kith and kin, or the alluring comfort of personality cults. However, personal politics, by its very nature as institutionally unbound, leads to persistent factionalism, improvisation, and instability. Mobutu Sésé Seko might have wished he had chosen a different vocation when the end seemed nigh, but he was also complicit in his own demise by not ceding any authority to a constraining institution.

The persistent concern of uncertainty is why scholars now observe that autocrats routinely surround themselves with political institutions like legislatures, judiciaries, and especially political parties (Gandhi 2008). Indeed, political parties have become the cornerstone in the study of authoritarian institutions. One of the longstanding findings in political science is that party-based forms of autocracy survive considerably longer than their military or personal brethren (Geddes 1999). Similar studies have found persistent correlations between single-party authoritarianism and regime longevity (Brownlee 2007), a reduced number of military coups (Cox 2009), and even stronger records of economic growth (Keefer 2007). Cross-nationally, it is now rare to find an authoritarian regime in power for more than 10 years that has not created a support party of some kind.[3] Party-based authoritarianism, and for that matter election-based authoritarianism, is the modal form of contemporary autocratic governance.

Recent scholarship also suggests that ruling parties provide a spectrum of benefits to autocrats. First, a ruling party is simply another tool of authoritarian control used for its coercive and distributional ends. In this sense, it is primarily beneficial because of its organizational features. For instance, Levitsky and Way highlight a party's ability to act as a tool of public monitoring and electoral mobilization, which often acts as a substitute for state power (2010, 62). Presumably, parties with larger countrywide presence can gather information on dissidents, mobilize voters to the polls, deter opposition parties, and even facilitate electoral fraud. Regimes might also invest in formal mobilizing structures like youth wings or party cells. Parties are also the means through which resources might reach voters, especially when autocrats can use their monopolistic control of public goods or the budget cycle to distribute patronage

---

[3] According to Barbara Geddes, by 2004 63 percent of autocratic regimes held regular multiparty elections, including 93 percent of former single-party regimes (2006).

strategically by rewarding supporters and punishing detractors (Greene 2007, Blaydes 2011). In certain settings elaborate party machinery can be used to distribute clientelistic resources more effectively and provide the means for monitoring voting compliance.[4] Moreover, the party itself is an additional distributional resource an autocrat can employ. Positions of prestige within the party or in the legislature can be used to co-opt elites and create more enduring political coalitions (Arriola 2009).

Second, some parties go beyond these simpler organizational faculties by shaping elite career incentives. As Jason Brownlee writes, parties lengthen the "time horizons on which leaders weigh gains and losses" (2007, 12). Or, as Milan Svolik notes, "cooptation via authoritarian parties breeds an enduring rather than momentary stake in the regime's survival" (2012, 164). The reason for this is the potentially hierarchical nature of parties, which provides a system of rewards and advancement that requires persistent investments of time and resources from participants, usually starting at a very early age. In this sense parties are institutions that create sunk costs in terms of privileges accrued and time invested, which raises the costs of defection. When a party lacks these features, an elite need not necessarily invest time into the party. Rather, they might use their personal influence to promote themselves, perhaps serving in the legislature one day but somewhere else the next. In this scenario, continued loyalty depends more on the availability of various patronage positions. By contrast, with a hierarchical party, if resources become scarcer and promotion is not guaranteed, elite loyalty might persist because of the time already invested and the perceived future career opportunities.

Third, parties can also provide the means through which rulers signal the credibility of their commitments to their followers. This is different from the question of regime cohesion. Cohesion is often inherited or derivative of a shared ideology, past, or identity. Moreover, cohesion might only apply to a narrow segment of the regime (Levitsky and Way 2012). Credibility, on the other hand, refers to the methods by which regimes persistently bind themselves to some formal rules and processes that smooth

---

[4] There is a large literature on party machines, clientelistic linkages, and vote buying largely derived from the Latin American experience (Kitschelt 2000, Schaffer 2007). It should also be noted that, perhaps unintentionally, a party's organizational ability to mobilize voters also signals strength and permanence to potential defectors. In fact, autocrats might have an incentive to create supermajorities rather than minimum winning coalitions to signal the immovable nature of the regime. Studies show that supermajorities can maintain elite loyalty (Magaloni 2008) and also possibly deter military intervention (Geddes 2006).

exchanges with supporters. The specific institutional features of parties that foster credibility are not necessarily clear or uniform. Jason Brownlee notes that credibility emerges from the presence of a "sustainable system for members to settle disputes and exert influence" (2007). Looking at the Mexican PRI, Beatriz Magaloni emphasizes the importance of competitive and fair primaries, especially for executive positions (2006). Lisa Blaydes makes similar insights regarding legislative elections in Egypt, which were more competitive and signaled to elites that they had a fair shot of attaining office (2011). Philip Keefer stresses that parties preserve credible commitments when they maintain intra-party transparency and focused expectations through the institutionalization of practice (2007). The point is that credibility provides elites not only with career paths, but takes steps to ensure that those career paths are stable over time.

CREDIBLE RULING PARTIES AND ELECTORAL AUTHORITARIAN CONTESTATION

I push this literature forward by expanding the concept of a credible ruling party and linking it to electoral authoritarian contestation. I use the term credible party to convey when a ruling party sustains features that bolster expectations of regular and fair exchange between a regime and its followers. For elites this means primarily stable career paths, and for voters the persistent delivery of desired goods. It is not that the party itself is credible, but rather the relationships it develops with elites and voters are. It is also a concept that is distinct from simply institutionalization, and instead looks at four unique dimensions: the party's physical size, decisional autonomy, internal democracy, and the breadth of its social commitments.[5] A more detailed conceptualization is provided in Appendix B, but all of these features of ruling parties are coded based on their development during the single-party era so as to single out their impact during elections. The choice to think of a specific party "type" clearly has tradeoffs.[6] While there is no specific boundary across which

---

[5] Institutionalization refers to entities that become reified and acquire organizational and social stability, often termed behavioral routinization and value infusion (Huntington 1968, Levitsky 1998, Randall and Svåsand 2002a). The term institutionalization is often mentioned in discussions of authoritarian parties, but without much empirical reference besides party age (Geddes 1999, Brownlee 2007). A party can be institutionalized, but not physically large or internally democratic.

[6] The term "credible party" does not appear in other literature on party typologies (Panebianco 1988, Kitschelt 1994, Gunther and Diamond 2003). The literature on party

a party becomes credible, using a party type helps with the process of theory building and maintains some degree of parsimony. Moreover, the evidence presented from a select number of cases validates the conceptual choices here. Regimes with what I consider credible ruling parties behave as expected during elections. The same can be said for regimes without credible parties.

Physical organization helps ruling parties build credible relationships with elites. Hierarchical parties with considerable sub-national presence and affiliated mass-mobilizing organizations can guarantee more positions to elites, but also importantly assure elites that their positions are secure. As mentioned, parties are useful organizational tools, which signal to elites that the regime can compete effectively and will likely go undefeated in an election. In Tanzania, TANU famously created thousands of party cells for each ten homes in rural and urban areas. These institutions not only helped the regime reach voters, but also reduced the influence of individual parliamentarians in securing voter support. By contrast, the ruling party in Kenya tended to end at the district, which meant that the regime depended on the popularity and wherewithal of its legislative candidates to get out the vote. Consequently, elite defection had a crippling effect since the regime could not guarantee to other elites that the party's infrastructure would compensate and mobilize voters. The smaller the physical size of the party the more likely, all things being equal, that elite defection will cascade.

Credible ruling parties also retain relatively stronger decisional autonomy. When ruling parties operate somewhat independently of other political institutions like the presidency, elites are provided with more voice and control over their own affairs. This fosters credibility because it ensures stable expectations regarding what the rules of the game are, and gives elites the chance to express their grievances and help adjust the party's direction as needed. At a minimum this entails some basic level of party institutionalization, but more importantly, internal procedures that are followed by the party. For instance, credible parties hold more frequent and open national congresses where elites can debate and vote on party bylines or elect party officials. When ruling parties use national congresses as ceremonial occasions rather than deliberative affairs, they do not foster the same level of credibility. In the case of Cameroon,

---

typologies was also important in early work on African single-party regimes (Hodgkin 1961, Zolberg 1966, Morgenthau 1967, Coleman and Rosberg 1970). The issue is that while these typologies capture important information regarding parties, they tend to focus on ideology and do not address the specific context of authoritarian parties.

national congresses have historically simply been opportunities for the party to rubber stamp directives issued by the president. This left elites much more skeptical of the ruling party and their role in the regime.

A third critical element of credible ruling parties is the presence of competitive and transparent processes for the nomination of candidates. The literature on party primaries notes differences in their inclusiveness (Hazan and Rahat 2010); however, the Africanist literature generally distinguishes between competitive and plebiscitary primaries (Collier 1982). In the latter, a slate of candidates is handpicked by the president or the party's National Executive Committee and presented for an up and down vote in the central committee. This weakens credibility since it keeps recruitment and promotion decisions opaque. For instance, in Cameroon it was common for the Cameroon People's Democratic Movement (CPDM)'s Central Committee to overturn local primaries in favor of more politically connected candidates. By contrast, in competitive primaries the party delegates or members vote for their preferred candidates. Ruling parties can promote even more credibility when they ensure that merit and fair competition is considered. This was evident in Tanzania, where dissatisfied nominees could lodge complaints with an adjudicating body within the party. This logic also extends to how parties nominate their presidential candidates. In other words, internal democracy increases the credibility of ruling parties because it ensures fair and repeated competition.

While many of these features of credible parties have been noted elsewhere, I further contend that parties also build credible exchanges with citizens, and in the context of elections, voters. Parties, and especially single-party regimes, have the opportunity to establish enduring and credible systems of transaction with defined political constituencies. These patterns are often categorized as wide vs. narrow and regular vs. temporary forms of social incorporation.[7] In the African context narrower coalitions prioritized urban constituents over rural ones, or cash and export-crop farmers over food-crop and subsistence-based peasants (Bates 1981). Ethnic bias also limited the breadth of a regime's social commitments, unless that ethnic bloc was sufficiently large as to constitute a real majority (Elischer 2013). This includes parties that were supposedly multiethnic in name like the CPDM or Kenyan African National

---

[7] Social incorporation is cornerstone in studies of state building and regime development. See for instance the arguments regarding the role of labor incorporation in corporatism and democratization (Collier and Collier 2002, Rueschemeyer, Stephens, and Stephens 1992), and broader class incorporation in determining regime types (Moore 1966, Waldner 1999, Bellin 2000).

Union (KANU), but there was evidence of a disproportionate distribution of resources within the ruling coalition. On the other hand, more widely incorporative parties such as TANU reduced the salience of ethnicity in resource allocation and instead reached into the countryside. Broadly conceived rural communities like subsistence peasants were by far the largest constituency in pre-independence Africa.

These patterns influence the ability of ruling parties to build credible relationships with voters. Narrow incorporation leads to perceptions of bias in resource allocation, and the beneficiaries of government largesse can change suddenly. This can involve the distribution of club goods like schools, health facilitates, and infrastructure. It also extends to the allocation of political appointments, or might include state-level pricing schemes. For instance, in Kenya the perception grew in the 1980s that Kalenjin maize farmers were provided with preferential government pricing, which signaled a shift from policies that previously benefitted the Kikuyu coffee and tea growers (Lofchie 1994). This does not encourage expectations of consistent exchange, since the credibility of this relationship depends on the identity of those in power. If a cabinet member is dismissed, this might signal a sudden decline in resource allocation to a specific region or ethnic group, and the party's promises seem less credible. By contrast, consistently wide distributive commitments foster expectations of regularity with the party in power, independent of who the president or a specific legislator is.

Importantly, the emergence of a credible relationship with citizens should not imply ideological support (although it might), but rather the consequence of longstanding interactions with the regime. I consider the motivations of citizens across contexts as quite similar: to gain access to clientelistic resources, rather than clear policy preferences (Wantchekon 2003). Whether the fact that a citizen repeatedly shows up to endorse the ruling party is indicative of their real preferences is debatable. And indeed, there is substantial scholarship on the question of preference falsification in authoritarian settings.[8] A public demonstration of support is the first step in gaining access to government resources, so it might not be sincere. However, the important part of this relationship is its consistency, not its authenticity. Widely incorporative parties might simply have made

---

[8] The literature on preference falsification in authoritarian settings has primarily been used to explore the collapse of communism and the onset of political revolution (Kuran 1997, Kalyvas 1999). Recently there have been attempts to explore this factor in contexts of closed authoritarianism (Malesky and Schuler 2011) and electoral authoritarian settings (Frye et al. 2017).

it clear to voters that the devil they know through a long and imperfect historical relationship is better than the devil they don't know.

The presence or absence of a credible ruling party generates a number of specific causal process observations and comparative implications, which are examined in detail in Chapters 5 and 6. These relate primarily to the ways in which ruling parties manage elite competition, mobilize social support, and shape opposition decision-making:

The Management of Elite Competition: Credible ruling parties are more competent at managing elite competition, and consequently at preventing defection. Within individual cases, when regimes have credible parties we should observe the operation of actual internal party institutions that impact how elites relate to the party. The institutional mechanisms in place should reduce elite tensions, and make the appearance of overt grievance less common. Parliamentary and presidential nomination systems should follow clear procedures, and credible parties will be more adaptive to internal disputes that might arise during the nomination process. The institutional autonomy of the party means that conflict resolution means can be offered independent of the interests of the president or other influential figures in the regime. Elites in credible ruling parties should note the integrity of the party's internal structures and the fairness of its nomination processes as factors that sustain their loyalty and longer-term investment in the party.

Less credible parties will not demonstrate these same features. Absent institutionalized mechanisms for selecting candidates or managing elites, disputes and factionalism should be much more overt. Nomination processes should be contentious moments associated with more expressed criticism and elite defection. Candidates should state their disappointment with the party's internal processes, the absence of a level playing field or transparency during nominations, and the lack of any meaningful or satisfactory recourse. This insight extends to presidential selections, which should generate significant conflict within regimes without credible ruling parties. With higher levels of actual and potential elite defection, the regime must fall back on core supporters and expend manipulation and resources to entice elites back into the fold. In comparative perspective, regimes without credible ruling parties are more susceptible to elite defection during moments of similar regime vulnerability that might arise due to economic crisis or strong opposition mobilization.

Electoral Mobilization and Support: Credible ruling parties have an advantage when it comes to mobilizing voters. This is partially due to their larger organization across the country. Credible parties should be able to muster significant, although not necessarily dominant, vote shares across most areas of the country, while less credible parties will not. There should not be many areas of the country that are at least not minimally touched by the ruling party, or many areas of the country where the ruling party wins miniscule percentages of the vote. Voter mobilization is also strengthened by the broader social commitments that credible parties make. Since these parties have made historical commitments to a wide range of citizens, this should correspond with levels of electoral support.

Without credible ruling parties there are likely to be vast areas of the country where the incumbent has negligible voter support. This is because in the absence of party infrastructure that can mobilize voters, the defection of an elite can precipitate massive voter defection. This voter defection should also mimic the narrower social incorporation of the regime. The most consistently lowest levels of support should come from constituencies that view themselves as the victims of distributional bias and inconsistent promises from the ruling party. This means that to win elections the regime needs to depend heavily on a narrow and core base of support, which in these contexts primarily means ethnic cohorts. There should be a strong correlation between the ethnic identity of voters and support for the regime, which will supersede the importance of other factors such as more objective material conditions. As with enticing elites back to the party, regimes with less credible ruling parties will need to expend resources to attract back large voting blocs.

Opposition Contestation: A corollary of these observations is that the credibility of ruling parties also impacts patterns of opposition contestation. Since credible ruling parties can retain elite support more easily, this makes it difficult for opposition parties to recruit popular politicians. Instead, it forces them to train new generations of party leadership and focus on party building. We would also expect opposition parties that face credible parties to note the size of the ruling party as a factor during elections, while in other scenarios oppositions might more often cite the role of the security services or state officials. Likewise, since credible ruling parties enjoy wider and more sustained levels of popular support, it makes it difficult for opposition parties to expand their operation and it limits their outreach efforts. We should find that opposition parties are not only hindered by their material shortcomings, but by their limited appeal in regime strongholds. On the other hand, the logic of ethnic-party building is more likely to permeate oppositions when regimes are more narrowly incorporative and themselves dependent on the support of smaller ethnic blocs.

A central question emerges from this discussion – if credible parties are so beneficial to the survival of autocratic rule, why don't all autocrats create them? There is no simple answer. Credibility requires substantial institutional investments, compromise, and vision. Some work has looked at the origin of credible parties through the lens of elite conflict and the availability of state patronage. High degrees of elite discord without resources at regime inception can lead to more credible parties since a ruler is forced to make institutional concessions to create a coalition (Smith 2005, Brownlee 2007). Other work contrasts state capacity with the power of an autocrat's "launching organization," which often means a political party (Slater 2010, Hanson and Sigman 2013). Different balances of power at inception can push rulers on different pathways of regime construction and combinations of carrots and sticks. Strong parties might emerge because the state is powerful and can curtail political opposition and mobilize financial resources, or strong parties might emerge out of preexisting powerful organizations used to overtake the state.

The literature on African politics also provides some insights into the origins of political institutions. For instance, Joel Barkan and Frank Holmquist have traced different regime linkage strategies to the structure of peasant society and the progress of commercial agriculture (Barkan and Holmquist 1989). In Adrienne LeBas' work on opposition parties in Kenya, Zambia, and Zimbabwe, she notes that preexisting structures like labor unions often provided a stable foundation for opposition parties. Likewise, opposition parties that drew stark rhetorical lines in the sand between themselves and their opponents were more capable at maintaining group cohesion (LeBas 2011). On the other hand, Rachel Riedl traces incumbent authoritarian strength in the face of democratization pressures to different legacies of regime building (Riedl 2014). Regimes that brokered with traditional elites could control the transition to elections, which generally led to a more stable party system.

My approach is to focus more on the consequences of different institutional arrangements during the multiparty era, rather than their origins. There are elements of comparative historical analysis and path dependence to this argument.[9] Decisions and developments at regime inception lock autocrats into certain institutional pathways that have real staying power. The factors that shape these choices are influenced by structural

---

[9] By comparative historical analysis I am referring to a vast body of work that examines how macro-social phenomenon vary across space and time, investigates the origin and consequences of political institutions, and takes historical explanation and the role of time seriously. For more, see, Mahoney and Rueschemeyer (2003), and Pierson (2004).

conditions, but they cannot be reduced to them. These institutional features replicate themselves over time because there are sufficient members who benefit from their maintenance, and it becomes very difficult to move from a specific pathway of institutional evolution. Elections then serve as an exogenous shock that lets us observe patterns of continuity or disruption from the single-party era. While this is an argument primarily about legacy, I nonetheless stake out some speculative ground on origins in Chapter 4, which discusses the evolution and features of ruling parties in the three cases.[10]

THE ROLE OF INTERNATIONAL ACTORS
IN DEMOCRACY PROMOTION

The end of the Cold War fundamentally reshaped the international context of regime development. With the United States at the forefront, democracy promotion as a stated foreign policy goal took on much greater centrality (Carothers 2000, Cox, Ikenberry, and Inoguchi 2000, Schraeder 2002). Particularly, there have been three noticeable trends: the growth of the democracy assistance sector (Finkel, Pérez-Liñán, and Seligson 2007), the documented rise of election observation as a global norm (Kelley 2012b), and the use of conditionality and sanctions as tools to foster better governance (Levitsky and Way 2010, Donno 2013a). Consequently, there is a robust research program and growing debate over the ability of external actors to foster regime change. Much of the concern is over whether external actors can determine complex outcomes such as democratization, but even if we take into consideration a more limited result, such as changes in electoral competition, there are disagreements over the conditions under which external actors can and choose to make a difference.

Take for instance the growth in election observation, where there have been dramatic changes since the end of the Cold War. While in 1986 only 10 percent of elections were monitored, by 2004 that rate rose to 80 percent (Kelley 2012b, 17). Election observation is not costless to autocrats, and experimental evidence suggests that the presence of election

---

[10] There is a considerable body of work that similarly investigates the impact of single-party legacies in the post-communist setting (Ishiyama 1997, Kitschelt et al. 1999, Grzymala-Busse 2002), but only limited extension to African single-party regimes (Ishiyama and Quinn 2006). This design also mimics the logic used by Robert Putnam in *Making Democracy Work*, where different legacies of civic identity were put to the test with a set of government reforms in the 1970s (Putnam 1994).

observers can lead to more competitive outcomes (Hyde 2011). But, not all election observation missions are created equally, nor are they always willing or able to report on electoral misconduct. International observer missions from the United States are more likely to be critical, and international observation works best when paired with a robust domestic effort. Likewise, there can be a built-in bias for stability, or a preference for a peaceful rather than a necessarily credible election. Therefore, the impact of international election observation is conditional on the goals of donor countries and the context of observation.

Consider also the evolution of the democracy assistance sector during the past few decades. In the United States the National Democratic Institute (NDI), the International Republican Institute (IRI), and the United States Agency for International Development (USAID) provide electoral assistance, legal consultation, party training, and civic-education programs across the globe. In Europe, various foundations support similar democracy assistance efforts. International organizations such as the United Nations Development Program (UNDP), and the International Institute for Electoral Assistance (IDEA) are some of the latest additions to this global community. However, the efficacy of these endeavors is debatable. Statistical evidence shows that democracy assistance can empower comparatively weak political actors and improve certain indicators of democracy (Finkel, Pérez-Liñán, and Seligson 2007, Cornell 2013). On the other hand, there is evidence that democracy assistance creates unintended consequences by weakening state capacity and limiting the autonomy of political actors (Roessler 2005, Jarvik 2007). A major criticism of democracy assistance has been its often unfocused and rigid methods. Thomas Carothers laments the "one size fits all" approach of party assistance (Carothers 2006), while others note that democracy assistance is distributed unevenly and lacks national-level diplomatic engagement. Between 1990 and 2003 US democracy assistance in Africa was four times lower than in Eastern and Central Europe (Finkel, Pérez-Liñán, and Seligson 2007).

Finally, an external actor's ability and willingness to use conditionality or diplomacy varies. Conditionality rests on the assumption that international actors can provide something of material value to a regime, such as aid, development assistance, foreign investment, or desirable membership in a regional or international organization like the European Union. It refers to what Susan Hyde calls the desire of a regime to seek international benefits, or what Levitsky and Way conceive of as Western leverage. On the other hand, diplomatic engagement is typically rhetorical, and appeals to a regime's normative and legitimacy concerns (Hafner-Burton 2008, Lebovic and Voeten 2009). In the post–Communist context, high-level diplomatic engagement from figures like Secretary of State Madeline Albright and individual ambassadors were important factors. Similarly, in Latin America, democratic transitions in the Dominican Republic were driven by threats from the Clinton administration to downgrade diplomatic ties, and in Nicaragua by a threat to suspend assistance (Donno 2013a). Yet, as with election observation and democracy assistance, the impact of these tools varies. For instance, not all countries are economically sensitive to external threats. The absolute size of an economy, the extent of bilateral ties, the time-horizons of elites, and the degree of regional coordination all shape the capacity to enforce conditionality (Stokke 1995, Crawford 1997, Emmanuel 2010).

Importantly, the extent of international involvement depends not only on the perceived utility of such action, but also on foreign policy interests. External actors might have the incentive to maintain the status quo or block external attempts at election observation, democracy assistance, or conditionality. In some cases, powerful actors like Russia or China act as clear authoritarian patrons (Bader, Grävingholt, and Kästner 2010, Burnell and Schlumberger 2010, Vanderhill 2012). But, even potentially democratic patrons such as the United States, Great Britain, or France are uneven in their commitments. Fundamentally, competing foreign policy goals limit the degree of support for democracy promotion. Since the end of the Cold War, concerns with regional stability and national security have at times trumped democracy promotion. Economic interests also oftentimes lie at the heart of these dilemmas. Taken to an extreme, Western countries can become involved in democracy prevention rather than promotion, or act as significant authoritarian patrons themselves (Brown 2005, Brownlee 2012).[11] This is evident in Africa, where the integral role of French patronage in a number of countries is exemplified by the quote from Omar Bongo at the top of the chapter. Historical ties between Gabonese elites and French economic entities limited the willingness of France to use conditionality. More recently, US concerns with the war on terror have conditioned commitments to democracy promotion and economic reform. For instance, the United States now maintains

---

[11] Some of this discussion builds on Levitsky and Way's use of the term "Black Knight" to describe an external actor who counters Western efforts at democracy promotion. However, in practice, a Black Knight is simply an external actor that faces a conflicting foreign policy dilemma and decides to err on the side of the status quo.

a significant military presence in Djibouti for operations against the terrorist group Al-Shabaab (Bollee 2003).[12]

INTERNATIONAL PATRONAGE AND ELECTORAL
AUTHORITARIAN COMPETITION

The concern here is limited to the observable impact of international patronage on competition. The assumption, which is taken up in greater detail in Chapter 7, is that international action carries with it some consequence, and that in the immediate post–Cold War era several African countries were sensitive to international pressure. Choices regarding the level of international intervention are primarily shaped by fluid perceptions of strategic interest. Moreover, international actors are likely to intervene more strongly if they thought their efforts were bearing fruit. The counterfactual to consider is not whether more international action would have helped a country make greater strides toward democracy. Instead, the counterfactual is whether changes in the actual level of international commitment would have left an electoral authoritarian regime with more or less manipulative tools that would help it rebuild vote share. In other words, did international actors exacerbate problems of authoritarian uncertainty in the absence of credible institutions?

As with the term credible ruling party, the boundary between democratic and autocratic patronage is unsettled. By democratic patronage, I refer to whether a country is subject to combinations of strong democracy assistance, aid conditionality, and diplomatic engagement. By autocratic patronage I refer to explicit or implicit support for the incumbent regime, whether by financial or military aid, rhetorical support, or a reluctance to utilize the noted tools of democratic patronage. Chapter 7 provides some comparative data that demonstrates real differences in international commitments to democratic and economic reform and establishes Kenya as the target of democratic patronage, Cameroon as the target of autocratic patronage, and Tanzania as fairly status quo. To some observers, what seems like democratic patronage might in fact fall short of measures that induce democratization, and therefore actually sustain regimes (Brown 2001). Again, my focus is not on such transformative ends, and the utility

---

[12] There are other factors that shape an external actor's willingness to engage in strong national-level democracy promotion. Levitsky and Way note the role of social, economic, and political linkages with the West. However, these linkages in Africa remain low compared to other regions (an average score of 0.17 compared to 0.56 in Europe).

of the measurement choices lies in the empirical analysis. There are a number of observable implications that validate the notion that differences in international patronage impacted an electoral authoritarian regime's range of manipulative maneuverability, and consequently their vote share.

Access to Manipulative Resources: International actors can impact the amount and specific types of manipulative resources an autocrat can employ during elections. This might include denying the regime the ability to fully manipulate elections, or fostering political reform that limits the ability of regimes to curtail political organization or censor opposition. Regimes that are sensitive to international legitimacy costs might also be hesitant to use physical violence out of fear of retaliation. Importantly, the denial of certain repressive resources does not mean full restraint, and might indeed push regimes into more overtly coercive practice. For example, political reforms partially secured through international pressure made the 1997 Kenyan election more open than in 1992, but there were still significant levels of fraud and ethnic violence. By contrast, when countries enjoy authoritarian patronage or the status quo, coercive and manipulative actions are likely to go unpunished or unnoticed, and might even expand.

Access to Economic Resources: The use of conditionality and diplomatic pressure means that autocrats might be deprived of some crucial resources needed to maintain patronage coalitions. This is particularly true in Africa, where the size of the public sector at the onset of the 1990s was substantial, and nearly every country entered negotiations with international lenders (IBRD 1994).[13] With strong democratic patronage, foreign aid might be withheld from a regime absent political and economic reform, incumbents might be compelled to engage in some structural reform of their economies, and foreign investors might be reluctant to invest. The lack of financial resources could also lead to popular grievances, since services and growth opportunities might be limited during protracted negotiations with international lenders. On the other hand, authoritarian patronage might stabilize regimes through side payments that mitigate the impact of economic crisis or conditionality imposed by other international actors. With more economic resources available, autocrats can overcome the weakness of their parties and entice elites and voters back into the coalition through patronage.

---

[13] By 1990, thirty African countries entered into structural adjustment agreements with the World Bank and International Monetary Fund. Fifteen of these countries had 75 or more state-owned enterprises, which accounted for approximately 20 percent of formal sector employment (IBRD 1994).

Opposition Empowerment: The influence of international actors extends to the ability of opposition parties to build support and offer credible alternatives. More democracy assistance programming gives opposition parties additional and smarter tools of electoral contestation. Beyond training in party building and election monitoring, democratic patrons can also support oppositions financially and rhetorically. As the case study of Kenya will demonstrate, international engagement and pressure helped convince the opposition that an election boycott in 1992 would be counterproductive. This prevented KANU from achieving a supermajority in the legislature. By contrast, autocratic patronage means that opposition parties have to rely solely on domestic sources of support. The opposition in Cameroon had no real relationship with an international patron, and lost ground by boycotting several elections. Consequently, it was much easier for the regime to coopt opposition figures and fragment the political landscape.[14]

THE CASE STUDIES: TANZANIA, CAMEROON, AND KENYA

The three cases of Tanzania, Cameroon, and Kenya provide demonstrable variation along the moving parts of my theory, which helps identify causal processes and explicate different types of electoral authoritarian contestation. All three countries were single-party regimes that emerged in the immediate years following independence in the early 1960s. All three countries were swept in global changes that provoked a transition to multiparty elections in the early 1990s. These elections revealed important differences in their sensitivity to the challenge of electoral uncertainty. In Tanzania electoral outcomes have been consistently hegemonic, but contestation has also been more tolerant. In Cameroon elections have been repressive and hegemonic, while in Kenya more manipulation did not coincide with strong vote shares and led to electoral defeat. Table 2.1 records some of these differences in competition with measures of incumbent vote share, and some other commonly used indicators that capture the toleration of electoral contestation like the protection of civil liberties, degree of electoral fraud, and extent of state violence.

These outcomes are not surprising given the different kinds of ruling parties that emerged in the postindependence period and solidified

---

[14] Relatedly, Leonardo Arriola presents the argument that financial liberalization in the late 1980s and early 1990s, which was sparked by international actors, also facilitated coalition building in African countries (2012).

TABLE 2.1. *Electoral competition in Tanzania, Kenya, and Cameroon*

Tanzania	CCM presidential vote share	CCM % seat share	Freedom house scores	Political terror scale	Election free & fair
1995	61.8%	80.2%	6.6	2.5	2.0
2000	71.7%	87.5%	4.4	3	1.7
2005	87.4%	88.8%	4.3	3	2.5
2010	62.8%	77.9%	4.3	2.5	2.6
2015	58.5%	73.4%	3.3	3	2.2
Kenya	KANU presidential vote share	KANU % seat share			
1992	36.4%	53.2%	6.6	4	1.3
1997	40.1%	51.0%	7.6	4	1.5
2002*	31.3%	30.5%	6.5	4	2.3
Cameroon	CPDM presidential vote share	CPDM % seat share			
1992	40.0%	49.0%	6.6	3.5	0.5
1997	92.6%	64.5%	7.5	3	0.7
2002	N/A	83.0%	6.6	3	1
2004	70.9%	N/A	6.6	3.5	1
2007	N/A	85.0%	6.6	3	0.9
2011	78.0%	N/A	6.6	2.5	1.3
2013	N/A	82.2%	6.6	3	1.5

Notes: Freedom House scores record the Political Rights and Civil Liberties in the year prior to the election. A higher number means less protection of those rights and liberties. Gibney's Political Terror Scale ranges from 1 to 5, with five indicating high levels of state violence. The measure of electoral freedom and fairness is from Varieties of Democracy (V-DEM) and ranges from 1 to 4 with four indicating a completely free and fair election. *=Electoral defeat.

in the decades that followed. At independence, TANU in Tanzania was clearly the predominant political organization in the country. The lack of ethnic politicization and the leadership skills of the nation's father figure Julius Nyerere facilitated the expansion of TANU from its urban birthplace into the countryside. However, upon gaining independence the state that Nyerere inherited was extremely weak. State administration was poorly staffed, revenues were limited, and the military was minuscule. Very quickly the broad-based alliance that buttressed TANU began to fray, culminating in an attempted military coup. Nyerere's recourse to this predicament was to elevate the party as an integrative institution. In contrast with some understandings of this moment in Tanzania history, Nyerere was not compelled into concessions to rival elites because he lacked patronage resources, but rather because he had a distinct vision for the party and a socialist agenda that reached the rural population and further subdued ethnic divisions.

This was not the pattern of regime evolution in Cameroon or Kenya. In these instances, colonial powers bequeathed moderately stronger state institutions – a potent coercive apparatus in Cameroon and a well-staffed civil administration in Kenya. In both cases there was also no unified political organization at independence. Ethnic divisions had become politicized during colonial rule, which led to a proliferation of parties. In Kenya, KANU reflected an alliance between the Kikuyu and Luo, while the Kenyan African Democratic Union (KADU) was representative of Kenya's minority tribes. In Cameroon, parties reflected north-south divisions and the country's heritage as both a British and French colony. The likelihood of a credible ruling party to emerge from this confluence was not high, nor were foundational presidents necessarily inclined that way to begin with. Instead, other parties were coopted or coerced, and eventually merged with the ruling party. Consequently, the party itself was relegated as a secondary institution compared to the presidency. Elites brought ethnic loyalties to the regime, which led to persistent perceptions of distributional bias. In Kenya this was to the Kikuyu under Jomo Kenyatta and the Kalenjin under Daniel arap Moi. In Cameroon the bias was directed toward the Fulani under Ahmadou Ahidjo and later toward the Beti under Paul Biya.

These cases were held up as paragons of stability, partially because they did not succumb to military coups, but also because they were able to stage leadership transitions away from foundational figures. Yet, these moments of transition actually provided early indications that differences in party credibility were a problem for these regimes. In Tanzania, Julius Nyerere stepped down as president in 1985, but remained chairman of the party. His successor Ali Hassan Mwinyi was elected in an organized party primary. Despite some opposition from stauncher socialists, there was little fanfare over his nomination.[15] By contrast, presidential transitions were demonstrably more contentious in Cameroon and Kenya.

---

[15] Edward A. Gargan. "Nyerere Steps Down But Keeps His Hand In," *New York Times* (November 3, 1985).

Ahmadou Ahidjo and Jomo Kenyatta essentially handpicked their successors, which led to significant backlash within the regime, calls for constitutional change, and eventually coup attempts.[16] Absent institutional legitimation, these new presidents were forced to use coercion and patronage to secure their hold on power.

The actual transition to elections also reflects differences in party credibility. By the late 1980s each regime was vulnerable due to combinations of economic decline, increased political corruption, and growing international pressure (Bratton and van de Walle 1997). While patterns of opposition mobilization differed, in each case there were prominent figures in opposition – many of whom were previous regime insiders – that appeared to offer viable alternatives. Yet, in Tanzania the transition was embraced and managed by the regime. In 1992, opposition parties were legalized and the regime provided a three-year timetable to prepare for elections.[17] By contrast, incumbents in Cameroon and Kenya were more skeptical of multipartyism and sensitive to its challenges. Their response to nascent opposition was violent, and they resisted any dialogue over a transition to elections or the process of holding elections. Parties were legalized under immense pressure, and in each case the regime tried to hold snap elections that would catch the opposition off guard and defer discussions of constitutional reform.[18]

The divergence in electoral competition cannot be explained by factors like opposition coordination, state capacity, or economic performance. The upper left panel of Figure 2.2 notes the opposition factionalization index in each country (note that data for Kenya in all panels ends in 2002). This captures the likelihood of randomly choosing two members of the opposition from different parties (Beck et al. 2012). It is an imperfect measure, since it only looks at parties with legislatives seats

---

[16] Jomo Kenyatta changed the constitution prior to his death in 1978 to ensure that his vice president, Daniel arap Moi, would succeed him. In 1982 a faction of the Kenyan Air Force attempted a coup. Ahmadou Ahidjo also changed the constitution to let his prime minister, Paul Biya, succeed him. Ahidjo resigned from the presidency in 1982 due to illness, but remained the party chairman. In 1984 members of the Presidential Guard attempted a coup against Biya.

[17] The key mechanism in Tanzania was the Nyalali Commission, which was established in 1991 to investigate the viability of a transition to multipartyism. The committee returned a recommendation of 40 reforms, many of which were not implemented prior to the first election (Hyden 1999).

[18] In Cameroon parties were legalized in 1990, but Biya resisted a national conference and withheld the election date until just weeks prior. In Kenya, Moi legalized opposition parties in December 1991, but only dissolved parliament in October 1992. Elections were scheduled for December, but only announced in November of that year.

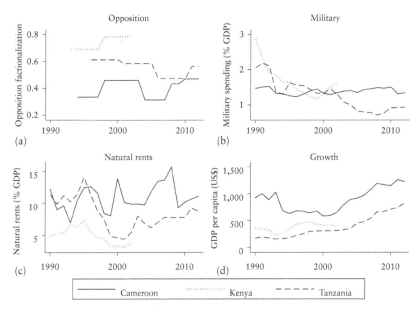

FIGURE 2.2. *A comparison of Cameroon, Kenya, and Tanzania along opposition factionalization, military spending, natural rents, and GDP Per Capita*
Sources: Beck et al. (2012), Bank (2014)

and does not account for specific electoral behavior like boycotts, which might temporarily reduce the level of factionalization. For instance, in Cameroon two major opposition parties boycotted the 1992 legislative election and therefore reduced the index to 0.33 in 1993. Still, the data does not indicate a consistent relationship with competition. In Kenya the opposition was more balkanized than in Cameroon or Tanzania, but elections were close and repressive. This factionalization helped the regime remain in power, but it does not explain the more competitive conditions to begin with. Opposition factionalization in Cameroon and Tanzania has hovered around continental averages, and at one point actually converged while competition differed.[19]

The other panels in Figure 2.2 look at measures of state capacity and economic growth, and also fail to differentiate these cases. It is difficult to find adequate cross-national measures of state capacity, especially in

---

[19] Opposition parties in each case have also uniformly failed to secure broad-based coalitions, with the exception of Kenya in 2002 and Tanzania in 2015. In 1995 and 2000 the CHADEMA party in Tanzania did not field presidential candidates and instead endorsed other figures, but this was not full coordination.

a region like Africa. Military spending and the share of natural rents in gross domestic product are the most consistent measures that address some of these capacities.[20] The data shows that military spending in each case declined in the early 1990s and converged at approximately 2 percent of GDP by the mid-1990s. The role of natural rents fluctuates with global markets, and Cameroon has pulled away since the 2000s due to increases in oil production. But, the data also shows that at crucial moments there was near convergence. Levels of economic growth are also poor predictors of competition. Each country started at different levels of development, but growth in the 1990s was nearly uniformly flat, and Cameroon and Tanzania have both grown steadily since the early 2000s (World Bank 2016).

The more convincing explanation for these differences in competition is the credibility-building features of ruling parties and the subsequent role of international actors. Fundamentally the ruling party in Tanzania has been able to persistently provide its own sources of elite conflict resolution and voter mobilization. One of the major challenges CCM faced during the multiparty era was whether it would be able to manage an increased factionalism within its ranks. In addition to new generational challenges, the growing influence of moneyed interests led to the perception that previously meritocratic avenues of advancement were closing due to rampant corruption. This placed the institutional strength of the party at loggerheads with the influence of personal networks that threatened to erode the very party institutions that had been the lifeblood of CCM for decades. In a sense, it was not a given assumption that CCM would not crack under the pressure of multipartyism, but rather a test of whether the party's institutions would prevail.

Remarkably, the party has repeatedly reasserted its independent influence over its factions, which has reinforced the credibility of the regime. This is evident in the ways the party has adapted to legislative primaries under conditions of multipartyism. Since 1995, when accusations of primary impropriety were at their highest, the party has adjusted by offering dispute mechanisms, setting clearer guidelines for nomination, overturning races, and ultimately opening up voting to a broader segment of the party. Defection at the legislative level is nearly nonexistent in Tanzania.

---

[20] The data in Africa on other measures of state capacity like the ability to tax or the effectiveness of government is inconsistent and has large gaps. Taking an average from the available data, tax revenue as a percentage of GDP was nearly uniform at 15 percent, and the World Bank's Statistical Capacity Indicator hovered at around 60. (Data on Kenya is unavailable.)

Most importantly, the party has consistently enforced its stated rules for presidential nomination, even at the risk of rejecting very popular candidates. Most starkly, in 2015 this meant denying Edward Lowassa's controversial candidacy due to violations of the party's bylaws on campaigning. This surprised many observers who anticipated that Lowassa's financial heft would secure the nomination. Lowassa defected to the opposition, but drew few other major players from CCM.[21]

The second challenge CCM faced was whether it could still rely on the support of significant numbers of rural voters that had possibly grown disillusioned with economic stagnation and the regime's embrace of economic liberalization. Nonetheless, there has been significant continuity in patterns of electoral support. Part of this is reflective of the party's organizational scale. Regime insiders and opponents both note that the regime can rely on thousands of party cells to mobilize votes. In real terms, this has meant that CCM rarely dips below the 50 percent vote-share mark in any district of the country. The other dependable part of CCM's vote has been the loyalty of many rural communities that were the direct beneficiaries of redistributive policies in the early 1970s. In these areas CCM's vote-share at times skyrockets to 80 percent. Voters in these areas are hesitant to embrace opposition parties because of their historical ties to the ruling party. The lower level of elite defection does mean that voter defection is less likely, but participants in these elections frequently note deeper sources of voter loyalty to CCM. It is not simply a matter of opportunism or ethnic voting, but derivative of a long period of repeated interaction with the party.

Regimes in Cameroon and Kenya were not as equipped for multiparty elections. In both cases a wave of elite defection shook the party during foundational elections. Since personal networks of influence had strongly permeated each party, there were no credible or meritocratic systems for nominating candidates. Political advancement in the party depended heavily on the decisions of the president, and the needs of various elites with closer ties to the president. With economic crisis, each regime had to tighten its ruling coalition, which inevitably meant pressure from certain constituencies – primarily ethnic cohorts – and the creation of starker winners and losers. This also made the party resistant to reform that might produce more transparency or democratic internal processes. In each case defection was preceded by calls for party reform that went

[21] Erick Kabendera. "Edward Lowassa ditches CCM for opposition party," *The East African*, July 28, 2015.

unheeded. In Kenya many defectors from KANU cited the manipulation of the 1988 primary, which dislodged several Central Province politicians, and the lack of reform in KANU prior to 1992. In Cameroon there was vocal protest over Biya's resistance to hold a national congress of the CPDM, and multiple accusations of primary rigging.

The consequences of weaker party credibility are clearly evident when we look at the issue of presidential succession. Daniel arap Moi and Paul Biya faced the end of their constitutionally mandated terms as president in 2002 and 2011, respectively. Neither KANU nor the CPDM had institutional structures for electing successors, which forced a real dilemma on each regime. In Kenya, Moi's option to retire and elevate Uhuru Kenyatta, the Kikuyu son of Kenya's first president, proved detrimental. It unleashed a strong backlash from other presidential contenders, another failed attempt at party reform, and ultimately the defection of more KANU elites. In Cameroon, it is also clear that the end of Paul Biya's term threatened to unravel the party. In recently uncovered private discussions, there was grave concern that Biya's choice of successor – whether another southerner or a northerner – would not be a consensus candidate and would tear the party apart, or even worse, lead to civil war. These fears were partially the reason the constitution was changed in 2008 to allow Biya to run for a third term.

These differences extend to the way these parties mobilized social support. Neither KANU nor the CPDM could brag about party real estate, and their parties generally ended at the district level. Likewise, voter alliances in each country were more overtly ethnic and not tied to the party itself. Perceptions of systematic bias and misallocation of resources toward specific groups and areas were strong. This meant that when an elite defected, the regime lost its main link with voters in the constituency. In both cases, there were large parts of the country where the regime could not even mobilize 20 percent of the vote. More importantly, the absence of persistent and wide-scale relationships with voters meant that when push came to shove regimes had to fall back on the support of ethnic cohorts. In Kenya, Moi only won overwhelming voter support in the upper Rift Valley and parts of the Far North, while in Cameroon Paul Biya's vote share mainly came from his Beti co-ethnics in South and Central Provinces. This inevitably meant that elections were going to be narrower.

To compensate for the weakness of their parties, regimes in Cameroon and Kenya had to become much more coercive. Their foundational elections were closer than in Tanzania, and manipulation likely helped them survive those challenging moments. Here the importance of international actors takes on greater significance. Kenya became the target of concentrated democratic pressure, primarily from the United States. Elections in Kenya were the most observed on the continent, economic privatization went further than in Tanzania or Cameroon, and international actors used direct pressure to force concessions from the regime. This pressure failed to fully limit the KANU regime, especially when it came to the use of violence, and the Moi regime remained brutal in the 1990s. But, democratic patronage constrained the range of tools KANU could employ. Former KANU elites recall the struggle to adapt to a more restrictive environment, and opposition actors recollect a sense of empowerment. Crucially, there is evidence that American pressure helped push Moi away from amending the constitution to avert a succession struggle.

Cameroon, on the other hand, was able to sustain a diverse range of manipulative tools due to international assistance. Important French loans and aid allowed Biya to pay civil service salaries prior to the 1992 election, and also helped the country weather economic crisis. French support deterred other actors from engaging in stronger democracy assistance or election observation, which was much lower in Cameroon than in Kenya or Tanzania. During negotiations with international lenders, the French were also instrumental in generating a steady flow of loans to the regime despite a comparatively smaller degree of reform. The public sector in Cameroon remained largely intact, which gave Biya an enormous resource that he could use to entice oppositions and compensate losers. After 2001, Cameroon's temporary position on the UN Security Council made it more important for American strategic interests. The conflict between American foreign policy goals came to a decisive point when Biya changed the constitution. The maneuver was overtly supported by the French, and according to recently revealed embassy documents, implicitly endorsed by the United States. As a result, the opposition in Cameroon has dwindled away.

Through this brief outline of the argument as it pertains to these three cases I have argued that ruling party credibility is a primary factor that differentiates structures of competition, and that international patronage is a secondary factor in contexts of weaker ruling party credibility. The argument is summarized in Table 2.2, and the specific moving parts are discussed in detail in the next chapters. Chapter 4 details how party institutions evolved differently in the three cases in terms of their credibility-building features. The impact of party credibility on elite behavior during candidate selection is discussed in Chapter 5. The legacy of social incorporation on voter mobilization is presented in Chapter 6, while Chapter 7 details the influence of international actors.

TABLE 2.2. *A two-stage theory of electoral authoritarian competition applied to the cases*

	Tanzania	Cameroon	Kenya
Regime Formation: *Did the incumbent build a credible ruling party?*	Yes	No	No
Elite Loyalty: *Do elites remain loyal to the regime or defect during vulnerable moments?*	Yes, regime takes steps to ensure credibility of selection processes	No, regime does not take steps to ensure credibility of selection processes	No, regime does not take steps to ensure credibility of selection processes
Voter Loyalty: *Do voters remain loyal to the regime or defect?*	Yes, regime maintains relationship with a broad constituency	No, regime must rely on narrower support	No, regime must rely on narrower support
Initial Electoral Competition	Tolerant and hegemonic	Repressive and non-hegemonic	Repressive and non-hegemonic
International Patronage: *Do international actors engage in strong democratic patronage?*	No, status quo oriented and not influential	No, party retains some ability to coerce and coopt	Yes, party loses some ability to coerce and coopt
Long-Term Electoral Competition	Tolerant and hegemonic	Repressive and hegemonic	Repressive and non-hegemonic

CONCLUSION

This chapter has offered a theory regarding the sources of differences in electoral authoritarian competition in former African single-party regimes. The central part of this argument is that the emergence of credible ruling parties in autocratic regimes has long-term consequences for regime stability and the management of electoral uncertainty. Through their ability to credibly shape elite career incentives and voter expectations, regimes with these parties are much less sensitive to the transition to multipartyism. In this sense, there is a great degree of continuity from the single-party era. Elites and voters remain loyal to the party, and the regime can contest elections with less fraud but nonetheless dominate the election. Tolerant hegemonies like Tanzania's are rooted in credible ruling parties.

By contrast, without these advantages elections are in fact much more challenging, and the endurance of electoral authoritarianism depends on contingent factors like the actions of external actors. I argue that the question of whether an international actor can influence competition is an empirical one. Existing theory predicts when external actors are more or less likely to intervene, but do not specify how their actions actually impact outcomes. At times, international actors can use a combination of tools to limit an autocrat's ability to use coercive strategies to deal with electoral uncertainty. This differentiates repressive yet hegemonic outcomes in Cameroon from repressive yet non-hegemonic outcomes in Kenya. The next chapter turns to a discussion of the concept of electoral authoritarianism and electoral competition in more detail, with an empirical application in Africa.

3

Electoral Authoritarian Competition
and the African Experience

The 2010 elections were competitive, with basic freedoms provided for, including freedom of association, freedom of movement, freedom of speech, and freedom of assembly ... at the same time there are still areas where concerns remain.

—Commonwealth Observation Report, Tanzania
General Elections (2010)

The Cameroonian government, for which President Paul Biya bears ultimate responsibility, took unusually extreme and illegitimate actions to ensure the president's victory. This led inexorably to the conclusion that the election was flawed to the point where its legitimacy and validity are called into question.

—National Democratic Institute Observation Report,
Cameroon Presidential Election (1992)

The era of electoral authoritarianism challenges not only our ideas about the nature of political change, but also our methods for identifying regimes. There are in fact two sets of conceptual challenges. First, we must situate the concept of electoral authoritarianism in relation to other forms of authoritarianism and to electoral democracy. Electoral authoritarianism is not simply the presence of elections under authoritarian conditions, nor is it a flawed democracy. There are sufficient violations of the democratic spirit so to render a regime as authoritarian, but elections still carry some meaning. Second, we need to develop ways to identify *intra-electoral authoritarian* variation in terms of competition. Electoral authoritarian regimes differ in their ability to marshal strong vote shares and in their propensity toward manipulation. These challenges are not easily addressed, since the standard methodological toolkit tends to eschew subjective judgments of regime features like freedom and fairness or competitiveness. Moreover, while there are issues regarding the quality of observational data on regime practices, there is also fundamentally no consensus over what constitutes a clear violation of democratic norms, or what makes a regime more or less competitive.

This chapter tackles these issues with an eye toward the African experience. I argue that electoral authoritarianism is a distinct form of authoritarian rule, but that some degree of subjectivity is inevitable when judging regime practices and when we conceptualize distinct regime types. This approach avoids classification standards that claim to be able to crisply differentiate regime types (Alvarez et al. 1996), and embraces the notion that conceptual choices are at times more art than science and must serve one's immediate research goals (Collier and Adcock 1999). Since I am more interested in authoritarian dynamics rather than democratization, I hold regimes to a fairly high democratic standard that avoids the "fallacy of electoralism." I also offer a conceptualization of electoral authoritarianism that builds on prior work and the most current data.

The second contribution of this chapter is to unpack the concept of electoral competition, and to identify configurations of electoral authoritarian competition. As noted earlier, there is some confusion over the term competitiveness, which can refer to the electoral outcome but also the electoral process. I maintain that these two dimensions of competition do not always operate in conjunction, and are equally important for studying electoral authoritarianism. I refer to the competitiveness of the outcome as the extent of *electoral hegemony* and the competitiveness of the process as the extent of *electoral toleration*. Regimes can be classified as either hegemonic or non-hegemonic, and as tolerant or repressive. Again, an element of unavoidable subjectivity remains a threat to these descriptive inferences, which I try to minimize by being explicit about my conceptual choices and by using the best possible data. I examine the role of incumbent vote share and a range of manipulative tools like physical violence, electoral fraud, exclusion, and censorship, to demonstrate a variety of experience in the sub-Saharan African context.

The end goal of this chapter is to situate electoral authoritarian competition in relation to other concepts, so that we can better examine electoral authoritarian trajectories and their relationship to authoritarian institution building. Figure 3.1 distinguishes between seven regime types, including four types of electoral authoritarian competition. Regimes that fall below the electoral threshold are considered *closed authoritarian*

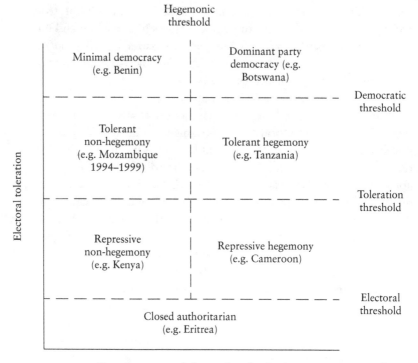

FIGURE 3.1. *Situating types of electoral authoritarian competition with examples from Africa*

regimes. This would include cases like Eritrea or Swaziland that do not hold regular elections. Countries that fall above the democratic threshold satisfy minimal conditions of freedom and fairness, and are therefore considered *minimal democracies,* such as Benin or Malawi. Between the democratic and electoral thresholds lies the range of electoral authoritarian regimes. When regimes combine hegemony with toleration they are called tolerant hegemonies, as in Tanzania, and when regimes combine hegemony with repression they are called repressive hegemonies, as in Cameroon. Regimes that are non-hegemonic but tolerant are coded as tolerant non-hegemonies, as was the case for a period in Mozambique, and regimes that are non-hegemonic but repressive are considered repressive non-hegemonies, as in Kenya. In addition, a democratic regime that falls to the right of the hegemonic threshold is considered a *dominant-party democracy,* such as Botswana or South Africa (Pempel 1990, Giliomee and Simkins 1999).

These regime classifications can be used to draw some broader descriptive inferences. Indeed, looking at the evolution of electoral authoritarianism in Africa since 1990 I find that periods of non-hegemony are relatively short. Likewise, most African electoral authoritarian regimes are – perhaps unfortunately – repressive hegemonies. However, there are an important number of tolerant hegemonies that require explanation. Electoral authoritarianism also arises in very different historical and institutional contexts. Repressive hegemonies are strongly associated with former military and personal regimes, while former single-party regimes evolved in more diverse trajectories. This corresponds with the major ideas laid out in the previous chapters. Ruling parties developed differently during the single-party era, and therefore shaped the way that autocrats subsequently competed in multiparty elections.

The chapter proceeds with a discussion of the concept of electoral authoritarianism and its relation to closed authoritarianism and minimal democracy. I offer some classification rules to help distinguish what electoral authoritarianism actually is. The chapter then breaks down the concept of electoral competition and uses data on incumbent vote share and manipulation from the Varieties of Democracy project (V-DEM) to measure hegemony and toleration in twenty-eight African electoral authoritarian regime periods since 1990. This dataset offers some of the most comprehensive and sophisticated information about regime practices in a large number of countries. The chapter then describes how electoral authoritarian sub-types have evolved since 1990, and examines the correlation between electoral authoritarian competition and former regime type.

SITUATING THE CONCEPT OF ELECTORAL AUTHORITARIANISM

While electoral authoritarianism is a form of hybrid regime, not all hybrid regimes are in fact electoral authoritarian (Schedler 2006b, 4–5). Nor is electoral authoritarianism simply the presence of elections under authoritarian conditions (Gandhi and Lust-Okar 2009). The notion of hybridity in these latter contexts refers to the incorporation of democratic elements into authoritarian regime practices.[1] Hybridity might include empowering legislatures with real decision-making that helps bind elites to a regime or signal credibility to international investors, but

---

[1] Another definition of authoritarian hybridity refers to the combination of different institutional bases of authoritarian politics, like "triple threat" regimes that are simultaneously single-party, military, and personalistic (Geddes, Wright, and Franz 2012).

this is not always accompanied by regular multiparty elections (Gandhi and Przeworski 2007, Wright 2008). Similarly, hybridity can also refer to the use of judicial institutions to either constrain or enable authoritarian behavior (Solomon 2007). In the Middle East, the term "liberalized autocracy" has been used to describe strategic advances and retreats in the level of political rights and civil liberties (Brumberg 2002). At times liberalized autocracies, particularly in the more open monarchies of the Middle East, do hold limited multiparty elections but under severe constraints, and in most cases executive power is uncontested (Lust-Okar 2004, Posusney 2004).

While these elements of hybridity are all important, there is something fundamentally distinct about electoral authoritarianism that distinguishes it as a regime type. As Andreas Schedler writes, electoral authoritarian regimes:

> Hold regular elections for the chief executive and a national legislative assembly. These elections are broadly inclusive (they are held under universal suffrage), minimally pluralistic (opposition parties are permitted to run), minimally competitive (parties and candidates outside the ruling coalition, while denied victory, are allowed to win votes and seats), and minimally open (dissidence is not subject to massive, but often to selective and intermittent repression. The elections are not, however, minimally democratic. (Schedler 2013, 2)

A number of key factors are highlighted by this definition that helps to situate the concept more clearly. First, elections are not simply a onetime occurrence to release social pressure or realign regimes, but are incorporated into the regular practices of regimes. The expectation from regime elites and opposition actors is that elections are to be a repeated game. While recurrent elections possibly reinforce democratic norms, the prospect of a future election necessarily shapes actor strategies in ways that are different from liberalized autocracies (Lindberg 2006a, 2009a). Second, electoral authoritarian elections open up all major national political offices to contestation, including the chief executive. The degree to which these offices are contested free and fairly does vary, but it means that there are far stronger focal points for oppositions to mount significant challenges and demonstrate their strength (Howard and Roessler 2006). Likewise, opening up executives for election forces new dynamics within regimes on how they manage issues like succession (Magaloni 2006).

While the distinction between electoral authoritarianism and liberalized autocracy is more easily discernible, the boundary with minimal democracy is essentially contested. Minimal definitions of democracy generally emphasize three procedural rules: executive selection, legislative selection, and party pluralism (Alvarez et al. 1996).[2] These standards are meant to prevent classification bias and eliminate the need to engage in subjective judgments regarding the freedom and fairness of elections. However, the growth of hybrid and electoral authoritarian regimes since the end of the Cold War necessitates moving beyond simply procedural accounts to an assessment of the electoral process itself (Schedler 2006b, 10). Indeed, some minimalist definitions of democracy arguably suffer from their own biases, likely toward democracy. The transition from "democracy with adjectives" to "autocracy with adjectives" reflects not just a semantic shift, but an academic refocus on factors largely ignored by the democratization literature, such as hybridity, authoritarian institutions, and the role of elections in authoritarian politics (Carothers 2002). To make these judgments regarding the quality of contestation easier, scholars now point to the increasingly strong data on elections, political rights, and civil liberties from media outlets, election observation missions, and the expert judgments of numerous outlets like Polity IV and Freedom House.

Yet despite the creation of what is essentially a cottage industry dedicated to measuring various aspects of democracy, significant challenges remain. For instance, Gerardo Munck argues that research on electoral authoritarianism is guilty of methodological sloppiness because there is incongruence between the concepts studied and the data employed (Munck and Verkuilen 2002, Munck 2006). Most prominently, organizations like Freedom House score countries' political rights and civil liberties rather than clearer dimensions of democracy such as participation and competition. Other data sources are unclear over how they aggregate individual measures, or how they maintain consistency across multiple years of observation. There are now several competing datasets that measure various aspects of electoral practice, such as the National Elections Across Democracy and Autocracy (NELDA) dataset (Hyde and

---

[2] There is a degree of disagreement over whether a fourth criterion, alternation, should be included in the definition of minimal democracy. While democratic norms cannot be truly tested absent a change of power, incorporating this rule ignores the experience of "dominant party democracies" that were prevalent in cases like Israel, Italy, and Japan for long periods of time (Pempel 1990, Giliomee and Simkins 1999). In addition, there is the risk of a "fallacy of turnovers." As several African cases exemplify, turnover does not a democracy make. For instance, after the Movement for Multiparty Democracy in Zambia defeated the ruling United National Independence Party (UNIP), the country remained electoral authoritarian for nearly a decade. President Frederick Chiluba attempted to change term limits and was indicted over 100 counts of corruption.

Marinov 2012), the Quality of Elections Data (QED) dataset (Kelley 2012), and the V-DEM project (Coppedge et al. 2017).

These new datasets all make important contributions, but there are still questions of data validity. Importantly, information on authoritarian settings is invariably more opaque, and measures rely on expert judgments. Coders commonly employ newspaper reporting, election observation missions, or their personal in-country experiences to assess freedom and fairness and electoral integrity. Indeed, observers and participants can come to very different conclusions, and election observers often hedge their statements for various reasons. Jonathan Hartlyn and Jennifer McCoy note the issue of "observer paradoxes," where due to resource limitations election observers are confined to short periods of observation and specific geographic regions (2006). Susan Hyde has shown how the presence of election observers creates incentives to mask certain types of fraud, and therefore skew an overall assessment of the election (2011). Adding concern is the fact that at times there is a motivation to downplay violations of the election. Judith Kelley examines the "shadow market" of election observation missions, often strategically invited by countries to overlook violations of election norms. An election monitor's special relationship with a host country can bias reports and encourage an emphasis on progress and success, rather than democratic shortcomings (2012b).

Compounding these issues of data is a fundamental, and in my opinion ultimately irreconcilable, debate over the actual minimal definition of democracy. Putting aside questions over whether regimes should be measured as types rather than as continuums, there is no consensus on what elements of democracy must be violated, and to what extent they must be violated, to render a country nondemocratic. On the extreme, democracy is fairly easy to gauge and assess. In instances like Kenya during the 1992 election, when fraud and violence were so prevalent before, during, and after the election, it is easier to designate a regime as nondemocratic. Likewise, not many experts would disagree that Equatorial Guinea or Belarus are nondemocratic regimes. The more challenging cases are those that most approximate conceptions of a minimally democratic regime. Importantly, it is not just a question of whether violations are subtler and therefore more difficult to detect – i.e., a problem of measurement – but opacity over what it means to be democratic. Consequently, scholars diverge over what they consider to be the population of electoral authoritarian regimes. In Levitsky and Way's 2010 survey of competitive authoritarianism, they admirably move away from simple aggregate measures to code their own cases. Yet, they also employ a fairly strict definition of democracy, and any violation of their chosen criteria of freedom and fairness, civil liberties, and a level playing field renders a regime nondemocratic (365–8). A shift of the threshold between democracy and autocracy from a 3 to a 4 on Freedom House's political rights scale similarly alters the study population (Morse 2012). New data does not necessarily solve the disagreement over concepts.

IDENTIFYING ELECTORAL AUTHORITARIAN REGIMES

I use a number of classification rules to designate regimes as closed authoritarian, electoral authoritarian, minimal democracies, or as unclassified/other. These rules are summarized in Table 3.1, and while they do not proclaim to identify regimes without issue, they do help build consensus and avoid some of the perils of conceptual stretching. First, as noted, if a regime does not hold multiparty or multicandidate elections for both national legislatures and executives it is considered "closed authoritarian." This is a basic requirement that differentiates the concept of electoral authoritarianism from other forms of authoritarian hybridity. Second, since regularity is also emphasized as a central element of electoral authoritarianism, I maintain that a country must hold at least two consecutive elections for it to be classified. Regimes that have not held a second election, whether under electoral authoritarian or minimally democratic conditions, are considered "unclassified." Notably, this also includes regimes that have had turnover, but not yet held a second election. The idea here is not to overstretch the definition of either minimal democracy or electoral authoritarianism to instances where we simply do not know enough about regime practices.[3] Third, if a regime is embroiled in some state of internal conflict like a civil war or military coup it is coded as "other."

The more challenging component is the conceptual distinction between minimal democracy and electoral authoritarianism. I utilize the coding scheme developed by Howard and Roessler, which combines the Freedom House Political Rights (PR) score with the Polity IV (Piv) aggregate score (2009). Elections years with a lagged PR score of 3 or higher and Piv score of 6 or lower are considered authoritarian. By contrast, elections years with a lagged PR score of 2 or lower or a Piv score of 7 are considered

---

[3] A country is back-coded as democratic to the moment of electoral transition if the subsequent election was minimally democratic. For instance, in Ghana the 2000 election removed the NDC from power and the 2004 election was minimally democratic. Therefore, Ghana is considered an electoral democracy from 2000 onwards.

TABLE 3.1. *Classifying electoral authoritarian regimes*

Regime type	Classification rules
Electoral Authoritarian	Elections for executive and legislature AND Held at least two consecutive elections AND Does not meet minimal democratic threshold (PR > 2 and Piv < 7)
Minimal Democracy	Elections for executive and legislature AND Held at least two consecutive elections AND Meets minimal democratic threshold (PR < 3 or Piv > 6) -OR- Elections for executive and legislature AND On democratic threshold (PR = 3 or Piv = 7) AND Meets two turnover test
Closed Authoritarian	No elections for executive and legislature
Unclassified	Elections for executive and legislature AND Has not held at least two consecutive elections
Other	Election years held under conditions of internal conflict or other interruption

Notes: PR is the Freedom House Political Rights score and Piv is the Polity aggregate score. A two-turnover test is when an incumbent loses an election twice. "Other" includes years of conflict due to civil war or coup, transitional governments, and external occupation.

minimally democratic.[4] In recognition of the "two turnover" test, borderline regimes that nonetheless have seen incumbents lose elections twice are also recognized as minimally democratic (Huntington 1991).

There are a number of advantages to this approach. First, it provides two separate data assessments of broader regime practices across a wide swath of countries and time. The Freedom House score aggregates expert assessments of electoral processes, political pluralism and participation, and the function of government. The Polity IV score judges the competitiveness of political participation, the openness and competitiveness of executive recruitment, constraints on chief executives, and regulation of participation.[5] Second, it also uses data that is independent of my measures

---

[4] I use lagged measures to avoid including post-election improvements in political conditions that might get swept up in a score.

[5] Specifically, the Freedom House Political Rights score assigns weights to each component and aggregates into a 1–7-point scale, with 7 indicating the least protection of political rights. Scores for the individual components are only available for a limited period of

of electoral competition that are discussed below.[6] Third, it is an approach that has been used in several other research studies on electoral authoritarianism, and therefore allows some degree of comparability (Clark 2006, Lindberg 2006b, Schedler 2006b). The specific thresholds used here actually produce the greatest level of consensus across these previous studies (Morse 2012). Since I am interested in the authoritarian features of regimes, these choices also likely err on the side of authoritarianism.

From this classification I am able to identify twenty-eight country-periods of African electoral authoritarianism between 1990 and 2016. While most of the comparative data ends in 2016, the number of African electoral authoritarian regimes appears to be fairly stable. As of writing, of the twenty-eight cases eleven countries have exited electoral authoritarianism. In Kenya (2002), Ghana (2000), Nigeria (2015), Senegal (2001), and Zambia (2011) electoral authoritarian regimes were defeated at the polls. In Côte d'Ivoire (1999), Guinea (2008), Mauritania (2005), and Niger (2010) military coups ended electoral authoritarian tenures. In 2012, Central African Republic entered into a civil war that ended François Bozizé's ten-year stint as the president of an electoral authoritarian regime. In 2014, Burkina Faso's Blaise Compaoré was forced out of office after nearly twenty years in power following public protests that erupted after his attempt to amend the constitution and run for another term. This leaves seventeen cases that have been steadily electoral authoritarian, on average, for over twenty years.

UNPACKING THE CONCEPT OF ELECTORAL AUTHORITARIAN COMPETITION

Given the debate over the term competition in the context of electoral authoritarianism, it is important to unpack the concept into two major constituent parts.[7] I empirically examine the records of what I term electoral hegemony and toleration in all twenty-eight of Africa's recent electoral authoritarian regimes. I explain why an electoral authoritarian

---

time. The Polity IV score subtracts an autocracy scale from a democracy scale, both of which are weighted 11-point indexes.

[6] All of the identified cases of electoral authoritarianism also score below a 2.5 on V-DEM's index of electoral democracy.

[7] These distinctions are not just semantics, but shape the empirical population of cases and therefore theoretical insights. For instance, Levitsky and Way exclude cases where electoral contestation itself does not seem meaningful, what they call "hegemonic regimes." African cases like Burkina Faso, Chad, and Uganda are not discussed (2010).

regime might seek not just victory but actually large presidential and legislative majorities, and suggest some useful cutoff points for distinguishing hegemonic versus non-hegemonic regimes. I then discuss the inherent dilemmas in using manipulation during elections, and explain why regimes might be interested in maximizing electoral returns while minimizing more overt forms of manipulation. Using data from V-DEM I provide evidence that electoral authoritarian countries rely on different arrays of physical repression, electoral fraud, exclusion, and censorship. From these data I am to create a broader measure of electoral toleration that can differentiate between tolerant and repressive electoral authoritarian regimes.

The Authoritarian Advantages and Disadvantages of Hegemony

Authoritarian regimes at times aspire to not just win elections, but to establish some degree of electoral hegemony. At a basic level hegemony works by maintaining supermajorities in the legislative body, or generally speaking two-thirds of the seats, which prevents legal and constitutional change. Legislative majorities act as a gatekeeper against tangible future challenges and limit the utility of a central locus of opposition activism. Indeed, the end of single-party dominance in cases like Korea, Taiwan, and Mexico was heralded by reforms to the electoral process and constitutions, which occurred only after regimes lost their legislative majorities (Solinger 2001). At another level, electoral hegemony is less about these tangible benefits, and more about the projection of power. Garnering supermajorities in the legislature and strong presidential vote shares increases regime strength by signaling to elites that it is in their interest to continue and hitch their careers to the current regime (Magaloni 2006). The ability to marshal large numbers of voters at the polls might also deter other challenges from the military (Geddes 2006, Gandhi and Lust-Okar 2009). Within the context of African neo-patrimonial regimes, perceptions of presidential power help maintain what are at times tenuous multiethnic coalitions that hinge on the central role of the executive as a broker (van de Walle 2003).

However excessive electoral hegemony can be counterproductive, especially when outcomes appear over-determined. When presidents win 90 percent or 100 percent of the vote, the assumption generally is that elections have been manipulated to such a degree as to drain them of any competitive meaning whatsoever. For instance in Egypt, Hosni Mubarak's regime held fairly competitive legislative elections, but also infrequent presidential elections that were by most accounts sham and won by unbelievable margins (Blaydes 2011). It is not on the face of it clear why regimes hold elections with zero uncertainty. Monopolistic demonstrations of power are more often associated with single-party rule and seen as ways for regimes to momentarily renew legitimacy (Hermet, Rouquie, and Rose 1978). In other instances over-determined elections act as ceremonious occasions that made citizens complicit in perpetuating authoritarian rule (Wedeen 1999). While this degree of hegemony might serve some symbolic function, it does not really help autocrats overcome their informational uncertainties, and can in fact have unintended consequences. Frequent elections that have absolutely no meaning might spur oppositions into unexpected contentious escalation, as evident in the Arab Spring of 2011 (Bellin 2012).

Accordingly, there is no agreed upon standard for measuring electoral hegemony. Regimes differ in what they aim to gain from hegemony, and as Andreas Schedler writes, "electoral competitiveness is grounded in intersubjective (sic) perceptions" (2013, 206). Autocrats might aim for hegemony to mitigate uncertainty, but they might also want to make sure that elections signal some minimal level of credibility to both domestic and international audiences. Likewise, electoral outcomes need to be interpreted in lieu of actor expectations, which is itself derivative of specific country contexts and histories. We would need to know what the pre-election perceptions of various players were in order to decipher whether an election result reflects hegemony or not.[8] Is a 60 percent incumbent presidential vote share a sign of weakness and therefore greater competitiveness, or is it a demonstrative signal of power and regime longevity? It is impossible to know the answer to these questions without deep country knowledge, which limits the ability to make comparisons across cases.

This is also why the current literature presents so many definitions of hegemony. Most rely on some combination of legislative and presidential vote share (often referred to as a power requirement) and regime longevity. However, there is little agreement over what the specific threshold is between a hegemonic and non-hegemonic regime. In an overview of seven studies of electoral dominance conducted by Matthijs Bogaards, he found that thresholds for hegemony ranged from a simple plurality of seats to over 75 percent of seats and presidential vote shares. Likewise,

---

[8] In addition we should be aware of the impact of various election institutions on perceptions of electoral hegemony, particularly as plurality vs. majoritarian vs. proportional election systems create different expectations from election participants. For example, even though an incumbent might win the second round of a two-round presidential system, losing the first round might signal important vulnerabilities.

TABLE 3.2. *Classifying electoral authoritarian hegemony and toleration*

	Classification rule
Electoral hegemony	
Hegemonic	Wins at least two consecutive elections
	Maintains two-thirds of the legislative seats OR 70 percent of the presidential vote
Non-Hegemonic	Wins at least two consecutive elections
	Maintains less than two-thirds of the legislative seats AND 70 percent of the presidential vote
Electoral toleration	
Tolerant	Scores above 0.4 on the index of electoral toleration
Repressive	Scores equal to or below 0.4 on the index of electoral toleration

Notes: The data on elections comes from the African Elections Database. The electoral toleration score is an aggregate measure of V-DEM's indexes of physical violence, clean elections, freedom of association, and freedom of expression (Coppedge et al. 2017).

some scholars emphasize a duration of incumbency that ranges from a single election to twenty years in power (Bogaards 2004). In Roessler and Howard's work on electoral authoritarianism, a hegemonic regime was classified using a 70 percent threshold of seats or votes (2009, 112), while Larry Diamond uses a 75 percent threshold (2002). By contrast, Andreas Schedler's work does not emphasize vote share but margins of victory and opposition fractionalization (2013, 207–8).

Given this uncertainty over the definition of hegemony, which is inevitable in these types of exercises, my approach is to split many of the differences and test whether various thresholds alter the results to a meaningful degree. Likely, regimes are concerned with both control of the legislature and the projection of power. While margins of victory capture the relative capacity of an incumbent vis-à-vis their opponent, it obfuscates the importance of absolute majorities and can in fact be misleading. Theoretically, an incumbent can win an election by a large margin but still only win a plurality of the votes. Indeed, this was the case in Kenya during the 1992 election, when Moi won by a large margin of 10 percent, but still only secured 36 percent of the presidential vote. It would be a stretch to claim that Moi had successfully demonstrated electoral hegemony. As summarized in Table 3.2, I consider a regime hegemonic when it survives at least two elections (a minimum requirement for any regime classification), and during that time has either maintained a supermajority in the legislature or kept above 70 percent of the presidential vote. Otherwise regimes are considered non-hegemonic.[9]

Figure 3.2 summarizes trajectories of vote and seat share in the twenty-eight identified cases of African electoral authoritarianism. The reference lines notes the 66 percent threshold for interpretive purposes, but specific data can be found in Appendix A.[10] Most regimes have seen fluctuation in their vote and seat share over time, but hegemony is still the predominant competitive outcome. Hegemony is also generally sustained through both legislative control and strong presidential vote share. Only in the case of Congo-RoC, has there been a prolonged period of presidential hegemony without commensurate legislative hegemony. There are more instances where presidential vote shares have been non-hegemonic while legislatures have remained firmly in incumbent hands, as in Gabon, Gambia, Ghana, Seychelles, and Togo. Notably, with the exception of Rwanda, all the instances where presidential vote shares rose above 90 percent correspond with boycotts by the major opposition parties.

Non-hegemonic outcomes do appear to be transitional, but can still persist for long periods of time. In Burundi, Cameroon, Chad, Gabon, Guinea, and Mozambique non-hegemonic periods lasted one to two election cycles before regimes transitioned to hegemony. Similarly, in Central African Republic, Kenya, Niger, and Zambia, periods of non-hegemony were preludes to transitions away from electoral authoritarianism. In Kenya and Zambia this was to defeat at the polls, while in Central African Republic and Niger this was transition to a state of conflict. This is in-step with expectations regarding electoral hegemony that views low vote shares or narrow margins of victory as a temporary stepping-stone toward either authoritarian retrenchment or democratization (Roessler and Howard 2009). In other instances non-hegemony reflected temporary vulnerability as in Ethiopia between 2005 and 2009, Togo between 2005 and 2009, and Zimbabwe between 2002 and 2012. In Nigeria, the People's Democratic Party teetered back and forth between non-hegemony and hegemony, and eventually lost power in 2015. Only in Congo-DRC has Joseph Kabila's electoral authoritarian regime persisted without presidential or legislative hegemony.

---

[9] It is also important to be wary of interpreting too much from election results when oppositions have boycotted them, since this might artificially inflate incumbent vote shares.

[10] To further probe the robustness of these results I also considered a 75 percent threshold for presidential vote share. The only results that change are for Nigeria between 2010 and 2013, which would be coded as a "non-hegemonic" rather than "hegemonic."

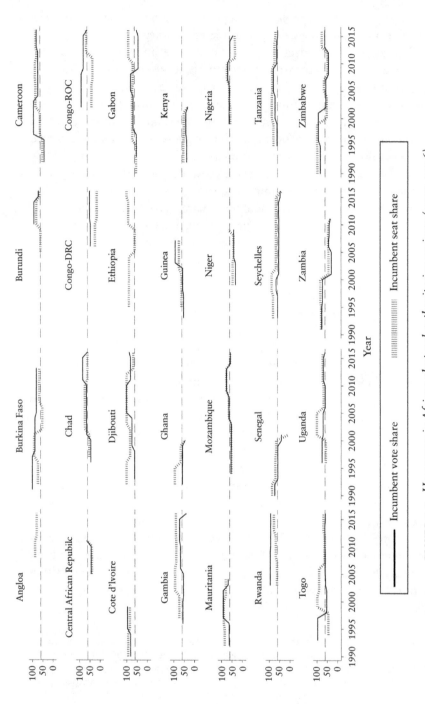

FIGURE 3.2. *Hegemony in African electoral authoritarian regimes (1990–2016)*

Notes: Hegemony is defined as either two-thirds seat share or 70 percent vote share, but the dashed reference line marks the 66 percent threshold for interpretive purposes. The data comes from the African Elections Database.

The Menu of Manipulation and Electoral Toleration

The challenges of electoral uncertainty mean that incumbents must manipulate the electoral process to some degree. But, since regimes enter elections with very different tools of contestation and knowledge of their own vulnerabilities, the risk of elections to incumbents diverges, and therefore so does the menu of manipulation. At times manipulation might be used to actually secure electoral victory from the jaws of defeat, while at other times it might be employed more strategically to win individual regions or seats, or to create the supermajorities that underpin hegemony. Autocrats must also balance the need to mitigate uncertainty against the need for elections to remain minimally credible and against the unforeseen costs of repression. An election that is too constrained might not serve other autocratic needs. Similarly, the operating assumption is that incumbents would prefer to win elections with less overt and less severe tactics. It is not controversial to assume that if an incumbent could win hegemonic vote shares with less manipulation they would, since repression risks backlash.

The menu of manipulation that shapes the toleration of electoral contestation is in fact quite broad, and goes beyond the election itself. As Andreas Schedler notes, we can identify broader institutional manipulations that autocrats use to mitigate authoritarian uncertainty. Outside of elections autocrats can shape legislatures, courts, and local governments. For instance, autocrats might weaken legislatures by limiting their formal powers, or through executive control of central positions like the speakership. Judges might not be guaranteed tenure, and could be appointed without review. Similarly, in many cases local governments are not elected but centrally appointed, and are often highly dependent on the central government for resource allocation. In some instances, regional governors and even mayors are simply extensions of autocratic power (Schedler 2013, 64–6). These institutional checks on uncertainty indirectly impact electoral contestation too. A judge might deny a petition from an opposition party and certify fake results, or a governor might limit the number of permits opposition parties have to hold rallies. But, they are still just indirect measures, or rather the institutional mechanism through which certain forms of manipulation might occur.[11]

---

[11] Looking at the data from Africa's electoral authoritarian regimes there is some diversity. The V-DEM data has a measure of judicial empowerment, legislative empowerment, and regional government empowerment that ranges from 0 to 1. These measures tend to follow trends in other manipulative practices, but there are some exceptions. For instance, legislatures in Kenya and Uganda are not very constrained, but other forms of

I build on Andreas Schedler's work on the menu of manipulation and differentiate between four major arenas: physical violence, electoral fraud, exclusion, and censorship (2013, 275). These forms of manipulation are rank ordered according to their severity. The assumption is that overt forms of manipulation that violate the clearest norms of contestation are the most severe. Physical violence most often happens in plain view and strongly infringes on basic human and civil rights. Fraud can be less visible at times, but is also a fairly overt form of manipulation. Exclusion of opposition groups and civil society is generally a very visible form of norm violation, but not as harsh as physical violence or electoral fraud, while censorship of media and information is both less visible and less severe. Admittedly, within each category of manipulation there is quite a bit of leeway. Electoral fraud can include overt actions like ballot stuffing, but also more subtle manipulations like rigging the voter registration or vote buying (Lehoucq 2003, Calingaert 2006). Censorship can include repression against journalists, but could also involve burdensome legal and financial requirements on newspapers and radio stations. Similarly, exclusion can include overt restrictions on political parties and civil society, but also a broader disrespect for civil liberties and the rule of law.

The data for these elements of electoral toleration come from the V-DEM indexes of physical violence, clean elections, freedom of association, and freedom of expression. The V-DEM indexes combine numerous individual measures into an aggregate index using Bayesian factor analysis that ranges from 0 to 1. The physical violence index measures freedom from torture and freedom from political killing. The clean elections index combines measure of election management body capacity, voter registration integrity, vote buying, voting irregularities, voter intimidation, election-related violence, and a general measure of freedom and fairness. The freedom of association index captures the extent to which both political parties and civil society organizations are regulated and repressed, while the freedom of expression index examines the government's respect of print and media, internet censorship, journalist harassment, freedom of discussion, and academic freedom. While this is not an exhaustive list, the V-DEM data touches on the most important theoretical elements behind the term electoral toleration.[12]

---

manipulation are comparatively high. In Congo-DRC, Ethiopia, and Gambia manipulation is high, but local government is more empowered. In Côte d'Ivoire and for a period of time in Zimbabwe judiciaries were empowered while manipulation remained higher.

[12] I also looked at other measures that capture exclusionary practices like freedom of religion, repression of religion, domestic freedom of movement, and international freedom

The V-DEM data is also unique for its exceptional validity, and its impressive breadth of coverage. The dataset encompasses all African states, with information dating back to the year 1900. For each country V-DEM hires at least five experts to code data, which allows for strong inter-coder reliability.[13] V-DEM further looks for convergent validity by testing their measures against other aggregate datasets like Freedom House and NELDA. The data also allows for more nuanced comparisons by using measurement scales that range from 0 to 1, and by providing coders with the ability to state their level of confidence in any specific judgment. While not immune to all the perils of coding time-series cross-national data, the V-DEM takes strong steps to avoid bias, and is in many ways the best data on the market today. In comparison, NELDA's unit of observation is an election, and it uses a dichotomous measure of outcomes. This makes it difficult to measure nuanced differences in competition across time. Similarly, a dataset like the QED analyzes elections based on election observation reports, does not use country experts, and has only limited coverage in Africa.

Figure 3.3 shows the average score for each V-DEM index across a country's electoral authoritarian period, with lower scores reflecting worse conditions. What these data show is that electoral authoritarian regimes employ very diverse menus of manipulation, and therefore are unequally tolerant of electoral contestation. Using the sample averages as the benchmark, which do vary from index to index, there are only a handful of cases that persistently repress, cheat, exclude, or censor to a high degree: Angola, Chad, Congo-RoC, Ethiopia, Gambia, and Guinea. In other cases, specific manipulative tools are stressed more heavily to constrain elections. For example, electoral authoritarian regimes in Mauritania and Uganda do not employ comparatively high levels of censorship, but do commit relatively high degrees of violence, fraud, and exclusion. In Zimbabwe there are stronger protections for freedom of association, in Djibouti less violence, and in Rwanda less electoral manipulation than the sample average. In Kenya the menu of manipulation consists primarily of physical violence and electoral fraud, while

---

of movement. There are more restrictions on religion in Chad, Congo-RoC, Congo-DRC, Djibouti, Ethiopia, Gambia, Mauritania, Rwanda, and Uganda. Likewise, freedom of movement is more curtailed in Central African Republic, Chad, Congo-RoC, Congo-DRC, Ethiopia, and Kenya. However, these regimes were already considered sufficiently repressive, so adding this data simply makes them more repressive.

[13] The V-DEM data uses item response theory. The point estimates provide the most useful pieces of evidence when considering trends across time, and they mitigate some of the uncertainty due to inter-coder reliability issues.

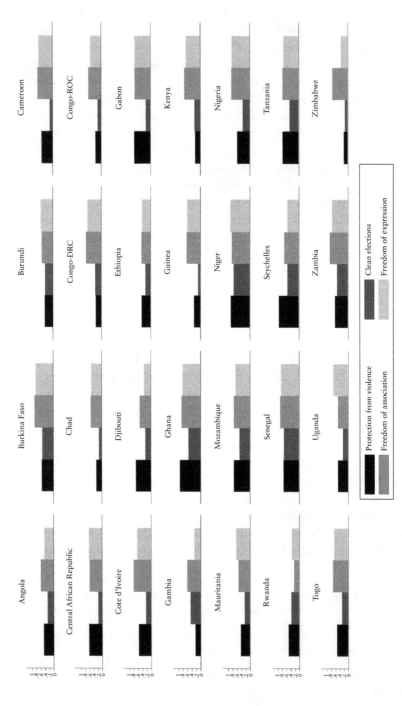

FIGURE 3.3. *Types of manipulation in African electoral authoritarian regimes (1990–2016)*

Notes: Data comes from version 6.2 of the Varieties of Democracy Project (Coppedge et al. 2017). Each measure is an index that aggregates relevant variables using Bayesian factor analysis. The mean scores are 0.52 for political violence, 0.32 for clean elections, 0.66 for freedom of association, and 0.60 for freedom of expression.

Legend:
- Protection from violence
- Freedom of association
- Clean elections
- Freedom of expression

Côte d'Ivoire, Gabon, Nigeria, and Togo rely strongly on high levels of electoral fraud. In a fairly tolerant place like Seychelles, there is actually a level of censorship that is above the sample average.[14]

Moving from these individual indexes of manipulation to an aggregate assessment of electoral toleration is not straightforward. Since not all forms of manipulation go together, we need to account for differences in the intensity of manipulation within any specific index, and differences in the configuration of manipulation across these indexes. We cannot simply aggregate the different indexes of manipulation because we need to address the divergent impact of individual practices on electoral contestation. A regime that physically represses to a strong degree, but is nonetheless fairly tolerant of organization and expression is qualitatively different from a regime that does not commit too much violence but strongly curtails organization and expression. Harsher violations of electoral norms through physical violence and electoral fraud should be given more weight when assessing the degree of electoral toleration.

My classification of electoral toleration utilizes both an additive and multiplicative index that assigns different weights to the individual manipulative indexes. To create an index of electoral toleration, I take the average of the weighted average of the indexes of physical violence, clean elections, freedom of association, and freedom of expression, and the interaction between those four terms.[15] The multiplicative side of the equation holds all indexes as equally valuable and necessary for electoral toleration, while the additive side of the equation lets in some substitutability across the individual indexes. I assign greater weight to physical violence and clean elections than freedom of association and freedom of expression. The results only differ slightly when the individual components are assigned equal weights of 0.25. I use the sample average of electoral toleration (0.4) to indicate the threshold between repressive and

---

[14] To further probe the validity of these measures I compared them to NELDA's measure of election-related violence (NELDA33), allegations of fraud (NELDA47), and evidence of opposition harassment (NELDA15). Since NELDA uses a dichotomous measure I used the V-DEM mean score for each index as a benchmark. NELDA ranks a number of cases as lower on violence (Chad, Gambia, Guinea, and Rwanda) and fraud (Angola, Chad, Gabon, Mauritania, and Togo). Data from the CIRI Human Rights Data Project on Physical Integrity validates the V-DEM measures of violence. Data from QED is more limited, but confirms the V-DEM coding for Togo.

[15] The aggregation formula looks like this: Electoral Toleration = 0.5 × (Physical Violence × Clean Elections × Freedom of Association × Freedom of Expression) + 0.5 × (0.4 × Physical Violence + 0.3 × Clean Elections + 0.15 × Freedom of Association + 0.15 × Freedom of Expression). This builds off of the aggregation techniques emphasized by V-DEM to create their Polyarchy Index.

tolerant electoral authoritarian regimes (see Table 3.2). To classify regime periods rather than just the general trend, I look at toleration in the two years prior to an election (see Appendix A).

This classification, when applied to African electoral authoritarian cases (Figure 3.4), indicates consistency across time and correlates with commonly held expert views of electoral conditions in these countries. Electoral toleration has consistently been repressive in Angola, Burundi, Cameroon, Central African Republic, Chad, Congo-DRC, Congo-RoC, Côte d'Ivoire, Djibouti, Ethiopia, Gabon, Gambia, Guinea, Kenya, Mauritania, Rwanda, Uganda, and Zambia. On the other hand electoral contestation has been tolerant in Burkina Faso, Ghana, Mozambique, Senegal, Seychelles, Tanzania, and Zambia. Only in Burkina Faso did electoral conditions improve from repression to toleration. Gabon, Nigeria, and Togo have teetered close the toleration threshold. In Togo the regime became significantly more tolerant of contestation after the 2005 election, which also corresponds with the death of president Gnassingbé Eyadéma and the growth of greater international pressure on the regime.[16] In sum, there is variation in terms of electoral hegemony and electoral toleration within the sample of African electoral authoritarian regimes.

TRAJECTORIES OF AFRICAN ELECTORAL AUTHORITARIAN COMPETITION

The two dimensions of electoral competition – hegemony and toleration – can be combined to classify electoral authoritarian competition in twenty-eight cases of African electoral authoritarianism. Figure 3.5 demonstrates how electoral authoritarian competition has evolved since 1990. A pessimistic conclusion from this data is that the predominant form of electoral authoritarianism in sub-Saharan Africa is a repressive hegemony. Repressive hegemonies are quite stable in Cameroon, Djibouti, and Gabon. In Ethiopia, Nigeria, Togo, and Zimbabwe repressive hegemonies have experienced brief dips into repressive non-hegemony. In Côte d'Ivoire, Gambia, Guinea, and Mauritania repressive hegemonies

---

[16] Note that in the case of Tanzania data is aggregated from both the mainland and Zanzibar. On Zanzibar there is less toleration of open contestation. Likewise, the score for Gabon rose after 2010, which corresponds with the death of Gabon's long-standing president Omar Bongo. However, the data from V-DEM is only available to 2015 and does not account for the deteriorating electoral conditions since the controversial 2016 election, which was rejected by the opposition (Staff, "Gabon Constitutional Court Upholds Ali Bongo's Disputed Re-Election," *The Associated Press*, September 24, 2016).

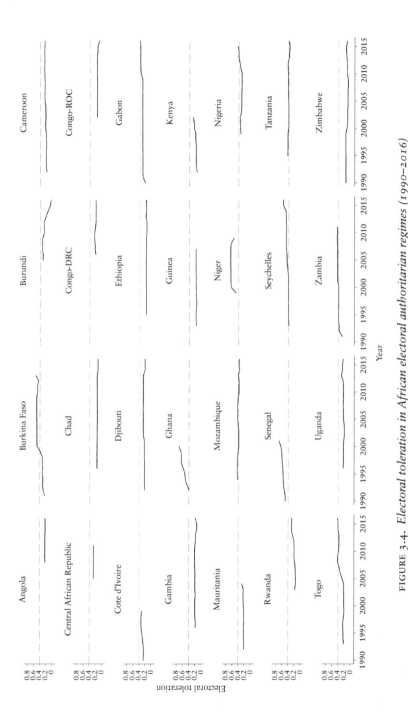

FIGURE 3.4. *Electoral toleration in African electoral authoritarian regimes (1990–2016)*

Notes: The reference line indicates the threshold between a tolerant and repressive regime (0.4). The electoral toleration score is an aggregate measure of physical violence, clean elections, freedom of association, and freedom of expression. All data is from V-DEM (Coppedge et al. 2017).

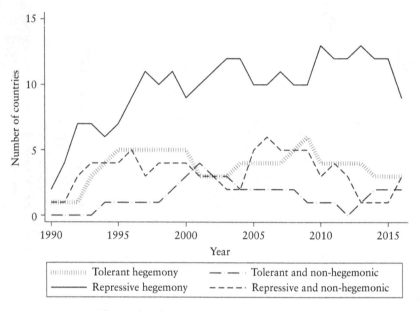

FIGURE 3.5. *Electoral authoritarian competition in Africa (1990–2016)*
Note: Combining the classification rules for hegemony and toleration creates
the specific regime types.

ended following military coups. Only in Burkina Faso did a repressive
hegemony become a tolerant hegemony, and no repressive hegemony has
directly democratized. By contrast, tolerant hegemonies only occur regularly in a handful of countries – Burkina Faso, Mozambique, Senegal,
Seychelles, and Tanzania. In Burkina Faso the tolerant hegemony fell to
a military coup in 2014, while in Zambia a tolerant hegemony became
non-hegemonic in 2001 when the Movement for Multiparty Democracy
won just 43 percent of the seats and Levi Mwanawasa 30 percent of the
vote. Tolerant hegemonies in Ghana and Senegal transitioned into electoral democracy. Notably, tolerant hegemonies do not seem to regress to
repressive hegemonies.

As expected, non-hegemonic regimes are much more dynamic. Only
38 percent of repressive non-hegemonies and 52 percent of tolerant non-
hegemonies remained as such after an election. Periods of repressive non-
hegemony were mostly interlude to a return to repressive hegemony. For
instance, Burundi, Cameroon, Chad, Gabon, Gambia, and Nigeria all
began as repressive non-hegemonies after their foundational elections,
but then became hegemonic following second elections. In a few cases
repressive non-hegemony predated a transition to an unclassified regime,

as in Central African Republic following the 2012 civil war and Guinea following the 2008 military coup. Repressive non-hegemonies have only lost elections in Kenya, while Congo-DRC is the continent's longest lasting persistently repressive non-hegemony. On the other hand, tolerant non-hegemonies are also more often prelude to some kind of regime change. For example, Niger's tolerant non-hegemony collapsed following a military coup in 2010. In both Nigeria and Zambia tolerant non-hegemonies lost power at the ballot box. Only in Mozambique has the regime vacillated between tolerant hegemony and tolerant non-hegemony.

In summary, the diversity of African electoral authoritarianism is real. While repressive hegemonies are the modal sub-type of electoral authoritarianism, a considerable number of regimes do exist for prolonged periods of time as tolerant hegemonies. Repressive hegemonies are more likely to transition via some form of unconstitutional change like a military coup, while tolerant hegemonies are more likely to experience turnover via elections. Periods of non-hegemony are relatively short, and repression appears to be a winning strategy for most. Repressive non-hegemonies are more likely to become repressive hegemonies than tolerant non-hegemonies are to become tolerant hegemonies. Tolerant non-hegemonies were more liable to transition following electoral defeat. However, some of this indeterminacy might simply reflect heterogeneity. African tolerant hegemonies include former single-party states in Tanzania, military regimes in Ghana, and regimes that emerged after defeating other autocrats, as in Zambia.[17] Repressive hegemonies similarly include former single-party states in Cameroon, military regimes in Gambia, and heavily personalized regimes in Congo-RoC. The next section briefly explores whether there is a relationship between electoral authoritarian competition and the regime type that preceded it.

THE INSTITUTIONAL UNDERPINNINGS OF
ELECTORAL AUTHORITARIAN SUB-TYPES

Electoral authoritarianism is not only diverse with regard to its competitiveness, but also with regard to the historical and institutional context

---

[17] There is a case to be made that Ghana was in fact a tolerant non-hegemony. In 1992 incumbent Jerry Rawlings won 58 percent of the vote and the ruling party, the NDC, won 98 percent of the seats, but the opposition boycotted the legislative election. In 1996 Rawlings only won 57 percent of the vote and the NDC captured just 66.5 percent of the legislative seats, which places it right on the boundary between hegemony and non-hegemony.

it emerges from. The major argument of this book is that among the former single-party regimes of Africa differences in ruling party credibility was a primary factor that differentiated tolerant hegemonies from repressive hegemonies. This insight does not necessarily carry when we consider other electoral authoritarian settings. In cases like Rwanda, electoral authoritarianism materialized out of a brief period of military rule following the Rwandan Patriotic Front's defeat of the radical Hutu regime in July 1994. In the Gambia, Lt. Yahya Jammeh led a group of officers on a coup in 1994. Two years later the Gambia began to hold regular unfair elections. In Congo-DRC Joseph Kabila succeeded his father's heavily personalized regime and began to hold elections in 2006 following the end of the second Congolese civil war. In Zimbabwe, Robert Mugabe and the Zimbabwe African National Union (ZANU) ascended to power following the Lancaster Agreement that ended the Rhodesian Bush War. There was no regime interlude, and the 1980 election marks the beginning of Zimbabwe's electoral authoritarian path. These are very different electoral authoritarian origins than a transition after a prolonged period of single-party rule.

One way to test for the impact of institutional origins is to examine the correlation between electoral authoritarian competition and the prior regime type. Based on the categorization of autocratic regimes developed by Barbara Geddes and colleagues, I identify prior regimes as party-based, military-based, personal, or other (Geddes, Wright, and Franz 2012).[18] A party-based regime is one that has existed for at least ten years and where a major political party has operated. A prior military regime is one that originates in a military junta or rebel movement that gains political control and establishes an interim military government. In some cases a military regime might create a ruling party, but unless it is in existence for more than ten years the regime is still considered military. A personal regime is one where a prominent individual or family controls most aspects of politics. A party might exist, but it is generally devoid of any meaning. "Other" is a residual category that includes electoral

---

[18] I make slight amendments to the original coding to reflect what I consider a more accurate description of prior regime type. In Burkina Faso, Central African Republic, Chad, Gambia, Ghana, and Guinea I recode the prior regime as military-personal rather than personal. In each case presidents came to power either via military coup or insurgency. I recode Cameroon and Togo as party-personal rather than personal to reflect the continued importance of ruling parties. The Geddes et al. data is also missing for Djibouti and Seychelles, and I code both as a party-based form of authoritarianism.

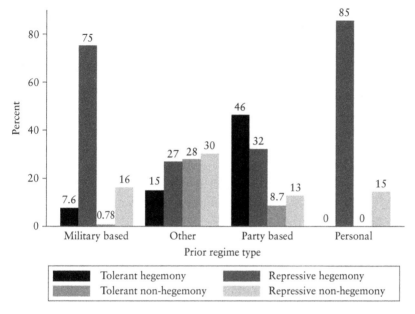

FIGURE 3.6. *Prior regime type and electoral authoritarian competition in Africa*
   Note: Regime types are based on Geddes, Wright, and Franz (2012).

authoritarianism that originates from different or unclear origins like an interim regime.[19] The results are presented in Figure 3.6.

The evidence here suggests that institutional origins do have some significant impact on electoral authoritarian outcomes. Military-based and personal regimes are rarely associated with tolerant outcomes, and most often lead to repressive hegemonies. This is to be expected given the theory of autocratic institution building presented in this book. Military and personal regimes are not equipped with ruling parties that might be used to operate more effectively or retain elite and voter support. These kinds of regimes are therefore comparatively more vulnerable to the detrimental effects of elections, and generally have developed much more pronounced coercive institutions that can be used to repress opposition. In fact, the only military regime that transitioned to a tolerant hegemony was in Burkina Faso, but only following a period of repressive hegemony. The "Other"

---

[19] "Other" is the prior regime in Niger, Nigeria, Zambia, and Zimbabwe. For example, in Nigeria the death of General Sani Abacha in 1998 led to an interim military government led by Major General Abdulsalami Abubakar. Abubakar oversaw a quick transition to elections, which were won by the formerly imprisoned Olusegun Obasanjo and the People's Democratic Party.

category correlates with diverse outcomes, which is understandable given that the category refers to many different settings. Zambia's transition to a tolerant hegemony after defeating United National Independence Party (UNIP) in 1991 is very different from Zimbabwe's transition to a repressive hegemony at the end of the Rhodesian Bush War.

However, the fact that party-based authoritarianism is linked not only to a greater likelihood of hegemony, but also to both tolerant and repressive hegemonies supports the theory presented in Chapter 2. The major argument was that ruling parties actually diverged in their ability to serve authoritarian needs during elections. Indeed, several of these single-party regimes in reality resembled personal regimes rather than institutionalized party-based systems with credible ruling parties.[20] At times, parties existed in theory but they lacked the organizational breadth or internal structures to exude credibility. In other words, we can say that tolerant hegemonies are strongly rooted in party-based authoritarianism, but not that all party-based authoritarianism leads to tolerant hegemonies. Differences in electoral authoritarian competition can only be adequately explained with closer attention to the specific elements of authoritarian institution building, not just across broader regime types but within those types as well.

CONCLUSION

This chapter has outlined some of the basic theoretical and empirical challenges with regard to the study of electoral authoritarianism, and has offered some useful means for both identifying electoral authoritarian regimes and for measuring differences in competition. I have tried to situate the concept of electoral authoritarianism into some broader debates regarding the subjective nature of regime classification, and have unpacked the concept of electoral competition to refer to the electoral outcome (hegemony) and the electoral process (toleration). Combined, these two dimensions of competition can be used to classify electoral authoritarian competition. When applied to the range of African electoral authoritarian regimes since 1990, we discover a diversity of experience and that repressive hegemony is the predominant form of electoral authoritarian

---

[20] One way to broadly examine this issue is to use Geddes' et al. finer-tuned regime distinctions. And indeed, "party-personal" regimes never transition to tolerant hegemonies but transition to repressive hegemonies 70 percent of the time. On the other hand, purely "party-based" regimes transition to tolerant hegemonies 66 percent of the time and to repressive hegemonies 16 percent of the time.

competition. However, this chapter has also highlighted an important distinction between tolerant hegemonies and repressive hegemonies.

Another major conclusion from this chapter is that in addition to the range of electoral authoritarian outcomes, we need to consider the multiplicity of historical and institutional settings in which electoral authoritarianism originates. This is true across broader regime types and within them, especially in the category of party-based authoritarianism. A concern with scope conditions has shaped the rest of this book's focus on former single-party regimes and differences in ruling party credibility. In the next chapters I use the cases of Tanzania, Cameroon, and Kenya to demonstrate divergence in ruling party credibility during the single-party period, and to trace the impact of these differences to electoral authoritarian contestation. Likewise, I show how international patronage can further influence electoral competition in the absence of credible parties. Later, I return to the broader category of party-based authoritarianism to show how the results travel outside of the original three cases.

4

The Structure and Origins of Ruling Parties in Tanzania, Cameroon, and Kenya

The party in Tanzania has maintained its vitality ... it is not an institution that remains dormant most of the time, resuscitated only to mobilize voter support for an election. Rather, it is centrally involved in candidate screening and selections, and consequently work in the party is often a useful basis for aspirants to higher office.

—Joel Samoff (1987)

Like the CNU, the CPDM has annex organizations like the youth and women's wings. Its structures are a carbon copy of the past from the lowest organ (the cell) to its highest organ (the national congress). Like the CNU, the CPDM is highly elitist.

—*Historic Dictionary of Cameroon* (2010)

The ruling party Kenya African National Union (KANU) is inactive and even ineffectual. No annual party conference or election of office bearers has taken place in a long time. At the General Elections in October last year, the party cannot be said to have played a big role, apart from accepting or rejecting the nominations of candidates. After that it was each candidate for himself and the party was largely ignored.

—*The Weekly Review*, Nairobi (February 8, 1975)

My theory of electoral authoritarian competition depends on the emergence of very different regime configurations during the single-party era. The central dilemmas of autocratic rule under conditions of elections are more easily managed with credible ruling parties. This chapter's main task is therefore to empirically demonstrate these differences in ruling parties across the three cases of Tanzania, Cameroon, and Kenya. As noted in Table 4.1 and described in detail, by the onset of multipartyism

TABLE 4.1. *Measuring ruling party credibility in Tanzania, Cameroon, and Kenya*

Case	Physical size	Decisional autonomy	Internal democracy	Social incorporation	Ruling party credibility
Tanzania	Large	High	High	Wide	High
Cameroon	Medium	Low	Low	Narrow	Low
Kenya	Small (medium)	Low	Moderate (low)	Narrow	Low

Note: Kenya's score for physical size increased and score for internal competition decreased during Daniel arap Moi's tenure.

in the early 1990s there were notable differences in terms of physical infrastructure, decisional autonomy, internal democracy, and the breadth of social incorporation. Only in Tanzania did the ruling party develop institutional features that would clearly foster credibility. By contrast, regimes in Kenya and in Cameroon were much more presidentially centered and the role of ethnicity was key in preserving ruling coalitions. While changes occurred in each of these parties in the immediate years prior to elections – generally following presidential succession – the ruling parties retained their key features prior to elections.

Earlier accounts of single-party regimes in Africa made distinctions between mass and patron, pragmatic and revolutionary, and centralized and decentralized parties (Coleman and Hodgkin 1961, Rosberg 1970). These classifications often overstated the extent to which political parties were physically present. As Henry Bienen noted, "the characteristics attributed to political systems in Africa were often based on images that African parties wanted to convey to the world and themselves, rather than any objective reality" (Bienen 1978, 41). This led Samuel Huntington to argue that African single-party systems were uniformly weak, since they lacked the prerequisites to push sweeping social agendas or to institutionalize into recurring political patterns (Huntington and Moore 1970, 12–13). Immanuel Wallerstein questioned whether ruling parties in Africa served any representative function at all. Party activity was often dormant and secondary to the role of informal institutions and patronage. Wallerstein called this reality the "no-party" state (1966). These concerns found empirical validation rather quickly as many of Africa's new political entities succumbed to military coups.

As single-party regimes in Africa amazingly persisted, more attention was given to underspecified cross-regional variation. Ruth Collier noted that some single-party regimes were plebiscitary rather than competitive. These differences were predictive of whether regimes would solidify long-lasting coalitions or move toward more overt patronage and competitive clientelism (Collier 1982). Bratton and van de Walle expanded on this insight and specified more distinctions in the extent of competition and participation during the single-party era. From this variation they drew conclusions regarding the trajectories of public protest and democratic reform in the early 1990s (Bratton and van de Walle 1997). Similarly, building on work that examines the role of local powerbrokers, Rachel Riedl stresses two strategies of authoritarian power accumulation in Africa – elite incorporation versus state substitution, which shaped democratic transitions and the stability of subsequent party systems (2014).[1]

My focus on credibility incorporates insights from the literature on authoritarian politics to provide a different perspective of the single-party era in Africa. Indeed, little attention is generally given to the actual credibility of ruling institutions. Brokered regime outcomes, where political parties might be secondary institutions, involve the distribution of patronage to important elites. One expectation is that during transitions to elections or democratization local elites that emerged as key players in sustaining the regime will remain loyal for purely material reasons. This assumption is challenged given differences in ruling party credibility and uneven access to coercive and material resources. As my cases show, some brokered regimes were unable to prevent elite and voter defection. Likewise, state substitution strategies, which can involve elevating a ruling party, are assumed to be prone to failure because they do not eliminate socially important leaders and require immense amounts of resources to continually operate. Once again, these assumptions are debatable given the empirical record and role of credibility in sustaining institutions. At times powerful ruling parties minimized the influence of social elites through their commitments to a broader social constituency, or because they utilized the integrity of their internal structures.

While my concern is primarily in classifying differences in ruling party credibility and exploring their impact on electoral authoritarian competition, some elaboration on institutional origins is unavoidable. Hence, a secondary goal of this chapter is to stake out some tentative ground

---

[1] For similar work on the social basis of postcolonial African states see Boone (1994), Young (1994), Herbst (2000), and Bayart (2009).

on the factors that lead to the creation of credible authoritarian institutions and allow their reproduction over time. I claim that strategies of regime building cannot be reduced to a single structural factor. I specifically stress the importance of two intersecting variables – inherited state capacity and the extent of organized political competition. Both factors limited or expanded the range of choices that leaders had at independence. But, I also emphasize that while some paths of institutional evolution were constrained, all regimes faced similar challenges of regime consolidation. Therefore, the eventual pathway chosen must also reflect on the role of leadership. Julius Nyerere, Ahmadou Ahidjo, and Jomo Kenyatta were starkly different people, with distinctive worldviews, time horizons, personal interests, and leadership skills.

This makes the postindependence moment a real critical juncture that set regimes on certain paths, which then became difficult to move off from.[2] These cases suggest that the credibility that was fostered by Tanzania's ruling party persisted because a sufficient number of elites benefitted from its maintenance, but also because the institutions themselves developed a stake in keeping their own autonomy. Over time, Chama Cha Mapinduzi (CCM) became the site of observable conflicts between elites who wanted to undermine credible systems of exchange to benefit themselves, elites who did not have the same level of resources (or were ideologues) and wanted the party to retain its credibility, and the actual people who worked for the party. During the single-party era this came to a decisive point following the transition from Julius Nyerere to Ali Hassan Mwinyi. The party underwent significant changes, but retained key features that enhanced credible exchanges. However, these tensions persisted into the electoral period, forcing the party to constantly reassert its autonomy over individual factions.

By contrast, the pathways chosen in Cameroon and Kenya made it very difficult for presidents to consider erecting a credible ruling party. In

---

[2] The literature on critical junctures is conflicted over whether during these points in time there must be complete unpredictability, meaning that many different paths could have theoretically been equally chosen. Previous events and structural conditions can in fact bias one pathway over the other, and the assumption of unpredictability requires burdensome counterfactual assumptions or historical regress to "true" junctures (Mahoney 2000, Page 2006). My approach is to use the postindependence moment as a critical juncture in the sense that it necessitated decisions over what regimes would look like. This is also similar to Lieberman's "periodization" strategy that breaks down institutional analysis into distinct phases, including the consequence of different institutional configurations and the uneven role of exogenous shocks like elections on institutions (Lieberman 2001).

each case a sufficient number of elites had habituated into a less predictable system of exchange with the regime, which created real entrenched interests. In Cameroon, Paul Biya saw himself as a reformer and offered a "New Deal" that promised to transform the ruling party and bring in new and younger blood. This effort fell victim to pressure from elites who saw access to the regime in starkly zero-sum terms. Similarly, throughout the 1970s in Kenya there were calls for party reform, but it was nearly impossible, or in Kenyatta's interest, to make meaningful change to the Kenya African National Union (KANU) because of elite pressure. Kenyatta's successor, Daniel arap Moi, faced similar demands from elites who felt excluded from the previous system. His supposed revitalization of KANU needs to be seen as a way for him to develop some authoritarian tools to manage the unstructured factionalism that plagued the party, rather than a sincere attempt at constructing a credible institution.

The chapter proceeds by breaking down the single-party era into three time periods and discussing each case sequentially. The first period examines the unique challenges of postindependence state building and the set of circumstances faced by distinctive foundational leaders. The chapter then details the process of regime and party building that followed with an emphasis on credibility building mechanisms. Specific attention is given to the aforementioned dimensions of credible ruling parties: physical size, decisional autonomy, internal democracy, and social incorporation. Finally, the chapter discusses leadership transition and the period of reform that preluded the reintroduction of elections in order to highlight patterns of continuity and persistence.

THE COLONIAL HERITAGE AND THE CHALLENGES OF REGIME CONSOLIDATION

Independence leaders in Tanzania, Cameroon, and Kenya faced severe challenges of governance that forced them to make decisions about how to organize ruling institutions. As elsewhere in Africa colonial powers made limited investments in state institutions, which made the projection of power uniformly difficult (Herbst 2000). Each regime had to administer vast territories and respond to striking social diversity and demands placed upon the state. In the case of Cameroon, the tricky process of unification between the former British and French colonies exacerbated these issues. While space precludes fuller discussion of the origin of party institutions, these cases bring to the fore three major factors that shaped decision-making in the immediate postindependence era. First, there were moderate differences in state capacity, especially in terms of the development of coercive institutions and the civil administration. Second, the extent of organized political division differed, often due to the politicization of ethnic identity and the power of new elites that emerged under colonialism (Boone 1994, Posner 2005). Third, the three foundational leaders reflect dramatically different backgrounds, ideologies, and political orientations.

Weak States, Unified Organization, and Visionary Leadership in Tanzania (1961–1966)

The state that Julius Nyerere inherited from the British was perhaps the most limited of the three cases. Tanzania lacked a large administrative center from which to govern. Under the Germans there were multiple governmental locales, most prominently in northwestern Kigoma, central Tabora, and northeastern Tanga. Only in 1925, under the British mandate and the governorship of Sir Donald Cameron, did Dar es Salaam become the locus of political authority. Indirect rule in Tanzania elevated opaquely chosen chiefs to head Native Authorities, and by most accounts this fueled large resentment from more independent traditional leaders and economic cooperatives (Austen 1968, Coulson 1982). It also meant that there were very few Africans in the civil administration at independence. By one account 25 percent of posts were simply left unmanned after colonialism (Iliffe 1969). Similarly, the state was dependent on difficult to collect poll taxes and the taxation of cash crops like coffee and sisal (Fjeldstad and Therkildsen 2008). Finally, the state had very little coercive capacity and the Tanganyika Rifles was British officered and consisted of just 2,000 men. In 1964, the military mutinied against their officers, which necessitated external British involvement and the creation of the Tanzania People's Defense Forces essentially from scratch (Parsons 2003).

While the state was weak, the political vehicle that Nyerere headed, the Tanganyika African National Union (TANU), was by far the predominant political institution. The core of the movement was the Tanganyika African Association (TAA), an urban-based organization that consisted primarily of schoolteachers and junior civil servants, like its leader Nyerere. TANU quickly expanded into the countryside to become the most recognized political institution. There is some consensus that the absence of a sufficiently large ethnic group, commercial class, or White settler community made the expansion of TANU into the countryside much easier.[3] Likewise, the British and Germans both used Swahili as the lingua franca, which facilitated the process of alliance building with other chiefs, rural peasants, and cooperative leaders. Subsequently, by the end of the 1950s TANU boasted nearly 500 branches and a remarkable two million members. During the last colonial election of August 1960, TANU won all but one of the legislative seats, and Julius Nyerere was subsequently named Prime Minister (Temu 1969).[4]

However, this early electoral success should not be construed to mean that TANU was an all-powerful organization. Rather, as Henry Bienen notes, TANU's early successes were largely derivative of its popularity rather than its organizational resources. The party lacked finances, and membership quickly declined after independence. Likewise, while a popular figure, Nyerere faced pressure from TANU's numerous branches and influential chiefs that previously headed Native Authorities. The Local Government Amendment Act of 1962 reappointed many Native Authority chiefs as local government administrators in an effort to calm tensions. Likewise, the office of Prime Minster was replaced with a more powerful president. There were also seeds of religious dissent, especially from the All-Muslim National Union, which criticized TANU over the lack of Muslim legislative candidates (Bienen 1970, 57–71). These centrifugal pressures, combined with the 1964 military coup, meant that there were real challenges to political authority after independence that would require some change in regime configuration.

Nyerere's recourse to invest in the ruling party is derivative of these circumstances, but also cannot be reduced to them. The figure of Julius Nyerere looms large in Tanzanian historiography, and there are not many African leaders that have been the subject of such debate, if not much actual biographical work (Molony 2014).[5] There is a tendency to romanticize Nyerere's legacy. Some accounts downplay the coercive elements of

---

[3] Tanzania is home to over one hundred ethnic groups, the largest being the Nyamwezi-Sukuma (approximately 20 percent of the population). However, many of Tanzania's ethnic groups were not discernably hierarchical, which reduced the salience of ethnic identity. While there were perceptions of ethnic bias in favor of specific groups (the Haya and Chagga in particular), they were not sufficiently large as to constitute effective political blocs. Similarly, British indirect rule produced no major ethnic political organization that could form the basis for a rival political party.

[4] The only other parties to register vote share during this period were the short-lived United Tanganyika Party, and the more nationalist African National Congress.

[5] Molony's recent volume on Nyerere's early years is an exceptional contribution, and he notes the dearth of biographical materials on Nyerere. For other accounts of Nyerere's life see, Iliffe (1973), Smith (1973), Graham (1975), Hatch (1976), and Brennan (2014).

his political philosophy, while others overstate the influence of his rural upbringing (Coulson 1982, 24). As the son of a Zanaki chief, Nyerere was relatively privileged and attended British colonial schools. But, as Nyerere himself was prone to emphasize, he was not part of an elite class and grew up in fairly deprived circumstances. It is clear that Nyerere took an early liking to academics and to Catholicism. He attended the prestigious Makerere College in Uganda, and following a three-year stint as a schoolteacher in Tabora, travelled to Edinburgh to obtain a master's degree in economics and history. This period spent in the United Kingdom appears to have been critical in forming the bedrock of Nyerere's political philosophy and activism. It was then that he began to write more seriously about egalitarianism, the paramount role of education, the relationship between Western principles of socialism and democracy, and the values of African traditional society. While reading John Stuart Mill and Adam Smith, Nyerere developed his own ideas about one-party democracy, the path to independence, and ultimately his socialist ideology of *ujamaa*.

This made Nyerere a clearly intellectually driven leader with a genuine interest in activist and transformational politics. And indeed, the changes that Nyerere made to TANU under the guise of *ujamaa* are so profound that they were clearly not inevitable, but forged. The absence of a more powerful state or stronger political rivalry might explain why Nyerere did not have to broker with other elites or centralize power in the presidency. However, it does not explain the distinct character and scale of the ruling party (Miti 1980). Nyerere had to make tough and risky decisions that alienated several political rivals. For instance, Oscar Kambona, a key figure in the independence movement, was exiled in July 1967 over his opposition to *ujamaa*'s economic nationalization. Two years later TANU co-founders Bibi Titi Mohammed and Michael Kamalize were arrested and tried for treason (Mwansasu 1979, Mwakikagile 2006). Nyerere's ability to transform the ruling party must also reflect his leadership skills and distinct use of ideology. He appeared to be genuinely committed to a more internally democratic – if monopolizing – ruling party, and could draw followers with him to support that vision.

Coercive Capacity, Multi-Ethnic Politics, and Coalition-Building in Cameroon (1960–1965)

Along many indicators the postcolonial site in Cameroon was weak. During colonialism Anglophone Cameroon was neglected, and most administration and budget allocation took place from Nigeria.[6] In Northern British Cameroon the British relied on indirect rule by appointing Fulani chiefs (*lamidos*) or Bamileké chiefs (*fons*) to head Native Authorities. In Southern British Cameroon it was more difficult to identify local authority figures, and there was more direct British administration.[7] However, by the time of unification there was practically no African administration in Southern British Cameroon, taxation was minimal, and there were likely less than 150 Africans under arms (Johnson 1970, 201–5). The situation was only moderately better in French Cameroon. Many major administrative duties were housed in Brazzaville, and the French were reluctant to incorporate too many Africans into local government. The Civil Commissioner of Cameroon appointed regional administrators, who were nearly invariably non-African. The few Africans in the civil service were drawn primarily from the Douala, Bassa, Bamileké, and Beti populations. Concurrently, officially recognized councils of notables and a tiered system of chiefs akin to indirect rule helped the French reach some of the rural population, but did not produce an effective administration (Le Vine 1964).

Relatedly, pre-independence Cameroon was home to several political parties that reflected the country's more pronounced ethnic and regional divisions.[8] One source of division was between British and French Cameroon, but there were also important rifts within each unit. In British Cameroon, the Kamerun National Democratic Party (KNDP) resonated more with the northwestern grasslands, while the Cameroon People's National Convention (CPNC) was associated with the southwestern coastal people (Johnson 1970, 257–85). In French Cameroon, there were clear north-south divisions, which loosely paralleled a Muslim-Christian divide. The Cameroonian Union (UC) dominated the north and was led by Ahmadou Ahidjo, and represented his own Muslim and Fulani

---

[6] At the end of German colonialism Cameroon was divided between the British and French. The British received a mandate over the smaller territory bordering Nigeria, then called British Northern and Southern Cameroon. In 1961 Southern Cameroon elected to reunify with French Cameroon, which created the Federal Republic of Cameroon. Northern British Cameroon integrated with Nigeria. Ahmado Ahidjo was the Republic's first president, and John Ngu Foncha became Vice President and Prime Minister of the state of West Cameroon (Johnson 1970).

[7] According to Victor Le Vine this was to protect the commercial agricultural sites established by the Germans (1964, 195–9).

[8] There are over 200 ethnic and linguistic groups in Cameroon, but the most important clusters can be loosely broken down as follows: Bamileké/Bamoun (8 percent), Bassa/Duala/Bawkeri (12 percent), Fang/Ewondo/Beti (18 percent), Fulani (14 percent), and Kirdi (18 percent).

background. In the South there were several parties, such as the Union of Peoples of Cameroon (UPC), which was firmly rooted in the Bassa, Douala, and Bamileké populations (Joseph 1977). Other southern parties included the Ewondo-based Cameroon Party of Democrats and the Beti-based National Action Movement (Kofele-Kale 1986). In 1955 a radical wing of the UPC party launched an insurgency against the French, which persisted into the postindependence period.[9]

This reality left Ahidjo in a precarious situation – he faced an ongoing uprising, strong centrifugal pressures from other parties and elites, and had limited state resources.[10] Two factors seem to have exerted strong influence on his decision to centralize power in the presidency rather than create a credible institution. First, the UPC rebellion left Ahidjo with comparatively stronger coercive capacities. To combat the UPC the French High Commissioner Pierre Messmer created emergency zones and augmented the Cameroonian military with a significant *gendarmerie*. The French also created a strong intelligence gathering service called the *Service des Etudes et la Documentation* (Takougang and Krieger 1998, 39–40, Kamga 2015). This gave Ahidjo a very different set of tools than Nyerere had in Tanzania, and even Jomo Kenyatta did in Kenya. Ahidjo could use coercion to cajole other elites into a ruling coalition and did not have to cede any institutional reform to the ruling party.

Second, Ahidjo himself was not inclined toward a more institution-building approach. There are not many biographical records of Ahidjo's earliest years. His father was apparently a Muslim Fulani chief, but he was raised by his mother, a former slave. Ahidjo's intellectual journey is also much more prosaic than Nyerere's – he did not excel in the colonial education system, did not travel abroad, and did not spend time writing. Instead, after secondary school at the *École Primaire Supérieur* in Yaoundé, he joined the civil service as a radio operator. It was during this period, while travelling across the country, that he became interested in independence politics and began to develop some thoughts on the multiethnic nature of Cameroon. In 1946, Ahidjo ran successfully for office in the territorial legislature with his party the "Friendly Association of Bénoué." In 1956, Ahidjo failed to win a seat on the Assembly of the

---

[9] A definitive account of this period and the UPC rebellion is provided in Joseph (1977).
[10] Ahidjo was also not a consensus leader in Cameroon. In 1957 Andre-Marie Mbida of the Party of Democrats was elected Prime Minister of Autonomous French Cameroon and Ahidjo was selected as Minister of Interior. Disagreement between Mbida and the French led to his forced resignation a year later, and the French backing of Ahidjo as premier (Bayart 1978a).

French Union, which seemed to instill in him a greater sense of political realism. He gained the reputation of a rather shrewd and autocratic northern politician, who was able to cajole and intimidate other northern leaders into a broader base that eventually became the Cameroonian Union.[11] While he was Deputy Prime Minister he did not curry much national prestige, and depended on his personal relations with other elites to gradually expand his support. Therefore, while circumstances seemed to preclude a credible ruling party from emerging, the specific configuration the regime took also reflected Ahidjo's unique leadership style and assessment of the coalitional nature of Cameroonian politics.

The Civil Administration, Divided Politics, and Elite Interests in Kenya (1963–1965)

In Kenya we find another unique set of initial circumstances that ultimately led to the weakening of the ruling party. In comparative terms, state capacity in Kenya at independence was much stronger. As the crown jewel of British East Africa, and with a substantial White settlement, the civil administration in Kenya was one of the oldest and largest on the continent. Colonial governors in Kenya retained the power to appoint Provincial Administrators and District Commissioners, and these figures were bestowed with crucial functions such as tax collection, juridical oversight, and the maintenance of law and order. Importantly, the civil administration could be used to restrict political activity by refusing permits, limiting fund raising, and overseeing elections (Okumu and Holmquist 1984).[12] The power of Provincial and District Commissioners also kept Native Authorities weaker than in other British colonies, and indeed the extent of indirect rule in Kenya was comparatively lower (Lange 1995). Commenting on the strength of the civil administration, Daniel Branch and Nic Cheeseman note that by independence "the Kenyan state, and particularly the executive, had far greater non-coercive resources with which to overcome the dialectics of its role" (2006, 16).[13]

---

[11] Most of this assessment of Ahidjo's early years comes from Bayart (1978a), Jackson and Rosberg (1982), and Glickman (1992).

[12] Branch and Cheeseman refer to this outcome as a "pact of domination" that bonded an African elite into a system of control that mimicked the direct control of the colonial governor (2006, 22).

[13] An authoritative account of the colonial period can be found in Berman (1990). On the legacies of the colonial era, and specifically the civil administration, see also Gertzel (1970).

At the same time political divisions were much starker and defined than in Tanzania. Some of these divisions were ethnic, but also mirrored nascent class identities.[14] KANU did not completely dominate the electorate at independence, and faced challenges from its major rival the Kenyan Democratic African Union (KADU).[15] KANU and KADU represented different multiethnic coalitions, with KANU more representative of the Kikuyu and Luo, and KADU of the smaller tribes such as the Kalenjin. But, there were important divisions within ethnic communities. The Mau Mau Emergency of the 1950s pitted Kikuyu squatters against colonial settlers in Central Province, but also against other land-owning Kikuyu. Moreover, there were important divisions within the Luo community between a fairly cohesive labor movement led by Tom Mboya, and champions of the landless like Chief Oginga Odinga. In fact, Odinga was a close ally of Mau Mau activist and Kikuyu Bildad Kaggia (Widner 1994, 41–52). Similarly, the term "Kalenjin," to which Daniel arap Moi was ostensibly a key representative, was itself fairly novel, complicated, and masked important intra-group differences that were quite pronounced at independence (Lynch 2011).

The civil administration offered Jomo Kenyatta a way to mitigate the pull and tug of these powerful political rifts, but his aversion to a stronger political party also comments on his inherent conservatism and perhaps even ethnic chauvinism. Kenyatta attended missionary schools and converted to Christianity at an early age, while still initiating fully into Kikuyu life. This seems to have instilled in him a belief in the need for Kenyans to transform themselves into a more Western model of personal achievement, but also the conviction that the Kikuyu intrinsically exemplified the type of enterprising Kenyan he envisioned. This is further evident in Kenyatta's simultaneous activism in broader liberation politics and Kikuyu welfare. His thesis and book *Facing Mount Kenya* is a study of the Kikuyu and a forceful critique of British colonialism. During his fifteen years in the United Kingdom Kenyatta maintained an engagement with the Kikuyu Central Association and other African progressive

---

[14] The majority of Kenyans are Kikuyu, who are related to the Embu and Meru and reside largely in Central Province. These groups constitute approximately 30 percent of Kenyans. Other groups include the Luhya of Western Province (14 percent), Luo of Nyanza (13 percent), Kalenjin of the Rift Valley (11 percent), Kamba of Eastern Province, and smaller groups like the Somali, Masaai, and Mijikenda (Throup and Hornsby 1998).

[15] A number of smaller regional parties also existed, such as the African People's Party, the Baluhya Political Union and the Coast People's Party (Bienen 1974). KANU retained the upper hand as far as numbers were concerned and won eighty-three seats versus KADU's thirty-three in the 1963 general election (Sanger and Nottingham 1964).

figures.[16] When Kenyatta returned to Kenya he was welcomed as a national hero, but also as a champion of the Kikuyu.

Two other factors shaped Kenyatta's reluctance to reshape KANU into a more credible institution. First, since he had spent so much time abroad he returned to a movement that was largely not of his own making. Kenyatta's imprisonment during the Mau Mau period also meant that he was not directly involved the foundation of KANU. To counter this Kenyatta often referred to himself as the *mzee*, or elder statesman who stood above the fray of party politics. This contrasts with Julius Nyerere, who is often admirably referred to as *mwalimu*, or teacher. Second, Kenyatta was personally allied with land-owning elements of the Kikuyu elite, primarily through his marriage to his third wife Grace Wanjiku and fourth wife Ngina Kenyatta (Jackson and Rosberg 1982, Widner 1994, 55). Both women were daughters of Kikuyu chiefs from the wealthy Kiambu district. It is therefore unsurprising that Kenyatta resisted some calls for economic redistribution, even when they came from elements of his own Kikuyu base. Kenyatta's impulse and personal interest was toward a more market-based model of economic growth that benefitted the land-owning coffee and tea farmers of Central Province (Barkan 1984b). It also further explains his reluctance to transform the party into something he could not completely control.

REGIME BUILDING AND THE EMERGENCE OF
DIFFERENT RULING PARTY CREDIBILITY

From these junctures three very different parties developed. Only in Tanzania did a credible ruling party emerge in response to the need for political stabilization. This involved immense investments in party institutions and the development of internal processes that gave elites voice and leveled the playing field. Likewise, *ujamaa* provided the needed backdrop that led to the creation of a truly large constituency for the ruling party, namely rural peasants. By contrast, in Cameroon coercion was used to gradually centralize power in the office of the presidency. While the party maintained some interesting organizational features it did not foster credibility or widen its social base. In Kenya the ruling party was perhaps the weakest. The Provincial Administration was used to great effect to eliminate political opposition, and the party atrophied in the

---

[16] During his time in the United Kingdom Kenyatta travelled briefly to the Soviet Union and married a British woman, Edna Clarke, with whom he had a son.

years that followed. The stability of the regime depended on the loyalty of elites, who generally represented important ethnic groups.

Creating a Credible Ruling Party in Tanzania (1967–1985)

With the Arusha Declaration of 1967 Nyerere proclaimed *ujamaa* as Tanzania's new national socioeconomic policy. In the immediate years that followed, TANU underwent fundamental and wide-sweeping changes. Resources from nationalization were diverted toward expanding the infrastructure of the party. The party's National Executive Committee was paid salaries commensurate with members of parliament, and was required to meet every few months. The party's secretariat was expanded to house nine new functionary offices – the disciplinary committee, ideology and political education, foreign affairs, organization, finance, administration, social services, economic planning, and defense and security. Money was also used to create the TANU Youth League (TYL) and the Kivukoni Party Leadership College (Tordoff 1967). Villages with more than 250 members were considered a TANU branch, and branches were established in workplaces with more than fifty people. All branch secretaries (who acted simultaneously as the civil ward executive officer) were required to undergo three months of party training. By the mid-1970s there were an incredible 7,200 TANU branches throughout Tanzania (Mwansasu 1979, Okumu and Holmquist 1984).

TANU developed other important structures that gave it a real nation-wide presence. TANU maintained a number of affiliated organizations like the Union of Tanzanian Workers (JUWATA), Cooperative Union of Tanzania (CUT), Tanzanian Youth Organization, Tanzanian Parent's Association, and the Union of Tanzanian Women. TANU elites saw these organizations as important vehicles for translating the principles of *ujamaa* into reality (McHenry 1994, 53). However, far more critical than these mass mobilizing organizations was the grassroots network of party cells created for every ten homes, known as *nyumba ya kumi*. The importance of cells cannot be overstated, and it was a massive and unparalleled effort on the continent. Cell leaders (*mbozi*) were paid modest sums to ensure a stable institutional structure. Cell leaders were responsible for transmitting TANU policies, collecting party dues, registering new members, and keeping tabs on citizens (Ingle 1972, Samoff 1974).[17] As Joel

---

[17] The *mabozi* were also prominent members of their communities and often fulfilled important social roles too. Several surveys conducted in the 1970s found that the

Barkan notes, TANU party cells provided a system of linkage between the periphery and the center that was more durable than the potentially personal ties between MPs and constituents (Barkan 1984a, 86).

Internally, TANU developed specific institutions that signaled credibility to participating elites and leveled the playing field. The party was given significant decisional autonomy, evident in the power afforded to party positions and the regularity of national conferences. Following independence, the civil administration was simply amalgamated with equivalent positions from within the party. For instance, regional Executive Officers simultaneously acted as TANU regional Secretary-Generals. In 1973, a process of decentralization reinforced the roles of regional and district party chairmen, who began to direct major development programs (Maro and Mlay 1979). Party congresses were also held regularly every five years at the national, regional, and district levels. These became intriguing events where written agendas were followed and recorded, and elites could have some say over the bylaws of the party (although ultimate decisional authority still rested with Nyerere). Indicative of the party's autonomy, the central committee members were elected directly by the national party congress, not the president. This practice was replicated at lower levels of the party (Mwansasu 1979, 184).[18]

TANU's semi-competitive primary system also fostered credibility. Every five years during primaries numerous candidates could vie for nomination through their local branch, and were subsequently screened by their Annual District Conference. Prospective candidates were expected to make presentations and answer questions about their political past and adherence to party principles. After a vote, TANU's executive committee reduced the list of nominees to just two candidates. On average, the party rejected 10 percent of candidates and at times some constituencies ran without competition (McHenry 1994). During campaigns the platforms were essentially the same, and candidates were forbidden from using private resources. To differentiate candidates, one ran under the symbol of a house (*nyumba*) and the other under the hoe (*jemba*). Likewise, at election meetings candidates were forbidden from using tribal language and had to communicate in Swahili (Hyden and Leys 1972, Samoff 1987).

---

majority of a cell leader's time was spent on issues like marital disputes and land disagreements (Miller 1970).

[18] One consequence of strengthening the party was a weaker legislature. In fact, Nyerere had originally suggested completely eradicating the legislature, which the party rejected (Miti 1980). For more on the Tanzanian legislature during single-party rule see van Donge and Liviga (1986a,b).

This fairly meritocratic system was supplemented by the Leadership Code of 1967, which forbade TANU officials and elected representatives from engaging in secondary business endeavors. The code was enforced infrequently to purge members, but curtailed widespread use of individual-level clientelism in Tanzania (Barkan 1984a).[19]

TANU also developed a credible system for selecting the highest positions in the party, including the presidential nominee. Beginning in 1983, TANU's chairman and vice chairman were both elected through a secret ballot at the party's national congress.[20] In 1985, the party, by then called CCM, institutionalized a system for selecting the president. Members of the party could nominate themselves if they were age eligible, had gathered 250 signatures from party members, obtained a university-level education, and could pay a monetary deposit. The party's Central and Executive Committees vetted candidates before presenting them to a vote in the party's National Congress. A majority rule further strengthened the credibility of the system. If no one candidate reached the 50 percent mark in the first round, the bottom candidates dropped out and a second round of voting was held. This system would later elect Ali Hassan Mwinyi as Julius Nyerere's successor (Samoff 1987, 149).

Finally, the party solidified credible exchanges with a wide social constituency through its major social and economic policies. Central to this was the use of *ujamaa* to construct collective villages (*ujamaa vijijini*). Nyerere envisioned these villages as opportunities to extend the party into the countryside and popularize its socialist agenda. Villages were expected to participate in collective small-scale agriculture. The efficacy and aftereffects of villagization and *ujamaa* itself have been heavily debated. By 1978, approximately nine million Tanzanians were living in collective villages (Mascarenhas 1979). Economically the program was a failure, and as Goran Hyden notes it failed to capture the peasantry or break the "economy of affection" that shaped rural life (Hyden 1980). Likewise, *ujamaa* involved a crackdown on agricultural cooperatives and private shops in favor of communal and state-owned enterprises

---

[19] The primary system was fairly effective at renewing political blood in the legislature, and between 1960 and 1985 each parliament rotated on average over half of its members. Likewise, this is not meant to convey that life within TANU was without its rewards or that corruption was absent. In fact, cabinet positions and national executive council membership were fairly secure jobs despite repeated cabinet shuffles (Between 1960 and 1984 there was only one year without a cabinet shift.). Elites who penetrated the upper echelons of TANU were likely to stay there.

[20] Roger Carte. "Changes to the Constitution of the Party," *Tanzanian Affairs* (January 1983).

(known as Operation *Maduka*). The results were drastic food shortages, near famine, and underproduction of export agriculture. Between 1965 and 1980 agriculture in Tanzania grew at an anemic 1.6 percent (Lofchie 1994). *Ujamaa* was a major culprit in the economic crisis that beset Tanzania in the late 1970s (Tripp 1997).

However, the political consequences of *ujamaa* are much more nuanced since it was in reality not a uniform policy. Between 1967 and 1972 villagization was encouraged rhetorically, mainly through ideological prodding. This stage was emulative of the Israeli kibbutz movement and spearheaded by the TYL. Nyerere utilized a wide range of persuasive tools at hand such as the Catholic church and state education system, and eventually lived himself for nearly a year in a model village in Dodoma region. Between 1972 and 1974 villagization was motivated primarily through material inducements. TANU and the TYL would provide needed development resources like roads, schools, and health dispensaries. Likewise, the colonial-era poll tax was abolished and school fees waivered for those who moved into villages. According to TANU records, these incentives were deliberately extended to subsistence-based rural areas with little cash-crop production, coastal towns where the sisal trade had collapsed, and along the TAZARA railway linking Morogoro and Mbeya.[21] This stage of *ujamaa* was fairly successful in these geographic areas, even where cash farming was more established. For instance, by 1972 Hyden notes that in Iringa region "all capitalist farming ... had come to an end" (Hyden 1980, 102). This implied a major investment of party infrastructure and a transfer of state resources to large swaths of the rural countryside, without consideration of narrower factors like ethnic identity. Unlike in other African countries, Tanzania actually experienced rural rather than urban bias (Stren, Halfani, and Malombe 1994). The party's commitments to peasants and workers were not mere rhetoric, but backed by actual policies and institution building in the least developed areas of the Tanzanian countryside (Lofchie 1994).

Villagization evolved into a much more forceful phase between 1974 and 1978, and this too had distinct political consequences. Frustrated with the slow progress of villagization in other areas of the country, by 1974 Nyerere declared that all Tanzanians would be required to reside in *ujamaa* villages by the end of 1976, by force if necessary. Most notably,

[21] United Republic of Tanzania. 1970. "The Economic Survey Annual Plan for 1970–1971." Dar es Salaam, Tanzania: Government Printer; United Republic of Tanzania. 1972. "The Economic Survey Annual Plan for 1972–3." Dar es Salaam, Tanzania: Government Printer.

the strongest resistance to villagization was in areas where cash and export farming was comparatively more entrenched and established, particularly coffee, sisal, and cotton growing in northern and northeastern Tanzania. Ironically, these regions were also the backbone of TANU during the independence movement. In this sense *ujamaa* essentially reversed this historic relationship since forced villagization was economically disastrous for these commercial sectors. As Michael Lofchie notes, farmers in Arusha, Kilimanjaro, and the Lake Zone soon found themselves "pariahs in their own nationalist party" (Lofchie 1994).

Presidential Centralization and a Limited Party in Cameroon (1966–1982)

In the immediate years following independence Ahidjo took advantage of the emergency powers left by the French to centralize power in the office of the presidency. Ahidjo used ambiguously defined "states of warning" and "states of emergency" thirteen times in the interim period before independence. These powers were further entrenched in the constitutional committee of 1960, and later extended to the entire territory of French Cameroon (Kamga 2015).[22] Unification with British Southern Cameroon in October 1961, gave way to a new "Supreme Law," which provided the president with a monopoly over decision-making that was extended every six months until 1972.[23] This allowed Ahidjo to rewrite elements of the constitution nearly singlehandedly, and cajole other parties to join a "Grand National Party," which ultimately became the Cameroon National Union (CNU). Likewise, Ahidjo weakened the federal structure and created urgency for a unitary state that gave the president more powers. Ahidjo appointed the major state-level administrative figures and could divert resources from Anglophone Cameroon (Johnson 1970, 200–13). Unsurprisingly, in May 1972, a referendum passed nearly unanimously to abolish the federal state.[24]

---

[22] Strangely, one of the French advisors to the constitution making process was political scientist Maurice Duverger (Kamga 2015). The new constitution slightly changed the terminology to include "state of exception" and "state of emergency."

[23] For more on the process of unification see Johnson (1970), Le Vine (1971), and Kofele-Kale (1980).

[24] In 1969 the constitution was changed to give Ahidjo the power to appoint the Prime Ministers of Western and Eastern Cameroon, and in 1970 it was changed again to allow the Vice President (an elected position) to act simultaneously as Prime Minister. Subsequently Ahidjo nominated pro-unitary state advocate Solomon Muna as his Vice Presidential candidate, and appointed him Prime Minister of West Cameroon.

Soon after, the process of political centralization continued apace. The positions of Vice President and Prime Minister were summarily eliminated, and Ahidjo restructured Cameroon into seven provinces administered by presidentially appointed governors. Each governor could further select Senior Divisional Officers (*prefets*), Sub-Divisional Officers (*sub prefets*), and district heads (Takougang and Krieger 1998, 44–50). In tandem, Ahidjo added new and important coercive tools to the security state left by the French. In 1975 the *Service des Etudes et la Documentation* was converted into the *Centre National de Documentation* (CND), its interrogative functions exported to the notoriously violent *Brigades Mixtes Mobiles*, and a Presidential Guard was created (largely officered by northerners). Ahidjo commanded all military units, and Cameroon became a comparatively much less open country than Kenya or Tanzania (DeLancey 1989, 55). For several years even travel across regions required government-issued passes (Takougang 2004b, 77–8).[25]

Consequently, the party itself was used primarily for its coercive ends and failed to develop credible features. Organizationally, the original UC was actually quite robust in northern Cameroon. Indeed, one reason the UC was able to contest so effectively in the north during colonial territorial elections was its established local party organization that permeated down to a cell level (Azarya 1976, 52–4). Yet, following the creation of the CNU this infrastructure expanded unevenly to other parts of the country. The CNU mimicked the territorial administration with forty-nine party sections, numerous sub-sections, and local committees that corresponded with the territorial department, arrondissement, and quarter or village. However, the CNU had no regional party structure, reflecting the primacy afforded to provincial governors. Nor is it clear how institutionalized and permanent these lower levels of the party actually were. Early resistance from southern politicians stalled efforts at party expansion and local committees were generally poorly attended events (Bayart 1978b).

The CNU was not, however, completely abandoned as a party. Its governing structures – the National Congress, National Committee, Central Committee, and Political Bureau – operated continuously and were renewed on a regular basis, albeit in a plebiscitary manner. These party organs were in fact expanded in the early 1970s in a brief attempt at party revitalization (Bayart 1978b, 80). The party had an established party school directed for years by the noted partisan Joseph Charles

---

[25] Other coercive legislation included the Anti-Subversion Act (1962) and the Press Law (1966), used to essentially kill private media in Cameroon (Eko 2004).

Doumba. The CNU also built two major affiliated wings, the Youths Cameroon National Union and the Women of Cameroon National Union, which were replicated down to the department level. These institutions comprised 45 percent and 23 percent of party membership, respectively (DeLancey, Neh Mbuh, and DeLancey 2010, 86–7). The CNU also exerted some control over affiliated trade and labor unions, particularly the *Union Générale des Travailleurs du Cameroun*, although this relationship was at times quite tenuous (Takougang and Krieger 1998, 75–8).

Yet, in contrast with the moderate organization of the party the CNU did not develop internal institutions that would produce credibility. Ahidjo's impetus was consolidation and centralization, and that involved limiting the autonomy of the ruling party. This has led some observers to consider single-party Cameroon as quite "Gaullist" in nature, and Ahidjo akin to classic African "Big Men" (Joseph 1978). The presidency was the locus of power, and ran an expansive office with a parallel cabinet and special delegates dispatched to select government ministries (DeLancey 1989, 57). This limited the autonomy of the party and its legislative bloc, which had little say over national policy. Party life between single-party elections was not very visible or vibrant. Beginning in 1969, the CNU started to hold national congresses every five years, but these were largely orchestrated moments for Ahidjo to declare policy, rather than a forum for open discussion among party elites. By-laws were not always followed, and congresses remained ceremonious rather than substantive.

Elite competition was also tightly regulated, and the rules of the game were unclear. General elections were held every five years, but the CNU retained a single district that covered the entire country. Voters elected representatives via a plebiscite of pre-approved candidates from the party's Central Committee. The selection criteria were idiosyncratic and related more to perceived loyalties and personal connections rather than merit. Likewise, cabinet shuffles were frequent and individuals had very little chance of serving in the same ministry for over four years (DeLancey 1989, 60). Nor were there any mechanisms for executive succession. In 1979 Ahidjo changed the constitution to ensure that his Prime Minister Paul Biya – a position only reinstated a few years prior – would be his successor, rather than the President of the National Assembly. When Ahidjo stepped down this generated backlash and a petition to "change the Prime Minister" and replace Biya with a northerner. Since Ahidjo remained chairman of the CNU, there was also a bifurcation of authority that led to a severe political crisis. Biya implicated Ahidjo in an anti-government plot, and forced him to resign and self-exile in Paris (Le Vine 1986, 35–40, DeLancey 1989, 65–71).

Finally, the party did not establish credible relationships with widespread social constituencies. There was no real commitment to rural development, despite Ahidjo's promises of a "Green Revolution." Allocations of monies to the National Fund for Rural Development (FONADER) were meant to stimulate *ujamaa*-style pioneer villages, and encourage youth settlement in rural areas. However, in reality FONADER led to a strong sense of urban bias since most rural citizens did not have the wherewithal to complete the application process for loans. Urban citizens leveraged their advantages and political connections to purchase farmland. Over time, rural development basically meant larger agrobusinesses (Ndongko 1986). Virginia DeLancey has similarly documented declines in agricultural productivity due to misaligned pricing schemes that paid farmers below market rates for export crops like cocoa and coffee. Indicative of the failure of the Green Revolution, Cameroon experienced one of the highest rates of urbanization in Africa, reaching 36 percent by 1982 (1986).

Likewise, there was evidence of ethnic bias within the ruling coalition. Interestingly, during the Ahidjo years this was not reflected in cabinet or political appointments, which were allocated proportionally by province, with the exception of the military and security services (Kofele-Kale 1986).[26] Yet the north received a disproportionate amount of development resources under the guise of balanced development to address historical discrepancies across regions. Development policy under Ahidjo became known as "Garoua First," in reference to his northern hometown. For example, an extensive road network and airport were built in the north, while there was still no road linking the major commercial hubs of Yaoundé and Douala. Popularly, the allies and beneficiaries of the north became known as "Garoua Barons," playing on historical north-south divisions. Notably, Eastern Province received little state investment despite similarly dire starting economic conditions (DeLancey 1989, 62–3). Exacerbating these tendencies was also the perception of Anglophone discrimination in various circles, referred to ominously as the "Anglophone problem" (Kofele-Kale 1986, 64–8). After unification, the central government diverted trade through the Douala river port

---

[26] Only Littoral province, the bastion of the Bamileké, was persistently underrepresented in public appointment. One argument is that in exchange for their economic freedom the Bamileké implicitly agreed to stay out of national politics (Arriola 2012).

rather than the more accessible Anglo port of Limbe. Many businesses in Limbe subsequently closed (DeLancey 1989, 75–6). There were also perceptions of cultural bias in sectors like university language requirements, and concern that Anglophones did not hold major cabinet positions.

Presidential Control and Ruling Party Decay in Kenya (1966–1978)

After independence Jomo Kenyatta utilized his control of the Provincial Administration to force his major political rival KADU into a merger with KANU.[27] What followed was a gradual decline in the importance of the ruling party as a central institution of governing. The national level of the party rarely met and was grossly understaffed. During the first postindependence years, the party headquarters in Nairobi actually had no phone service and was in debt for £20,000 (Bennett 1966, 339). Discussions of revitalizing the national level of the party failed. There was a short-lived party school (the Lumumba Institute) that dissolved brusquely after its creation. At the 1966 KANU congress in Limuru, Kenyatta's notion of party reform was to create and handpick nine new vice-presidential positions (Widner 1992, 57). At both the Mombasa (1970) and Nakuru (1975) congresses there were proposals for party reform, which included consolidating the vice-presidencies, creating an independent KANU chairman, reviving KANU's parliamentary group, and expanding the party secretariat.[28] These proposals never materialized, and KANU failed to even hold an internal party election between 1966 and 1978. To make things worse, KANU only had an interim Secretary General for most of the 1970s (Okumu and Holmquist 1984, 62–3).[29]

The situation was not much different at other levels of the party. For KANU the branch was the only real visible sub-national element, although smaller divisions did exist on paper (Mueller 1984). KANU's branches

---

[27] Kenyatta used the Provincial Administration to limit the implementation of Kenya's original constitution, which had established a federal structure (the *majimbo* constitution). At the same time he campaigned heavily for national unity and a single party. KADU members were deprived of development funds and ultimately the party dissolved and the constitution was changed to create a unitary state, with Kenyatta as President and former KADU leader Daniel arap Moi as Vice President. For more on this period see Gertzel (1970).

[28] Staff. "Is KANU to be revitalized?" *The Weekly Review* (June 30, 1975), Staff. "Another Hope of Revitalization in Nakuru" *The Weekly Review* (July 28, 1975).

[29] Constitutionally, KANU was required to hold internal elections every two years. Elections scheduled in 1973 and 1977, following the Mombasa and Nakuru congresses respectively, were cancelled. In the latter the election was cancelled just a day before it was scheduled, after delegates had already arrived.

numbered in the hundreds, compared to the thousands in Tanzania, and a membership drive in 1970 to recruit one million members fell far short of those goals.[30] At the branch level, elections were intermittent and unorganized and often resulted in internal coups. Financial transgressions were widespread, and branch chairmen would habitually buy membership cards in bulk and distribute them to supporters to bolster perceptions of branch strength (Okumu and Holmquist 1984, 62–3). Likewise, there were very few party-affiliated sources of mobilization. Kenya had relatively strong labor unions at independence, but they were schismatic over national policy issues. In 1965 Kenyatta dissolved the existing labor unions and consolidated them into the Central Organization of Trade Unions (COTU). But, as Adrienne LeBas notes, COTU was separated from party mobilization and the "ruling party never viewed unions as a key channel for communication" (2011, 104).[31] By the mid-1970s reform-minded members of KANU, such as the outspoken J.M. Kariuki, began to publicly proclaim that KANU had become moribund and was "driven into obscurity."[32]

Concurrent with KANU's weak infrastructure, the party failed to develop significant internal sources of credibility. The party remained entirely subservient to the office of the president and lacked real decisional autonomy (Widner 1992, 53–67). Indicatively, one of Kenyatta's first decisions was to end monthly consultative meetings with KANU's parliamentary group. Further symptomatic of the party's subservient position was the fact that it was so difficult to hold a party congress or an internal election. Other constitutional amendments further bolstered the president's dominant position. For instance, the 6th amendment of 1966 stated that the constitutional protection of movement, association, and expression would not be compromised if the president exercised his power under the Preservation of Public Security Act and the Detention Act. Kenyatta often utilized executive control over the civil administration

---

[30] Staff. "Is KANU to be revitalized?" *The Weekly Review* (June 30, 1975).

[31] Other organizations that could have been used to bolster the organizational capacity of KANU, such as the Kenyan Farmer's Association or the National Council of Churches of Kenya were not utilized. Indeed, under Kenyatta mass-mobilizing institutions emerged outside of KANU along ethnic lines. The most infamous was the Gikuyu, Embu, and Meru Association. At one point the latter was described as the "only well-organized mass movement in Kenya ... with properly elected national district members and with regular meetings." Staff. "Gema Speaks out on Politics" *The Weekly Review* (March 19, 1975).

[32] Staff. "Death of J.M. Kariuki" *The Weekly Review* (March 17, 1975).

to restrict KANU political gathering, registration of political groups, and the flow of development funds.[33]

KANU did, however, maintain fairly competitive party primaries, but in many ways they actually weakened the credibility of the party. Under Kenyatta, parliamentarians were encouraged to develop their own personal linkages with constituents through a policy known as *harambee*, or self-help. MPs were allowed to organize their districts for local development projects, and received matching funds in return. The only stipulation was that local leaders could not engage in any ideologically motivated behavior or threaten Kenyatta's position. As Joel Barkan notes, the challenge for MPs was "to create a political base that is large enough for the regime to value and coopt, but not too large for the regime to fear" (Barkan 1984a, 78). Parliamentary elections were held every five years, and there were few limitations on who could run for office. But, better-connected and wealthier candidates clearly had an advantage. Indicatively, there were comparatively fewer parliamentary backbenchers in Kenya than there were in Tanzania (40–50 percent in Kenya versus 60–70 percent in Tanzania), and turnover was significantly lower. Between 1969 and 1978 turnover in Kenya ranged between 41 and 58 percent, compared to 64 and 80 percent in Tanzania (Barkan 1984a). Barkan has further noted that this system of recruitment, while competitive, reinforced a multi-tiered system of patronage with the undisputed president at the apex. The system relied heavily on personal relationships, and was therefore fairly rigid, prone to breakdown and inconsistency, and did not foster a sense of credibility or managed expectations.[34]

Executive succession was not, however, institutionalized in any meaningful way under Kenyatta. The Kenyan presidency had no defined term limits set until 1991, and there was no process within the party for choosing or selecting a successor besides the constitutional provision that the Vice President succeeded him in the case of death or resignation. Point in fact was the tenuous transition from Kenyatta to Moi in 1978. While

[33] Under Kenyatta the system was *de facto* single party. There was an attempt to create a new party in 1966 when Bildad Kaggia and Oginga Odinga left KANU to create the populist Kenya People's Union (KPU). The party was shut out by the civil administration from the 1966 by-election (known as the "little general election"), and in the local government elections of 1968. Provincial governors were instructed to declare all KPU candidates disqualified, and in 1969 the party was declared illegal. Part of the KPU's lament was the weak status of the ruling party KANU.

[34] Jackson and Rosberg refer to the Kenyan regime as an aristocracy, where Kenyatta surrounded himself with an inner court of fraternal Kikuyu politicians from Kiambu who had risen to political prominence with him (1982, 99).

Moi was groomed for years as a likely successor, his ultimate selection sparked significant backlash from within Kenyatta's inner circle. As in Cameroon, there was a failed "change the constitution" movement that arose in response. Some KANU members went as far as to attempt and stack the scheduled 1977 party elections against Moi, which were eventually postponed by Kenyatta to avoid a crisis (Widner 1992, 110–29).

Finally, KANU did not develop strong bonds with broad segments of the population. Under Kenyatta the perception of Kikuyu domination in politics and the economy was widespread. Kenyatta's inner circle was mainly from Kiambu District, and referred to as the "family." This included three of Kenyatta's brothers-in-law, two nephews, a son, and a daughter (Widner 1992, 76). Kikuyu elites were overrepresented in the cabinet (~30 percent), usually controlled key portfolios such as agriculture and security, and held the majority of prominent posts in the civil administration. During Kenyatta's tenure, the Kikuyu also increasingly dominated the security forces and the officer corps (Hornsby 2012, 232–56). Arguably, the overrepresentation of Kikuyu in these institutions was suggestive of the community's better starting conditions in terms of education and economic wellbeing, but what matters was the perception of ethnic bias on part of Kenyan citizens (Barkan and Chege 1989).

These observations extend to the actual distribution of economic goods, and in particular land. Various land reform programs in Central Province and the mixed districts of the Rift Valley such as the Million Acre Scheme, Haraka Program, and Shirika Scheme, were created to address historical issues of inequality and landlessness.[35] However, by 1977 land still remained highly concentrated in a few hands, and particularly with the Kikuyu. As Shem Migot-Adholla notes, rural development policy emanated from the "needs to diffuse insurgency during the Mau Mau revolt," but "supported the better placed, more enterprising, and often wealthier individuals" (Migot-Adholla 1984, 207). Since the Kikuyu had more economic and political wherewithal, they were able to purchase the most profitable tea, coffee, and horticultural farms. Similarly, the distribution of *harambee* funds reflected ethnic bias since it benefited those who already had the means to raise local funds (Barkan and Holmquist 1989). By 1972 a scathing report by the International Labor Organization highlighted the growing regional discrepancies in

---

[35] Land issues were not limited to the Rift Valley and Central Province but were most pronounced there. Coastal land was also highly valued and Kenyatta issued a presidential edict that banned sales in Coastal Province without presidential approval. For more on these land distribution schemes, see Harbeson (1973) and Leo (1981).

welfare and the disproportionate gains of Central Province (Widner 1992, 77–83).[36]

CHALLENGES OF LEADERSHIP SUCCESSION
AND POLITICAL CHANGE

In all three cases ruling institutions faced challenges with the transition to a new generation of leaders and the onset of regional economic crisis in the mid-1980s. Consequently, there were important reforms made to the size and structure of ruling parties. In Tanzania, Ali Hassan Mwinyi oversaw a restructuring of CCM and opened its doors to new business interests. This challenged the cohesion of the party's internal structures and stressed its historic social coalition with rural peasants. In Cameroon, Paul Biya offered a "New Deal" that included promises to liberalize the CPDM's rigid nomination processes and to hold more national congresses. In Kenya, Daniel arap Moi oversaw an important expansion of the party and took it upon himself to revitalize some of KANU's dormant structures. But, what is remarkable in each case is how difficult it was to fundamentally change once on a specific pathway of institutional development. CCM retained the key elements that made it a credible party, while in Cameroon and Kenya promised reforms to the party stalled and gave way to even more presidential dominance, internal authoritarianism, and ethnic bias.

One reason for this continuity is that in each case there were sufficient elites in place who had a stake in maintaining the system. In Tanzania, reform and the incorporation of business reflected Ali Hasan Mwinyi's priorities, but also created backlash from many devoted socialists, including Nyerere. Likewise, by the time of these changes there was a large and dedicated party bureaucracy that had a stake in the process of reform. By contrast, in Cameroon and Kenya the zero-sum nature of elite competition meant that attempts at party reform generated resentments from perceived losers, and from elites that felt it was their turn to helm the ship of state. Once an attempted coup plot was discovered in Cameroon, the process of reform reversed, and the ruling coalition became more overtly favorable to southern ethnic elites, rather than the north as under Ahidjo. In Kenya, an attempted military coup prodded Moi to bolster aspects of the party as tools of political control, which meant it did not increase its credibility building potential. Likewise, the orientation of the regime

---

[36] Perceptions of bias also extended to the distribution of government loans and educational policies. See Cooksey, Court, and Makau (1994).

became more explicitly toward the Rift Valley and the minority groups that had not been part of the original KANU alliance.

New Business Interests and Party Reform in Tanzania (1985–1992)

Economic crisis was a significant factor that spurred Mwinyi to make changes to CCM. The state of the Tanzanian economy throughout the 1980s was abysmal, and this forced the government into a lengthy process of structural adjustment with international lenders.[37] Privatization of state-owned resources, the liberalization of the public sector, and cutbacks to social service made it necessary for the party to rethink its financing structure, ideological outlook, and relationship with nascent business interests. By 1988, it seemed as if CCM had essentially renounced *ujamaa* as an explicit ideology, although it still maintained an official commitment to peasants and labor.[38] Furthermore, throughout the 1980s it also became clear that the Leadership Code put in place by Nyerere was frequently violated, and that numerous figures were involved in corruption and black market activities (Tripp 1997). In 1990 the Leadership Code was officially abolished. This reflected the emergence of a new class of elites in CCM, many of whom were not as wedded to the party's ideological heritage.

The process of reform involved significant input from the party, and many of the changes actually served to strengthen CCM. In response to donor demands, in 1985 Mwinyi began to extricate the party from the state. This began by offering high-level CCM members a choice – keep your government job or party position, but not both. As a result, the party was left with a much more dedicated permanent staff than before. The bulk of reforms were delegated to CCM's Secretary General, Horace Kolimba. After his appointment in 1991, Kolimba worked with the party secretariat on downsizing CCM, implicitly in preparation for multipartyism. The party's nine secretaries were deemed redundant and pared down to just three offices: economic planning, mass mobilization, and finance. Likewise, as CCM moved away from state socialism, in 1992

---

[37] Nyerere reluctantly accepted these reforms in 1980 with a short-lived National Economic Survival Program. Mwinyi oversaw a larger three-year IMF sponsored Economic Recovery Program in 1985 and an Economic and Social Adjustment Program in 1989. Nyerere remained critical of the rapid pace of liberalization under Mwinyi and eventually resigned from CCM in 1990. See Campbell and Stein (1992), Costello (1996), and Temu and Due (2000).

[38] Mwinyi's tenure is often referred to as the age of *ruksa*, or permissiveness. This is in reference to the pace of economic liberalization.

Kolimba dismantled party branches in the workplace, army, and police (Mmuya and Chaligha 1994). Finally, two of CCM's affiliated mass mobilizing organizations, the JUWATA and CUT, were delinked from the party. However, the JUWATA was simply replaced by the Organization of Tanzanian Trade Union (OTTU). The CUT was more successful at staking out independent ground (Tripp 2000).

Other changes were heavily debated at CCM's 1992 Chimwaga Congress, which brought together the party's national congress and representatives of the party's major supportive organs. A key compromise that emerged from the Chimwaga Congress was to scale back on some of the party's infrastructure, while investing in novel tools that could help CCM compete in elections. CCM's immense cell system was supplemented with a novel institution called the *wakereketwa*, or party militants (known as the *maskani* on Zanzibar). These cell-level organs were more ad hoc than the *nyumba kumi*, and developed and used primarily for campaigning and contesting elections. A number of new mass mobilizing organs also came out of Chimwaga, with the specific goal of increasing voter turnout. Among these were the Tanzanian One Theater, the CCM Motorcycle Club (*Umoja wa Wapanda Pikipiki*) and the Youth Commanders of the Party (*Makamanda wa Vijana*). These organizations travelled the country to popularize CCM and its candidates prior to the foundational election. By the multiparty elections, CCM was a leaner but meaner party, and retained impressive real estate (Mmuya and Chaligha 1994).[39]

Another development that came out of Chimwaga was conflict over the inclusion of perceived corrupt and new business interests. For the first time in its history, CCM allowed business elites to join the Central Committee and participate in party primaries. This created significant backlash, and an unprecedented official censure from the OTTU and CUT. Many in the party vocally criticized the party secretariat for the decision, and made clear their fear that the historical sources of CCM's credibility – fair competition and a commitment to rural constituencies – were at risk (Baregu 1994, Kaiser 1996). There were no changes made to the candidate selection process or the basic bylaws of the party, but these developments meant that elections would be a test of whether CCM's internal processes and wide social incorporation would endure. Indeed, as discussed in the next chapter, since multipartyism primaries have increasingly become contentious sites, with some elites committed

---

[39] The details and impetus for these changes were revealed via anonymous interviews conducted with members of CCM's national secretariat in 2010.

to working around CCM's nomination process and other keen on seeing the rules enforced.

The CPDM and Stalled Party Reform in Cameroon (1983–1990)

Paul Biya's ascension to the presidency signaled a new central node in the governing multi-ethnic coalition, which jeopardized the position of many former regime elites. Early in his tenure Biya promised "rigor and moralization" in public life, and called for public sector reform and increased efforts to combat corruption. This threatened many Ahidjo-era politicians, and was likely a key catalyst behind the failed military coup of April 1984 (Le Vine 1986). Biya's response to the coup involved some important reform measures that injected new vitality into existing party infrastructure. The Political Bureau and Central Committee were expanded, and the party was rechristened in 1985 at the Bamenda Congress as the Cameroon People's Democratic Party (CPDM). During the subsequent party elections of 1986, half of the party's section presidents were replaced, as were large majorities of the women and youth wing leadership (Takougang and Krieger 1998, 81). While new blood in the party was important, it was not a huge investment in the party's organization, and did not address the absence of a regional party structure.

The Bamenda Congress also promised a "New Deal" that would increase the party's autonomy and make internal processes more transparent. However, outside of the Bamenda Congress itself subsequent CPDM congresses were still held irregularly, and were actually less vociferous than during the Ahidjo-period (DeLancey 1989, 73–6). Biya also retained the essential elements of the Ahidjo security state. The notorious CND was simply rededicated as the *Direction Général d'Etudes et de la Documentation*. None of the draconian laws from before were removed from the books, and press freedoms continued to be highly monitored (Takougang and Krieger 1998, 77–92). Further weakening the party, the position of Prime Minster was abolished between 1984 and 1991. Elite recruitment only became slightly more open under Biya. As part of the New Deal, Biya seemingly introduced competitive elections for party positions and primaries for legislative nomination. Yet, while party cadres welcomed these developments, the CPDM's Political Bureau still wielded significant influence over the nomination process. Biya also made provisions for a presidential primary, but the prerequisites were so burdensome that in practice it made real internal competition impossible. Candidates would need to present a petition with 500 signatures from each of

Cameroon's ten provinces, and from elected officials in the legislature and Central Committee of the CPDM (Takougang and Krieger 1998).

What did substantially change was the general social orientation of the ruling party, which also explains why reforms to the party were so piecemeal. Biya faced significant pressures from his southern and central cohorts to deliver resources and political prestige. The flip from north to south has been referred to as the ascendancy of the "Beti Mafia" over the Garoua Barons of the Ahidjo era. Biya initially continued Ahidjo's commitment to regional balance in political appointments, but over time the Beti and related groups came to dominate much of the government, security forces, and civil administration (van de Walle 1994, Takougang 2004a, 108–16). Likewise, Biya did little to redress tensions between Anglophone and Francophone Cameroonians. For instance, in September 1983 the Ministry of Education made French the required language for a bachelor's degree, which sparked student protests at the University of Yaoundé. Biya also changed the name of the country from the United Republic of Cameroon to the Republic of Cameroon, a move perceived by many Anglophones as a slight and new attempt at cultural hegemony (Konings and Nyamnjoh 2004).

As multiparty elections neared the CPDM bared significant resemblances to the CNU, and the coercive presidential regime erected by first President Ahmadou Ahidjo. Paul Biya's presidential powers overshadowed the party, which itself was not a very transparent or credible institution. Elite loyalty to the party came mainly through the promise of financial reward and fear of reprisal. As Mark DeLancey writes of the CPDM, the essence of the ruling party was the "cohesion of a few important people, each of whom brought his/her loyalties to the party" (1989, 52). Or, in the words of Jean-Françoise Bayart, by the end of the 1980s the CPDM was, like the CNU, a hegemonic and highly elitist party (Bayart 2009). The multiethnic and strong regional forces in Cameroonian politics continued to shape the distribution of resources, which strived for balance on paper but remained skewed in perception toward the president's own cohort.

Attempts at Party Revitalization in Kenya (1979–1991)

The changes to KANU that occurred under Kenyatta's successor Daniel arap Moi are the subject of some considerable scholarly debate. The impetus for Moi's reforms was perhaps initially sincere. But, ultimately they were less about creating a credible ruling party and more about fostering new tools of coercive control (Hornsby 2012, 331–79). One reason was that Moi faced much more stressful economic conditions than Kenyatta, with the end of the cash crop boom of the 1970s. But, fundamentally it was the perceived shift in ruling coalition from the Kikuyu toward the Kalenjin, Luhya, and other minority ethnic groups that limited reform. Moi was already fearful of Kikuyu dissent during the transition process from Kenyatta, but the attempted coup of August 1982 reified in his mind a real peril. At the same time there was immense pressure to reorient public policy toward the Rift Valley. This meant that while the actors changed, the essential contours of the Kenyatta regime and ruling party remained the same, if not more autocratic.

One of the first steps Moi took to reform KANU was to reintroduce internal party elections in 1978, after a nearly ten-year absence. These elections were repeated again in 1986 and 1988, and did allow new blood into the party. Relatedly, early on in Moi's tenure he directed an attempt at reinvigorating KANU's moribund infrastructure. At the time KANU had just 281 branches, and Moi required all of them to open bank accounts, submit financial statements to the party's national treasurer, and to raise the membership fee from 2 Ks to 5 Ks.[40] Party branches were required to build on plots of land issued by the government.[41] Moi further set the lofty goal of increasing KANU membership from a few hundred thousand to eight million people within a few years. KANU began to create new party branches, with grassroots nomination of candidates for five rather than two-year limits. Likewise, Moi required that civil servants become party members, banned ethnic welfare organizations, and purchased the *Nairobi Times* as the official mouthpiece of KANU.[42]

These seem like impressive changes, but it is not obvious whether they gave Moi considerable more leverage on the ground or built credibility. While Moi issued directives, the actual construction of physical party buildings at the district level and below were uneven.[43] Likewise, after the attempted coup the decisional autonomy of the party weakened even

---

[40] Office the President. Delegates to the KANU Provincial Conferences on 18th November 1978 (November 10, 1978).

[41] Office of the National Treasurer. "Kenyan African National Union Governing Council Meeting Notes" *KANU 1/3(252).* (March 25, 1980).

[42] Staff. "KANU: A Real Powerbase" *The Weekly Review* (October 14, 1988).

[43] In an interview with KANU's Secretary General in 2012, it was indicated that KANU continued to hold real estate, but it was less clear how many physical buildings the party actually owned. Poor record keeping, particularly after the party's defeat in 2002 made it difficult to assess the actual infrastructure of the party on the eve of elections. Nick Salat (KANU Secretary General). Author Interview. Nairobi. (August 7, 2012).

further. Between 1982 and 1990 there was an increase in executive orders, the use of the General Service Unit, and detention without trial.[44] Moi also used the Provincial Administration to actually circumvent KANU during elections. It was more common under Moi for the administration to deny KANU party meetings. Compounding this were changes in KANU's nomination process, which became much more opaque. During the 1983 General Election, there were widespread accusations of fraud, and several regime insiders were likely rigged out of their seats. The most important innovation Moi introduced was the elimination of the secret ballot in favor of a malleable queuing system. During the 1988 KANU party elections, the perception from numerous elites was that queuing allowed Moi to remove Central Province branch chairmen like Kenneth Matiba and Martin Shikuku.[45] The same system was used during the KANU legislative primaries, but with the added stipulation that candidates who won 70 percent of the primary vote could run unopposed, and that only candidates who won at least 30 percent of the vote could actually run. Infamously, Charles Rubia's opponent in Straehe District was elected without contest with 70.5 percent of the primary vote (Hornsby 2012, 456–8). Exacerbating the opacity of the party, a new national disciplinary committee purged many rivals from the party. The committee proved so unpopular that it was dissolved in 1987 after just twenty-one months in existence (Hornsby 2012, 400–1).

As in Cameroon, this coincided with clearer changes in the distributive commitments of the regime. This was evident in public appointment and the composition of cabinets. For instance, between 1978 and 1991 there were twelve dismissals and five forced resignations from cabinet in favor of Moi loyalists (Throup and Hornsby 1998, 46). Likewise, Moi replaced all but one of Kenya's Provincial Administrators and nearly half of the District Commissioners. There was also evidence that larger public salaries and parastatal management positions shifted toward the Kalenjin and minority tribes. The transition toward a narrower social coalition also meant a divergence of state resources away from Central Province to the Rift Valley. Public expenditures on roads, health, water, and education

---

[44] Moi's tenure is associated with a number of draconian laws that increased the power of the presidency, such as the Vagrancy Act, which allowed Moi to arrest youths in urban areas with no proof of employment or abode, or the Outlying and Special Districts Act that gave the civil administration the power to employ travel restrictions and curfews. Likewise, Moi infamously weakened the judiciary and eliminated tenure for the attorney general, state-controller, auditor-general, and judges.

[45] Staff. "Election: 1988" *The Weekly Review* (February 25, 1988).

all changed, as did patterns of *harambee* contributions (Mbithi and Rasmusson 1977, Widner 1992). The most significant adjustment was a swing in public policy from pricing schemes that supported coffee and tea producers in Central Province, to those that protected grain and cereal growers in the upper Rift Valley and Western Kenya. As Michael Lofchie documents, the price index for wheat nearly tripled, while total production of wheat grew by 30 percent (1994, 158). Moi also tempered the autonomy of coffee and tea producers by banning the Kenyan Farmers Association and replacing it with the Kenya Grain Growers Cooperative Union. These policies led to an unprecedented, but also ultimately unsustainable, economic boom in the upper Rift Valley.[46]

CONCLUSION

This chapter has demonstrated how following the critical juncture of postindependence presidents took their regimes and ruling parties in very different directions. Only in Tanzania did the party develop features that we would consider credibility building, while in Cameroon and Kenya parties were either used primarily for organization, or completely neglected as ruling institutions. Despite moderate changes, these essential patterns persisted with the transition to new leadership and in preparation for economic and political reform. Indeed, it became quite difficult for regimes without credible ruling parties to forge new institutions. Resistance from older elites accustomed to a looser style of politics, or demands from new constituencies in anticipation of gains from the state meant that in a real sense parties actually became less credible and more autocratic. On the other hand, in Tanzania the party showed signs of resistance to the apparent erosion of its credibility following the incorporation of business interests, and allowed some real modernization of its national and grassroots organization. By the multiparty era, differences across these three cases were still quite evident.

However, the period of single-party rule provides a poor test of the resilience of these different regime configurations. With opposition parties legally or in practice banned, the incentives for elite defection were very low. A regime could persist with a weaker political party if it could

---

[46] Similarly the largely Maasai pastoralist communities of Kenya benefitted from the Moi government's economic policies through the divergence of development aid and the creation of the Ministry for Reclamation and Development of Arid and Semi-Arid Lands (Hornsby 2012, 439–40).

maintain a system of material rewards, coerce opponents, and keep a monopoly over political space. All that would change with the transition to multiparty elections that swept the African continent. Since this change corresponded with declines in economic resources and the opening of new political space, it laid bare the essential features of these regimes and the ruling parties they had built. As the next chapters show, this had real consequences for how each regime managed elite competition in the era of elections, as well as their ability to translate social constituencies into stable voting blocks.

5

Ruling Party Credibility and the Management of Elites

> CCM members are a humorous bunch – not strictly religious and much more involved and participatory.
>
> —Author Interview with Anonymous CCM MP (2010)

> Careers are made and unmade in this party and even in the state of Cameroon through the sheer will of Mr. Paul Biya. The rest of the people in the party are stooges, who are struggling to avoid contradicting the prince and protect their daily bread.
>
> —Le Messager, July 19, 2006 (Author Translation)

> During the single-party era KANU reigned supreme ... With the reintroduction of the multiparty system anyone, for instance, who may feel shortchanged in the forthcoming election could individually defect to another party or carry with him or her most of his or her supporters who almost invariably are members of his or her ethnic group.
>
> —The Weekly Review, June 1, 1998

The inception of multiparty elections provides new incentives for elite defection, which tests the endurance of party structures put in place under single-party rule. As noted in Chapter 4, in reaction to the critical juncture of postindependence regimes in Tanzania, Cameroon, and Kenya embarked on quite different strategies of regime construction in terms of the credibility fostering features of their ruling parties. This chapter traces a major implication of this variation with regard to the ability of regimes to shape elite incentives after the transition to multiparty elections. We should observe real differences in the degree of expressed elite grievance, internal factionalism, and consequently the amount of elite defection.

The ability of regimes to use ruling parties to manage elite competition during contentious moments like presidential succession or legislative primaries will also differ. Importantly, this elite defection should relate to differences in ruling parties, not the extent of regime vulnerability and the immediate material motivations for defection.

The claims and evidence presented here are rooted in my argument that credible ruling parties shape elite careers. Elite loyalty and regime splits are a major source of uncertainty for autocrats, who must manage very disparate social forces, often with very limited resources. Ruling parties help mitigate some of that uncertainty by providing clearer and more stable career trajectories that require considerable investments of time. Credible parties go a step further by leveling the playing field, institutionalizing practice, and providing elites with some control over their own affairs. During elections a more credible party like Chama Cha Mapinduzi (CCM) can independently enforce rules and ensure repeated contestation within the party. Loyalty is rooted in longer-term perspectives regarding the efficacy of remaining within the ruling party. By contrast, less credible parties like the Cameroon Peoples Democratic Movement (CPDM) and Kenyan African National Union (KANU) depend largely on their ability to compensate elites and coercively deter defection. Elites that feel the nomination process has been unfair to them, or that they have no recourse, are more likely to express grievance and have less incentive to remain loyal to the ruling party.

By directing attention to the internal processes within ruling parties I push back on some of the standard explanations in the literature on defection and regime breakdown, which focuses more directly on simple opportunity costs and the impact of regime vulnerability (Haggard and Kaufman 1995, Rakner and van de Walle 2009). According to these arguments, elite defection is rooted mainly in short-term changes like economic crisis, the availability of viable alternatives, and perceptions of regime decline. This is a view of autocracy that is largely transactional and considers elites as purely opportunistic. Elites lend their support to a regime as long as they receive something of immediate material value in return. Applied to our three cases, what should determine the extent of elite defection is the degree of crisis that precedes an election and the flexibility afforded nascent opposition. My approach does not ignore these material opportunities, but I find that elites are more likely to weather difficult times and continue to hitch their wagon to a regime when institutions are in place that foster credible exchange.

One way to validate these contentions is to observe the actual behavior of party institutions and elites, and to see whether this corresponds with the theoretical expectations that each case generates. The chapter relies on a range of evidentiary materials that provide case-level causal process validation of the role of credible ruling parties in managing elite competition. Using secondary sources, media reporting, and field interviews with elite participants, I show how the ruling party in Tanzania repeatedly reasserted its independent influence and responded to elites, even when there was really no material risk of defection. At the same time, the absence of credible institutions led to persistent dilemmas and even crisis in Cameroon and Kenya, which forced more coercion as a means to sustain ruling coalitions. This is evident even when the likelihood of elite defection was not very high to begin with. Specifically, presidential succession impacted regimes in Cameroon and Kenya quite acutely. The counterfactual is that if regimes in Cameroon and Kenya had credible parties, we would not observe the same extent of internal elite tension.

A second source of causal inference comes from the comparison of cases during similar moments of regime vulnerability, and observing whether there are differences in elite defection. This requires a clearer definition of the term regime vulnerability. In other work, vulnerability has been described as a set of factors that causes regimes some concern over their hold on power (Bunce and Wolchik 2011, 38). One issue with this categorization is that it subsumes the very institutional feature this study is interested in. Tanzania's credible party made the regime less vulnerable because it could more easily retain elite and voter support.[1] To observe the impact of institutional credibility we need a measure of vulnerability that is more exogenous. I focus on two specific factors that were mentioned in the introduction: economic uncertainty and opposition mobilization. Economic decline reduces the amount of patronage resources and public support for regimes. Similarly, opposition mobilization – whether from civil or political society – increases perceptions of regime weakness and reduces the costs of defection. Foundational elections are particularly vulnerable moments, since they open up political alternatives for the first time. But, I also note whether opposition parties boycotted an election, which reduces regime uncertainty, or whether there was a uniquely popular candidate who could mobilize support.

---

[1] Bunce and Wolchik refer to this dimension of regime vulnerability as regime institutionalization. However, as indicated in Chapter 2 the term credible party incorporates institutionalization along with other factors like physical size and internal rules of competition.

By elite defection I refer specifically to high-level officials such as incumbent members of parliament or senior members of the ruling party.[2] It is also important to make a distinction between elite defection and regime vulnerability. I note how some defection is often a precursor to opposition mobilization, which increases regime vulnerability (Bunce and Wolchik 2011, 39–40). As discussed in the cases, many opposition parties were founded by former regime elites who had long been out of power, and at times a major defection significantly strengthened the opposition. However, defection can also cause a cascade effect by rapidly increasing perceptions of vulnerability, and therefore exacerbating the problem of defection (van de Walle 2006). To avoid conflating the process of elite defection with regime vulnerability, I limit comparative observations to defections that occur in the early stages of an election period. More specifically, in order to capture elite defection that is related to perceptions of institutional credibility, the most important time frames to consider are when ruling parties set guidelines for internal competition and during candidate selection. Defection that occurs in the aftermath of an election is not considered in the comparative measure.[3]

As summarized in Table 5.1, elite defection does not always correspond with the extent of regime vulnerability. Most explicitly, foundational elections are considered uniformly stressful for regimes and offered perhaps the most substantial moment for elite defection. In each case economic crisis, declines in regime legitimacy, and new opposition parties challenged incumbents in novel ways. Yet, levels of elite defection clearly diverge, which corresponds primarily with differences in ruling party credibility. Note that in Cameroon vulnerability differs between the presidential and legislative election because of the opposition boycott of the latter. During subsequent elections we lose some comparative leverage since regime vulnerability declines. However, we can make comparative insights when all three regimes were at moderate levels of vulnerability (Tanzania in 2010 and 2015, Cameroon in 2011 and 2013, and Kenya in 2002). Once again, differences in ruling party credibility differentiate the

---

[2] Tracking the extent of elite defection is also not necessarily straightforward. There is no clear record of elite defection and some burden of proof on establishing the *absence* of elite defection. This identification process depends heavily on secondary source materials from each country, research into individual elites, and by comparing parliamentary membership across election periods. Multiple journalistic sources from each election period were consulted.

[3] Also note that in each case there were no legal hurdles on elites that prevented them from returning to the party. And indeed, in each case following elections there was generally a wave of defections back to the ruling party.

TABLE 5.1. *Regime vulnerability and elite defection in Tanzania, Cameroon, and Kenya*

Country	Election period	Regime vulnerability	Elite defection
Tanzania	1992–5	High	Low
Cameroon*	1990–2	Low/high	Low/moderate
Kenya	1990–2	High	High
Tanzania	2000	Low	Low
Cameroon*	1997	Low	Low
Kenya	1997	Moderate	Moderate
Tanzania	2005	Low	Low
Cameroon	2002–4	Low	Low
Kenya	2002	Moderate	High
Tanzania	2010	Moderate	Low
Cameroon	2007	Low	Low
Tanzania	2015	Moderate	Low
Cameroon	2011–3	Moderate	Low

Notes: The first election period refers to the time between the legalization of multiparty elections and foundational elections. Subsequent election periods refer to the nearest presidential and legislative elections. In Cameroon the March 1992 legislative elections were boycotted by the opposition, which reduced vulnerability. *Major opposition parties boycotted the election.

extent of elite defection. One key difference in this latter period is that the absence of defection in Cameroon is linked to the international context discussed in Chapter 7.

The chapter proceeds by looking at how ruling parties in each case managed elite relationships during three key time periods: foundational elections when regime vulnerability was high, interim periods when regime vulnerability was low, and following the emergence of new challenges that increased vulnerability to moderate levels. For each period I justify my account of regime vulnerability by discussing the material conditions in terms of the state of the economy and opposition mobilization. I then detail observed differences in expressed elite grievance, the utilization of party institutions, and observable high-level elite defection.

THE CHALLENGE AND DIVERGENT RESPONSE TO FOUNDATIONAL ELECTIONS

While the specific circumstances differ, foundational elections arrived in each case at the culmination of a period of economic and political crisis that left regimes vulnerable. In Tanzania, decades of state intervention and economic stagnation compelled the country into negotiations with international lenders and painful structural adjustment (Campbell and Stein 1992). In Cameroon, a global drop in oil prices, combined with persistent economic mismanagement and high levels of corruption plunged the country into a tailspin (Konings 1996). Severe economic crisis also took a toll on Kenya, made worse by strong international pressure and a six-month suspension of balance of payments by the Paris Club. At the time, all three countries had fairly large public sectors that were major sources of government revenue. Structural adjustment, while ultimately uneven in its impact, was nonetheless a real shock that compelled the privatization of many state-owned enterprises, the liberalization of some banking, and a temporary reduction in the size of the civil service (IBRD 1994). On the eve of multiparty elections, growth per capita was −1.6 percent, −6.6 percent, and −1.9 percent in Tanzania, Cameroon, and Kenya respectively. Likewise, economic crisis corresponded with a sharp spike in price inflation. Cameroon was hit worst, and in 1991 the Consumer Price Index (CPI) jumped 47 percent. Faring not much better, the CPI rose 10.4 percent in Kenya and 22.4 percent in Tanzania (World Bank 2016).

The introduction of multipartyism also revealed substantial tensions within each regime, and led to the formation of significant political and civil society opposition. A major difference across the cases was the extent of popular mobilization. In Tanzania, the path to multiparty elections was much more top-down and managed, and there was no sustained popular protest movement against CCM (Hyden 1999). This does not, however, suggest that there was no meaningful opposition. Economic liberalization made clear a growing and deep factionalism within CCM over the future ideology of the party, and concern with the growth of corruption and personal networks of influence. As one astute Tanzanian observer succinctly put it, the 1980s brought to the fore the "idealists, the overtly corrupt, and the wannabe corrupt."[4] Exacerbating these tensions was the end of Ali Hassan Mwinyi's second term in office, which forced a succession dilemma on the regime. Indicative of CCM's internal factionalism, in 1995 an astonishing seventeen candidates vied for the party's presidential nomination (Mwase and Raphael 2001).

While there was less popular mobilization, the legalization of parties led to the formation of some very effective and credible alternatives, which

---

[4] Mwesigu Braegu (Campaign Chair, CHADEMA). Author Interview. Dar es Salaam (November 12, 2010).

drew heavily on former regime insiders with quite deep financial pockets.[5] The chairman of Chama cha Demokrasia na Maendeleo (CHADEMA), Edwin Mtei, was Minister of Finance in the 1970s and had ties to wealthy coffee planters in the Kilimanjaro region. The mainland chapter of the Civic United Front (CUF) was founded by human rights activist James Mapalala, but also attracted former CCM elites like Musobi Mageni (Lands Minister, 1972–5) and Economic Advisor Ibrahim Lipumba. The party's ties with financial interests from Zanzibar and its appeal with the Muslim coast gave it significant coattails (Chege 1994, 62–4). Crucially, in April 1995 the former Home Minister Augustin Mrema dramatically defected from CCM to join the National Convention for Construction and Reform-Mageuzi (NCCR-M) as its presidential candidate. Mrema was a popular figure, and his defection was a clear signal to other possibly disgruntled elites that leaving the party was safe.[6] NCCR-M became CCM's major contender in the foundational election with nationwide support, including in many rural areas.

In Cameroon and Kenya opposition parties could similarly draw on significant resources, but popular mobilization was also much stronger. Paul Biya's resistance to elections precipitated violent clashes with opposition protestors, particularly in the Anglophone North West. After reluctantly legalizing political parties in 1990, popular pressure continued and culminated with a six-month nationwide strike called the "ghost town" or *villes mortes* campaign (Takougang and Krieger 1998, 89–114).[7] Cameroon's new opposition parties relied heavily on former regime insiders and the business community, and aligned along distinctive ethno-regional grounds. The Social Democratic Front (SDF) and its candidate John Fru Ndi grew out of the Anglophone North West, and Fru Ndi himself had only recently left the CPDM in 1988 (Krieger 2008). The National Union for Democracy and Progress (NUDP) was firmly rooted

---

[5] There was an important civil society component to regime opposition too. By 1990, the National Committee for Constitutional Reform (NCCR) had brought together many of Tanzania's leading academics, lawyers, and human rights activists. The NCCR-M was the political descendent of the NCCR, and in 1995 was the largest opposition party (Mmuya and Chaligha 1994).

[6] Mrema was a vocal critic of Ali Hassan Mwini and corruption in CCM. In 1995 he was expelled from government, but remained a member of CCM. Staff. "The Mrema Phenomenon" *Tanzanian Affairs* (May 1991), Staff. "Dismissal of Mrema Transforms Political Scene" *Tanzanian Affairs* (May 1995).

[7] In 1990 opposition activity was strongest in the Anglophone North West and led to a number of regime crackdowns. New political parties and civil society groups briefly came together into the National Coordination of Opposition Parties and Associations.

in the Fulani north, and its leader Bello Bouba Maigari was an Ahidjo-era Prime Minister who self-exiled to Nigeria in 1984. Importantly, prominent business interests affiliated with the Bamileké ethnic community initially sided with the opposition, which gave it significant resources to contest foundational elections (Arriola 2012).[8]

Kenya's pathway to multipartyism was similarly marked by popular mobilization and the construction of sound political alternatives by former regime insiders. By 1990, political opposition to Moi was multifaceted and included a younger generation of activists and lawyers from outside of KANU (known as the "Young Turks"), along with church groups and expelled KANU elites like Kenneth Matiba, Charles Rubia, Oginga Odinga, and Martin Shikuku. Moi himself was embroiled in political scandal following the mysterious death of Foreign Minister Robert Ouko. A violent crackdown on a large opposition protest on July 7, 1990 (known as the *saba saba* protests) put more pressure on Moi and exacerbated tensions within the regime. By August 1991, the major opposition leaders had coalesced into the Forum for Restoration of Democracy (FORD), and continued to press for elections, which were legalized just a few months later. FORD ultimately split into two rival political parties, which made defection from KANU perhaps a riskier choice, but popular pressure against the regime remained comparatively strong.

Elite Loyalty during Tanzania's 1995 Foundational Election

It is evident that CCM's institutionalized presidential primary system helped manage elite competition and curtailed defection. The internal processes laid out previously were strictly followed, which provided a predictable and fairly level playing field. CCM's Central Committee vetted all seventeen candidates and recommended six based on the agreed upon criteria of perceived electability and their record of public integrity. The party's National Executive Committee provided a second set of eyes on the final list, and based on internal preferential voting nominated three to face the party's national congress. These were Benjamin Mkapa, considered Nyerere's favorite, Finance Minister Jakaya Kikwete, a popular youth candidate, and Prime Minister Cleopa Msuya, who was also part of CCM's older guard. Notably, this vetting process eliminated several important

---

[8] Adamou Ndam Njoya, a Bamoun chief and former minister, founded the Cameroon Democratic Union (UDC). Exiled Ahidjo-era politicians reinstated the Littoral-based UPC, and a formerly jailed Kirdi politician, Daikole Daissale, founded the Movement for the Defense of the Republic (MDR).

figures like Lands Minister Edward Lowassa. According to some public opinion polls, Lowassa was a frontrunner but dropped from consideration due to opposition from Nyerere and swirling rumors of his involvement in corruption. Other veteran CCM members, such as the Speaker of the Parliament Pius Msekwa, CCM's Vice Chairman John Malecela, and former CCM Secretary-General Horace Kolimba, likewise did not make the final cut (TEMCO 1997, 66–7, Mwase and Raphael 2001, 251–3).[9]

Subsequently, there was a one-month campaigning period and near uncertainty over who the ultimate presidential candidate would be. As the sitting Prime Minister, Cleopa Msuya could marshal significant state resources to campaign in numerous regions. Likewise, Kikwete could tour the country as part of his responsibilities as Finance Minister. Mkapa was a comparatively lesser-known figure, but he benefited from the support of Julius Nyerere and sitting president Ali Hasan Mwinyi. At CCM's national party congress on July 22, 1995 there was no clear frontrunner and voting was forced into a second round between Mkapa and Kikwete. Mkapa only narrowly won the second ballot by 686–638 delegates (Mwase and Raphael 2001). Kikwete was appointed Foreign Minister and encouraged to run again in 2005, while Msuya was re-elected as an MP without a government portfolio and ultimately retired in 2000. The crucial fact to recall is that neither Kikwete, nor any of the other primary losers, defected to the opposition despite their own popularity and the availability of relatively strong alternatives. The fairness of the process and the opportunity to contest again clearly mattered.

This pattern of elite loyalty was largely mirrored during the legislative primaries, despite several disputes over the integrity of the nomination process. Per CCM's guidelines, candidates could recommend themselves through their district branches, and as with the presidential nomination they went through a process of preferential voting by party delegates. In 1995 there were over 800 CCM candidates, ranging from three to fifteen per constituency. By the end of the primary forty sitting members of parliament were on the sidelines, including two former ministers and five former CCM regional commissioners (TEMCO 1997, 73–8).[10] Some

---

[9] Edward Lowassa remained in parliament and became a Minister for State in the Vice President's Office for Environment and Poverty. He would later become Minister of Water and Livestock Development and then Prime Minister. Pius Msekwa remained Speaker of the Parliament until 2002, and then became CCM's Vice Chairman until 2012. Horace Kolimba died in 1997.

[10] This data is also derived from, Staff. "Winners and Losers" *Tanzanian Affairs* (January 1996).

of the losers made accusations of vote buying, and criticized the National Executive Committee's occasional use of veto power during nominations to vet candidates. CCM responded fairly sporadically to these allegations by rerunning primaries in some constituencies but not others. Yet, the record of defection before and after CCM's primaries is amazingly sparse. Despite popular expectations, "virtually none of the established figures in CCM ... changed sides."[11] There were some reports of defection at the grassroots level, and some of the non-incumbent CCM primary contenders left for other parties. For instance, Stephen Wasira of Bunda claimed he had been rigged out of his primary against incumbent Joseph Warioba, and defected to the NCCR-M.[12] However, the observable record indicates that just six incumbent MPs switched sides. Besides Augustin Mrema, no other prominent figures left CCM.[13]

Disillusionment and Defection during Cameroon's 1992 Foundational Election

In Cameroon foundational elections brought to the fore significant resentments in response to the incoherence of the ruling party and the absence of clear nomination guidelines. Unsurprisingly, one of the first figures to leave the CPDM was John Ngu Foncha – the former leader of the Anglophone KNDP, architect of Cameroonian unification, and Vice President of the CPDM. In June 1990, Foncha cited the government's recourse to violence, but also his own personal disillusionment with the ruling party. According to Foncha, he was systematically denied an audience with Biya and believed he had become "an irrelevant nuisance."[14]

---

[11] Staff. "Election Guide" *Tanzanian Affairs* (September 1995). The lack of defection was so remarkable to observers that both Julius Nyerere and Benjamin Mkapa used it as a talking point during their campaign stops (Mwase and Raphael 2001).

[12] Daniel Mjema. "Wasira: Warioba Alinkimbiza CCM 1995" *Mwananchi* (September 25, 2014). Wasira eventually returned to CCM.

[13] Based on author calculations by examining incumbents in the 1990 legislature and comparing the names to candidates in the 1995 election across all parties. The former incumbents and their constituencies are Edith Mallya Munuo (Kawe), Mustafa Juma Wandwi (Musoma Urban), Ndembwela Ngunangwa (Njombe South), Symphorian Nelson Lutter (Kibaha), Frank Tarimo Kisinane (Siha), and Ali Saidi Mtaki (Kongwa). Three defectors left for NCCR-M, two to CHADEMA, and one to the CUF.

[14] Staff. "Party Vice President Resigns in Protest" *Foreign Broadcast Information Service* (June 13, 1990). It should also be noted that another Anglophone elite, President of the National Assembly Samuel Muna Tandeg, defected earlier in 1988 and later joined the SCNC with Foncha.

Foncha did not affiliate with a political movement until he joined the South Cameroonian National Council (SCNC) in 1994.

There was also pressure from the CPDM's Northern and Littoral-based politicians for internal party reform. This progressive wing included several figures Paul Biya had recruited as part of his New Deal. For example, Henri Hogbe-Nlend, the well-known CPDM President of the Paris Section, defected to the UPC and criticized Paul Biya's nomination as the party's presidential candidate without deliberation or contest. Hogbe-Nlend argued that the CPDM operated in an undemocratic manner, and lamented what he saw as a defunct CPDM Central Committee and Political Bureau.[15] Concurrently, the CPDM's Assistant Secretary General, François Sengat Kuo of Douala began to organize reform-minded voices in the CPDM who self-identified as the *Courant des Forces Progressistes*, and eventually called for Biya's resignation (Takougang and Krieger 1998, 133). In February 1992, Sengat Kuo left the CPDM claiming that:

The advent of multipartyism necessitates a revision of the strategy and structures of the party; but the president who is the only one who can call an extraordinary congress has obstinately refused.[16]

Soon thereafter, five more senior members of the progressive wing defected from the CPDM: Thomas Melone (President, Sanaga Maritime Section), Victoria Tomed Ndando (CPDM Women's Wing President), Garga Haman Hadji (Minister of Public Function), Delphine Tsanaga (former Minister of Social Affairs), and Sameul Eboua (Chairman of Cameroon Airlines).[17]

On the other hand, the record of elite defection prior to the March 1992 legislative election is much more vague. One major factor that contributed to this was the opposition's decision to boycott the election, which meant that there was really no safe place to defect to.[18] The only

---

[15] Staff. "RDPC Dissident Condemns Right Wing, Biya" *Foreign Broadcast Information Service* (March 1, 1991).

[16] Tikum Mbah Azonga. "Biya's Test Elections" *West Africa* 587 (March 2–8, 1992).

[17] Michel Lobe Ewane. "These Men Who Are Challenging Biya" *Jeune Afrique Economie* 142 (May 1991).

[18] Reporting on CPDM primaries is sporadic and there are no public records of primary races. Likewise, the Ministry of Territorial Administration (MINAT), which oversaw the 1992 election, did not report the names of the contenders, just their affiliated parties. Also note that Cameroon uses a mixed system, and some constituencies use multi-member districts with Closed List Proportional Representation. Therefore, different electoral lists often compete against each other.

noteworthy legislative elite defection was that of Jean-Jacques Ekindi nearly a year earlier. As president of the CPDM's Wouri Section, which is in the commercial hub of Douala, Ekindi was a fairly influential member of the party. His resignation came after he attempted to sponsor a slate of candidates and was denied by the CPDM's Central Committee. From Ekindi's perspective, this was clear rigging by conservative elements in the party who wanted to sideline him.[19] Ekindi defected from the CPDM to create his own party, the Progressive Movement, and he challenged Biya in the presidential election with the support of much of the former reform wing of the CPDM.

Besides this, evidence of elite defection during the process of legislative selection is paltry. It is fairly certain that in the Anglophone North West there was extensive grassroots defection to the SDF. Likewise, Ndam Njoya's Cameroon Democratic Union (UDC) party banked on his traditional title and weakened the CPDM's infrastructure in Foumban. When another senior prince of the region, Ibrahim Mbombo, broke ties with the CPDM and endorsed Njoya, other junior princes and local party rank and file followed suit. This led Joseph Takougang and Milton Krieger to note that in the buildup to the 1992 election the CPDM resembled a "calving iceberg," while the opposition remained dynamic and unified (Takougang and Krieger 1998, 132). Yet, it is difficult to pinpoint specific numbers, and other reporting notes that defections did not amount to a mass exodus from the CPDM, but rather a "wait and see approach" because of the opposition boycott.[20] Nonetheless, while there might not have been significant defection, the inaugural election revealed quite deep elite resentments.

Party Crisis and Defection during Kenya's 1992 Foundational Election

Elite defection during foundational elections was the most consequential in Kenya. Amidst widespread accusations that KANU had failed to reform internally or address the faulty nomination process that had plagued the 1988 election, the legalization of opposition parties sparked a tidal wave of defection. Between December 1991 and January 1992, KANU lost at least eleven senior figures to the FORD party. The most famous of these defectors was KANU's chairman and representative from Alego

---

[19] Jean-Jacques Ekindi (Former CPDM Section President, Wouri). Author Interview. Douala (August 4, 2015).

[20] Philippe Gaillard. "The Paralyzed State" *Jeune Afrique* (March 27–April 2, 1991).

District in Nyanaza, Peter Oloo-Aringo. Just weeks earlier, Oloo-Aringo had voiced his own skepticism of multiparty elections.[21] On Christmas Day, 1991 KANU suffered another serious blow when Minister of Health Mwai Kibaki left KANU to form the Democratic Party (DP). Up to that point, Kibaki had publicly declared his faith that KANU would reform, but cited the stalled investigation into the death of Robert Ouko as a facilitating factor for his defection.[22] During the two weeks that followed Kibaki's defection, many prominent Kikuyu personalities left KANU, as well as other figures from the Coast, Rift Valley, Nyanza, and Eastern provinces.[23] One of these defectors, John Keen from Kajiado North in the Rift Valley, echoed a statement shared by others, arguing that KANU "had become a nightmare" full of little "godfathers dictating business."[24]

Defections picked up again once parliament dissolved in October 1992. After parliament disbanded, 10 percent of KANU's incumbent MPs defected *before* their scheduled primaries (Throup and Hornsby 1998, 296–7). This deluge of defectors included much of KANU's Kikuyu support from Central Province, but a fair number of MPs from other regions. KANU's legislative primaries were an incoherent mess, and there were frequent accusations of impropriety and corruption. In a move that likely strengthened local party bosses, Moi allowed KANU branches to

[21] The other first wave defectors were Minister for Manpower and Development Njoroge Mungai (MP Westlands), former Vice President Josephat Karanga (MP Kasarani), former Foreign Minister Munuyua Waiyako (former MP Kasarani), Chief Secretary for the Civil Service Geoffrey Kariithi (MP Gicuhugu), Matu Wamae (MP Mathira), Maina Wanjigi (MP Kamukunji), Peter Kabibi Kinyanjui (MP Kiuyu), James Njenga Mungai (MP Molo), Raymond Ndong' (MP Rangwe), and John Michuki (former MP Kangema). Njoroge Mungai returned to KANU 5 weeks after his defection. This information was sourced from: Staff. "Former Cabinet Minister Leaves KANU" *Foreign Broadcast Information Service* (December 1991), Staff. "Nine Officials Leave KANU for FORD" *Foreign Broadcast Information Service* (January 1992). See also Throup and Hornsby (1998, 187).

[22] Staff. "Kibaki Says Resignation Related to Ouko Inquiry" *Foreign Broadcast Information Service* (December 1991).

[23] Among the Kikuyu who defected after December, 1991 were Minister of Science and Technology George Muhoho (MP Juja), Minister for Agriculture John Gachui (MP Gatanga), and Assistant Minister for Cooperative Development Njenga Karume (MP Kiamba). From the coast the DP drew Eliud Mwamunga (former MP Voi), Mohammaed Jahazi (former MP Mvita), and John Safari Mumba (former MP Bahari). From the Rift Valley it brought in John Keen (former MP Kajiadjo North), Samuel arap Ng'eny (MP Aldai), and Charles Murgor (MP Keiyo). From Nyanza the DP attracted James Nyamweya (former MP Nyaribari-Masaba), and from Eastern Province it brought in Frederick Kalulu (MP Mbooni). These names are sourced from Hornsby (2012, 488–99), Throup and Hornsby (1998, 95).

[24] Mwenda Njoka. "Twists and Turns" *The Weekly Review* (January 10, 1992).

choose their own method for selecting candidates – either by the infamous queuing system that Moi introduced in 1986, or by a secret ballot. There was such confusion at the local level that participants challenged the results in nearly two-thirds of constituencies. This led to the creation of a special KANU Nominations Appeals Tribunal, which was an ad hoc institution created in response to the messy primaries, not an established part of KANU. The Tribunal ordered repeated nominations in forty-three constituencies; however, KANU's Secretary General Joseph Kamotho unilaterally cancelled several of these rerun races.

In total, between the legalization of opposition parties in December 1991 and the election held a year later, I calculate that an astonishing 25 percent of KANU's incumbent MPs had defected to the opposition.[25] Regime vulnerability definitely explains some of this, and there was clearly a cascade effect as more elites defected. But, the absence of credible primaries and the inability of the party to self-reform exacerbated elite tensions that had grown under single-party rule. The foundation of these elite disputes was the narrow ethnic social incorporation of KANU under Kenyatta and Moi, and the simultaneous weakening of party institutions that could foster credibility.

ELITE DEFECTION AND RULING PARTY CREDIBILITY IN TIMES OF STABILITY

After foundational elections all three regimes faced considerably less threatening environments, but the impact of differences in ruling party credibility is still apparent. In Tanzania, the 2000 and 2005 elections were conducted from a position of relative regime strength. Economic conditions had stabilized significantly, and the opposition's likelihood of electoral success diminished substantially when Augustin Mrema bitterly defected to the Tanzanian Labor Party (TLP). The CUF and its candidate Ibrahim Lipumba became the opposition frontrunners in 2000 and 2005, but given their stronger ties to Zanzibar this left no credible mainland opposition to speak of.[26] In Cameroon, oil prices recovered and structural adjustment stalled. The opposition further deteriorated when

---

[25] Author calculations based on comparing sitting MPs in 1988 to party candidate lists in 1992.

[26] One factor that did potentially make CCM more vulnerable in 2000 was the death of Julius Nyerere the year before. As the ideological father of the party, some viewed his leadership as a key factor that kept the ruling party's internal institutions intact.

it again boycotted the 1997 presidential election. In 2004, an opposition coalition disbanded just months prior to the scheduled presidential election. Senior members of the NUDP, MDR, and UPC parties also joined government in 1992, which left a fractured SDF as the only real political alternative. Finally in Kenya, while economic conditions only improved mildly, splits within the opposition strengthened KANU's position. Between 1992 and 1997 several FORD and DP supporters actually defected back to KANU (Hornsby 2012, 545–6).[27]

Continued Ruling Party Adaptability in Tanzania (2000–2005)

Despite the lower level of vulnerability, this period provides some additional observations of how a credible party interacts with elites. First, in 2005 CCM's presidential succession system was once again put to the test, this time with eleven candidates.[28] As in 1995, the process was followed to the letter of the law. On May 1, 2005 the party's Central Committee reduced the number of candidates to five: Jakaya Kikwete, who had run in 1995, Minister of Transport Mark Mwandosya, veteran CCM member Salim Ahmed Salim, sitting Prime Minister Frederick Sumaye, and the Minister of State for Planning Abdallah Kigoda. During this initial process the former Prime Minister John Malecela was surprisingly dropped from consideration. In response, Malecela utilized the appeals process within the party, and made a formal request to reconsider his candidacy, claiming that he "was like a bulldozer than can clear the road" of other weaker candidates (TEMCO 2006, 28–9). His appeal was denied, but Malecela remained a member of parliament and CCM's Vice Chairman. In later deliberations within CCM's National Executive Committee, Kigoda and Sumaye were also eliminated. Kigoda stayed on as a minister, and Sumaye resigned from government to become a Goodwill Ambassador to the United Nations.

Kikwete was considered the frontrunner given his continued popularity with younger voters, his close loss in the 1995 primary, and the endorsements of the sitting president Benjamin Mkapa. Nonetheless,

---

[27] Economic conditions in Kenya were comparatively weaker than in Tanzania and Cameroon, but improved from 1992. Between 1994 and 1996 there was an average 2 percent growth in GDP and inflation rates fell to 5 percent (World Bank 2016).

[28] There was essentially no contest in 2000 since Benjamin Mkapa was the incumbent, and the internal norm was to allow presidents to contest two terms. Only Eugene Munasa submitted papers to challenge Mkapa, but he was rejected by CCM's Central Committee because he did not have a college degree.

deliberations in CCM's national congress were actually quite vociferous, and debate opened up over the dismissal of Frederick Sumaye by the National Executive Committee. Several CCM members assumed that a sitting Prime Minister would be the party's natural candidate. While the party's decision on the final three candidates was not overturned, the internal deliberations are revealing and forced the candidates to do more outreach and campaigning. Kikwete won the primary in the first round with 1,027 delegate votes to Salim's 476 and Mwandosya's 122.[29] This process once again demonstrates the remarkable persistence and evenhandedness of CCM's presidential nomination system. Even if the incentives for defection were relatively low, all the other participants accepted the outcome.[30]

Second, CCM's legislative primaries gained credibility in response to demands from members for more intervention during the nomination process. The July 2000 primary was well organized, but also fairly dramatic with new accusations of vote buying and some boycotts of election results. One important change that impacted the credibility of primaries for the worse was the legalization of *takrima*, or gift giving by candidates during elections. Many younger CCM primary contenders saw *takrima* as an overt form of election bribery that reduced the competitiveness of primaries and benefitted the wealthy. In response to this criticism, on August 13, 2000 CCM took the drastic step of actually banning forty sitting MPs from participating in the election due to violations of the party's campaign guidelines. Benjamin Mkapa, who had pushed for the legalization of *takrima*, was forced to endorse the committee's decision. As Mkapa stated, the party's reaction was in response to "the rich who used their financial muscle in an attempt to privatize the Party for their personal gain."[31] Again, while the incentive for defection was relatively low, the large number of incumbents defeated during the primary would theoretically compel some CCM elites to stake their careers elsewhere. Yet, only one incumbent MP, Hashim Abdallah Sagaaf of Dodoma Urban, defected to the CUF. The record further indicates that just two former incumbent MPs defected: Lumuli Kasyupa of Kyela to the CUF

---

[29] Staff. "Eleven CCM Candidates Fight for Presidency" *Tanzanian Affairs* (May 2005), Staff. "Election Guide" *Tanzanian Affairs* (September 2005).

[30] Salim Ahmed Salim returned to his previous position as president of the Julius Nyerere Foundation, and Mark Mwandosya remained in parliament and became the Minister for the Environment in the new Kikwete administration.

[31] Staff. "Elections 2000" *Tanzanian Affairs* (September 2000). Among those who were banned were two ministers, one deputy minister, a former ambassador, and a former High Commissioner in London.

and Ndembela Ngunangwa of Njombe South to the TLP (TEMCO 2001, 55–60).[32]

The 2005 legislative primary was contented similarly, and marked by a fairly high level of competition. Approximately ten candidates competed within CCM for each constituency (TEMCO 2006, 31), and once again accusations of corruption and the illicit use of *takrima* flourished. CCM's National Executive Committee was once again involved in vetting candidates and investigated numerous accusations of procedural impropriety. Fifty incumbent MPs were eliminated during the 2005 primary, some by voters, some by vetoes from CCM, and others in rerun primary contests.[33] Many opposition parties banked on a wave of defection to follow CCM's primaries, which once again did not materialize. My research shows that just one incumbent MP, Njelu Kasaka of Lupa, left CCM for the CUF, but he returned shortly thereafter to the ruling party (TEMCO 2006, 34). In 2005, several primary losers actually took to the media to deny rumors of their imminent defection, and reassert their loyalty to CCM.[34] Notably, in April 2006, *takrima* was finally deemed illegal by Tanzania's High Court, although the practice continued informally.[35]

Elite Wrangling and Failed Party Reform in Cameroon (1997–2007)

The period of stability that followed foundational elections in Cameroon corresponds with less elite defection, but also with continued evidence of severe internal tensions and elite grievance over the lack of internal democracy and the absence of presidential primaries. This came to a fairly dramatic climax when Biya's candidacy was surprisingly challenged prior to the 1997 election. Biya expected that he would be nominated without contest at the CPDM's Ordinary Congress in December 1996. But on

[32] This was also verified with an author calculation that compares the 1995 parliament to the 2000 candidate lists. This was Ngunagngwa's second defection. He left for NCCR-M in 1995 and returned to CCM shortly thereafter.

[33] Staff. "Election Guide" *Tanzanian Affairs* (September 2005). Among those who were banned from competition were Minister of Energy and Minerals Daniel Yona, former CCM Secretary General Lawrence Gama, former Finance Minister Simon Mbilinyi, and Deputy Foreign Minister Abdulkadeer Sharif. Yona was jailed over corruption in 2015. Lawrence Gama, a noted military veteran, died in 2009. Simon Mbilinyi joined a Tanzanian NGO, and Sharif was appointed by Kikwete to lead the "Brand Tanzania Initiative."

[34] Michael Okema. "Today the Road to Riches Lies through CCM" *The East African* (September 7, 2005).

[35] Michael Okema. "Judges Refuse to Entertain 'Hospitality' Law" *The East African* (May 9, 2006).

October 21, 1996 Victor Ayissi-Mvodo, an Ahidjo-era politician and former Minister of Territorial Administration, came out of retirement to oppose Biya's candidacy. Mvodo's relationship with Biya was notoriously tense, and he gave an extensive and critical interview to the newspaper *Le Nouvelle Expression*, where he expressed the need for new party leadership and internal reform (Tangwa 2010, 153–4). Mvodo also sent a letter to the CPDM's congress denouncing what he called the "institutionalization of a monopoly by the President of the Republic over the destiny of our party, and thus that of the State and the entire nation."[36] After Biya was endorsed as the CPDM's candidate, another challenge arose in April 1997 when the Minister of Health and Biya's personal physician Titus Edzoa resigned from the CPDM. Edzoa made known his opposition to the CPDM's uncompetitive and rigid nomination process, and condemned Biya's own personal fortune. There was coordination between Mvodi and Edzoa, and discussion of forming a new political party to challenge Biya.

Mvodi and Edzoa's defections were surprising to some, given that they were from ethnic groups and regions that were historically part of Biya's coalition. Both were Ewondo (a sub-group of Beti) from Central Region, while Biya himself was a Bulu-Beti from Southern Region. This made the succession appear as an internal struggle within the major pillar of the ruling coalition. Edzoa had specifically noted his demotion from Secretary-General of the Presidency to Minister of Health, and the problem of stable careers in the CPDM as a precipitating factor. In an interview he gave at the time Edzoa noted:

He [Biya] calls one of you and says, "I'm going to appoint you to such a position." ... You start working, then he calls your friend and tells him how bad you are working and promises your post to him. Then he tells you that your friend has pressured him to take your post ... How can he demonstrate that he is not the origin of your fall? You are obliged to quarrel, and this sets up an unhealthy climate, a climate of mistrust and animosity.[37]

However, others see Edzoa's defection as a pure power play, since it was assumed he was associated with major corruption scandals like awarding a public contract to dredge the Douala port to a company that he owned.

---

[36] Delphine Fouda. "Biya, adversaires et supercheries" *The African Independent* (November 30, 2009). Mvodo also wrote a book titled *Projet de rederessement et d'esperance* (Project for Redress and Hope), and created a think tank called Cameroon 97.

[37] Jules Romuald Nkonlak. "Cameroun – 1997–2014: Retour sur l'affiare Titus Edzoa" *Le Yaoundé* (February 24, 2014).

The regime's reaction to these developments was swift and coercive. On June 21, 1997 Victor Mvodo died of an apparent pulmonary embolism while in Paris, although rumors of government involvement were widespread (Smith 2008). In late April, Edzoa's passport was rescinded, and in May the Prefect of Mfoundi threatened that he would need to take action to counter Edzoa's political agitation for the sake of public safety. On May 6, Edzoa and his campaign manager Michel Atangana were placed under house arrest, and on May 12 Atangana was arrested by a special unit of the police and kept in administrative detention for fifty-six days. A letter from the Secretary-General of the Presidency directed an investigation into Atangana over his alleged involvement in a road project scheme and the liquidation of the Cameroonian chapter of the Bank of Credit and Commerce International. On July 3, 1997 Edzoa was also arrested and both he and Atangana were charged with public embezzlement. Leaked wire taps published in local newspapers suggest that there was a coordinated effort directed from the president's office to steamroll Edzoa. In October, Edzoa and Atangana were sentenced to fifteen years in prison. Both were later tried on a second charge in 2012 and sentenced to another twenty years in prison, but pardoned by Biya in 2014.[38] Undoubtedly, this harsh reaction to the presidential challenge was a signal to other potential defectors to stay put.

Elite dissent also grew notably more visible prior to the 2004 presidential election. One of the more interesting developments was an unverified report released on June 4 that Paul Biya had unexpectedly died while in Switzerland. It is unclear who sparked the rumor (some suggested that Biya's opponents in the CPDM had), but it spread quickly and apparently many Cameroonians took it seriously enough that they began the process of adapting to a post-Biya world. There were sporadic reports of CPDM members making large cash withdrawals, troop deployments to the Yaoundé Airport and presidential palace, and gossip that Biya's son Frank had sold his home and fled the country.[39] The Minister of Communications Jacques Fame Ndongo was forced to go public to counter the rumors and warn that "to gear up for the process of selecting a successor would be equivalent to casting seeds to the wind, and thus starting a tempest in a peaceful forest."[40] While a fairly odd circumstance, it does

---

[38] Ibid.

[39] Staff. "L'attitude de Paul Biya Après Avoir Appris sa "Mort" Comment le Pouvoir a Organisé la Riposte" *La Nouvelle Expression* (June 10, 2014), Ntemfac Aloysius Nkong Ofege. "Biya Returns from the Dead" *African Independent* (June 15, 2014).

[40] Christopher Bouisbouvier. "Communications Minister Queried on President's Death Rumor" *Jeune Afrique L'Intelligent* (June 20–26, 2004).

shed some light on the absence of institutionalized means of succession within the party, and the power of a simple rumor to shake things up.

A more pronounced development was the emergence of yet another progressive wing in the CPDM, this time led by the influential Bamileké Chief, Pierre Mila Assoute. In 2003, this group published a white paper titled *Livre Blanc du Groupe la Modernisation Du RDPC*, which outlined necessary party reforms, including competitive presidential primaries. Assoute claimed to have the support of 100 Central Committee members and sub-section party presidents.[41] He further warned in a letter to the CPDM's Central Committee of a party split if a statutory Ordinary Congress and Central Committee meeting were not held to elect new party officials and revitalize the party.[42] In an interview, Assoute noted that there was "a dictatorship in the party," and that at the CPDM congresses "they [party conservatives] would go somewhere behind, write documents, and come and read it to the people and they clap."[43] When Assoute's bid to contest the presidency was denied by the CPDM, he resigned and ran with an opposition party. Assoute later self-exiled to France.

There was also pressure from Biya's northern allies, although not directly from within the CPDM. In September 2002 the NUDP members of government and some northern CPDM members published a memorandum critical of the government's neglect of the north, called the *Mémorandum sur les Problémes du Grand North*. While ostensibly this was done to address regional imbalances in development fund allocation, the undercurrent was the growing debate over Biya's succession, and the question of whether the presidency would return to a northerner. By 2004, many of the NUDP signatories to the memorandum left government and joined the embryonic National Coalition for Reconciliation and Reconstruction (CRRN). The CRRN ultimately failed to nominate a consensus presidential candidate in 2004, but it did draw one senior defection from the CPDM, the former Minister of Posts and Telecommunications, Sanda Oumarou. The defection was short-lived, and Oumarou later returned to the CPDM.[44]

---

[41] Staff. "Money in the Pipeline" *Africa Confidential* 44, 16 (2003).

[42] Charly Ndi Chia. "Central Committee Member Wants Biya to Step Down" *Post Tribune* (September 16, 2004).

[43] Ibid.

[44] The CRRN also unsuccessfully attempted to draw the recently sacked Finance Minister Edouard Mfoumou as their presidential candidate. Mfoumou later proclaimed his support for Biya, and in a bizarre press conference compared him to his own personal savior. The rumor was that he was coerced into making the statement. See Essama Essomba.

Turning to the legislative elections it is difficult to discern widespread elite defection between 1997 and 2007, but internal dissent over the CPDM's nomination process was still apparent. One major development was that while during party primaries delegates at the section level voted for candidate lists, the CPDM's Central Committee increased its use of a distributed party circular that often overturned these results (referred to as the CPDM's *investiture* in its candidates). According to insider accounts in the CPDM, this was done ostensibly to remove unpopular candidates or figures that might have violated party guidelines, but in practice it was also likely used to position influential, wealthy, and connected individuals in the legislature. For example, following the 1997 CPDM primary, Albert Dzongang of Littoral Province defected from the CPDM to form the Popular Development Party. Dzongang, a former CPDM stalwart, claimed that there was a deliberate attempt to rig him out of his seat in order to make room for a Bamiléké politician.[45] His was the only major legislative defection in 1997.

CPDM primaries in 2002 and 2007 were particularly controversial and led to the downfall of many prominent figures. In 2002, approximately eighty incumbent legislatures lost their seat during the primaries, which translates into an astonishing 68 percent turnover rate. For example, it was reported at the time that Antoine Ntsimi of Lékié was rigged out of his position in order to position Jean-Bernard Ndengo Essemba and his supporters. Likewise, there was a report that Speaker of the National Assembly Cavaye Yéguié Djibril had actually lost his seat in Mayo-Kani, but was eventually declared the winner by the CPDM's department president.[46] Subsequently, there were reported conflicts between the CPDM's Secretary-General Charles Doumba, who was technically responsible for the primaries, and Gregoire Owona, the increasingly influential Minister-Delegate for Relations with the Assemblies.[47] René Sadi replaced Doumba as Secretary-General in April 2007 after growing concerns with his health.

"Je Dois Tout Au President Biya" *Cameroon Tribune* (September 20, 2004). This account is also detailed in (Arriola 2012, 189).

[45] Albert Dzongang (Former MP CPDM). Author Interview. Douala. (August 5, 2015). Dzongang ran in the 1997 election as a presidential candidate, winning just 1.2 percent of the vote.

[46] Léger Ntiga. "La Chute Des Baobabs" *Le Messager* (May 15, 2002), Staff. "Investitures: Bon Nombre De Grosses Pointures Du RDPC N'ont Pas Passé Le Cap Des Primaries" *Le Yaoundé* (May 30, 2002).

[47] Asong Ndifor. "CPDM in Crisis: Has Charles Doumba Resigned?" *The Herald* (May 25, 2003).

The 2007 legislative primaries were even more contentious and at least ninety incumbent CPDM MPs lost their primary races. This time the CPDM left less time for primary campaigns, and raised the financial requirement from 50,000 CFA to 500,000 CFA. This created a backlash in the party, and some accused the CPDM of limiting its ranks to the wealthy.[48] The CPDM Central Committee also continued to use its *investiture*. At times this appeared to garner some support from members. For instance the party dropped the MP for Ngoketunjia Sud, traditional chief Fon Doh Gahgwanyim III, after he was convicted of murder but released on medical grounds. Yet in the primary race that followed, Emmanuel Banmi's candidacy was overturned in favor of Gahgwanyim's favored candidate Sixtus Gabsa, who had not even filed paperwork. Violent protests, a dispatched CPDM reconciliation committee, and an appeal with the Supreme Court forced the CPDM to accept the original primary result.[49] On the other hand, in Mfou and Afamba in Central Province Jean-Marie Assene Nkou's primary victory was overturned in favor of Dieudonne Ambassa Zeng's electoral list. In Nde in West Province, Jean-Claude Feutheu successfully appealed the CPDM to overturn his primary loss to Jean Ketcha, which led to an outbreak of violence between their campaign staffs.[50]

Despite these tensions, there is no real evidence of massive legislative elite defection between 1997 and 2007. As noted, the external environment did not provide a safe environment for disgruntled elites, but the paltry of findings is nonetheless revealing. The level of elite dissatisfaction was particularly acute in 2007, and forced the CPDM to dispatch the Prime Minister Ephraim Inoni and Secretary General René Sadi on a reconciliation mission to counter threats of defection. Yet, it is difficult to pinpoint how primary losers were compensated, and my research into individual MPs only indicates that they did not run on an opposition party's ticket when they lost a primary. Rumors suggested that some losers were paid "consultancy fees," or were appointed to other state positions. In addition, the fear of violence – both physical and financial – appears to have swayed some losers to keep their concerns to themselves.[51] As Paul

[48] Samuel Mack-Kit. "Elections 2007: Encore Une Victoire Annoncée Poue le RDPC" *Mutations* (May 24, 2007).

[49] Chris Mbunwe and Kni Nsom. "Violent Demonstrations Grip Balikumbat as CPDM Dumps Banmi" *Cameroon Post* (June 5, 2007).

[50] Alexander T. Djimeli. "Législatives 2007: Voici Les Listes Du RDPC" *Le Messager* (May 28, 2007).

[51] U.S. Embassy, Yaoundé. "Cameroon Elections: Campaign Kicks into High Gear" Wikileaks Cable: 07YAOUNDE894_a (July 18, 2007).

Abine Ayah noted in 2007, "The party hierarchy has the right to invest in whichever candidate it wants, no matter whose ox is gored."[52]

Party Factionalism and Legislative Defection in Kenya (1997)

The period that followed Kenya's foundational election was marked by continued internal factionalism and an inability to assert institutional integrity. Unlike in Cameroon, this corresponds with more moderate levels of regime vulnerability and therefore also higher levels of elite defection. Prior to the 1997 election, two rival blocs within KANU were clearly evident and often referred to as "KANU A" and "KANU B." The former represented a more moderate and reform-minded group of KANU leaders that included figures like Simeon Nyachae, William ole Ntimama, Musalia Mudavadi, and Kalonzo Musyoka. KANU B reflected a more hardline wing, with figures such as Nicholas Biwott and George Saitoti. Put in other terms, KANU A wanted to see a broadened KANU alliance and outreach to minority ethnic groups like the Kisii, Luo, and Luhya. On the other hand, KANU B was more prone toward a narrower alliance that would maintain the dominant role of the Kalenjin by making overtures to the Kikuyu (Hornsby 2012, 582–96). However, lurking behind this factionalism was also maneuvering over whom Moi's eventual successor would be if he abided by term limits and stepped down in 2002.[53]

Tensions within KANU also gave rise to a brief reform movement, similar to that in Cameroon, that called for new party elections in order to reinvigorate the party. North-Eastern politician Al Haji Ahmed Khalif, along with the support of thirty-five sitting MPs, led this effort. Their opposition was specifically directed at regime insiders, particularly Kikuyu that had lost their elected position in 1992 but continued to wield significant influence. As Jeffrey Steeves writes, their criticism was that "the elected leaders of KANU have been completely forgotten in the patronage structures that gravitates around State House" (1997, 48–50). Khalif argued that a party election would help remove them. While the KANU A and KANU B divisions were more about succession wrangling, this division between reformers and insiders reflected a growing rift between the major tribes that were associated with KANU and the smaller ones like the Somali (Khalif's own ethnic group), Samburu, and Kamba. Moi's

---

[52] Chris Mbunwe and Kni Nsom. "Violent Demonstrations Grip Balikumbat as CPDM Dumps Banmi" *Cameroon Post* (June 5, 2007).

[53] Staff. "Moi's Last Lap" *Africa Confidential* 39, 4 (1992).

response to this dissent was to threaten party expulsion and reshuffle his cabinet in favor of KANU B elites.

There was also little improvement in the conduct of the 1997 primaries. In their election observation report, the Institute for Education in Democracy characterized KANU primaries as utter "chaos" and wrote that the party chairman often handpicked candidates regardless of the voting outcome (1997). Others observed that the KANU primaries were "a shambles, marred by violence, malpractice, and incompetence" (Hornsby 2012, 606). The use of queue voting in particular, which was at the discretion of the local KANU branch, led to numerous challenges that stalled because it was virtually impossible to recount these elections. By the November 27 deadline, KANU had finalized less than half of its legislative slate. Flooding in North Eastern and Eastern Province also led to delays and primary cancellations without the knowledge of KANU's Central Committee.

Consequently, there are reports of approximately 100 KANU legislative candidates that switched parties. These defectors mainly included non-incumbent candidates who might have run for office for the first time in KANU's fairly open primary. It was not uncommon for candidates to nominate themselves simultaneously on multiple party lists. However, the list of elite defections in 1997 also included a number of former MPs who had lost in 1992 and ran again, as well at least nine incumbent MPs.[54] Among the KANU defectors was Julia Ojiambo, the former MP for Funyula and KANU's Director of Women and Youth Affairs. Ojiambo lost her legislative seat to Moody Awori in 1983, but continued to contest the primary in 1988 and then again in 1992. By 1997, she finally decided to defect from KANU and join the FORD-K. She notes a general frustration felt by others regarding KANU's shoddy nomination process:

I decided to stay in KANU to play the game again. We went through the whole primary campaign, only to be told afterwards that the certification of candidacy had already been given away and offered to Awori ... Accusations were leveled against me, labeling me a security risk. But there was nothing they could possibly find against me ... This was the reward for what I did for KANU.[55]

---

[54] According to available records these were John Safari Mumba (MP Bahari), Samuel Gonzi Rai (MP Kinango), Kassim Bakari Mwamzandi (MP Msambweni), Dairus Msagh Mbela (MP Wundanyi), Kipatrus arap Kiror (Belgut), Samson ole Tua (MP Narok South), Frederick Cheserick (MP Marakwet East), Protas Momanyi (MP Bonchari), and Hussein Maalim Mohamed (MP Dujis). Based on author calculations comparing the 1992 parliament to the 1997 party candidate lists and public records.

[55] Julia Ojiambo (Former Senior Member of KANU). Author Interview. Nairobi. (July 27, 2012).

NEW CHALLENGES OF PRESIDENTIAL SUCCESSION
AND OPPOSITION MOBILIZATION

Following this interim of relative stability, a number of key developments increased the incentives for elite defection and presented regimes with new challenges. In Tanzania, the 2010 election was held in the aftermath of the global financial crisis and in the context of very public corruption scandals that racked CCM.[56] Factionalism within CCM also led to the formation of two overt rival groups: the so-called reformers led by parliamentary speaker Samuel Sitta, and the conservatives led by former Prime Minister Edward Lowassa and CCM's Secretary General Yusuf Makamba.[57] Making matters worse, for the first time in a decade there was an opposition with large popular appeal: Wilibrod Slaa and the CHADEMA party. In 2015, CCM faced even stronger pressure to crack down on public corruption, and took a real blow to its public image when it failed to provide promised constitutional reform. During CCM's presidential primary that year an astonishing forty-two people contended, and for the first time ever the opposition formed a national coalition called *Ukawa*. This made the 2015 election perhaps the ripest moment since 1995 for elite defection. However, during both the 2010 and 2015 election, elite defection did not translate into a mass exodus.

Cameroon also suffered from the repercussions of the global financial crisis, even if by 2011 it was able to secure greater access to aid and was more insulated from international pressure (see Chapter 7). The most significant challenge the regime faced was the end of Biya's constitutionally mandated term in 2011. By 2008, the CPDM began to internally discuss whether there was a viable alternative candidate, and several party elites began to consider the possibility of abolishing term limits to prevent a party rift. Indicatively, in January 2008 Biya privately discussed changing the constitution with US Ambassador to Yaoundé, Janet Garvey, and claimed that it was a necessary step to prevent the party from tearing itself apart. On April 10, 2008, amidst the most widespread public protests seen since the early 1990s, the constitution was amended, paving the way for Biya to run again in 2011.[58] It was under

---

[56] Between 2005 and 2010 Tanzania was rattled, among others, by the Bilali scandal, Barrick Gold Mine Scandal, BAE radar scandal, and the Richmond Affair. See, Staff. "Fight Against Corruption – Allegations" *Tanzanian Affairs* (January 2008).

[57] Staff. "Rift in CCM Now in the Open" *Tanzanian Affairs* (January 2010).

[58] U.S. Embassy, Yaoundé. "Biya Tells Ambassador He Plans Constitutional Change" Wikileaks Cable: 08YAOUNDE103 (January 31, 2008).

these conditions of more moderate vulnerability that the 2011 and 2013 elections were contested. There were again rumblings within the party and some notable defections, but not to the same levels seen during the foundational election.

Finally, the 2002 Kenyan election provides in many ways the best evidence for the impact of weaker party credibility. That is because regime vulnerability did not change much between 1997 and 2002, and by many indicators it actually slightly decreased. By 2002 international pressure on the Moi regime had subsided to a degree, and the economy showed signs of strength and positive growth. Importantly, in 1999 long-standing opposition figure Raila Odinga took his National Democratic Party (NDP) and joined the KANU government. In March 2002 the NDP went so far as to merge with KANU and form what was called "New KANU" (Steeves 2006). This was a real blow to opposition efforts, made worse when they formed two rival alliances that threatened to split the opposition vote: the National Alliance Party of Kenya (NAK) and the Kenyan People's Coalition. Consequently, some public opinion polls at the time actually indicated an easy KANU win in December.[59] Therefore, it was not clearly the strength of the opposition that drew defectors, but the inability of the party to manage presidential succession.

Reasserting the Party in Tanzania (2010–2015)

In 2010 elite defections once again did not materialize, and the capacity of the party to respond to elite concerns remained impressive. While in 2010 there was no challenge of presidential succession to cope with, CCM beefed up its support of credible legislative primaries. The major innovation was the introduction of open primary voting to all CCM members, and not just party delegates. This was in response to major criticism from younger party members that vote buying and corruption still plagued the nomination process. As a result of this influx of new primary voters, an unprecedented seventy-seven incumbent MPs were not on CCM's ticket.[60] These primary losers once again included fairly prominent CCM elites like John Malecela, his third such rejection in recent history. Yet, despite this large turnover in CCM's legislative slate, there are records of just three mainland incumbents who left CCM: Fred

---

[59] National Democratic Institute. "Kenya's 2002 Election" *NDI Election Watch* (October 8, 2002).

[60] Mike Mande. "CCM Old Guard, Incumbents Routed in Party Primaries" *The East African* (August 9, 2010).

Mpendazoe (Kishapu), Chacha Zakayo Wangwe (Rorya), and former CCM presidential nominee John Shibuda (Maswa).[61] The defection of former MP Sikitu Philip Chibululu, who was known as the "Mandela" of CCM, also drew national headlines.[62] Otherwise, there were reports of just nine other non-incumbent CCM primary losers who switched sides, which made the seemingly dramatic 2010 election actually not that out of the ordinary for CCM. One CCM member who lost their primary criticized John Shibuda and endorsed the primary process, noting "as a politician you should learn to give in ... Sometimes you must agree with what the party's hierarchy has decided."[63]

Similarly, CCM coped with the immense challenges of 2015 by utilizing its nomination process once again to produce a consensus candidate. In response to the opposition's challenge in 2010 and the growing outrage over public corruption, in 2012 CCM produced new nomination guidelines that gave an ethics committee considerable input into its slate of candidates (*Kanuni za Unogozi na maadili Toleo la Mwaka*). Legislative candidates were still selected by preferential voting, but local ethics committees now screened candidates prior to their endorsement by the National Executive Committee. This also held true for presidential aspirants, who had to submit documents and financial disclosures to the national ethics committee. Importantly, the ethics committee input was on the level of advice, and final decisions over candidacy were still up to the National Executive Committee and the vote of the National Congress.

This became very relevant in 2015 when the crowded presidential field was overshadowed by the nomination of Edward Lowassa. To recall, Lowassa ran unsuccessfully in 1995, and later backed Kikwete for president in 2005. However, in 2008 he was implicated in the "Richmond Scandal," a large-scale corruption scheme involving Tanzania's energy sector. Lowassa was not charged, but was dismissed as Prime Minister and later lost his seat on CCM's National Executive Committee.[64] Yet, Lowassa was clearly a popular politician, with deep roots in Arusha Region and strong support from the more conservative elements of CCM. With large support showing in public opinion polls, and an apparently

---

[61] Bernard Lugongo. "Mpendzaoe: Why I Have Quit CCM" *The Citizen* (March 31, 2010).
[62] Frederick Katulanda. "'Mandela' of CCM Defects and Joins CCJ" *The Citizen* (March 31, 2010).
[63] Frank Kimboy and Bernard Lugongo. "I'm Decamping to CHADEMA, Says Shibuda" *The Citizen* (August 18, 2010).
[64] Tom Mosoba. "Lowassa Implicated in Richmond Scandal" *The Citizen* (February 7, 2008).

limitless bankroll, Lowassa began his presidential campaign in early 2014. According to unofficial reports, he spent approximately $10 million to secure over 750,000 endorsements, even though the minimum was just 450.[65] There were a number of other influential candidates in 2015. These included Lowassa's major rival and the Parliamentary Speaker Samuel Sitta, sitting Prime Minister Mizengo Pinda, Vice President Mohammed Bilal, Foreign Minister Bernard Membe, and a young rising star in the party, January Makamba. Likewise, the 2005 candidates Mark Mwandosya and Frederick Sumaye ran again. However, while reports suggested that Pinda or Membe had some public support, Lowassa was clearly the candidate to beat.[66] Lowassa expected his popularity, long history with the party, endorsement spending, and personal rapport with Kikwete to clear the competition and pave the way for his nomination.

The issue was that Lowassa's candidacy brought to the fore the factionalism that had plagued CCM for decades. There was a clear personal rivalry between Samuel Sitta and Lowassa, but also real disagreement among other CCM elites over whether a Lowassa nomination would hurt or help the party's prospects in the near and long-term. Some evidence suggests that Kikwete and other CCM bigwigs like former president Benjamin Mkapa were actually leaning toward the less controversial Bernard Membe.[67] Others took issue with Lowassa's violation of CCM's guidelines on early campaigning, which specified a narrow window of time for soliciting endorsements in early 2015. Lowassa was not the only candidate to campaign early or spend lavishly on party endorsements, but he went far beyond any one other candidate. In February 2014, CCM's new ethics committee issued a warning to six candidates to cease early and illegal campaigning, and placed them under a twelve-month monitoring period.

As CCM's ethics committee vetted candidates in July 2015 more questions arose over Lowassa's nomination and his violation of party guidelines. Following closed deliberations in the Central Committee, both Lowassa and Sitta's names were amazingly dropped from consideration, along with nearly the entire slate of senior candidates. Bernard

---

[65] These estimates were compiled from various sources by the blog www.mtega.com and can be found at https://docs.google.com/spreadsheets/d/1rA5mH1JL_dnfiHaUcys RuGYou1LQmHKGiVhXu4Bmsek/edit#gid=0

[66] Jenerali Ulimwengu. "Lowassa's Juggernaut Rolls on, and Mwalimu Can't Stop Him This Time" *The East African* (July 4, 2014), Songa wa Songa. "Lowassa, Slaa, Still the Most Preferred Candidates" *The Citizen* (November 13, 2014).

[67] Jenerali Ulimwengu. "The Man Who Would Succeed Tanzania's President Kikwete" *Africa Review* (February 23, 2014).

Membe and January Mkamba passed the Central Committee, but were later dropped following the National Executive Committee deliberation. This was not a unanimous decision, and three Central Committee members took the unprecedented step of publicly demonstrating their disapproval and criticism of the new ethics committee's input.[68] The final three candidates nominated to CCM's National Congress were a relatively unknown trio: Minster of Works John Magufuli, Minister of Justice and Constitutional Affairs Asha-Rose Migiro, and African Union Ambassador to the United States Amina Salum Ali. But, all three finalists were consensus figures who were not associated with corruption scandals or any of the major factions within CCM. Magufuli won the final nomination with 87 percent of delegate votes.

Lowassa unsuccessfully protested the decision within CCM, but then defected to join CHADEMA as their presidential candidate. This was the first time that a presidential contender had defected from CCM, and the most significant elite defection since Augustin Mrema joined NCCR-M back in 1995.[69] However, despite media predictions and some hyperbolic reporting, what is notable is that there was again no mass exodus of elites from CCM. It is true that at the local level many CCM supporters, especially in Lowassa's Arusha stronghold, left the party.[70] However, there are reports on fairly few senior defections. Lowassa's fellow CCM primary contender Frederick Sumaye also joined CHADEMA, as did the incumbent MP for Kahama, James Lembeli, and Special Seat MP Esther Bulaya.[71] Likewise, this early wave of defection included four CCM Regional Chairmen: Mgana Msindai (Singida), Khamis Mjega (Shinyanga), Onesmo ole Nagole (Arusha), and John Guninta (Dar es Salaam).[72]

---

[68] Damas Kanyabwoya. "Fallout within Tanzania's Ruling Party as Former Prime Minister is Eliminated from Nomination Race" *The Citizen* (July 11, 2015).

[69] Erick Kabendera. "CCM Fallout Looms as Lowassa Left out of Presidential Race" *The East African* (July 11, 2015), Salma Said. "CCM Breaks Silence on Lowassa's Decamping" *The Citizen* (August 1, 2015). There were rumors that Lowassa forced the National Executive Committee to drop Bernard Membe from consideration as a way to balance the scales, and accusations that Lowassa was prepared to spends hundreds of thousands of dollars to bribe members of the National Executive Committee.

[70] Peter Saramba. "Exodus Hasn't Shaken Us, CCM Chief Declares" *The Citizen* (July 21, 2015).

[71] Katare Mbashiru. "Lembeli Defects to CHADEMA" *The Citizen* (July 22, 2015), Louis Kolumbia. "Sumaye Decamps CCM, Joins Ukwawa" *The Citizen* (August 22, 2015).

[72] Bakari Kiango. "Defections Won't Weaken CCM" *The Citizen* (August 15, 2015), Jaston Binala. "Defections may 'Dent' CCM's Image" *The East African* (August 15, 2015). Mgana Msindai returned to CCM in 2016, along with former defector Fred Mpendazoe. See, Staff. "The Hero and Two Prodigal Sons" *The Citizen* (July 31, 2016).

Elite loyalty also persisted during CCM's legislative primaries that year, which was particularly competitive with over 2,700 contenders. Turnover was not as acute as in 2010 (approximately fifty incumbent MPs were eliminated), but as in previous elections old guard politicians did lose their seats, including eight deputy ministers. CCM's National Executive Committee reran contests in nine constituencies following reports of election irregularities and vote buying attempts. In three cases CCM simply overturned local results and nominated the second or third place winners following allegations of vote buying. In a new development, Tanzania's national election observation committee began to evaluate party primaries, and concluded that 88 percent of CCM's races met minimal democratic standards (TEMCO 2015, 89). After the primaries, five incumbent MPs defected, to opposition parties: Dr. Makongoro Mahanga (MP Sengerea and Deputy Minister of Labor), Goodluck ole Medeye (MP Arumeru-West and Deputy Minister of Lands), Said Nkumba (MP Sikonge), Dickson Kilufi (MP Mbarali), and Luckson Mwanjale (MP Mbeya Vijinini).[73]

The nomination of Magufuli clearly signaled to CCM's cadres that it was taking a stance against corruption, but also that the party's institutions mattered. In another sense, the rejection of Lowassa reflects CCM's immense confidence in the primacy of the party over popular and well-known personalities. This appears to have been a miscalculation by Lowassa, who expected his defection would draw out far more disgruntled elites.[74] Lowassa framed his defection as the result of growing autocracy within CCM, which was ironic given the accusations leveled against him and the steps CCM had taken to reinforce procedural integrity. And indeed, the evidence suggests that by rejecting Lowassa's candidacy the party actually deterred more defection by assuaging other elites' concerns over the longer-term integrity of the party.[75] Magufuli's clean public record and abidance by party rules helped retain the support of key CCM figures like Samuel Sitta and Bernard Membe.[76] Not even

[73] Peter Elias. "Mahanga Amfuata Lowassa CHADEMA" *Mwananchi* (August 3, 2015), Staff. "Said Nkumba ahama CCM, ajunga CHADEMA" *Mwananchi* (August 13, 2015), Lauden Mwambona and Godfrey Kahango. "Lowassa: Sitaki Mchezo" *Mwananchi* (August 15, 2015).

[74] Staff. "Why Lowassa Lost in CCM Nomination Battle" *The Citizen* (July 14, 2015).

[75] Peter Nyanje. "Magufuli Tactics Paid Off for CCM" *The Citizen* (November 4, 2015).

[76] Samuel Sitta became Minister of Transportation and died in 2016, January Makamba became a Minister of State in the Vice President's office, Mohammed Bilal, Bernard Membe, Mark Mwandosya, and Mizengo Pinda all retired from politics, Asha-Rose Migiro remained at the UN, and Amina Salum Ali remained at the AU.

the sitting president Kikwete, who quite possibly favored Lowassa or Membe, could exert their will over the party's various committees and its institutionalized internal processes for nominating candidates.

Succession Challenges and Continued Party Tensions in Cameroon (2011–2013)

Biya's ability to amend the constitution was a critical factor that deferred decisions on presidential succession, but it did not alleviate the fundamental problems inherent to the CPDM as an institution. To several CPDM insiders, the constitutional change was simply a way to buy time for Biya to plan his exit and choose a suitable successor. But, as time progressed it became obvious that absent some mechanism for choosing a consensus candidate, any choice would send ripples throughout the party. Some senior CPDM elites discussed these matters quite openly with US Embassy staff in recently revealed conversations. In March 2009, Vice Prime Minister and Minister of Justice Amadou Ali spoke alarmingly with Ambassador Janet Garvey, and told her in unambiguous terms that it would be unacceptable to him and other CPDM elites for Biya to nominate another Beti or Bamileké.[77] In May 2009, the Minister for Territorial Administration, Marafa Yaya, reinforced this sentiment and suggested that Biya's attempt to handpick a successor would lead to a severe political crisis, and possibly even a military coup.[78]

This dissent within the CPDM was not resolved prior to the 2011 presidential election, when it became clearer that Biya would not actually resign. On January 3, 2011 former CPDM stalwart Paul Abine Ayah (MP Manyi South) resigned, and joined the People's Action Party as their presidential candidate. Ayah was the only reported CPDM defection prior to 2011. At the time Ayah stated that he feared for his life and found that:

The very CPDM that prides itself with practicing advanced democracy seems to connive at, or perhaps, even encourage the ruthless condemnation of rudimentary practices of democracy such as declaring one's candidacy for a post within the party.[79]

---

[77] U.S. Embassy, Yaoundé "Cameroon's Justice Minister Says North Will Support Biya, but not another Beti or Bami" Wikileaks Cable 09YAOUNDE256_a (March 12, 2009).

[78] U.S. Embassy, Yaoundé. "Biya's Succession Uncertain, Says Senior Cameroonian Minister" Wikileaks Cable 09YAOUNDE482_a (May 29, 2009).

[79] Emmanuel Kendemeh. "Hon. Ayah Paul Abine Quits CPDM" *Cameroon Tribune* (January 10, 2011). In early 2017 Ayah was arrested under suspicious conditions and put into a military tribunal over his alleged involvement with protests in South East Province.

Others who were rumored to oppose Biya's candidacy from within the CPDM soon found themselves entangled with the state over alleged corruption. In 2012, Marafa Yaya and the former Prime Minister Ephraim Inoni – both apparent Biya rivals – were arrested for their alleged connection with the "Albatross" embezzlement scheme to pocket money from the government purchase of a jet.[80] In 2016, Yaya and Inoni were sentenced to twenty and twenty-five years in prison, respectively.

Some of this internal drama culminated at the CPDM's Ordinary Congress in September 2011. Prior to the congress Saint Eloi Bidoung II, the Secretary of the CPDM's Mfoundi Section, and Tobie Ndi, a senior member of the CPDM's Nyong and So'o Section, challenged Biya's candidacy. Bidoung argued that he was going to use the congress as an occasion to stop elitism in the party and "cleanse the CPDM of the demons of conservatism, who have been fighting hard to make sure the party and the nation remain stagnant."[81] Both of their petitions were unsurprisingly reneged prior to the congress. During the congress itself, the Minister of Public Service and Administrative Reform, Rene Ze Nguele, voiced public opposition to Biya's chairmanship of the party, but not his presidential candidacy.[82] Biya was subsequently elected unanimously by a public show of hands in the congress.

In the legislative primaries two years later there was again large-scale turnover (~70 percent) and strong criticism of the CPDM's *investiture* prerogatives. Earlier in 2013 Biya had issued a new presidential circular that directed the CPDM's Central Committee to abolish primaries and use the *investiture*, but nonetheless consult local party militants.[83] The process led to some of the most vociferous backlash the regime had seen. Over 250 petitions were filed with the party. Charles Eyené of Ocean in South Province criticized that the "CPDM today is more a gathering of

---

[80] Staff. "Cameroon's Marafa Yaya Jailed in 'Albatross' Case" *BBC News* (September 22, 2012). These two figures also joined former Foreign Affairs Minister Jean-Marie Mebara as defendants in this case. Mebara was arrested in August 2008, also following rumors that he planned to challenge Biya in 2011. See George Mbella. "Atangara Mbella Still in Detention" *Cameroon Tribune* (May 6, 2012).

[81] Yerimi Kini Nsom. "I'll Cleanse CPDM of Delinquents, White Collar Thieves – Biya Challenger" *Cameroon Post* (July 24, 2011).

[82] Georges Alain Boyomo. "Congrese du RDPC: Duel Surréaliste Entre Paul Biya et René Zé Nguélé" *Mutations* (September 19, 2011). Per discussions with CPDM elites in 2015, Nguélé's challenge might have been pure show, to demonstrate to critics that the CPDM did actually practice internal democracy and Biya did not run unchallenged for a fourth term.

[83] Le Président National. Circulaire N°03/RDPC/PN DU/05 Juillet 2013 (July 5, 2013).

bandits, a business, a mafia."[84] Françoise Ngono Menkoe of Haut Nyong condemned members of the local *investiture* committee who were themselves running for office. The CPDM President of the Lom et Djerem Section argued that she was given instructions from Yaoundé to secure a list led by Kombo Gbéri for purely ethnic reasons.[85] Similarly, in Dja and Lobo a Fang Chief complained to the CPDM's Deputy Secretary General that "the Bulus want to grab all the elective positions at the expense of the Fangs."[86] There were also reports that some local CPDM chapters were pressured by ministers to accept lists with their wives on them.

However, elite defection in 2011 and 2013 was virtually nonexistent. This bucks some of the theoretical expectations. While on the one hand the absence of a credible ruling party made questions of presidential succession and legislative nomination relatively dramatic and challenging, the external conditions seemed more conducive given the aftereffects of economic crisis and the popular mobilization against the regime in 2008. The crisis did not parallel the extreme stress of foundational elections, but nonetheless lowered the ostensible costs of defection. Embedded in this discussion is the relative ease through which the regime in Cameroon could expend coercive measures to counter challenges during later elections and rebuild elite support. These issues are further elaborated upon in Chapter 7, but what is important to keep in mind is that the party was clearly not used to prevent dissent, and in many ways the weakness of the party was the source of substantial elite grievance.

Presidential Succession and Party Crisis in Kenya (2002)

Despite the relatively improved position KANU found itself in prior to the 2002 election, the inability of the party to select a consensus presidential candidate proved to be the regime's Achilles' heel. For various reasons, Moi acceded to step down from office and not seek a constitutional amendment to run for another term.[87] The prospect of the end of the Moi era sent ripples throughout KANU. Already in 1999 a key ally from

---

[84] Staff. "Legislatives et Municpales 2013: Le RDPC Laminé Par Les Investitures" *Camnews* 24 (July 19, 2013).

[85] Olinga Ange-Gabriel. "Risques d'Implosion. RDPC: Jusqu'ou Peut Aller Paul Biya" *Le Messager* (July 30, 2013).

[86] Yerima Kini Nsom. "2013 Twin Elections: CPDM Candidates Flood Party Secretariat with Petitions" *Cameroon Post* (July 20, 2013).

[87] There were in fact rumors that Moi would attempt to amend the constitution and run again. See the discussions in Ajulu (2001), Kanyinga (2003), and Ndegwa (2003).

the Kisii community and potential successor, Simeon Nyachae, defected from KANU to join FORD-P in apparent response to his demotion to the Ministry of Industry (Hornsby 2012, 662–4). The creation of New KANU broadened the party's social appeal, but it also made the question of succession much more opaque. Moi pulled a card from Jomo Kenyatta's playbook and amended KANU's constitution to appoint four KANU Vice-Chairs. These were filled by potential successors that corresponded loosely with a number of Kenya's major ethnic groups: Musalia Mudavadi (a Luhya), Noah Ngala (a Mijikenda), Kalonzo Musyoka (a Kamba), and Uhuru Kenyatta (a Kikuyu). Raila Odinga, a Luo, was appointed as New KANU's Secretary-General, while Joseph Kamotho, another Kikuyu, and George Saitoti, a Maasai, were the main losers of the party's rearrangement (Steeves 2006, Hornsby 2012, 671–5).

Postponing the question of succession was a short-lived strategy. The choice of successor was still ultimately Moi's, and any selection absent a credible institutional rule would signal a shift in the distribution of state resources and prestige. While the party could consult, it came down to jockeying among the numerous potential candidates. For various reasons Moi saw Uhuru Kenyatta, a Kikuyu and the son of Kenya's first president, as a young and potentially consensus figure who could deliver Central Province while maintaining the bulk of Moi's own Kalenjin support. Despite protestations from other KANU elites, this choice was formally announced on July 28, 2002 and followed by a countrywide publicity tour popularly referred to as "Project Uhuru." Moi's intention was to have Kenyatta's nomination simply endorsed at KANU's scheduled October delegate meeting in Kasarani by a public show of hands. There was to be no real party deliberation, or any competitive process for selecting the successor.

Unsurprisingly, this precipitated a strong backlash from the other presidential aspirants who demanded free primaries and a secret ballot. Shortly thereafter, seven KANU members – the four KANU Vice Chairs, plus Raila Odinga, William ole Ntimama (MP Narok North), and Moody Awori (MP Funyula) – created the "Rainbow Alliance." The alliance's explicit goal was internal party reform and a competitive presidential primary prior to the party's national congress in Kasarani.[88] When Uhuru Kenyatta was nominated without challenge as KANU's presidential candidate on

---

[88] National Democratic Institute. "Kenya's 2002 Election" *NDI Election Watch* (September 4, 2002). Other senior KANU figures like George Saitoti and Joseph Kamotho were also affiliated with this reform group.

October 12, just two days later the Rainbow Alliance left KANU and joined the small Liberal Democratic Party (LDP).[89] The LDP later joined the NAK to form the famous National Rainbow Coalition (NARC) that ultimately defeated KANU. It is important to recall in this timeline that the NARC coalition really only came together *after* the defection of the Rainbow Alliance from KANU. Given the economic and political conditions at the time, which made KANU externally less vulnerable than in previous elections, the Rainbow Alliance's defection was a risky move. It was propelled by deep elite resentments in KANU over the absence of any institutional integrity in selecting their presidential candidate.

Between the defections of the Rainbow Alliance, the dissolution of parliament, and KANU's legislative primaries, approximately thirty incumbent KANU MPs, or 15 percent of the entire legislative slate, left to join opposition parties.[90] The extent of defection was a surprise to some expert observers, who expected KANU to expend immense resources to deter them (Throup 2003). The question of why the KANU regime could not utilize more coercive power is important, and it clearly shaped the environment for defection. As discussed later, there were crucial external limitations on the KANU regime that made it difficult for the regime to stave off defections in 2002. In addition, as the likelihood of an opposition victory became clearer, signaled by rapidly changing public opinion polls and the growing momentum of the NARC coalition, so did the likelihood of elite defection. By the KANU primaries it was likely clear to many that they were on a sinking ship. Still, the fundamental break is rooted in the institutional inabilities of KANU to credibly shape elite careers and manage competition.

CONCLUSION

This chapter has demonstrated that differences in ruling party credibility influenced the ability of electoral authoritarian regimes to manage elite competition and retain elite loyalty, especially during moments of comparative vulnerability. The causal process observations from each case and the contrast across cases suggest that the presence of decisional autonomy and competitive party primaries can overcome fairly strong

---

[89] Njeri Rugene and Jeff Otieno. "We are Ready to Quit KANU Says Rainbow" *Daily Nation* (September 3, 2002).

[90] Based on author calculation that compares the 1997 legislature to the candidate rolls in 2002.

party factionalism, and also respond quicker to the demands of its members for political reform. This is particularly evident with regard to how
each regime coped differently with the challenge of executive succession,
and the divergence in the extent to which the party intervened in legislative primaries to ensure procedural integrity and provide members with
more predictability and voice. Tanzania's remarkable record of elite loyalty stands in contrast with the patterns in Cameroon and Kenya.

This chapter's main finding that credible ruling parties help ensure
elite loyalty during multiparty elections relates back to some of the major
claims made earlier in this book. If the central concerns of authoritarianism are institutional and informational uncertainty, and these uncertainties are exacerbated by the greater ease of exit provided by multiparty
elections, then credible parties offer a very useful solution. Regimes with
credible ruling parties do not need to expend the same degree of manipulation or patronage to retain the loyalty of their members. As discussed in
Chapter 4, there are unique historical origins to these types of institutions,
but these legacies are in fact very long-lasting and difficult to rewrite,
even with the impetus of electoral contestation. To stave off defection,
regimes without credible parties had to have the wherewithal to play a
more traditional autocratic game of carrots and sticks. Cameroon was
more adept at this game than Kenya and this is discussed in Chapter 7,
but the next chapter will show how credible ruling parties were also able
to retain much stronger voter loyalty in the face of elections.

6

Ruling Party Credibility and the Sources of Voter Support

CCM has a grasp on their minds, starting with the 10-house cell.
—Author Interview with Mwesiga Baregu, CHADEMA
Campaign Manager (2010)

You cannot discard these tribal and ethnic influences because if you are not able to assemble and organize a nation, if identities are not daily stuck to a national view and national progress, then you go back to your tribe, because it's easy.
—Author Interview with Jean-Jacques Ekindi,
Former CPDM Chair of the Wouri Section (2015)

Bear in mind the ethnic structure of Kenyan politics. What Moi was able to count on was how to shape the ethnic communities to back him.
—Author Interview with Musalia Mudavadi,
Former Vice President of KANU (2012)

This chapter explains how credible ruling parties influence the degree to which regimes can rely on persistent and widespread voter support during elections. As with elites, the incentives for voter defection vary from election to election and depend on factors like the state of the economy and the power of the opposition. However, I argue that what primarily shapes electoral authoritarian vote share is the ability of a regime to bank on historical and institutional linkages with citizens. As noted, credible parties often bring with them massive organizations that can be used to reach voters and insulate them from opposition appeals. Likewise, credible parties are those that have been consistent in their redistributive commitments and appeal to widely conceived communities, namely rural peasants. This allows regimes to get out the vote, but crucially also to bank on a consistent voting bloc. By contrast, without credible ruling parties the likelihood of voter defection grows. These regimes lack the local organization necessary to mobilize voters, and depend on the continued support of narrower social groups like ethnic cohorts.

These differences in ruling party credibility lead to a number of key observable implications in the three cases of Tanzania, Cameroon, and Kenya. First, we should notice significant spatial variation in the distribution of incumbent vote shares. In Tanzania, CCM should be able to persistently mobilize substantial levels of electoral support throughout the country because of their stronger infrastructure. This does not mean that CCM is able to dominate every part of the country, or that there is no opposition to CCM, only that the party should remain minimally competitive in most sub-national locations. By comparison, in Cameroon and Kenya there should be large swaths of the country where the ruling party cannot muster minimal vote shares. This is because these regimes cannot compensate for the loss of voter support by leveraging local infrastructure. Cascades of voter defection leave these regimes uncompetitive in many areas of the country.

Second, within each case the sub-national distribution of vote share should correspond with patterns of social incorporation established under single-party rule. In Tanzania, sub-national areas of consistently stronger support should coincide with investments made under *ujamaa* villagization between 1973 and 1975. To recall, this was a benchmark period for CCM when it offered club goods in exchange for political support. This should hold up even when controlling for possible confounders like ethnicity, levels of socioeconomic development, government provision, and opposition access. In Cameroon and Tanzania the expectations are different since no real commitment was made to rural constituencies. Rather, the major source of linkage between the regime and constituents was through ethnic appeals. Therefore, in Cameroon the areas of consistent regime support should come from southern and central regions that share the same ethnic background as Paul Biya. In Kenya, the areas of strongest support will likely be from Moi's Kalenjin co-ethnics and related groups. In both cases, the pull of ethnic identity in shaping voting outcomes should withstand the influence of the same possible confounding factors.[1]

---

[1] There is a question of whether presidential or legislative vote share would offer a better measure of ruling party credibility. Presidential candidates cannot always rely on local popularity and therefore need more infrastructure and historical legacy to get out the vote. On the other hand, given the restrictions on presidential elections in some countries,

Third, how participants view the process of contestation should differ depending on whether there is a credible party or not. This is primarily investigated through the perspective of opposition parties, who should note very different barriers to effective contestation. In Tanzania, the expectation is that opposition parties will highlight CCM's massive party infrastructure as a factor that hinders their own expansion, particularly into rural areas. Likewise, we expect that opposition actors will make investments where they think they can connect with voters, which will not be in areas where CCM has historical linkages. In Cameroon and Kenya participants should not define competition in the same terms. Since ruling parties generally ended at the district, we do not expect participants to note the role of ruling parties in helping to mobilize voters. Likewise, the role of ethnic identity, which is central in how ruling parties construct electoral outcomes, should not be lost on participants. Opposition actors will have to comport to the same logic of electoral contestation as ruling parties, and find ways to create rival multiethnic coalitions.

While this study is not as engaged with the fascinating literature on the sources of politically relevant ethnic identities in Africa (Posner 2005, Ferree 2010, Elischer 2013), it does contribute to a growing interest in the varied sources of voter motivation in the African context. Recent scholarship has provided a much more nuanced picture regarding the mixed motivations of African voters, by moving away from national level analysis to survey research that examines individual-level incentives. While ethnic mobilization remains substantial, some African voters are more influenced by clientelistic appeals (Wantchekon 2003), populism (Resnick 2012), and some degree of retrospective and prospective voting (Hoffman and Long 2013, Weghorst and Lindberg 2013). Ethnic identity tends to become more salient as elections become more competitive (Eifert, Miguel, and Posner 2010), and incumbents wield a range of distributional goods that vary from vote buying to various club goods, which might be valued differently by specific constituencies (Kramon and Posner 2013).

I add to this literature by presenting novel sub-national data that pit different theories of voter motivation against the impact of social incorporation, and bridge individual and national-level studies by drawing attention to unexplored variation in the sub-national context. One

---

voters might feel they have very little choice but to vote for the incumbent. Legislative results are often responsive to very idiosyncratic factors, such as local popularity, rather than party credibility. I present information on both presidential and legislative elections.

expectation is that lower levels of socioeconomic development and stronger government provision will reinforce clientelistic and retrospective voting independently of affinity factors such as ethnicity or historical ties with a ruling party (Blaydes 2011). By contrast, another perspective sees voter motivation rooted more in notions of prospective voting and access to information about political decisions (Mattes and Bratton 2007, Conroy-Krutz 2013). The argument here is that it is not social incorporation, but instead access to an opposition party – whether because population densities are higher, incumbents are weak, or turnout is generally higher – that shapes vote shares. My data confirm some of these mixed voter motivations, but the role of social incorporation still exerts a strong and independent impact on voters in all three cases.

A primary source for this chapter comes from the collection of extensive constituency and district-level data on elections, social incorporation, and a variety of controls.[2] This is done to map out spatial differences in incumbent vote share, but also to statistically model the relationship between vote share and various causal factors. In a sense then, I am using finer-grained quantitative sub-national data to validate a more macro-causal process regarding the impact of credible ruling parties. For Tanzania I gathered historical sub-national data on the proportion of the population resident in *ujamaa* villages between 1973 and 1975, and in all three cases I developed measures of the ethnic composition of districts. In each case efforts were made to find the most comparable and consistent sub-national data on socioeconomic development, at least two measures of government provision, and various measures of opposition access.

The major challenge with this design is the availability of consistent sub-national data across repeated electoral periods. In an ideal world, similar data would be accessible for every single election so that we could provide a baseline and account for change. However, despite extensive fieldwork efforts, that quality of data is simply not uniformly available. Government information is only gathered at irregular intervals, generally corresponding with a national census.[3] Moreover, the type of data

[2] While election data was available at the constituency level, other data is generally gathered at the district level. Therefore, the constituency level data was aggregated to the district level. Rather than use average percentages across constituencies, I calculated the raw vote counts, which provides a much more accurate representation of voting outcomes at the district level. Adjustments were made to address changes in the size and number of districts across time.

[3] Tanzania held a population census in 1978, 1988, 2002, and 2012. But, detailed sub-national data is really only available in the 2002 census. Kenya held a population census in 1989 and 1999, but collected slightly different information on socioeconomic

that governments collect at the sub-national level differs within and across countries. For example, some governments collect sub-national information on access to health facilities, while others do not. In the case of Cameroon, the constituency-level 2004 presidential election results have completely disappeared from public record, and there are large gaps and dissimilarities in the type of data collected by regional governments.[4] One region might measure the ratio of the population to health clinics, while another might measure the ratio of the population to doctors. This makes matched between-country comparisons impossible since the available measures differ.

The solution to these issues is imperfect, but nonetheless provides some real insights. First, since I cannot create a true panel structure, I consider the entire electoral authoritarian period as a whole. This means using the average incumbent vote share across multiple elections as the dependent variable. To account for regional differences and the nested nature of the data I employ a random effects multi-level regression model in each case. It is important to note that incumbent vote shares at the district level are not always consistent, and there are fluctuations from election to election. However, this temporal variation is not systematic, but rather related to factors unique to each election. For instance, in the 2005 Tanzanian presidential election there was no viable opposition candidate. This absence likely inflated CCM's vote share in opposition strongholds. Similarly, by 2011 Paul Biya had coopted a number of opposition elites, which helped the regime generate significant vote share in oppositional areas. Taking the average vote share, rather than focusing on a narrower range of elections, mitigates these fluctuations and demonstrates where regimes have geographically maintained the most consistent levels of support and opposition.

Second, to complement this snapshot I use measures of the independent variables that provide the closest approximation of their average value across the electoral authoritarian period. For instance, the analysis

---

development in each census, and only in 1999 was there more complete sub-national recordkeeping. Cameroon held a census in 1978, 1987, 2005, and 2015, and, as in Kenya, data on only a limited range of indicators was collected regularly.

[4] To find the 2004 presidential election results in Cameroon I consulted four main sources: the Ministry of Territorial Administration, the National Archives, individual political parties, and the Supreme Court. The Ministry of Territorial Administration could only produce results from a handful of constituencies. The records at the National Archives were missing, as were several major newspapers from the month of the election. Individual political parties did not have the information. The Supreme Court, which certifies results, hinted that it had the results but required some form of payment that could be considered bribery.

of voting outcomes in Tanzania examines the 1995–2010 period. The available sub-national data was from the 1988 census, the 2002 census, and the 1999 regional development reports. The latter two data sources are the most comprehensive and closest to the median year 2002. When data was available for every election, I calculated the average across the studied electoral authoritarian period. A major assumption here is that factors like levels of socioeconomic development and government provision were lower prior to the median year and higher afterwards, so that their values near the median year approximate the mean value for the sampled period. In other words, the level of literacy in 2002 likely reflects the average level of literacy between 1995 and 2010.

A number of additional tests were conducted to support these choices. For each case I conducted a small panel analysis at the district level. The data is much more limited and allows for only two points of comparison. For instance, a panel of Kenyan elections includes the 1992 and 1997 elections and data on socioeconomic development from the 1989 and 1999 population census. The results from these smaller panel analyses largely validate the findings discussed below regarding the role of social incorporation. I also constructed alternative measures of the independent variable that use different averages. For example, rather than use the literacy rate in 1999 as an independent variable in Kenya, I calculated the average literacy rate between 1989 and 1999. Finally, I also limited the dependent variable to the year closest to the independent variables. In Tanzania I tested the correlation between vote shares in 2000 and data from 1999 to 2002. Once again, the data is more limited, but the results still confirm the main findings from the comprehensive analysis. Therefore, to present the most detailed account of voter motivation in electoral authoritarian regimes I use the abovementioned inferential strategy.[5]

The sub-national analysis results are independently confirmed by information from field interviews with elite participants in each country. Repeated and in-depth conversations revealed important and consistent information regarding party strategies and decision-making with regard to voter mobilization. While interviews with regime elites can be unproductive and at times uninformative, several subjects were far removed from actual political events, while others spoke on conditions of anonymity.

---

[5] Another stipulation drove this analysis. In each case there are significant differences between urban and non-urban settings. In a series of models I interacted a dummy variable for "urban" with major predictors and preformed a Wald Test. The tests were significant, indicating that major urban areas behave very differently (they are generally much more competitive). Therefore, these observations are excluded from the analysis.

Through these interviews I was able to construct a better picture of what ruling party organization actually looked like, and how regimes reached out and mobilized voters. On the other hand, interviews with opposition elites can suffer from hyperbole. The predominant answer I heard regarding opposition weakness was some version of "we need resources," or "the election is rigged." Yet, when pushed to consider the challenges of voter mobilization it became apparent that opposition elites were acutely aware of the power of ruling party organization, the divergent receptiveness of certain populations to opposition messages, and the role of ethnicity.

The chapter proceeds by exploring the cases of Tanzania, Cameroon, and Kenya in sequence. For each case I consider the average spatial distribution of sub-national votes, and supplement that data with field interviews to assess the ability of regimes to leverage their party's organization to mobilize voters. I then conduct within-case statistical analyses of district-level incumbent vote shares to substantiate variation in sub-national support for the regime with their assumed bases of social incorporation. These findings are supplemented with field interviews and narratives that examine the impact of social incorporation on regime behavior, electoral contestation, and opposition campaign decision-making.

ELECTORAL MOBILIZATION AND THE LEGACY OF *UJAMAA* IN MULTIPARTY TANZANIA

Figure 6.1 depicts CCM's average presidential vote share between 1995 and 2010, which demonstrates both the strength of the party's organization and the legacy of its social incorporation.[6] On the mainland there are remarkably no areas where CCM's average district vote share has dipped below the 50 percent mark, and very few areas where CCM has won on average less than 60 percent of the vote. These districts tend to be more urban and are geographically concentrated in the north. Slightly more competitive districts are also found in Arusha (Arusha Urban, Karatu), Kagera (Bokuba Urban), Kilimanjaro (Hai, Moshi Rural, Moshi Urban, Rombo), Mwanza (Ukerewe), and Shinyanga (Bariadi, Maswa, Meatu). Outside of these areas we must assess CCM's presidential support from already strong levels of support. In 38 of 119 mainland districts, CCM's

---

[6] As noted earlier, the discussion is focused entirely on mainland Tanzania. Politics on the islands of Zanzibar are distinct in their history, the evolution of party structures, and therefore patterns of electoral mobilization, which tend to be more oppositional and competitive. The data is from United Republic of Tanzania (1997, 2001, 2006, 2011).

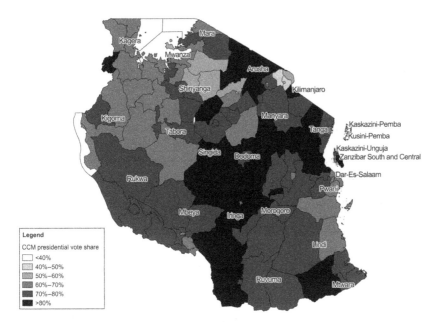

FIGURE 6.1. *Average CCM district-level presidential vote share (1995–2010)*
Source: Author created map with qGIS software based on constituency-level voting data

presidential vote share ranges on average from 60 to 70 percent. These less competitive districts tend to be concentrated in urban areas and in the northern regions bordering Lake Victoria. By contrast, the forty-five mainland districts where CCM wins between 70 and 80 percent of the presidential vote are dispersed throughout the country. The twenty-eight most supportive CCM districts, with vote shares on average above 80 percent, are mainly concentrated in central and southern regions of Dodoma, Iringa, Singida, and Tanga.[7]

This corresponds with expectations regarding CCM's unique advantages as a credible party. The party's extensive mobilization infrastructure – particularly the previously mentioned ten-house cell network – could be utilized during elections to assemble significant segments of the population through legal and extra legal means. Regime

---

[7] Looking across time for fluctuations in support, CCM generally had much stronger support across the board in 2000 and 2005, when there was no clear opposition front-runner. In 1995 Augustin Mrema likely attracted disproportionate oppositional support in Kilimanjaro. In 2005, Ibrahim Lipumba drew support away from traditional CCM strongholds along the coast, while in 2010 Wilibrod Slaa drew support away from CCM areas in Arusha and Manyara.

and opposition elites alike cite the strength of CCM's grassroots structure. Moreover, the impact of the wider pattern of social integration as developed through *ujamaa* is validated through within-case statistical analysis. The strongest areas of CCM support are precisely those that were the direct beneficiaries of the regime's redistributive policies, namely the more subsistence-based rural populations of the center and south. The northern areas bordering Lake Victoria, which were the major losers under *ujamaa*, are the regime's strongest opponents. These sub-national differences appreciably shape how opposition parties contest elections.

The Ten-House Cell Structure and CCM's Electoral Advantage

It is very difficult to account for the specific size and impact of CCM's ten-house cell network, and the election data presented here is clearly an imperfect proxy. Other quantitative evidence we have is based on surveys and a select number of experimental efforts. One study conducted between 1995 and 1997 found that CCM likely had an astonishing 38,121 operating party cells, and that party cells were by far the most familiar political office to citizens (Mukandala 2000). This was not based on formal accounts from the party, and the study did not reveal much about how the party cells were utilized to mobilize voters. One study surveyed ten-house cell members and found that voters do in fact behave differently in response to interviewer questions when the ten-house cell leader was present (Croke 2016). Whether the change in response was due to fear of reprisal or an expectation of future reward is unclear, and the study itself was limited to Dar es Salaam and would be difficult to replicate elsewhere.

The best evidence on the effectiveness of the ten-house cell structure comes from political participants themselves. Leaders in CCM at both the national and regional level note that the ten-house cell network is a major boon during elections, and is utilized primarily to organize rallies and register voters. As under single-party rule, *balozi* still tend to be members of the community who continue to perform services like paying for funerals or weddings. *Balozi* are also still paid modest salaries to ensure institutional continuity. As a member of CCM's secretariat in Arusha told me, "the cell leader knows all the voters, members, and their issues. They are directly with the people. If they do their job we win, if they don't we lose."[8] Another CCM member of parliament noted the interconnectedness

---

[8] Anonymous #TZ13 (Senior CCM Member). Author Interview. Arusha. (October 31, 2010).

of CCM's massive organization, observing that "CCM has strong roots and branches that are well connected from the cell to the district, to the region, to the national level."[9] In conversations with elites in CCM's national political affairs office, the scope of the cell structure was assumed to be stronger and more persistent in rural areas, where the population is perhaps more stable. Since residences change so often in urban areas it is more difficult to rely on a persistent *balozi* in cities.[10]

Importantly, the strength of CCM's infrastructure is not lost on opposition parties either. CCM's robust organization is often referred to as the regime's "network," and it is something that opposition parties generally and consciously try to emulate in their own party-building efforts. The pioneer opposition party on this account was the CUF, and by 2005 they claimed to have built a parallel party structure to CCM's in every village in Tanzania, which also extended down to the ten-house level.[11] The utility of this strategy is empirically uneven and fails for many reasons, namely financing. As a senior CHADEMA advisor conveyed to me about their own efforts to create a rival grassroots network, "our branch employees are not paid like in CCM and often they close their chapters and go work for CCM."[12] This is a standard lament heard from many opposition elites interviewed, who struggle to recruit local leadership and find that their own cell leaders are easily coopted by CCM. Indeed, many in the opposition believe that their own party cells pop up for the express purpose of garnering CCM's attention and an eventual bribe.

CCM's network is frequently cited as a primary hurdle to effective contestation. In Arusha, the chairman of CHADEMA told me that their inability to compete was rooted in the fact that "the ruling party has facilities, strong finances, and 100 percent network in the country from the national level to the ten-house cell level."[13] One reason is that the

---

[9] Anonymous #TZ3 (Senior CCM Member). Author Interview. Dar es Salaam. (October 18, 2010).

[10] This is based on a number of conversations with an anonymous member of CCM's Political Affairs office between October and November 2010. This member, who introduced himself simply as "Mr. Mishana," was fairly open about the organizational deficiencies of the cell structure, and was a key gatekeeper for other conversations with CCM elites.

[11] Ibrahim Lipumba (Chairman, CUF). Author Interview. Dar es Salaam. (December 3, 2010).

[12] Kitila Mkumbo (Senior Technical Advisor, CHADEMA). Author Interview. Dar es Salaam. (October 27, 2010). CHADEMA's effort at party expansion was known as "Operation Sangara," and was an attempt to train party leadership at the grassroots.

[13] Marigu Samson Mwigamba (Regional Chairman for Arusha, CHADEMA). Author Interview. Arusha. (November 13, 2010).

network can compensate for weaker candidates. As the Secretary General of the NCCR-M expressed:

We don't have very many buildings, and we are not in every constituency. Building a network is cumbersome. CCM has the network, it can field candidates who are not very strong but still get the votes. We need good candidates ... Any [CCM] candidates in Dar es Salaam will get at least 30%, in Mtwara 20%, Tanga 40%, and Ruvuma 50%.[14]

In contrast with CCM elites, many opposition members note that the cell network is particularly useful for vote buying and opposition intimidation. There are frequent stories of cell members vandalizing opposition offices or tearing down signs and flags. However, the role of the *balozi* as a straightforward problem solver and "get out the vote" tool is palpable among the opposition. As the Secretary General of the United Democratic Party (UDP) summarized:

They have leadership at the 10-house level so it is very easy for CCM to converse and transmit what has been passed on from higher up. He [the balozi] can go door to door and check for voting cards, ask people what their problems are ... This is especially true in rural areas.[15]

This validates much of what was conveyed by members of CCM themselves regarding the role and size of the ten-house cell structure.

Interestingly, the strength of CCM's ten-house cell system can at times also be a source of weakness if the cell leaders themselves become disillusioned with the ruling party. One of the more interesting accounts of this came from CHADEMA's enigmatic young member of parliament for Kigoma, Zitto Kabwe. In 2010 Kabwe was a rising star within CHADEMA and a national personality due to his strong advocacy for anti-corruption measures and appeal with youth voters. Kabwe attributes his success in Kigoma to, among other things, a unique ability to leverage his familiarity with the ten-house cell structure. Kabwe notes:

It is compulsory for people to know their 10-house cell leaders. I knew this. During my election I used CCM's 10-house cell leaders! CCM members who are 10-house cell leaders who were loyal to Zitto! I met almost 100 10-house cell leaders from one ward, which we won more than any other ward.[16]

---

[14] Samweli Ruhuza (Secretary General, NCCR). Author Interview. Dar es Salaam. (November 22, 2010).

[15] John Nkolo (Secretary General, UDP). Author Interview. Dar es Salaam. (November 11, 2010).

[16] Zitto Kabwe (CHADEMA MP, Kigoma Rural). Author Interview. Dar es Salaam. (November 29, 2010).

This demonstrates not just the importance of the size of the ten-cell network, but also its perceived direct connection to electoral success at the local level.

An Analysis of Sub-National Voting in Multiparty Tanzania

The strength of CCM's infrastructure helps explain why vote shares did not slip into uncompetitive territory across vast areas of the country, but the subtler sub-national variation in electoral support highlights the importance of social incorporation. To assess this I gathered district-level information on socioeconomic status (literacy), government provision of club goods (access to health facilities and access to piped water), and exposure to opposition parties (population density, CCM incumbency, and voter turnout). As a measure of social incorporation I calculated the percentage of the population that resided in *ujamaa* villages between 1973 and 1975. To recall, 1973 is a watershed year that separates a more benign version of *ujamaa* from a more violent form. The first period predominantly involved the use of selective material inducements targeted at the most under-developed areas of Tanzania. The second period involved the forced relocation of millions of Tanzanians and a more direct attack on the commercial cash-crop sector. We expect a correlation between vote share with villagization in 1973, but not in 1975.[17]

While ethnicity is generally not considered politically salient in Tanzania, it is worth exploring as a further control (Barkan 1994). Tanzania is home to over one hundred ethnic groups, but most are comparatively small. The Sukuma and the related Nyamwezi of Mwanza and Shinyanga regions is the largest ethnic bloc at approximately 20 percent of the population, but they are not considered politically relevant due to their looser social structure (Afrobarometer 2005). The literature cites two groups as politically relevant – the Haya of Kagera and the Chagga of Kilimanjaro. Each group is relatively small, at less than 5 percent of the population, but they are associated with historical perceptions of domination in educational resource allocation, public sector employment, and

---

[17] Data on socioeconomic indicators and government provision comes from United Republic of Tanzania (1998, 2002). Data on opposition access is extrapolated from United Republic of Tanzania (1997, 2001, 2006, 2011). Data on *ujamaa* villagization was gathered from Mascarenhas (1979) and Hyden (1980) and from the following primary source: United Republic of Tanzania, *The Economic Survey Annual Plan for 1972–1973* (Dar es Salaam: Government Printer, 1973). The correlation between access to piped water and access to health facilities is 0.4.

success in private enterprise following independence. Both groups were also likely the main losers of resource allocation under *ujamaa*, and are often considered the foundational strata of opposition parties in NCCR and CHADEMA (Mmuya and Chaligha 1994). I gather data on whether a district's population is more less homogenously Chagga, Haya, or Nyamwezi-Sukuma. Districts dominated by any other ethnic group are coded as "Other," and "Mixed" districts, which are the most common and correspond with the average CCM presidential vote share, are used as the reference category.[18]

The results in Table 6.1 confirm that CCM's average district-level vote share between 1995 and 2010 has been shaped by the historical legacy of *ujamaa*. Models 1 and 3 report the impact of the social incorporation variables, while Models 2 and 4 add the various controls. The percentage of the population resident in *ujamaa* villages exerts a strong and independent effect on CCM's presidential vote share. As expected, the measure of villagization in 1973 is significant with a high degree of confidence, while the measure of villagization by 1975 is not. A 1 percent increase in the proportion of the population residing in collective villages by 1973 leads to an approximately 0.17 percent increase in CCM's presidential vote share. Notably, this finding does not hold up as strongly in legislative elections, which is to be expected given that local contests are influenced by numerous other factors. In addition, ethnicity is not a clear motivating factor in Tanzanian elections. The coefficient on "Chagga" is significant and correlated with substantially less support for both CCM presidents and legislative candidates. But, the largest ethnic identifier, Nyamwezi-Sukuma, exerts no significant influence. The Chagga are a major opposition ethnic group, and their motivation appears to transcend their experience with more coercive *ujamaa* villagization and immediate economic factors. However, the group is too small to significantly shape the final electoral outcome in any meaningful way.

The evidence also suggests that CCM voters are not traditionally clientelistic: they are not from the most underdeveloped portions of Tanzania, and are not directly motivated by differences in government provision of desired club goods like piped water or health services. This stands up to different permutations of the range of club goods citizens might seek and

---

[18] The district data on ethnic composition was available from government regional reports (United Republic of Tanzania 1998) and a British survey conducted in the 1950s (Tanganyika 1956). This helped plot the spatial distribution of groups with the assumption that ethnic composition has remained fairly stable. Supplemental data was found in Gahnström (2012).

TABLE 6.1. *Random effects multilevel regression of average CCM vote shares*

	(Model 1)	(Model 2)	(Model 3)	(Model 4)
	Presidential vote share	Presidential vote share	Legislative vote share	Legislative vote share
Social Incorporation Variables				
%Pop. in Ujamaa Village (1973)	0.15*	0.17**	0.14	0.15*
	(0.06)	(0.05)	(0.08)	(0.07)
%Pop. in Ujamaa Village (1975)	−0.03	−0.02	−0.03	0.00
	(0.03)	(0.02)	(0.04)	(0.03)
Chagga	−16.39**	−16.52***	−16.74*	−15.45**
	(5.31)	(4.31)	(6.78)	(5.46)
Haya	−7.45	−2.40	−4.47	2.68
	(6.29)	(5.66)	(8.22)	(7.17)
Nyamwezi-Sukuma	−5.12	−1.76	−7.31	−5.21
	(3.51)	(2.97)	(4.55)	(3.77)
Other	0.14	2.04	−1.66	−0.87
	(1.93)	(1.75)	(2.50)	(2.22)
Socioeconomic Variables				
Literacy Rate (2002)		0.16		0.10
		(0.10)		(0.12)
Government Provision Variables				
Pop./Health Clinic (2002)		−0.00		−0.00
		(0.00)		(0.00)
%Pop. With Piped Water (2002)		0.03		0.06
		(0.05)		(0.06)
Access Variables				
Log Population Density (2002)		−1.98*		−2.19
		(0.93)		(1.18)
Average %CCM Incumbents		0.08*		0.18***
		(0.03)		(0.04)
Average Voter Turnout		−0.20		−0.22
		(0.13)		(0.17)
Constant	74.22***	82.99***	71.86***	79.80***
	(2.63)	(11.53)	(3.37)	(14.62)

(*continued*)

TABLE 6.1. (continued)

	(Model 1)	(Model 2)	(Model 3)	(Model 4)
	Presidential vote share	Presidential vote share	Legislative vote share	Legislative vote share
Observations	98	96	98	96
Clusters	20	20	20	20
χ^2	16.78	41.12	11.94	42.93
Prob > χ^2	0.01	0	0.06	0

Notes: The dependent variable is CCM's average district-level presidential vote share in Models 1 and 2 and CCM's average district-level legislative vote share in Models 3 and 4. Standard errors are reported in parentheses. Only non-urban and non-Zanzibar districts are reported. ***$p < 0.001$, **$p < 0.01$, *$p < 0.05$.

to different measures of socioeconomic development.[19] There is, however, some evidence that opposition access influences CCM vote shares. Increases in population densities translate into lower CCM vote shares in presidential elections, but not legislative ones. Likewise, marginal differences in CCM's incumbency lead to a 0.08 percent increase in presidential vote share and a 0.18 percent increase in legislative vote share. This is in line with expectations that CCM itself, rather than any individual member of parliament, is the key factor that shapes credible relationships with voters. As will be seen in Cameroon and Kenya, incumbency does not have the same effect. In those cases who the candidate is, not just what party they belong to, influences voters.

I contrast these factors by plotting the predicted CCM presidential vote share against specific variables, while holding all other variables at their sample mean and excluding Chagga-dominated districts (Figure 6.2). Panel A shows that in average districts, more *ujamaa* villagization increases CCM's vote share by up to approximately 15 percent. On the other hand, Panels B and C demonstrate that in districts with average levels of *ujamaa* villagization increases in literacy and access to piped

---

[19] In unreported models formal employment, poverty, and the percentage of households with mud floors were also included. All can convey states of socioeconomic development and the degree of government provision. Only employment had a small yet significant effect on CCM vote shares. None of the variables altered the coefficient on *ujamaa* villagization.

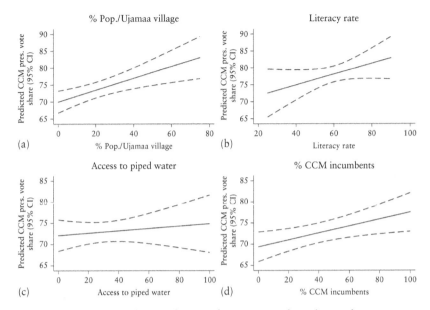

FIGURE 6.2. *Select predictors of CCM's presidential vote shares*
Note: Dotted lines represent the 95 percent confidence intervals. All other variables are held at their means in each sub-graph, and Chagga districts are excluded.

water possibly improve CCM vote share, but the confidence intervals at either tail end are too wide to make a definitive conclusion. In Panel D the smaller impact of CCM incumbency is demonstrated. To further illustrate the independent impact of *ujamaa*, I modeled CCM vote shares in districts with low levels of literacy, access to piped water, and villagization. The predicted CCM presidential vote share was 56 percent. By contrast, in modeled districts with low levels of literacy and access to piped water, but high degrees of villagization, the predicted vote share rises to 66 percent.

Participant Perspectives on Social Incorporation in Tanzania

The role of social incorporation came up frequently during interviews with Tanzanian elites. Opposition parties generally offer a supply-side story to explain their divergent patterns of electoral support, which the statistical evidence partially supports. Many parties claim that they lack the resources to expand and effectively compete with an entrenched political party. Therefore, they consciously embark on what they call a "Lake Zone" strategy. Since the Lake Zone in Northern Tanzania is where population densities are the highest, it is also the most cost-effective region to campaign in. Yet, the empirical analysis above indicates that while greater opposition access matters in legislative elections, it does not appear to matter much in presidential polls. Nearly every opposition elite I interviewed noted the distinct challenge of presidential campaigns in terms of the voter's receptiveness to message. As one activist noted, "we are strong where we go, but we go where we are strong."[20] To me this indicated a conscious concern with accessing CCM's core constituencies. The expansion to the Lake Zone is therefore not just a logistic consideration, but also due to perceived differences in voter openness to opposition messages.

During interviews differences in voter receptiveness between the Lake Zone and CCM's strongholds in the center and south were attributed to disparities in educational levels, the divergent heritage of missionary activity, and even democratic diffusion across international boundaries.[21] However, the role of *ujamaa* and its distributional consequences came up frequently. With regard to the north, the Deputy Secretary-General of the CUF Joran Bashenge made links to the role of cash-crop production and the higher levels of state repression that made the citizenry and local elites more distrustful of CCM and amenable to opposition messages. As Bashenge notes:

In the Lake Region you need to go back to history and independence. These regions were the big supporters of independence and the strong base for TANU. That revolutionary mindset continues to date. People are organized since then in cooperatives ... Cooperatives in the North and Coast have been the subject of CCM's policies of privatization.[22]

An opposition MP in Iringa Urban, at the heart of CCM's rural stronghold, also made links between the North and the cash crop economy, stating:

Understand the missionary history in the North. They were taught the gospel and economics and farming. In these areas [CCM strongholds], people were just taught the gospel. In the North they brought coffee and commercial crops. The ruling party is taking advantage of the miseducation (*sic*) of people.[23]

---

[20] John Mnyika (CHADEMA Interim Secretary General). Author Interview. Dar es Salaam. (October 25, 2010).

[21] As an additional control I ran the statistical models with a variable that measured the number of international borders per district, and student enrollment in primary, secondary, and post-secondary school. The results were all insignificant.

[22] Joran Bashenge (Deputy-Secretary General, CUF). Author Interview. Dar es Salaam. (November 15, 2010).

[23] Peter Simeon Mswiga (MP Iringa Urban, District Secretary General for Iringa, CHADEMA). Author Interview. Iringa. (November 26, 2010).

On the other hand, the feeling among the opposition is that voters in CCM's strongholds are beholden to the ruling party in deeply historical ways. For instance, Wilibrod Slaa told me that he thinks Dodoma, Iringa, and Singida are traditional "clienteles" of CCM.[24] This feeling was echoed by several other opposition elites in Dar es Salaam and elsewhere, who admit that despite investing significant party resources it is difficult to penetrate these specific regions. Joran Bashenge contrasts this experience to the cooperative legacy in the North:

> In areas where there were less cooperatives there is no interference from anybody and people don't know anything besides the party of Nyerere. During the election, radio and TV play Nyerere speeches in Dodoma, Singida, and Manyara.[25]

Freeman Mbowe of CHADEMA noted that "CCM's capital has for a long period of time been based on the politics of fear," which in this context meant fear of losing access to the central government.[26] John Nkolo of the UDP succinctly expressed these sentiments:

> As an MP candidate I had a difficult time talking with them. In 2000, one voter asked me if I was from Nyerere's party. I had to explain that he died and so forth. She told me that she would not vote for me since I was not from the party of Nyerere.[27]

Nkolo's anecdote was not the only one that referred to Nyerere's paramount influence in specific areas of Tanzania. From the opposition's point of view, large swathes of voters are simply inaccessible on a social and even psychological level.

ELECTORAL ISOLATION AND REALIGNMENT IN MULTIPARTY CAMEROON

The spatial depiction of Paul Biya's votes in Cameroon presents a very different picture than in Tanzania (Figure 6.3).[28] The data demonstrate

---

[24] Wilibrod Slaa (Secretary General, CHADEMA). Author Interview. Dar es Salaam. (November 18, 2010).

[25] Joran Bashenge (Deputy-Secretary General, CUF). Author Interview. Dar es Salaam. (November 15, 2010).

[26] Freeman Mbowe (Chairman, CHADEMA). Author Interview. Dar es Salaam. (December 4, 2010).

[27] John Nkolo (Secretary General, UDP). Author Interview. Dar es Salaam. (November 11, 2010).

[28] Election results were collected from the following formal sources: Ministre de l'Administration Territoriale (1992, 1997), Elections Cameroon (2011). However, since no formal records were available for the 1997 presidential election, 2002 legislative election, and

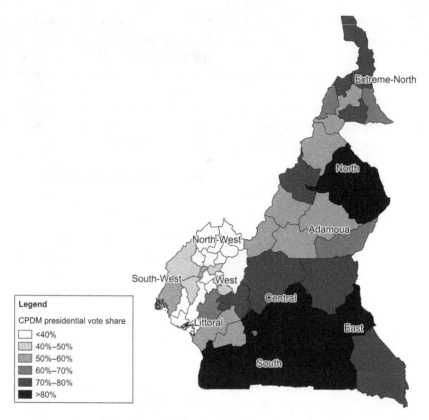

FIGURE 6.3. *Average CPDM district presidential vote share (1992–2011)*
Source: Author created map with qGIS software based on constituency-level voting data

that the CPDM is very uncompetitive in a critical number of departments. There are twenty-one departments where Biya has won on average less than 50 percent of the vote, and these departments are all located
in North West, South West, West, and Littoral Provinces. These regions
are where the major Anglophone communities reside, and are also the

---

2007 legislative election, I used the reported results in Michel Mombio. "Un Verdict
Inique" *Le Messager* (October 24 1997), Staff. "2002 Legislative Election Results" *Le
Yaoundé* (July 22, 2002), and Staff. "2007 Legislative Results" *Mutations* (August 13,
2007). I can only present the average of the 1992 and 2011 presidential elections. This
essentially bookends the period under discussion, but in many ways it reflects the low
and high points for the CPDM electorally speaking, and therefore provides a decent
assessment of average patterns of support. Data on the 1997 election would be misleading because of the opposition boycott, and as noted previously, data on the 2004
presidential election is missing.

locations of the UPC rebellion and much of the Bamileké community that joined the opposition in the early 1990s. In other regions of Francophone Cameroon the results are more mixed. Biya's core supporters are concentrated in the southern and eastern provinces of Cameroon, where there is no department that he won with less than 70 percent of the vote. The CPDM also retains significant support in Central Province, and only in the department of Mfoundi and Nyong et Kollo have presidential vote shares dipped below the 70 percent mark. However, in Adamoua, North, and Extreme North the average CPDM presidential vote share ranges between 50 and 70 percent. These are also the locations that have witnessed some of the largest shifts back toward the ruling party. During the 1992 election Biya won less than 50 percent of the vote in the majority of departments in these regions, and depended much more heavily on central, eastern, and southern voters.

This corresponds with expectations given the level of investment the ruling party made in establishing credible systems of exchange. The party's weaker organization and narrower social base made it vulnerable to voter defection along ethnic and regional lines. Despite some talk of party revitalization, the CPDM did not have the physical resources to compensate for the loss of voters, and therefore could not mobilize competitive levels of support in many areas of the country. Correspondingly, opposition groups rarely mention the CPDM itself as a hurdle, but rather stress the role of the presidency and the coercive apparatus. Likewise, within-case statistical analysis of sub-national voting reveals stronger clientelism and ethnic drive at the department level. What makes this interpretation a bit trickier is the fact that the CPDM and Biya have been able to realign their coalition by attracting greater northern support. As discussed in the next chapter, this corresponds with the greater leverage afforded Biya by the international community. But, this realignment still basically reveals the ethnic and brokered nature of regime building in Cameroon.

How Big is the CPDM? Participant Assessments of Party Strength

Unlike in Kenya, the ruling party in Cameroon supposedly retained greater physical assets that have helped it mobilize voters during elections. One plausible counterfactual to consider is that the CPDM's stronger support in the north is tied to the organizational reach of the party, rather than the logic of ethnic alliance making. Both conjectures can simultaneously hold, and indeed there are voices in Cameroon that argue that the CPDM plays the ethnic game, but might also not be as organizationally weak as some would otherwise believe. To recall, we can trace the CPDM's lineage back to Ahidjo and the UC. The UC was originally a regional party, and had built numerous party cells and local chapters throughout the north. But, the UC faced resistance when it tried to expand in the south, where other political parties were more firmly entrenched. This infrastructure might have survived the transition from Ahidjo to Biya, and partially explains why voter defection was more acute in Anglophone Cameroon where the UC had no physical presence at all. On the other hand, it might be that Anglophone identity pulls more voters away from the CPDM than the northern and Fulani signifier.

Several CPDM elites in fact do discuss party organization as a central reason they are so successful during elections, although they do not make direct ties to the UC and the veracity of their claims are uncertain. Elites often mention that the CPDM has retained an influential organizational secretary who is responsible for managing party branches, which is the most visible level of the party in Cameroon. Figures like Charles Doumba and his successor Emmanuel René Sadi are especially important and were tasked by the CPDM to maintain party activity at the branch level and resolve disputes over leadership and legislative selection. Sadi in particular was very active during the 2007 and 2013 legislative primaries, and was a key factor in an attempt to reassess the grassroots strength of the party. Prior to the 2011 election, the Cameroonian historian and political scientist Emmanuel Konde noted that:

The CPDM has won election after election ... principally because it is the best organized in the country. From the Cell, Branch, Sub-Section, Section, Central Committee, and Political Bureau, the CPDM is the only party in Cameroon that can boast an organization that is durable.[29]

A chief member of the CPDM's Secretariat also informed me that the lowest unit of the party, the cell, could be tapped into fairly easily from Yaoundé via established branch, sub-section, and section leaders.[30]

Yet, the utility of these party-building efforts are very unclear. As under single-party rule, sub-national party positions remained unpaid following

---

[29] Emmanuel Konde, "Why the CPDM Will Emerge Victorious in the 2011 Presidential Election" *Post News*, July 15, 2011.

[30] Anonymous #CM4 (Senior CPDM Secretariat Member). Author Interview. Yaoundé. (July 27, 2015). During fieldwork the author was presented with a roster of names and contact information, which was supposedly part of an attempt by the party to take stock of its infrastructure and create clearer lines of communication. The project was ongoing and therefore did not reflect on the prior period.

the transition to elections and the party did not develop a regional structure or even a permanent national office. Rather until 2016 the party's
secretariat only met sporadically at various locations throughout the
country, and used the major convention center in Yaoundé, the *Palais des
Congrès*, for occasional larger scale CPDM gatherings and conventions.
In other private conversations with several CPDM elites, their assessments of local party strength are generally uneven. One elite estimated
that there were only 500 subsections of the party throughout the country.
When pushed on the question of whether these sub-national levels of the
party physically existed he stated:

Where you want to find people working, if you go to villages and quarters you
know, when you go there, we do not have offices because you have meetings
in the houses of militants, that's where they usually meet. What I mean is that
in some villages you can find plaques, but the whole thing is that they meet in
houses ... It should be permanent, which it is not at all. It is empty. There is
nobody there. That I completely agree with you.[31]

In another revealing conversation with a member of the CPDM's national
organizational office, I was told that branches rather than cells were the
most visible aspect of the party:

And what is more visible is the branches. Because there are so many cells and it is
difficult to hold a meeting. So what has happened is that the cells are created generally when the party has been organized, but afterwards, they disappear. They
exist on paper, but when you go there sometimes, you don't find them again. You
don't find them. And mostly, the branches are really there.[32]

These comments from fairly prominent members of the CPDM leave the
impression that the party itself does not know what physical assets it
actually holds.

Many in the Cameroonian opposition likewise depict the CPDM as
more of a paper tiger, at least organizationally speaking. When asked about
the size of the CPDM, civil activist Matthias Owona Nguini noted that:

I don't think they [the CPDM] know because there is an anarchical development
of cells and subsections in the party because it is one of the means of political

---

[31] Anonymous #CM11 (CPDM Central Committee Member). Author Interview. Douala.
(August 4, 2015).
[32] Anonymous #CM4 (Senior CPDM Secretariat Member). Author Interview. Yaoundé.
(July 27, 2015).

struggle within the CPDM. And there is always a problem of validating the number of cells and subsections.[33]

Frequently opposition members note their interactions with traditional elites and chiefs, the civil administration, and the military rather than the CPDM's grassroots as a major electoral hurdle. One of the most prominent voices in the SDF, Joshua Osih, stated that:

At the grassroots level, there has never been something like the CPDM organization. The number you see them calling is the headmaster of the primary school. It's the doctor in the district hospital. It's the sub-divisional officer. Those are the branches of the CPDM at the grassroots level. There is nothing like a grassroots politician in the CPDM. It doesn't exist.[34]

Or, as Beatrice Anembom, an organizational secretary in the SDF, answered when asked what the primary local obstacle was to effective competition: "the government controls your blocs, your voting process."[35] These assessments stand in contrast with opposition statements from Tanzania, who also mention the state but always come back to the role of CCM's large cell network. All this suggests that while the CPDM maintains a possibly larger physical presence, it is still not likely the party's organization that is the key to its electoral successes or failures.

An Analysis of Sub-National Voting in Multiparty Cameroon

Sub-national data is much more constrained in Cameroon than in Tanzania, which requires some creativity in data collection and analysis. Similar department-level measures of socioeconomic development (literacy) and opposition exposure (population density, incumbency, and voter turnout) were gathered from election results, the 2005 population census, and regional socioeconomic development reports (MINAT 2000, Etudes de Population 2005). With regard to government provision, I use the proportion of the population that resides in homes with mud floors as a proxy for the delivery of adequate housing, and data on the ratio of population to infirmaries as a proxy for the delivery of health services. Data on these measures is the most consistent, but 20 percent are still

---

[33] Matthias Owona Nguini (Civil Society Activist). Author Interview. Yaoundé. (July 28, 2015).

[34] Joshua Osih (MP for Wouri, SDF). Author Interview. Douala. (August 3, 2015).

[35] Beatrice Anembom (Organizational Secretary, SDF). Author Interview. Yaoundé. (July 29, 2015).

missing. The reasons for these gaps appear random and due to administrative issues with data gathering in a number of key jurisdictions. For instance, in one department the government might gather data on the number of doctors per department rather than the number of clinics. As a solution I generate a multiply imputed dataset using a multivariate model to fill out the missing values. In comparison with a complete case analysis or an analysis that does not include this variable, the results are only moderately different.[36]

Data on the major indicator of social incorporation – ethnic identity – is available, although it did require some qualitative interpretation. Cameroon has over 200 identifiable ethno-linguistic groups, yet clearly not all are politically relevant. As discussed in Chapter 3, a major identity group is the Beti, which itself encompasses at least four sub-groups – the Ewondo, Bulu, Eton, and Fang. These groups are geographically concentrated in southern and central regions of Cameroon. I also consider the Bamileké, Fulani, and Kirdi to be distinct and important ethnic identifications, but combine the Bassa, Bakweri, and Douala into one group due to a shared heritage in the UPC rebellion and geographic association with the Littoral region. With regard to Anglophone Cameroon, the North West region is often lumped together under the broader linguistic grouping of "Grassfield" people, while the South West is considered more diverse. I argue that the Anglophone signifier is more important than these internal divisions. However, as will be discussed below, the Grassfield identity became relevant as a factor that explains the emergence of electoral hegemony in Cameroon over time. The "Other" category captures smaller politically relevant groups like the Baka and Bamoun, as well as other groups that dominate single departments like the Makaa, Gbaya, Dii, and Shawa Arabs. Once again the reference category is a mixed ethnic department, which constitutes approximately 14 percent of all departments and approximates the mean CPDM vote share.[37]

---

[36] In post-regression diagnostics the department of "Momo" (a stronghold of Anglophone resistance) exerted significant leverage and stood out as an outlier. It is therefore excluded from these models. It is also noteworthy that Cameroon uses a mixed electoral system, with some constituencies voted by first-past-the-post in single majority districts, and others by majoritarian vote in multi-member districts. This creates stronger incentives to consolidate around CPDM candidates. However, when I control for whether a district is single rather than multi-member there is no substantive impact on the results.

[37] The data on ethnic identity comes primarily from Lewis, Simons, and Fennig (2015), which lists numerous ethnic and linguistic identities by geographic location. With consultation from specialists in Cameroon, these groups were matched with the political departments.

As displayed in Table 6.2, ethnic identity clearly exerts a strong influence on voter choice in Cameroon. Holding all other variables constant at their mean and with an ethnically mixed department as the reference category, Anglophone departments register CPDM presidential vote shares that are on average 35 percent lower. Bassa/Bakweri/Douala and Fulani departments also vote for Biya at comparatively much lower rates than in mixed departments. As expected, the homogenously Beti departments register voters for Paul Biya at approximately a 13 percent higher rate than in mixed departments. However, ethnic considerations do appear to have a less consistent impact during legislative elections. Only the Bassa/Bakweri/Douala departments are persistently oppositional, and most are located in Littoral province, which is home to the major commercial city of Douala and UPC rebellion. The difference between presidential and legislative elections is likely because the CPDM's electoral dominance became more secure over time. A legislative protest vote based on ethnic identity made little sense, while presidential elections still offered moments to express voter grievance.

Other variables do not carry much causal weight in Cameroon, and there are some counterintuitive results regarding the impact of clientelistic motivations. The provision of a department-level good like adequate housing appears to correlate with lower levels of support for Paul Biya. One interpretation is that this measure is not really capturing a government-provided club good, but rather is an indicator of socioeconomic development. Therefore, as theories regarding clientelism generally predict, low information voters from areas with less socioeconomic development are more supportive of Biya. Keeping all other factors constant at their mean, in departments with mean access to better housing the predicted presidential vote share ranges between 60 and 80 percent. In departments with the least mud floor homes this range decreases to 50–85 percent, while in departments with the most mud floor homes the range increases to 65–95 percent. More direct measures of government provision like access to a health facility are surprisingly not good predictors of presidential vote shares. However, this might be due to the more challenging data availability and the smaller sample.[38]

---

[38] Models were also run with measures of formal employment and the male–female ratio. Neither was statistically significant or altered the significance of other coefficients. The correlation between health access and mud floors is 0.47. There is very little correlation between these two variables and the male–female ratio or employment.

TABLE 6.2. *Random effects multilevel regression of average CPDM vote shares (multiply imputed data)*

	(Model 1)	(Model 2)	(Model 3)	(Model 4)
	Presidential vote share	Presidential vote share	Legislative vote share	Legislative vote share
Social Incorporation Variables				
Anglophone	−33.81**	−35.10***	−19.70	−13.68
	(10.53)	(10.04)	(14.01)	(12.80)
Bamileké	−2.75	−9.14	9.33	10.76
	(6.90)	(7.09)	(9.36)	(9.94)
Bassa/Bakweri/Douala	−22.96***	−20.59**	−34.27***	−29.82**
	(6.93)	(6.81)	(9.39)	(9.65)
Beti	14.05**	12.85**	5.29	8.60
	(4.65)	(4.63)	(6.31)	(6.61)
Fulani	−12.81**	−11.32*	−9.70	−7.20
	(4.89)	(4.80)	(6.65)	(6.80)
Kirdi	−11.84*	−11.09*	−7.12	−1.56
	(5.09)	(5.24)	(6.91)	(7.45)
Other	0.44	−0.27	−3.69	−3.80
	(3.58)	(3.58)	(4.86)	(5.23)
Socioeconomic Variables				
Literacy Rate (2005)		0.24		0.11
		(0.16)		(0.21)
Government Provision Variables				
%Pop. with Mud Floor (2005)		0.27**		0.08
		(0.10)		(0.14)
Pop./Infirmary (1999–2000)		0.00		−0.00
		(0.00)		(0.00)
Opposition Access Variables				
Log Population Density (2005)		−0.48		−4.55*
		(1.49)		(2.08)
Average Voter Turnout		−0.03		−0.19
		(0.18)		(0.25)
Average %CPDM Incumbents		5.63		8.69
		(6.80)		(9.63)

(continued)

TABLE 6.2. *(continued)*

	(Model 1)	(Model 2)	(Model 3)	(Model 4)
	Presidential vote share	Presidential vote share	Legislative vote share	Legislative vote share
Constant	72.14***	41.78	71.97***	85.26**
	(5.52)	(22.30)	(7.39)	(28.18)
Observations	50	50	50	50
Clusters	10	10	10	10
F	9.93	6.43	4.37	2.67
Prob > F	0	0	0	0

Notes: The dependent variable is the average department-level CPDM presidential vote share in Models 1 and 2 and the average department-level CPDM legislative vote share in Models 3 and 4. Standard errors are reported in parentheses. Only nonurban departments included. ***$p < 0.001$, **$p < 0.01$, *$p < 0.05$.

Participant Perspectives on Ethnicity and Social Incorporation in Cameroon

The narrowness of the CPDM's social base compelled Biya to navigate a challenging ethnic arithmetic. While retaining his core Beti support, between 1992 and 2011 nearly every ethnic group in Cameroon increased its level of support for Biya and the CPDM's legislative candidates. Figure 6.6 plots the change in the CPDM's vote share by a department's ethnic composition across the electoral authoritarian period. The most pronounced shifts were among the Fulani and Bamileké communities, where CPDM votes increased by approximately 60 percent. This corresponded with Biya's cooptation efforts of elites who represent these groups. By 2004, the Fulani-based NUDP lost most of its legislative seats and joined the "Presidential Majority," which endorsed Biya's presidential candidacy (Diklitch 2002). As noted in Chapter 5, a similar tactic helped draw back the Bamileké support, and by 2004 Biya had won the endorsement of the two largest Cameroonian business organizations – the *Groupment Inter-Patronal du Cameroun* and the *Chambre de Commerce, d'Industrie, des Mines et de l'Artisanat*. While not a very

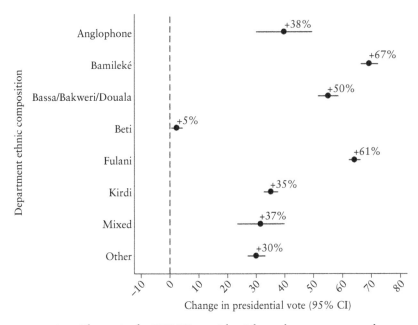

FIGURE 6.4. *Change in the CPDM's presidential vote between 1992 and 2011, by the ethnic composition of a district*
Note: Lines represent 95 percent confidence intervals.

large ethnic group, the Bamileké were at one point an important financial source for the opposition (Arriola 2012, 160–7).

While the Fulani and Bamileké are the basis of the CPDM's realignment after foundational elections, cooptation worked with other ethnic communities too, and surprisingly those groups that were central elements of the historical opposition to both Ahidjo and Biya. In April 1992, the UPC party split into factions, and the party's chair, Augustin Kodock, signed an agreement of cooperation with the CPDM. In 2002, Kodock was appointed Minister of State for Agriculture, and his faction of the UPC joined the Presidential Majority.[39] While still strongly oppositional, by 2011 Biya's electoral support from the Bassa/Bakweri/Douala departments had increased by 50 percent. The official line from the UPC is that the decision to ally with Biya in 1992 was for the sake of national unity, and to pressure the regime for reform from within. As the party's chairman related:

[39] Another faction of the UPC led by Henry Hogbe-Nlend joined the CPDM coalition after the 1997 election, when Hogbe-Nlend was made Minister of Science and Technology (Ngoh 2004).

We signed that alliance for democracy, to promote democracy, to promote free elections, to put in place the Senate, to change the law concerning security forces, to put in place the context where we can have freedom for NGOs, freedom for association, freedom for political parties, and so on.[40]

But, it is also clear that this was a strategic choice given the narrowness of the UPC's own social base in Littoral region, and the crucial cards that the regime held. As the UPC's chairman further stated:

You cannot tell someone who is in power "you have to go." He has the army. He has security. And also, you are not very sure that if he left power then you would have peace. No, no. It's not possible. So it is because of peace for this country that we signed this alliance.[41]

To coopt and divide elements of the Anglophone community Biya reinstated the position of Prime Minister, which an Anglophone has held ever since. But, he also took advantage of divisions within the Anglophone community and the growing gap between the North West and South West provinces. For instance, Biya publicly supported the South West Elite Association, which in 1996 merged into a broader movement called *Sawa*. The organization, which means "coast" in Douala dialect, articulated the grievances of "coastal people" vis-à-vis the SDF who were perceived as dominated by Grassfield and Bamileké people, and derogatorily referred to as the Anglo-Bami hegemony (Nyamnjoh and Rowlands 1998, Krieger 2008).[42] These efforts appear to have had some success, and Anglophone departments saw an approximately 40 percent shift in support for Biya between 1992 and 2011. However, this shift was slightly more pronounced in South West, and particularly in the more ethnically homogenous departments of Fako, Meme, and Ndian. Still, by 2011 Anglophone departments remained the most oppositional, with only an average 54 percent support for Biya and 59 percent for CPDM legislative candidates.

From the perspective of Anglophone politicians this was a clear ethnic calculus on the part of the CPDM, which has also influenced their own party building strategies. The former Secretary General of the SDF Tazoacha Asonganyi argued, "those ruling are called Betis and whatever. I think they still think that after this man [Biya], they can continue to rule.

---

[40] Bappoh Lipor Robert (Chairman, UPC). Author Interview. Yaoundé. (August 6, 2015).
[41] Ibid.
[42] A similar association, the North West Elite Association was also supported to place a wedge between the SDF and traditional rulers, or *fons*. These developments are referred to as the politics of *allogeny* and *autochtony* (Socpa 2006).

And this is the main challenge."[43] Joshua Osih reflected on what he called the "southern paradox," and claimed that southern regions are actually suffering economically, but "because a traditional ruler in the South gets an instruction in his dialect" they turn out the vote. He further noted: "what the CPDM does is they concentrate on the chiefs. They give them stipends. They give them money. They give them gifts."[44] Other opposition elites perceive similar cultural differences not just with the south, but also between other ethnic groups. As one member of the SDF told me:

> Let me put it this way. If you look at the history of Cameroon, in the West they are fighting people … You look at people from the North and [Ahidjo] put all his cohorts into big positions in the country … When Ahidjo left and Paul Biya took over, he realized there were too many people from northern regions … He decided to change, remove them, and put his own people … But we, the North West and South West, you already know that we are with the Anglophone culture who stand for the truth as fearless people, and we see, we want justice.[45]

To many in the opposition the ethnic nature of politics had compelled the SDF itself to become increasingly narrow in its appeal, which has factionalized the party's leadership.[46] Despite efforts and early successes at national-level party building, the SDF has not been able to shake its public image as associated with Anglophone interests and North West Province. Moreover, the membership in the party's Central Committee and National Congress has, over time, become more ethnically homogenous and Anglophone (Krieger 2008).

It is rare to find elite members of the CPDM discuss ethnic mobilization in such overt terms, which is unsurprising given the sensitivity of the subject. Most conversations with party elites involved references to the party's organization, its legacy as an independence-era institution that has secured peace for years, and its proclaimed record of success delivering for its citizens. It is, however, worth noting one standout occasion where a senior anonymous member of the CPDM's secretariat talked

---

[43] Tazoacha Asanganyi (former Secretary General, SDF). Author Interview. Yaoundé. (July 22, 2015).

[44] Joshua Osih (MP for Wouri, SDF). Author Interview. Douala. (August 3, 2015).

[45] Anonymous #CM15 (Senior SDF Opposition Member). Author Interview. Yaoundé. (July 29, 2015).

[46] A widely reported meeting between Paul Biya and the SDF's chair John Fru Ndi in 2010 signaled to many in the SDF a turn toward appeasement with the regime and recognition that the party had basically been reduced to an Anglophone alcove. Some in the SDF criticized Fru Ndi's meeting with Biya as the first step toward cooptation.

about social differences between voters based on their residence, and therefore their ethnic background:

Yes, there is a fundamental difference in the sense that in the South the fight is more within the party. You understand in the south. Where there is a campaign you come and say this is your mate. Vote for the system. In the North or North West, you have to convince because you talk and talk and talk and the reaction is poor. They are not convinced because they profess they stay in opposition. This is very fundamental.[47]

While not a "smoking gun" or direct evidence of deliberate ethnic mobilization, it does indicate an awareness of the ethnic calculus behind voting from within the CPDM. Moreover, this apparent confession came after lengthy discussions over the sources of the CPDM's voter support and their ability to effectively mobilize outside of their narrow comfort zone in the south. Combined with the oppositions' comments, the strategy of national-level ethnic alliance building, and the within-case statistical analysis, there is strong evidence that the CPDM cannot rely on a sufficiently wide basis of voters because of its legacy of narrower ethnic incorporation and weak credibility as a ruling party.

ELECTORAL WEAKNESS AND THE TRIUMPH OF ETHNICITY IN MULTIPARTY KENYA

Turning to the case of Kenya, between the years 1992 and 2002 the subnational voting patterns are quite stark (Figure 6.5).[48] Voting in Kenya fundamentally mimics the ethnic coalition put in place by Moi, and highlights the inability of the party to use infrastructure to generate minimal levels of support beyond those areas. In stark contrast with Tanzania, there are large areas of Kenya where KANU was nowhere near minimally competitive. KANU's support was mainly peripheral, and concentrated in the upper Rift Valley and Northeastern Province. In the bulk of districts in these areas KANU generally maintained over 70 percent of the vote, but did lose some support once Moi stepped down in 2002. KANU

---

[47] Anonymous #CM4 (Senior CPDM Secretariat Member). Author Interview. Yaoundé. (July 27, 2015).
[48] Constituency-level election data for 1992 and 2002 comes from Throup and Hornsby (1998) and IED (2003). The data for 1997 is from Staff. "Parliamentary Results by Constituency" *The Weekly Review* (January 9, 1998), and Staff. "Presidential Results by Constituency" *The Weekly Review* (January 9, 1998).

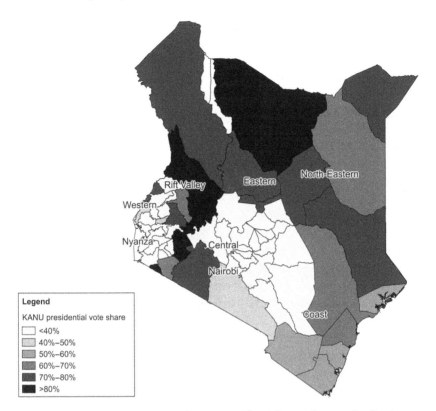

FIGURE 6.5. *Average KANU district presidential vote share at the district level (1992–2002)*
Source: Author created map with qGIS software based on constituency-level voting data

could also depend on strong vote shares in the Coast and parts of Eastern Province, but once again this declined in 2002. By contrast, vast areas of Central, Nyanza, and Western Provinces were consistently uncompetitive for KANU. In many districts in these areas KANU could muster no more than 15 percent of the vote in any election. Unlike in Cameroon, there are few oppositional areas that returned to KANU, and far more districts dropped considerably from their 1992 levels of support.

This corresponds with theoretical expectations given the serious short-comings KANU had as a ruling party and the extent of crisis it faced. KANU's weak organization and the absence of any real grassroots presence limited the party's ability to mitigate the downside of narrow social incorporation. When an elite defected from KANU, they took with them the bulk of electoral support. As in Cameroon, opposition figures rarely mention the party as a major threat during elections. Charles Hornsby writes regarding this period that "the ethnic sensitivities that had underlain politics in the single-party era became overt and self-reinforcing" (Hornsby 2012). The within-case statistical analysis and elite narratives find strong evidence for ethnic voting motivations and suggests more straightforward clientelistic motivations. Unlike in Cameroon, in KANU the narrow coalition further unraveled after the selection of Uhuru Kenyatta as Moi's successor.

The Nonexistent Party in Multiparty Kenya

While there was some ambiguity regarding the CPDM's infrastructure, the narrative that unfolds in Kenya is much clearer. Despite Moi's efforts at party reorganization in the 1980s, during elections KANU lacked the physical infrastructure at the grassroots to mobilize voters, and instead depended heavily on its members' personal networks. During my conversations with members of KANU's current secretariat, I was shown documents that demonstrated KANU's property holdings in every district. However, it was not clear whether there were actual buildings on this real estate. It was apparent that it was fairly common for KANU to rent temporary office space, or hold party-related events at a parliamentarian's home. Besides membership dues, party branches depended on locally available funds and could not count on support from the provincial or national chapters of the party. This meant that party branches continued to develop unevenly. Likewise, the branch level loosely corresponds with an electoral constituency or district, and there is no real record of a real grassroots or cell structure.[49]

I also inquired with a number of former KANU members of parliament whether they could rely on party facilities and assets to assist them during elections. The sample of interviews is not representative, but highly suggestive that the party was not a resource. One former KANU MP from Bonchari District recalled that during his 1997 campaign there was a KANU district headquarters, a district executive officer, and local chair. However, he recollected just a single KANU staff member at the constituency level, and they were not consulted on campaign strategies.

---

[49] Job Waka (Organizational Secretary of KANU). Author Interview. Nairobi. (July 18, 2012), Nick Salat (Secretary General of KANU). Author Interview. Nairobi. (August 7, 2012). During these interviews the subjects noted that many of KANU's records were destroyed after its defeat at the polls in 2002. As of the interview, the party's headquarters were in disarray and the party's archives had not yet been sorted.

In fact, he could not recall much activity at all at the district level of the party, noting that "KANU had structures in place and office bearers, but I don't remember them calling for elections and therefore vying for any post. For a long time internal elections were not held."[50] Another interviewed MP, who self-financed his entire campaign, stated that:

Offices were there, but they were very disjoined and not run by competent individuals or funded. KANU was a personal party. Support for any grassroots structure depended on the relationship between the locality and the president.[51]

This sentiment was echoed by other KANU elites who were interviewed and uniformly noted that the party essentially ended at the district. Consequently, when elites defected they took with them the primary mechanisms through which the party could reach voters.

From the opposition's point of view, many former activists in the FORD and DP parties likewise could not recall a KANU grassroots presence, and instead frequently commented on their interaction with the civil administration and informal coercive institutions. For instance, when asked about the major hurdles to campaigning at the local level, former FORD member Paul Muite stated: "The DCs, PCs, and Chiefs were the KANU party at the local level. KANU worked closely with the Provincial Administration."[52] Likewise, there were frequent references to personalized militias and extra-party groups like "Youth for KANU'92" or local gangs paid for by individual MPs. These informal groups were also associated with severe inter-ethnic violence in 1992 and 1997, and have been covered extensively in the secondary literature (Branch 2011, 222–7, Mueller 2011, Hornsby 2012, 490–3, 602–3). This is similar to the sentiments heard in Cameroon regarding the CPDM, and it stands in contrast with interviews conducted in Tanzania.

An Analysis of Sub-National Voting in Multiparty Kenya

The ethnic basis of voting in Kenya has been substantiated and explored quite thoroughly elsewhere, and by many accounts was a key factor during the electoral authoritarian period (Foeken and Dietz 2000, Ajulu 2002,

---

[50] John Opore (former KANU MP for Bonchari). Author Interview. Nairobi. (July 20, 2012).

[51] Moses Wetangula (former KANU MP for Sirisia). Author Interview. Nairobi. (July 17, 2012).

[52] Paul Muite (former Vice-Chair of FORD-K). Author Interview. Nairobi. (July 20, 2012).

Bratton and Kimenyi 2008). The ethnic orientation of voting in Kenya can be further substantiated through an analysis of district-level voting, while controlling for other factors. As in the other cases, district-level variables are regressed against the average KANU presidential and legislative vote share, and once again data availability drove some choices.[53] The one consistent measure of government provision was the percentage of homes with a mud floor. There is no measure of access to health facilities, which is a major good desired by African voters. Therefore, to account for multiple forms of government provision I also include a broader measure of the district-level poverty rate. This variable does correlate with both literacy and access to housing, but also potentially captures other factors like access to education, infrastructure, and health services.[54]

With regard to ethnicity, which is the basis of social incorporation, I utilize data on the ethnic composition of districts from the 1989 Kenyan census (Republic of Kenya 1994). While this is the most comprehensive data, the downside is that it assumed little demographic change in the 1990s. I consider the Kikuyu, Luo, and Kalenjin to be the most politically relevant ethnic groups, while remaining cognizant of the fact that these terms mask important internal variation. However, the test is whether these broader community signifiers can model KANU's district-level vote share while controlling for other factors. There are several other ethnic groups in Kenya that are politically relevant and mentioned in the secondary literature, but they must be consolidated in order to retain more statistical leverage. First, consistent with other work, I consider the Meru, Embu, Tharaka, and Nithi as "Kikuyu Allied" communities. Second, I lump together various communities that are considered "Swing Communities," meaning they were traditionally allied with Moi's KANU coalition but were not core supporters. These are the Kamba, Luhya, Kisii, and Mijikenda. Third, smaller ethnic groups like the Maasai, Samburu, Somali, and Turkana are consolidated as "Other." As before, the reference category remains the ethnically mixed district, which is the predominant district type and corresponds strongly with the mean KANU vote share.

The results in Table 6.3 substantiate these prior perspectives regarding the preponderance of ethnic voting in Kenya, but also highlight the

---

[53] The data on socioeconomic indicators and government provision comes from Republic of Kenya (2001), and IEA (2002).

[54] The correlation between the poverty rate and the percentage of homes with mud floors is 0.54. The same regression models were run without the poverty variable and with an additional measure of employment in the formal sector. Dropping the poverty variable does not significantly alter the results, and the coefficient on employment is insignificant.

TABLE 6.3. *Random effects multilevel regression of average KANU vote shares*

	(Model 1)	(Model 2)	(Model 3)	(Model 4)
	Presidential vote share	Presidential vote share	Legislative vote share	Legislative vote share
Social Incorporation Variables				
Kalenjin	27.24***	33.15***	25.91***	29.47***
	(6.09)	(5.13)	(5.24)	(4.98)
Kikuyu	−36.54***	−25.50***	−32.85***	−26.65***
	(9.91)	(4.99)	(7.12)	(4.85)
Kikuyu Ally	−28.61***	−14.37*	−24.61***	−15.99**
	(8.41)	(5.81)	(7.22)	(5.64)
Luo	−28.75**	−30.38***	−29.65***	−28.03***
	(8.90)	(5.05)	(8.57)	(4.90)
Other	2.21	−4.55	5.06	−1.29
	(5.86)	(4.03)	(4.99)	(3.92)
Swing Community	−12.73*	−9.15*	−7.81	−3.98
	(5.50)	(4.42)	(4.87)	(4.30)
KADU Won District (1963)	3.80	12.61***	3.19	7.43*
	(5.44)	(3.07)	(4.65)	(2.98)
Socioeconomic Variables				
Literacy Rate (1999)		−0.72***		−0.52***
		(0.16)		(0.16)
Government Provision Variables				
%Pop. with Earth Floor (1999)		−0.44**		−0.32*
		(0.14)		(0.14)
Poverty Rate (1999)		0.18		0.09
		(0.11)		(0.11)
Opposition Access Variables				
Log Population Density (1999)		−1.07		−0.57
		(1.68)		(1.63)
Average Voter Turnout		0.09		0.22
		(0.23)		(0.22)

(*continued*)

TABLE 6.3. *(continued)*

	(Model 1)	(Model 2)	(Model 3)	(Model 4)
	Presidential vote share	Presidential vote share	Legislative vote share	Legislative vote share
Average %KANU Incumbents		−0.05		0.04
		(0.06)		(0.06)
Constant	51.70***	120.88***	47.29***	88.20***
	(5.90)	(19.74)	(4.27)	(19.18)
Observations	65	65	65	65
Clusters	7	7	7	7
χ^2	50.46	108.5	56.97	95.93
Prob>χ^2	5.248	0	1.179	0

Notes: The dependent variable is %KANU presidential vote share in Models 1 and 2 and %KANU legislative vote share in Models 3 and 4. Standard errors are noted in parentheses. Only non-urban districts are included ***$p < 0.001$, **$p < 0.01$, *$p < 0.05$.

importance of other local factors. KANU's districts appear the most classically clientelistic from the three cases: they are less literate and more responsive to the extent of government provision. The effects of these variables are represented in the two subplots in Figure 6.6, which also reports 95 percent confidence intervals and keeps other variables at their mean. An increase in the literacy rate can significantly reduce KANU's vote shares by up to a striking 50 percent. On the other hand, districts increase their support for KANU presidents when they have more access to government services, in this case a lower percentage of homes with mud floors. Once again, the impact is quite substantive, and controlling for other factors reduces KANU's presidential vote share by nearly 25 percent. Interestingly, the variables that measure opposition exposure are insignificant. This is expected given the high degree of vulnerability that KANU found itself in, and the extent of elite defection prior to each election.

But, even when controlling for these confounding factors the role of ethnic identification cuts through. Homogenously Kalenjin districts register a 33 percent higher incumbent vote than in mixed districts. By contrast, Kikuyu and Luo districts provide KANU vote shares that are respectively 25 and 30 percent lower than in mixed districts. There is no consistent effect in districts with swing communities or other dominant ethnic groups, where motivations appear more mixed. To further probe this idea, I also controlled for the historic legacy of the KADU coalition,

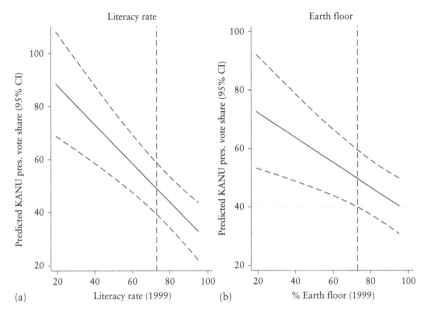

FIGURE 6.6. *Select predictors of KANU's district-level presidential vote shares*
Note: The dotted lines represent the 95 percent confidence interval.

which might capture not only differences in ethnic identity but variant perspectives toward historically controversial issues in Kenyan politics like federalism. The variable is meaningful, but fails to eliminate the statistical significance or importance of ethnic identity. Unlike in Cameroon, this pattern of ethnic voting is also consistent across presidential and legislative elections. This is again likely due to the fact that KANU remained more vulnerable between 1992 and 2002. In Kenya, legislative voters registered an opposition vote to KANU even when KANU nominated a local co-ethnic, since there was a greater likelihood that an opposition candidate could actually win.

Participant Perspectives on Social Incorporation in Kenya

The drastic consequences of narrow social incorporation were not lost on Moi. Between 1992 and 1997, KANU strived to retain the support of certain swing communities, while creating more homogenous districts in ethnically mixed areas. In 1991 and 1992, violent ethnic clashes in the mixed districts of the Rift Valley and the proclamation of exclusive "KANU zones" were widely perceived as instigated by incumbent KANU politicians. This violence led to the death of nearly 1,000 Kenyans and the displacement of approximately 250,000 people, mostly Kikuyu, Luo, and Luhya (Branch 2011, 199–215, Hornsby 2012, 490–2). In 1997, electoral boundaries were redrawn to create twenty-six new constituencies, largely along ethnic lines. Simultaneously, Moi reached out to swing community elites like Simeon Nyacahe (a Kisii) by reinstating him as a minister. Musalia Mudavadi's promotion as Finance Minister in 1993 was likewise viewed as an attempt to keep members of the Luhya community in the KANU fold (Hornsby 2012, 492–7, 586–612). Unlike in Cameroon, these attempts at realignment were not sustainable and did not form stable electoral majorities.

Opposition parties responded to Moi's coalition efforts by conforming to the same logic of ethnic politics. Despite attempts and aspirations to create broader-based national political parties, frequent opposition party splits were driven by personal ambition and even ethnic resentment within the individual parties. In particular, this refers to the gradual devolution of the initial FORD movement into FORD-K, FORD-A, and the NDP. One of the original "Young Turks" of early Kenyan opposition politics, Paul Muite, places the blame solidly on Luo resentment, stating: "Our intention was to create a national party. We wanted a party built on social democracy across Kenya. This was our vision, and it was a vision that was killed by [Luo] Raila Odinga."[55] Other elites interviewed referred to disagreements between Michael Wamalwa (a Luhya), Paul Muite (a Kikuyu), and Raila Odinga (a Luo) over the leadership of FORD. Ethnic identity became a key and deliberate lens through which to mobilize voters in a highly competitive and resource scarce environment. As Mukhisa Kituyi of FORD-K notes:

> You have limited resources and ask yourself should I spend across the country thinly or look for areas of maximal return. What informs current politics is that coalescing before elections, which cannot solve that dilemma.[56]

Ultimately, the logic of narrow social incorporation meant that KANU could not secure persistent electoral majorities, which came to a decisive turning point following the presidential transition of 2002. When Uhuru Kenyatta was selected as Daniel arap Moi's successor, this signaled a new redistributive commitment that raised latent ethnic resentments and fears.

---

[55] Paul Muite (former Vice-Chair of FORD-K). Author Interview. Nairobi. (July 20, 2012).
[56] Mukhisa Kituyi (former senior member of FORD-K). Author Interview. Nairobi. (July 18, 2012).

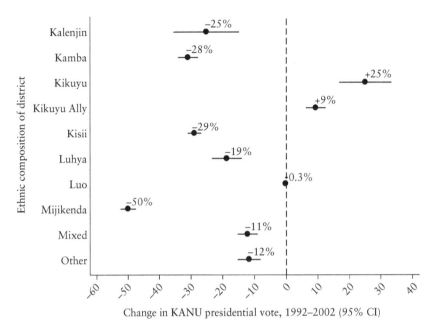

FIGURE 6.7. *Change in KANU's presidential vote between 1992 and 2002, by the ethnic composition of a district*
Note: Lines reflect 95 percent confidence intervals.

Unlike Biya, Moi did not have the same degree of centralized coercive and patronage tools, which translated into a significant defection of previously loyal KANU voters during the 2002 election. To capture this shift, Figure 6.7 plots the mean change in KANU presidential vote shares between 1992 and 2002, this time disaggregating "Swing Communities," into the relevant subgroups. While Uhuru Kenyatta predictably received 25 percent more of the Kikuyu vote, this was offset by a 25 percent reduction in the Kalenjin vote. However, the decisive shift was from the former swing communities of the Kisii, Kamba, and Mijikenda. Importantly, KANU lost nearly 50 percent of its support from the Mijikenda communities along the coast following years of unaddressed local violence and growing religious tension.[57] By 2002 a weakened ethnic alliance was no match for a unified opposition.

---

[57] The Mijikenda's dissatisfaction with KANU was evident earlier when local violence over land disputes along the coast was unaddressed by KANU. There was also evidence of religious tension between Arab Muslims and African Muslims. The opposition party *Shirikisho* drew much of the Mijikenda support away from KANU (Branch 2011, 222–7, Hornsby 2012, 602–3).

CONCLUSION

This chapter has presented a variety of data to validate the consequences of ruling party credibility on patterns of voter mobilization, and by extension electoral competition. Through spatial representations, within-case statistical analysis, and participant interviews I have demonstrated that credible ruling parties bring with them substantial real estate and wider historic social coalitions that translate into persistently high vote shares across large areas of the country. In Tanzania, the ruling party could rely on countrywide mobilization, and particularly the strong support of districts that were the primary beneficiaries of the regime's wider redistributive policies under single-party rule. On the other hand, when parties lacked those capacities, as in Cameroon and Kenya, voter support had to be manufactured by other means. In the context of narrow social incorporation in Africa, this meant the logic of alliances and ethnic party building, which permeated both the regime and the opposition.

A key unanswered question materializes from the discussion over the past two chapters: why was Biya more successful where Moi was not? While both Cameroon and Kenya started their electoral authoritarian experience in fairly similar dire straits, they evolved quite differently and only in Cameroon was electoral hegemony ultimately established via repression. The chapter has suggested that it was not differences in the party itself, but in the divergent ability of each regime to coopt elites and bring leaders of ethnic communities back into a ruling coalition. Biya could more easily utilize his power of appointment, and controlled significantly more state resources. Likewise, Biya could exert coercion more persistently and with fewer consequences. As the regime in Cameroon became more secure, posturing against the CPDM made less and less sense. In the next chapter I turn to the role of international actors in facilitating this process, and specifically show how differences in international patronage can have a direct impact on electoral competition.

7

The Electoral Consequences of International Patronage

I would have infinitely preferred evolution with Moi rather than revolution against him ... In some ways it seemed to me like I had no choice.
—Amb. Smith Hempstone, Rogue Ambassador (1997)

You know the French are locked in a battle, a cultural battle with the Anglo-Saxons. And they see the rise of an Anglo-Saxon, English-speaking president in Cameroon and say it is a challenge to French culture. And so they have done everything to ensure that the leadership of Cameroon remains French.
—Tazoacha Asonganyi, Former Secretary General, SDF
(Author Interview)

In this chapter I turn to the question of why repression produces electoral hegemony in some cases but not in others. As noted in previous chapters, the Kenyan African National Union (KANU) regime in Kenya was kept on its metaphoric electoral toes. Despite persistent violence and electoral fraud, this did not translate into dominating electoral victories. Kenya muddled through as a repressive non-hegemony, and eventually lost power in 2002. By contrast, electoral processes in Cameroon were similarly repressive, but over time this translated into significant electoral hegemony. By the 2013 election, the opposition in Cameroon was fairly isolated, and essentially confined to the internally divided Social Democratic Front (SDF) party. My argument is that these differences in competition can be linked to the role of international actors and their ability to exacerbate or ameliorate challenges of electoral authoritarian contestation without credible ruling parties. This is not an argument that claims that international actors act consistently, or that their endeavors necessarily lead to regime change (Donno 2013a). Rather, I claim that in certain circumstances international actors can have a marginal effect on electoral competition.

This is also an argument that pushes back on structural accounts of international behavior. In Levitsky and Way's study of competitive authoritarianism, an international actor's leverage is determined by a target country's political and economic vulnerabilities, as well as the presence or absence of readily apparent conflicting foreign policy goals (2010). For instance, an international actor has more leverage when a target country is aid dependent, but less leverage when there are conflicting foreign policy goals. This can muddle the picture since it conflates the ability and willingness of actors to intervene. For instance, Cameroon was in fact not immune to external pressure, but instead was frequently shielded from it by its patron, France. Likewise, both the ability and willingness of external actors to intervene is not static, but dynamic and evolves in tangent with changing notions of what the national interest is and what policies are most efficacious. Most clearly, the extent of American involvement in Kenya was not derivative entirely from their position of strength, but was also an actor-driven process and therefore contingent.

The approach of this chapter is to focus on how international patronage influences three major factors that shape electoral competition. First, I focus on the use of aid conditionality to reduce the size of the public sector and the availability of patronage appointments (van de Walle 2001). Within the context of African electoral authoritarianism the use of the state to sustain alliances and coopt opponents is important. While the record of donor-induced structural adjustment is mixed, it is not without influence, and there are differences across the cases. Second, I examine how international actors limited a regime's coercive capacity. Since the menu of manipulation is wide I look at how international actors responded to state violence, backed domestic processes of political reform, and contributed to local election observation capacities. Once again, while these commitments are not always consistent or equally effective, they vary across cases and carry some impact. Third, I analyze the consequences of diplomacy in terms of the extent of engagement with opposition parties and senior-level pressure leveled against regime elites.

The chapter begins by comparing all three cases along some broader measures of regime sensitivity, international patronage, and outcomes. This is done primarily to provide a baseline comparison that sets some of the similarities and differences across the cases in context. All three regimes began the multiparty period with significant degrees of aid dependency and sensitivity to international pressure, but experienced very different levels of direct democracy assistance, aid conditionality, and election observation. Consequently, there were further differences in the privatization of state-owned enterprises, the size of government, and the competitiveness of electoral processes. This comparison also highlights that international patronage is not as clear a factor in the case of Tanzania, where despite fairly status quo patronage the structure of competition has remained constant. The root of Tanzania's tolerant hegemony is its ruling party, not international patronage.

The main focus of the chapter is therefore the comparison of Kenya and Cameroon – the two cases where the absence of credible ruling parties made international patronage more consequential. To construct causal narratives that trace both the decisions of international actors to intervene or not and the specific impact on regimes, I draw from a diverse set of sources. In addition to secondary historical sources, I consulted memoirs and conducted in-depth interviews with various political elites who could comment from experience on the impact of international patronage. These interviews once again included several opposition figures who were at the frontline of electoral contestation and in direct contact with external actors. They also include key regime insiders who oversaw negotiations with donors and foreign embassies. Another major source of information comes from previously classified embassy documents from Cameroon, which provide credible and quite revealing insider information regarding American and French democracy promotion efforts. To clarify, this chapter is limited to the role of major international actors like the United States, France, and Great Britain.

COMPARING PATTERNS OF INTERNATIONAL PATRONAGE

Tanzania, Cameroon, and Kenya entered the multiparty era at moments of exceptional vulnerability, and remained quite sensitive to donor pressure throughout most of the electoral authoritarian period. As noted in Figure 7.1, Official Development Assistance (ODA) as a percentage of GDP varied across the three cases, but even in instances like Cameroon it is not meaningless and remained approximately 5 percent throughout its electoral authoritarian history. Likewise, the early 1990s were moments of immense vulnerability due to the severe regional economic downturn and move toward structural adjustment and austerity. In each case regimes entered into negotiations with international lenders and began significant reform of their economies and public sectors. One of

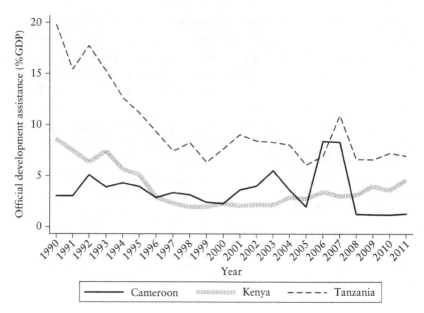

FIGURE 7.1. *Official Development Assistance (ODA) as percent of GDP in Cameroon, Kenya, and Tanzania (1990–2011)*
Source: World Bank Development Indicators (Various)

the reasons Cameroon was less aid dependent was its limited oil sector. But, while in 1990 oil revenues in Cameroon were approximately 30 percent of the country's export revenue, they constituted just 6 percent of the country's GDP. During the early 1990s oil revenues took a serious blow, and only surged briefly at the tail end of the decade and in the late 2000s to 11 percent of GDP.[1] Therefore, Cameroon could not bank on consistent alternative sources of finance, and needed international assistance to sustain its government.

Despite these similar sensitivities to external pressure, the range of tools that international actors employed differed. Figure 7.2 looks at patterns of democracy aid spending between 1990 and 2010.[2] While data is unavailable for Cameroon in the 1990s (USAID shut down their offices there in 1994), the comparative dearth of democracy programming is evident. A similar measure presented in Table 7.1 provides a sense of international

---

[1] For comparison, during the same period oil revenue was 30–40 percent of Gabon's GDP.
[2] This includes the following categories of aid: democratic participation and civil society, elections, human rights, legislatures and political parties, strengthening civil society, media and free flow of information, support to national NGOs (Tierney et al. 2011).

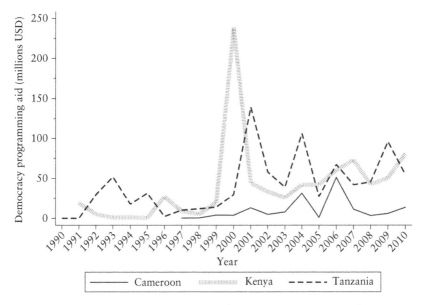

FIGURE 7.2. *Democracy programming aid in Cameroon, Kenya, and Tanzania (1990–2010)*
Source: Tierney et al. (2011)

and domestic election observation efforts. Once again, there is much less investment in Cameroon than in Kenya or Tanzania. In addition, the extent of election observation in Kenya is remarkable, and stands out even in broader continental perspective. As discussed later, the exponential growth of domestic election observation in Kenya is directly linked to the efforts of external donors, who funded, trained, and helped coordinate activities between groups. Note that approximately 210 international observers monitored the 2010 election in Tanzania, but many of these were deployed to Zanzibar in response to election violence in 2005.

Differences in international patronage are also apparent with regard to the use of bilateral and multilateral aid conditionality. Figure 7.3 compares patterns of total bilateral aid and concessional International Monetary Fund (IMF) lending in constant $US. In Kenya there was a steady decline in bilateral aid right up to the end of the electoral authoritarian period in 2002. There was a similar drop during this period in Cameroon and Tanzania, but importantly also a temporary spike in the early 1990s. In Cameroon, this was the result of an influx of important French bilateral aid that in many ways rescued the Biya regime from financial ruin. Importantly, bilateral aid in Cameroon rose significantly

TABLE 7.1. *Election observation in Cameroon, Kenya, and Tanzania*
(1992–2011)

Country	Election year	#International observers	Observer organizations	#Domestic observers
Cameroon	1992	19	NDI	N/A
Cameroon	1997	30	CW, IFES, OIF	600
Cameroon	2002	11	OIF	N/A
Cameroon	2004	31	CW, OIF	1,400
Cameroon	2007	22	U.S. Embassy	1,900
Cameroon	2011	10	CW, OIF	800
Kenya	1992	101	CW, IRI, NDI	438
Kenya	1997	N/A	NDI	28,000
Kenya	2002	204	CC, CW, EP, EU	20,000
Tanzania	1995	74	CW, IFES	N/A
Tanzania	2000	76	IFES, SADC	5,000
Tanzania	2005	40 (Mainland) 30 (Zanzibar)	SADC) (Mainland) NDI (Zanzibar) EISA (Zanzibar)	N/A
Tanzania	2010	230	CW, EU, EAC, SADC	7,000

Abbreviations: CC = Carter Center; CW = Commonwealth Secretariat; EAC = East
African Community; EISA = Electoral Institute for Sustainable Democracy in Africa; EP =
European Parliament; EU = European Union; IFES = International Foundation for
Election Systems; IRI = International Republican Institute; NDI = National Democratic
Institute; OIF = Organisation Internationale de la Francophonie; SADC = South African
Development Community.
Source: (Kelley 2012a).
For missing values the following available observation reports were consulted: Bakary
and Palmer (1997), OIF (1997, 2002, 2004, 2011), Commonwealth Secretariat (2010,
2011), EAC (2010), EISA (2005), EU (2010), NDI (2005), and SADC (2010).

in the 2000s despite no real significant economic or political reform.
Looking at international lending in Kenya, the period between 1994 and
2002 is categorized by net disbursements from Kenya *back* to the IMF,
meaning that Kenya paid more in interest payments on previous loans
than it received in new support. This coincided with deliberate aid conditionality on the part of the IMF. There was not a commensurate effort
to condition multilateral aid in Cameroon or Tanzania. In Cameroon, net
disbursements were zero during the early 1990s due to poor implementation of structural adjustment programs, but it successfully negotiated a
number of new aid packages in the following years. Once again, this was
despite limited progress in reforming the public sector.

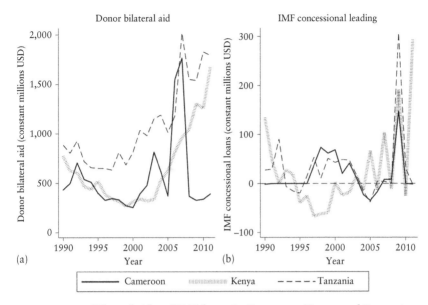

FIGURE 7.3. *Bilateral aid and IMF loans in Cameroon, Kenya, and Tanzania*
(1990–2010)
Source: World Bank (2016)

These different patterns of international patronage also had an impact on some broader measures of a regime's capacity to use clientelism. Figure 7.4 looks at the privatization of State Owned Enterprises (SOEs), and changes to the size of government cabinets.[3] Privatization took a much larger toll on Kenya's public sector than in either Tanzania or Cameroon. By 2000, nearly 40 percent of SOEs in Kenya were no longer under full government control. By contrast, Cameroon privatized less than 10 percent of its SOEs, and Tanzania less than 30 percent. Likewise, cabinet sizes in Kenya and Tanzania have shrunk or remained constant since the beginning of multipartyism, while in Cameroon it has expanded exponentially. By 2010, Cameroon had the largest cabinet on the Africa continent, with an array of ministers, presidential delegates, and secretaries of state. This left Cameroon in a much more privileged position to manage its ruling coalition and navigate the ethnic logic of alliance building.

Finally, there are also measurable differences in the competitiveness of electoral processes. Figure 7.5 depicts the V-DEM indexes for physical

---

[3] Cabinet size is also used in other work as a proxy for patronage capacity in African regimes (van de Walle 2001, Arriola 2012).

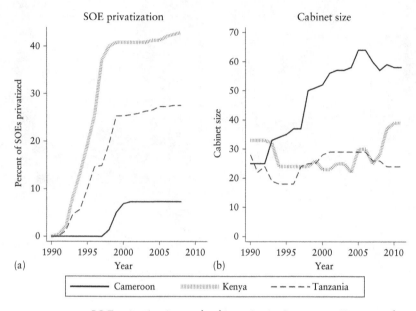

FIGURE 7.4. *SOE privatization and cabinet size in Cameroon, Kenya, and Tanzania (1990–2010)*
Source: World Bank (2009), Africa South of the Sahara (Various)

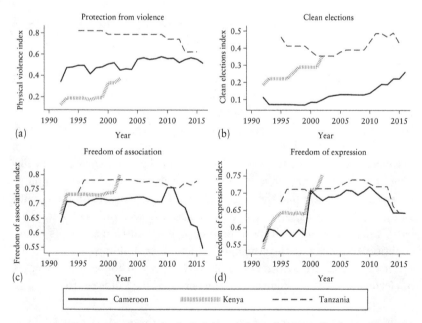

FIGURE 7.5. *Protection from physical violence, clean elections, freedom of association, and freedom of expression in Cameroon, Kenya, and Tanzania (1990–2015)*
Source: Coppedge et al. (2017)

violence, clean elections, freedom of association, and freedom of expression. Higher index scores reflect better protections and more tolerant electoral conditions. Tanzania's consistently more open electoral process is evident, with the exception of some negative change after 2010 that reflects conditions on Zanzibar. On the other hand, the contrast between Cameroon and Kenya stands out. In Cameroon there have been negligible improvements in electoral conditions. The only substantial change is in the freedom of expression. By contrast, in Kenya most indicators improved across the electoral authoritarian period, and remained above the levels measured in Cameroon. The one exception is the use of physical violence, which did improve prior to the 2002 election, but remained comparatively higher than in Cameroon or Tanzania. These changes in Kenya can be traced back to the international community's stronger efforts at democracy assistance and political reform.

The following sections provide a more detailed narrative of the relationship between international patronage and electoral authoritarian outcomes. From this brief comparison it is clear that different patterns of patronage emerged despite similar sensitivities, and that these differences likely had an impact on a regime's capacity to distribute patronage and manipulate the electoral process. The differences are starkest between Kenya and Cameroon, but the data also demonstrates that international actors were less influential in determining the broader parameters of electoral competition in Tanzania. In many ways Tanzania was the target of much stronger democratic patronage than Cameroon, with higher levels of democracy assistance and election observation. Likewise, while aid conditionality was not especially strong or consistent, there were meaningful declines in public sector spending. Yet, the story from Tanzania is one of consistent competition in comparatively more open elections with relative ease. Therefore, the following discussion focuses specifically on the impact of democratic patronage in Kenya and autocratic patronage in Cameroon.

DEMOCRATIC PATRONAGE AND THE SOURCES OF REPRESSIVE NON-HEGEMONY

Between 1992 and 2002 Kenya was the target of a potent combination of conditionality, democracy assistance, and diplomacy. Kenya held a comparatively more visible standing in the West due to its preeminence as the capital of British East Africa, the substantial British settler community, and the country's important tourism sector. Initially, the premise of strong international engagement was not a real priority in many Western governments. The British stressed continued stable relations with Kenya, and in 1991 the British Ambassador Sir John Johnson prepared to retire and become Moi's personal advisor. Similarly, the American position set out by the George H. W. Bush White House emphasized increased business investment in Kenya, not democracy promotion. However, there were also no obvious material constraints on international action or major conflicting foreign policy goals. Kenya relied heavily on foreign sources of finance, and it was only after the 1994 Rwandan Genocide and the 1998 embassy bombings in Dar es Salaam and Nairobi that regional security and the fight against international terrorism took central stage in Western circles.

Yet, in November 1991 the Paris Club suspended $350 million in financial assistance, which is often cited as a factor that aided the transition to multipartyism (Brown 2001, 731). What sparked this change is undoubtedly the violence of the Moi regime, but many observers note the direct influence of US Ambassador Smith Hempstone. Ambassador Hempstone had a famously dour relationship with Moi. In May 1990, after Hempstone delivered what he considered a fairly benign speech to the Kenyan Rotary Club, he was vehemently attacked in the Kenyan state-owned media for suggesting that the United States could condition aid to support democracy and human rights. One month later the Assistant Secretary of State for African Affairs Henry Cohen was dispatched to Nairobi to, per Hempstone, "smooth his [Moi's] ruffled feathers" and reset the relationship (Hempstone 1997, 94). Despite this, Hempstone remained a singular outspoken critic of Moi and KANU, particularly following the violent government reaction to the *saba saba* protest of July 1990. As Hempstone writes: "destabilization was a *possible* consequence of reform. But it was the *probable* outcome of trying to prop up the inequitable status quo, as the British were trying to do" (Hempstone 1997, 169).

In many ways US policy toward reform in Kenya appeared to follow Hempstone's lead. During a home-visit in October 1991, Hempstone discovered to his surprise that he was unable to meet with either President Bush or Secretary of State James Baker. Hempstone interpreted this as a personal slight and a direct consequence of his obstinacy toward Moi. Nonetheless, one month later Moi was dramatically uninvited from the opening of the second US–East African Trade Fair in Nairobi. Moi and other KANU elites were apoplectic and demanded Hempstone's recall. This forced the White House to make a critical decision on whether to back their sitting ambassador or try and return to more cordial relations with the KANU regime. Ultimately the White House issued a statement in support of Hempstone, and shortly thereafter also endorsed aid conditionality. It is not clear what drove this change in US policy, but Hempstone draws a direct link to his personal efforts with individual members of Congress and his strong public stance against Moi.

Other embassies shortly followed suit, and this began a prolonged, if inconsistent, period of democratic patronage. Some scholars like Stephen Brown argue that international donors actually helped keep Moi in power by endorsing flawed electoral processes, backtracking on aid conditionality, and emphasizing stability and economic reform over political transformation (Brown 2001). Others, such as Joel Barkan, think that international donors had "limited but significant leverage" that ultimately facilitated a change of power in Kenya (2004). The debate can be resolved by focusing on marginal changes in the competitive environment rather than transformation. Elections in 1992 and 1997 were severely flawed and accompanied by horrifying ethnic violence. However, international actors were able to extract some limited legal concessions, and helped put into place one of the most robust domestic election observation efforts on the continent. Similarly, donor-induced privatization was imperfect but went farther than in most African countries. Opposition actors in Kenya benefitted from active diplomacy at key moments, and there was high-level US pressure on Moi to abide by term limits. While donors could not fully constrain the regime, especially as it came to violence, they did make it more difficult for Moi to use all the tools at his disposal to rebuild electoral support. By the 2002 election and Moi's succession, KANU had even fewer cards left in its deck to coerce and coopt opponents.

Limiting Manipulation in Kenya: Political Reform and Election Observation

The Kenyan regime enjoyed some exceptional legal advantages that were assembled during the single-party era. Prior to the 1992 election there were numerous laws that impacted the opposition's ability to assemble, speak, and contest elections. For instance, the Public Orders Act allowed presidentially appointed District Commissioners to license public meetings. The Chief's Authority Act let local chiefs implement this law with little oversight or impunity. The Preservation of Public Security Act let the government indefinitely detain individuals, restrict travel, and censor the media on the shallowest of suspicions. Other measures like the Outlying District Act and the Special District Act gave the government the ability to restrict travel to what it deemed security sensitive areas, while the Vagrancy Act gave the police strong authority to search and seize property.

Importantly, the constitution also gave the president immense powers of appointment, including to the electoral commission (Ndegwa 1998).[4]

Donors were unable to make headway on constitutional reform prior to the 1992 election, and this directly impacted KANU's ability to compete. Reliable elections observers concluded that the president's control over the civil administration was likely utilized to commit substantial fraud (IRI 1993, NDI 1993). Other laws gave the regime the ability to exclude and censor opposition actors by regulating their freedom of association, movement, and expression. For example, in 1992 twenty-one meeting permits were denied by the administration, all for opposition party rallies. Several opposition members were placed under house arrest or had private meetings dispersed by the administrative police. Likewise, the creation of "KANU Zones" in North Eastern Province and parts of the Rift Valley further limited opposition movement. While Kenya has historically had a fairly active press, the regime sued several newspapers and closed down some radio stations. The regime also regulated civic education programs and some artistic expression it deemed too controversial (Ndegwa 1998).

These draconian provisions were the central targets of much opposition activity after the 1992 election. In mid-1997 the National Convention Executive Council (NCEC) was formed and brought together several civil society groups, church organizations, and political opposition to pressure the government into constitutional reform prior to the next election. The NCEC threatened to boycott the election if no meaningful progress was made. The government's response was remarkably violent, most infamously when it dispersed an opposition protest on the seventh anniversary of the original *saba saba* protests. This left over twenty people dead and scores injured. Many opposition figures, as in 1992, reported severe ill treatment and torture in Kenyan prisons. This subsequently led to a major rift between the NCEC's political support and its civil society component. Likewise, it left donors in a quandary over how to proceed, and made them concerned that violence might get out of hand.

Donors supported an effort to get parties to the negotiating table as quickly as possible, even if it meant that constitutional reform might not be comprehensive or ready in time for the 1997 election. In reaction to the government violence unleashed during the second *saba saba* protests,

---

[4] Ndegwa provides a superb survey of more of these constitutional provisions. He also notes that the electoral system required a presidential candidate win 25 percent of the vote in Kenya's eight provinces and established single-member plurality districts, which were advantageous to KANU (1998).

the United States pressured the IMF to suspend structural adjustment disbursements. This led to an immediate fall in the value of the Kenyan shilling and a quick rise in interest rates. When Moi remained defiant, other lenders cut their bilateral aid by some $400 million. Simultaneously, donors threatened to cut funding to the NCEC if they did not agree to come to the negotiating table (Brown 2001, 733). In August 1997, a new government-sponsored reform initiative called the Inter-Parties Parliamentary Group (IPPG) was formed (Hornsby 2012, 539–617). The IPPG was controversial and seen by some as a move to coopt the constitutional reform process.[5] However, it brought together moderate members of the regime and opposition, and compelled reluctant KANU hardliners to accede to a new process of constitutional reform (Hornsby 2012, 599).

The IPPG process set in motion a series of noteworthy piecemeal reforms. First, Constitution Amendment Bill No. 10 expanded the electoral commission from 11 to 21 members, and allowed the opposition to appoint some members. An omnibus bill repealed the controversial Preservation of Public Security Act, the Outlying Districts Act, the Vagrancy Act, and the Special District Act. The Chief's Authority Act was amended so that chiefs could no longer operate without writs of authority. The Public Orders Act was amended so that parties needed to only notify District Commissioners of public rallies, and removed licensing requirements from nonpolitical gatherings. Other laws like the Broadcasting Act were changed to allow more opposition airtime, and the Societies Act was altered so that the Registrar of Political Parties had to reply to requests within 120 days. Finally, the IPPG set out a longer-term constitutional review process through the Constitution of Kenya Review Commission Act (CKRC) (Ndegwa 1998, Ajulu 2001).

Some have criticized these reforms as not bold enough, and fault international donors for pressuring parties into joining the faulty IPPG process (Brown 2001). Indeed, most of the reforms were not in place prior to the 1997 election, and the playing field remained tilted toward the regime. Nonetheless, these changes limited the regime's maneuverability. For instance, the removal of the Public Orders Act meant that during the 1997 and 2002 election there were only a handful of incidents where District Commissioners denied meeting permits to opposition parties (IED 1998, 2003). As part of the CKRC, an impressive civic education campaign was launched prior to the 2002 election. The expanded Kenyan Election Commission, while not truly independent, was also seen

---

[5] Maina Kiai (Civil Society Activist). Author Interview. Nairobi. (July 13, 2012).

as far more credible during the 2002 election (IED 2003). Importantly, the prospect of future constitutional reform made it easier for opposition parties to negotiate between themselves. As Stephen Ndegwa notes, "had the constitutional process not been going on at the time ... it is virtually inconceivable that any opposition leader would have agreed to give up his or her slim chance at the imperial presidency" (2003, 154).

A second way international donors influenced the Kenyan regime's manipulative capacity was through a massive effort to improve the domestic capacity to manage and observe elections. Donor money funded much of the 1992 election. The United States paid for larger and more secure ballot boxes, trained polling agents, and provided actual ballots and indelible ink (Hornsby 2012, 510). Donors also supported the National Election Monitoring Unit (NEMU), a domestic observation coordination organ that trained over 5,000 observers.[6] In addition to NEMU, the 1992 election was observed by several foreign groups. Importantly, this did not prevent fraud but helped set a precedent.[7] According to the IRI observation report, up to three million Kenyans might have been disenfranchised due to registration issues (IRI 1993). According to calculations made by Charles Hornsby, result falsification impacted at least fifty seats, and Moi's vote share was inflated by approximately 250,000 votes. In some constituencies voters were deemed illiterate and a KANU agent would write their preferences down instead. In other constituencies, polling stations were actually taken over by KANU agents and observation teams were refused entry (IRI 1993, Hornsby 2012, 534–5).

However, by the end of the decade Kenya had the highest concentration of election observers on the continent, the vast majority of which were domestic. The NEMU was converted into the Institute for Education in Democracy, which had a much broader commitment to democratic and civil education in addition to election preparation and observation. The Kenyan Human Rights Council was likewise funded nearly entirely by Western donors. During the 1997 election there were approximately 28,000 domestic observers, nearly four times the amount in 1992 (Foeken and Dietz 2000). On the other hand, international election observation coalesced into the Donors for Development and Democracy Group, but

---

[6] Other domestic observation groups included the Bureau for Education, Research, and Monitoring, the National Council of Women of Kenya, and the National Committee for the Status of Women in Kenya.

[7] KANU denied entry to the National Democratic Institute, which only observed election preparations, the Carter Center, and a German observation group (Foeken and Dietz 2000).

as Stephen Brown notes, it deliberately withheld criticism of clear violations of the electoral process in order to maintain stable relations with
the Moi regime (2001). Yet, in 2002 domestic observation expanded yet
again with donor assistance. The Kenyan Domestic Observation Program
was created and made it possible to monitor every constituency in Kenya
and to finally conduct a parallel vote count (Hornsby 2012, 695). While
there were flaws in all of these elections, observations of fraud were
considerably lower in 2002 than in 1997 or 1992 (Carter Center 2003,
Commonwealth 2003, EU 2003, IED 2003).

These moderate improvements in the playing field and electoral process limited KANU's maneuverability, but are also overshadowed by
the regime's ability to use large amounts of violence. Between April and
May of 1992 armed groups, mainly in mixed ethnic areas bordering the
Kalenjin homelands, raided villages with the implicit aim of creating
more ethnically homogenous districts that would benefit KANU. KANU
elites funded these groups, which killed or displaced thousands of people (Throup and Hornsby 1998). A similar pattern emerged prior to the
1997 election; however, this time the violence was mostly confined to ethnically mixed Coastal areas. Likewise, in 1997 the government's response
to opposition protests were brutal, and between April and August the
General Service Unit reportedly killed over one hundred people (Ajulu
2001). Horrific stories of detention and torture in Kenyan jails were also
pervasive in the 1992 and 1997 elections (HRW 2002). However, by
2002 such political violence was largely absent, termed by some as the
"dog that did not bark in the night" (Brown 2004).

While international donors did respond to state violence in 1997 by
rescinding aid, they had more difficulty confronting the use of ethnic conflict for electoral gain. As Susanne Mueller notes, under Moi there was
a deliberate and gradual devolution of violence to numerous local youth
gangs and militias. Targeting these groups for sanction and linking them
to specific political backers is quite difficult (2011). By 2002, many of the
individuals who could mobilize these violent groups had defected to the
opposition following KANU's succession crisis (Brown 2004). Moreover,
such stark use of violence was in some sense derivative of the weak position KANU found itself in at the transition to elections, and was also
counterproductive. Ethnic violence might have secured some additional
seats for KANU in 1992 and 1997, but it worsened KANU's relationship with elites and voters from non-Kalenjin areas. Consequently, violence helped KANU survive elections but did not improve its competitive
position.

Limiting State Patronage in Kenya: Critical Public Sector Reform

Congruent with these efforts to restrict coercive capacity, Kenya was subject to donor pressure to restructure its economy and public sector. In 1987, Kenya negotiated an Enhanced Structural Adjustment Fund with the IMF, but had skirted the most significant structural reforms. At the time, Kenya had one of the largest public sectors in Africa with a sizeable civil service, over 200 SOEs that accounted for nearly 10 percent of GDP, and a record of poor public spending management. After the Paris Club withheld aid in November 1991, the Kenyan government made some gestures to lenders, for instance, by identifying some 130 SOEs for privatization, removing price controls on select commodities, and liberalizing its exchange rates. But, implementation of more significant reforms, and particularly privatization efforts, did not materialize.[8] After the 1992 election, Moi idly threatened that Kenya would abandon structural adjustment, but by November 1993 he was drawn back to the negotiating table. Despite no real progress on economic reform, Kenya secured a $850 million loan, $170 million in budget support, and some restructuring of approximately $700 million of its current debt (Hornsby 2012, 558–61).[9]

Between 1994 and 1997 there was continued back and forth between the Kenyan government and international lenders, but ultimately donor pressure forced a significant reduction in the size of the public sector.[10] This contributed to what Charles Hornsby has called the "de-patrimonialisation of the Kenyan economy" (Hornsby 2012, 629). By 1997, the Kenyan government had divested from over one hundred SOEs and reduced the civil service by approximately 33,000 people. The

---

[8] By late 1991 Kenya had privatized less than 10 percent of its SOEs. While it reduced the amount it spent on public wages, the civil services actually grew by 5 percent. Kenya's financial system was comparatively more liberalized than in other African states, with over twenty private banks. But, the Kenyan state maintained a majority stake in four banks and a minority stake in two banks. By late 1991 it had divested approximately 20 percent of the Kenyan Commercial Bank and removed controls over deposit and loan interest rates (IBRD 1994). For more on the Kenyan banking system see Arriola (2012).

[9] When negotiations with international lenders stalled in March 1993, the Kenyan shilling went into free fall and the Finance Minister Musalia Mudavadi was forced to restore price and foreign exchange controls and sell millions in treasury notes to cover the budget gap. This forced Kenya to acquiesce to some of the World Bank's demands and helped restore $85 million of aid in April.

[10] Part of the reason there was such vacillation after 1992 is that donor countries disagreed over the utility of aid conditionality. The United States, the Netherlands, and the Scandinavian countries were the most critical of Moi. However, Britain, Germany, and Japan at times used their leverage in multilateral donor institutions to remove political conditionality. The French and Italian were more ambiguous (Brown 2001).

government also stiffened fiduciary requirements on banks, reformed the financial management of some of its public utilities, and relaxed more price controls – particularly on the crucial maize industry that was a strong component of the Rift Valley's economy. This sent ripples throughout the KANU elite, and led to deep resentments and a sense of panic from those who were deeply entrenched in the public sector. As then Finance Minister Musalia Mudavadi recalled, this was a shock to KANU and fueled defection prior to the 1997 election:

> I presided over the most aggressive structural adjustment that could have possibly happened. I literally liberalized the economy, privatized parastatals, freed the exchange rate, and changed banking policies. It was necessary to do that because there were so many people who were married to the former regime and had a lot of political influence those days. So liberalization was like taking away what they knew how to deal with ... They were finding it difficult to operate in a liberalized environment.[11]

This is not meant to imply that public sector reform was comprehensive, only that it weakened KANU's grip on elites accustomed to state spoils. Indeed, Moi was able to continue and skirt many of the major changes lenders demanded without always losing access to international cash. In November 1994, the Paris Club donors committed another $800 million in aid and $200 million in budget support, but by late 1995 relations soured once again when the IMF suspended $90 million in Enhanced Structural Adjustment Facility (ESAF) payments after delays in the privatization program. Yet, by April 1996 there were again new pledges of bilateral aid, a new ESAF worth $216 million, and a new $127 million World Bank loan. This pledge was based on the promise that Kenya would restructure its National Social Security Fund, strengthen controls on public spending, further reduce and reform the civil service, better manage public utilities, and divest from some major SOEs like the Kenya Petroleum Refineries, Kenya Posts and Telecommunications, the National Bank of Kenya, and the Kenyan Commercial Bank (IMF 1996).[12] By October 1996, this new ESAF was also rescinded due to the slow pace of reform, and again surprisingly renewed in April 1997. Shortly thereafter all aid, including the remainder of the ESAF, was lost following the government's violent reaction to the second *saba saba* protests.

---

[11] Musalia Mudavadi (Former Finance Minister of Kenya). Author Interview. Nairobi. (July 25, 2012).

[12] There was also evidence that many SOEs were sold to KANU insiders and Moi himself at below market prices (Hornsby 2012, 566).

After the 1997 election the pace of both reform and aid subsided. This was despite high hopes in lending institutions that a new Kenyan reform team led by once-Moi opponent Richard Leaky could deliver tangible change. Indeed, by 1999 several SOE presidents were fired and slapped with corruption charges. In July 2000, Leakey successfully negotiated a new Poverty Reduction and Growth Facility (PRGF) worth over $200 million, and restructured $300 million of debt with the Paris Club. The PRGF promised some of the most significant cuts in the public sector since the 1994–6 period, and once again sent shockwaves throughout the KANU elite. Many figures took to the media and criticized the deal as "neo-colonial." Unsurprisingly, once again not all the reforms were implemented and the PRGF was reneged in December 2000. Leakey resigned and no IMF aid was provided again until after the 2002 election. Therefore, by the 2002 election KANU found itself in control of far less financial instruments to maintain a ruling coalition, and in more severe economic crisis due to the absence of steady bilateral and multilateral aid (Hornsby 2012, 629–49).

The Impact of Diplomatic Engagement: Term Limits and Empowered Oppositions

Democratic patronage also entailed high-level diplomatic engagement with the Kenyan opposition, and government actors also shaped the competitive environment. Smith Hempstone's early interaction with the "Young Turks" of the Kenyan opposition stands out as particularly unique in regional perspective. Hempstone was personally responsible for helping human rights lawyer Gibson Kuria gain asylum in the United States in July 1990. Hempstone claims that he actually escorted Kuria to the airport to avoid a possible assassination attempt (1997, 102–12). In November 1991, Hempstone housed Martin Shikuku in his public affairs counselor's home after a wave of arrests had swept up most of the opposition leadership. Later that month, Hempstone hosted a lunch with Deputy Assistant Secretary of State for African Affairs Bob Houdek and five members of the Kenyan opposition (Hempstone 1997, 250–6). It was also reported that British officials took Hempstone's lead and directly engaged with opposition leaders.[13] Many in the opposition recall a sense

---

[13] Peter Anyang N'yong'o (Foundational FORD Member). Author Interview. Nairobi. (August 1, 2012).

of personal debt to Hempstone (Brown 2001). Former KANU MP Julia Ojiambo summarizes this sentiment:

We needed a relentless fight. It was that feeling of confidence because there was an eye somewhere that would question what would happen if it did. Hempstone encouraged that eye. There was the impression that the international community was watching what was happening.[14]

Direct diplomatic engagement also had an impact on opposition decision making, particularly during the 1992 election. First, in July 1992 FORD and the DP threatened to boycott the election over the faulty voter registration. Opposition actors directly cite pressure from Ambassador Hempstone as a crucial factor that led them to renege on that commitment. Second, in December 1992, a week prior to the polls, the major opposition parties once again threatened to boycott the election and Hempstone intervened. Third, after the election, donors convinced opposition parties to take their seats in parliament. Donor insistence that opposition parties participate in a highly flawed electoral process for the sake of regional stability was controversial, and even gave Hempstone second thoughts. The argument is that stronger and clearer donor pressure might have leveled the playing field (Brown 2001). But, this views the impact of donors through the lens of democratization, rather than how they shape the competitive environment. One must consider the plausible counterfactual that if opposition parties had boycotted the foundational election – as they did in Cameroon – the regime would have won more seats and held more bargaining chips, particularly during the IPPG process. By contesting an unfair election, opposition parties prevented KANU from winning a decisive majority and establishing hegemony.

After Hempstone's tenure ended high-level diplomatic engagement ebbed and flowed. During the Clinton Administration, US Ambassador Aurelia Brazeal was instructed to reduce tensions with Moi and focus on regional stability and economic reform (Adar 1998). Opposition actors saw this negatively, although the economic reforms that were negotiated had an impact on the regime's competitive capacity. Brazeal's successor Prudence Bushnell was initially more engaged on issues of reform, especially after the regime's violent response to the second *saba saba* protests and the explosion of ethnic violence in the coastal areas. High-level diplomatic pressure forced the opposition and regime into the IPPG framework

---

[14] Julia Ojiambo (Former Senior Member of KANU). Author Interview. Nairobi. (July 27, 2012).

and led to the creation of new election observation measures prior to the 1997 election. However, the embassy bombings in 1998 returned issues of security cooperation to the forefront (Barkan 2004, Hornsby 2012, 660–1). For most of the 1990s British High Commissioners were also more likely to engage in "private rather than public diplomacy" (Cumming 2001, 264).

High-level diplomatic efforts increased during the period prior to the 2002 election, this time pressuring the regime over the question of succession. As Joel Barkan notes, the American stance during George W. Bush's administration was to ensure that elections would be held by the end of 2002, but without Moi as a candidate and without violence (2004). To achieve this Secretary of State Colin Powell made public statements that broadly endorsed term limits in Africa. These were seconded by more direct comments by Ambassador Johnnie Carson that urged Moi to hold the scheduled election, abide by term limits, and commit to the constitutional review process that began in 1997.[15] Behind the scenes there was also private diplomacy between Moi and the White House. In May 2001, Powell secretly met with Moi in Nairobi and pressured him to accept American conditions.[16] In June and November of 2001, Moi met with Vice President Dick Cheney, once at the White House and once again at the UN General Assembly, and was pressured to give up the presidency.[17]

It must remain conjecture why Moi ultimately decided not to run again in 2002, but as Chapter 5 showed it undoubtedly hurt KANU's competitive capacity and facilitated severe elite and voter defection. There were domestic imperatives that contributed to Moi's decision making, such as the fractured state of KANU, his past public commitment to term limits, and perhaps assurances that he and his allies would be protected by the successive Kibaki government (Brown 2004). Still, these factors were not all clear before Moi launched Project Uhuru in July of 2002. By contrast, many interview subjects mention the influential, if not decisive, role of international actors and especially Moi's concern with his own international reputation. Indeed, Moi was provided a fairly "soft landing" in the international community, and just prior to the 2002 election he

---

[15] Notably, during this period British diplomatic pressure also stepped up with the end of Sir Jeffrey James' tenure as High Commissioner. By November 2001, Kenya had censured James for pressuring the regime.

[16] Marc Lacey. "In Kenya Powell Repeats Call for a New Generation of Leaders" *The New York Times* (May 27, 2001).

[17] Musalia Mudavadi (Former Finance Minister of Kenya). Author Interview. Nairobi. (July 25, 2012).

was hosted and honored for his retirement by both President Bush and Prime Minister Tony Blair (Barkan 2004). Absent this international pressure and guarantees it is plausible that the succession crisis would have manifested very differently.

AUTOCRATIC PATRONAGE AND THE SOURCES
OF REPRESSIVE HEGEMONY

Cameroon entered the multiparty era with many of the same vulnerabilities as Kenya – a deteriorating economy in crisis, heavy government repression, and comparatively less but still significant aid dependency. Importantly, many of the conditions that allowed strong democratic pressure in Kenya were at play. From the United States' and other European countries' perspective, there were no immediate competing foreign policy goals in Cameroon. Indeed, after the NDI's dismal assessment of the October 1992 legislative election, the United States quickly withdrew aid and imposed strict conditionality. However, this international pressure was short-lived as it quickly became apparent that the Cameroonian regime benefitted from French autocratic patronage. French influence has been a constant factor for the past two decades, but was more overt during the 1990s. During the second half of Cameroon's electoral authoritarian period it is actually the United States that has alternated between the status quo and acting as an authoritarian patron. This is largely due to emerging foreign policy goals over the Iraq War and the global war on terror.

The origins of French support for Cameroon are multifaceted and have evolved since the colonial era (Atangana 1997). One impetus was to maintain pro-Paris elites in Cameroon so to facilitate investment and access to basic trade commodities. Likewise, France has navigated international politics as a medium-sized power by sustaining relationships with former colonies, which they can then leverage in international institutions (Cumming 1995, Emmanuel 2013). During the Ahidjo period, numerous treaties of economic and military cooperation were signed, and then renegotiated following reunification. Monetarily, the Cameroonian system is tied to the Franc through the Central Africa Franc Zone, which has facilitated an inflow of French investment and French input into policymaking. During the Ahidjo era, between 20 and 60 percent of all Cameroonian exports were to France, and between 45 and 55 percent of imports were from France. Under Biya, the relationship with the French appeared to cool somewhat; however, it was during this period that French oil investments became more profound. The French-owned oil company ELF-Aquitaine (later absorbed by Total), accounted for nearly 68 percent of Cameroonian oil production. Along with ELF, by 1990 there were approximately 200 French companies operating major businesses in Cameroon.[18]

On the other hand the global war on terror and the second Iraq War brought into focus conflicting American foreign policy goals. Between 2002 and 2003, Cameroon held a crucial temporary seat on the UN Security Council. This made Cameroon the target of serious US lobbying efforts to support a potential UN war resolution. Later in the decade, the United States sought Cameroonian opposition to the UN's Goldstone Report on the 2009 Gaza conflict between Israelis and Palestinians. It was during this period that the United States, while still ostensibly committed to democracy promotion and governance reform, began to view Cameroon through the prism of regional stability and as the gateway to Central Africa. During the 2000s, military cooperation between the United States and Cameroon increased, and bilateral aid was reopened. Importantly, in 2008 there was very little pressure upon Biya to refrain from amending the constitution and running for another term in 2011. While the United States remained the most vociferous foreign power critical of Cameroon's undemocratic behavior, it was not backed up with any other tools of democratic pressure. Importantly, the perception from within the US government was that they could have done much more to push for democratic reform.

Consequently, throughout Cameroon's electoral authoritarian tenure it has been the target of substantially less democracy aid and election monitoring. In important ways, despite reforms to election management, the regime's range of manipulative tools actually increased between 1990 and 2011 with the creation of new military units like the Rapid Response Brigade (BIR), which had international support. Likewise, with continuous access to French bilateral support and French influence with international lenders, Cameroon could skirt many of the most important reforms demanded as part of structural adjustment. As noted above, not only did cabinet size increase dramatically, but the reforms to the public sector were also minimal, and Biya retained control over literally hundreds of patronage positions. Finally, direct diplomatic engagement that could have been critical of Biya, raise the specter of reputational costs, or empowered opposition parties was notably absent.

---

[18] There are also significant cultural and economic ties between Cameroon and France. Importantly, the French also viewed John Fru Ndi, an Anglophone, as a potential threat to their interests. In 1992 the French Ambassador to Cameroon Yvon Omnes joined the Cameroonian government as a technical advisor to the president.

Autocratic Patrons and the Maintenance of Manipulation in Cameroon

Without strong international support, attempts at restraining manipulation in Cameroon remained largely symbolic. In 1991 following the *villes mortes* campaign, Biya agreed to create a Technical Committee on Constitutional Matters, which met intermittently between 1991 and 1995. However, since the SDF and Cameroon Democratic Union (UDC) parties had boycotted the 1992 election, Biya had little trouble passing a revised constitution in January of 1996 that held up the status quo. The state was conceived of as a decentralized yet unitary entity, and Biya retained the right to appoint regional governors and senior divisional officers. In addition, an included bill of rights was subject to the ambiguous "higher interests of the state," and left Biya with considerable access to the same emergency powers in place since the UPC rebellion. Other opposition suggestions like creating a vice presidency or a majoritarian election system were discarded. The recommendation that the president remain confined to two seven-year terms was included. Similarly, the new constitution provided for the creation of a Senate and Constitutional Council, but neither was actually created until 2013.

The aggressive attitude of the Cameroonian government toward opposition parties continued unabated, and is well documented by several human rights organization and in the United States' annual State Department reports on human rights. While in Kenya the 1997 *saba saba* protests led to international condemnation and pressure on Moi and the opposition to join the IPPG framework, there was no corresponding effort in Cameroon. During the 1997 campaign, North West and South West Provinces were similarly the sites of extensive violence and frequent detention. Both provinces were placed under curfew from March 27 to just weeks before the May election. Most remarkably, the SDF was denied entry into Center, North, Extreme North, Adamoua, and East Province until just May 3 (TI 2011).[19] Other notable instances of state repression include the 2002 criminalization and detention of the SCNC, the brief arrest of the authors of the 2003 "northern memorandum," the 2006 arrest of John Fru Ndi and other SDF members on charges of murder,

---

[19] One of the most remarkable sites of opposition repression was in the department of Mayo Rey in North Province. The traditional chief or *lamido* of Rey-Bouba explicitly warned that opposition parties were banned from campaigning in his department throughout the election campaign.

and the 2008 prohibition of all rallies and demonstrations in Littoral Province under the guise of the Preservation of Public Order Act.[20]

Similarly, freedom of expression remained much more constrained in Cameroon than in Kenya. Biya maintained control over the media and censorship through laws pertaining to defamation. In 1996, a new press law (Law 96/04) required all publications to pass a screening by provincial governors. Likewise, the government's control over media licensing helped to diminish the impact of the growing private media market. While in 2011 there were over 200 private newspapers and seventy private radio stations, only a few dozen operated regularly. Prominent examples of government intervention include the seizure of the newspaper *L'Expression*, the shutdown of Pius Njawe's popular Freedom FM radio station from 2003 to 2005, the temporary seizure of the major newspaper *Mutations* and the arrest of its senior editors in 2003, the closure of television stations Canal 2 and RTA in 2004, the mysterious death of *Cameroon Express* reporter Germain Cyrille Ngota in his prison cell in 2011. According to Reporters Without Borders, in 2011 Cameroon had the 8th worst freedom of the press in all of sub-Saharan Africa (Article 19 1997).

Notably, the "reformed" constitution did little to delink the executive from the coercive apparatus. As noted in Chapter 4, Cameroon has a comparatively larger military than in Kenya or Tanzania, in part due to the legacy of the UPC rebellion. As Jean-Germain Gros notes, the military in Cameroon is "probably one of the most politically potent in Africa" (Gros 1995, 120). The president retained control over the Presidential Guard, *gendarmerie*, police, and army brigades. In 2001, these capacities were enhanced with the creation of the BIR. Ostensibly formed to combat gang activity and banditry along Cameroon's frontier, the BIR was also a new and effective repressive force that could be used against the opposition (Diklitch 2002). Following the February 2008 riots in Yaoundé and Douala, the BIR reportedly killed over one hundred people. In total, it is estimated that the BIR is responsible for over 700 deaths, and used more extensively in urban areas than in rural zones or along the border.[21] The

---

[20] This is based on a careful reading of Amnesty International's country profiles and the US State Department's country reports on human rights practice in Cameroon. The 2006 murder charge leveled against Fru Ndi was over the death of Gregoire Diboule, an SDF supporter who was trampled to death at a rally. While Fru Ndi was released, the charges were not dropped until many years later.

[21] Staff. "Cameroon: Rapid Intervention Military Unit Strays from Its Mission" *IRIN News* (August 29, 2008).

BIR and the Presidential Guard received technical and military support from both the United States and Israel.[22]

Another crucial constitutional provision that did not change was the right of the executive, through the Ministry of Territorial Administration (MINAT) to redistrict based on the peculiar interests of any constituency. Because Cameroon has a mixture of single-member and multi-member districts, this gave Biya the leeway to shape the electoral system to the CPDM's advantage in ways that Kenya could not. The constitution allowed Biya to redefine constituencies based on their population *and* geographic size. While the size of parliament has remained a constant 180 members, the number of actual electoral constituencies has changed. Following the CPDM's narrow victory in 1992, the number of constituencies grew from fifty-six to seventy-four by increasing the number of single-member districts from four to twenty-three and the number of multi-member districts from forty-five to fifty-one. In 2007, Biya once again unilaterally redistricted *after* he had already convened the electorate. The number of constituencies rose to eighty-five in response to a new census that was never actually published.[23] The majority of these changes were in the oppositional regions of North West and South West Provinces. In 2007, nearly every multi-member constituency in North West was split into single-member districts, and the CPDM went from winning one seat in 1997 to nine seats in 2007 (Albaugh 2011).[24]

Finally, absent a major international effort to monitor Cameroonian elections or develop a domestic observation capacity, fraud persisted. After the controversial 1992 election, there were little improvements to the election process or any meaningful attempt to create a domestic observation capacity. In 1997, election management was still centralized in MINAT, which was perceived by most parties and international observers as highly biased and ineffective (Bakary and Palmer 1997). In 2000, the government

---

[22] The commander of both units was Colonel Avi Sivan, the former commander of the Israeli Special Forces unit *Duvdevan*. After retiring from the Israeli army, Sivan became a major advisor to Biya and helped secure extensive arms deals with the Israeli government. Sivan died in a helicopter crash in 2010. Georges Dougeueli. "Mort Du Monsieur Sécurité De Paul Biya Hélicoptère *Jeune Afrique*" (November 23, 2010).

[23] U.S. Embassy, Yaoundé. "While Not Pretty, Cameroon's Election Prep is Moving Ahead" Wikileaks Cable 07YAOUNDE741 (June 8, 2007).

[24] In comparative perspective, the impact of gerrymandering is much higher in Cameroon than in the other cases. According to calculations based solely on population size, some departments like Mfoundi or Wouri are underserved by approximately ten seats, while major rural departments in Central, East, and South are overrepresented by between five and eight seats.

created the short-lived National Election Observatory, which only managed the opaque 2004 presidential election (the results of which are missing). The National Election Observatory was summarily scrapped following accusations of rampant mismanagement and replaced by Elections Cameroon (ELECAM). While still presidentially appointed, ELECAM was the first sincere effort at creating a more professional election management body, and the first real international intervention in the electoral process. ELECAM was supported by the United Nation's Development Fund, which provided the cash to create an electronic voter registry. But, ELECAM was still ill prepared for the 2007 election, which remarkably was not observed by any international organization.[25] Only in 2011 did the European Union fund the local chapter of Transparency International to train and deployed some 800 domestic election observers (TI 2011).

Autocratic Patronage and the Protection of the Public Sector

Autocratic patronage also helped the CPDM and Paul Biya retain access to crucial state resources to fund a large patronage coalition. At the transition to elections, Cameroon's public sector consisted of approximately 150 SOEs, a large civil service, and one of the most centralized financial systems on the continent (IBRD 1994, Konings 2003). While Cameroon did not rely as heavily on foreign aid, the economic crisis of the 1980s took a heavy toll and forced Cameroon into negotiations with international lenders. In 1988 Cameroon signed an $80 million standby agreement with the IMF, and in 1989 it secured a $150 million structural adjustment loan with the World Bank. Both programs were conditioned on substantial reform to the public sector, and privatization was a key concern of international lenders (IMF 1991).

French intervention allowed Biya to skirt most of the required major structural reforms without any real economic consequence. This was particularly relevant during the 1991–1993 period, at the peak of Cameroon's political and economic crisis. Biya drew harsh international criticism for his violent response to the *villes mortes* strikes, which led to a sharp reduction in most bilateral aid. Following a disastrous NDI

---

[25] The US Embassy did send teams to each province and reported several issues with the election. In 2007 the Catholic Church also mustered approximately 1,600 observers through the National Commission for Justice and Peace, and the National Human Rights Commission sent approximately 300 observers. U.S. Embassy, Yaoundé. "Election on July 22: Nuts and Bolts and USG Observation" Wikileaks Cable 07YAOUNDE902 (July 19, 2007).

election observation report in April 1992, the United States and other donor countries like Germany ended all bilateral aid until real political reforms were initiated. American aid would not return to Cameroon until the 2000s. However, the French stepped in and tripled their bilateral support from $175 million to a peak of $425 million in 1993. In total, there was actually a net increase in bilateral aid during this period. Likewise, after much back and forth over the slow pace of implementation, Cameroon's agreements with the World Bank and IMF were suspended in 1992 before they had been fully disbursed. Once again, the French stepped in and directly paid Cameroon's external debt arrears with the World Bank (Konings 1996, Emmanuel 2013).[26] With no real imperative, progress on public sector reform was nominal. By 1994, Cameroon had divested from less than 10 percent of its holdings, and the civil administration grew by 5 percent. Banks remained heavily centralized and there was little improvement in the management of public funds (IBRD 1994).

During the remainder of the decade Cameroon successfully negotiated a number of large aid packages contingent on structural adjustment, but made only marginal changes to the broader contours of its public sector. In January 1994, the French helped negotiate a 50 percent devaluation of the CFA with the IMF. In return for the currency devaluation, the IMF agreed to an $81 million stand-by credit for Cameroon, and the World Bank entered into a new one-year $50 million structural adjustment loan. A $67 million additional IMF stand-by agreement was also signed in September 1995. Both programs were not fully drawn on, due to issues with the implementation of public sector reform. Regardless, by September 1997, and again through French influence, Cameroon entered a $162 million three-year ESAF (converted to a PRGF in November 1999) and successfully renegotiated nearly $2 billion of debt with the Paris Club. Between 1997 and 2000 Cameroon met several benchmarks of macroeconomic performance, and made important reforms to its budgetary process.[27] Likewise, key industries were privatized, such as the national electric supplier (SONEIL), the national palm oil company (SOCAPALM), and the national rail company (CAMRAIL). Competition

---

[26] In addition, $53 million of French aid was provided to pay for civil servant salaries, which had been drastically cut as part of Cameroon's agreements with the IMF and World Bank.

[27] Some notable developments were the reform of the tax code, the introduction of a Value Added Tax (VAT), and incorporation of oil revenues into the general budget. Between 1997 and 2000 Cameroon grew by an average of 4.5 percent and non-oil revenues grew by 3 percent.

was allowed into the telecom and banking sectors, the civil administration was downsized by several thousand personnel, and some new platforms for managing public finance were introduced. Yet, the breadth of privatization and public sector reform was limited and failed to address rampant corruption. As the IMF reported at the time, "the government continues to maintain numerous bank accounts rather than a single consolidated Treasury account; and the new Integrated Financial Management System remains underutilized" (IMF 2005).

Despite this limited progress, in 2000 Cameroon was again amazingly able to negotiate another $111 million four-year PRGF. In its review of this program, the IMF noted "significant fiscal slippages," privatization that fell far short of expectations, and extremely poor governance. The reasons were multifaceted. The IMF review notes issues with focusing too intently on benchmark performance criteria that measured fiscal performance, an unexpected growth in oil revenues that shielded the government from reform, and the continued proliferation of Cameroonian ministries that made implementation and monitoring difficult. However, the IMF also cited that the pace of reform slowed significantly prior to the 2004 presidential election (IMF 2005). Consequently, in October 2005, Cameroon signed a much smaller $26 million PRGF. In a review of this program, the IMF still observed slow progress on public sector reform. While gestures were made toward privatization of the telecom and transportation industries, the Cameroonian government received no receipts from privatization for the remainder of the decade. In 2009, following the global financial crisis, Cameroon amazingly received a $144 million Exogenous Shock Facility loan.[28]

Throughout the 2000s, Cameroon retained access to international lending from multilateral institutions, but also importantly regained access to lost bilateral aid. While French aid remained substantial throughout the 2000s, the United States and United Kingdom used bilateral aid to woo Cameroon's support for a UN war resolution on the Iraq War. This also represented a major pushback against France, who at the time encouraged Cameroon to vote against any war measure. During these negotiations both US Assistant Secretary of State for Africa Walter Kansteiner and President George W. Bush personally lobbied Biya with promises of increased bilateral aid under the Africa Growth Opportunity

---

[28] International Monetary Fund, "News Release: IMF Executive Board Approves US $144.1 Million Disbursement for Cameroon under the Exogenous Shocks Facility" *International Monetary Fund* July 2, 2009.

Act. Likewise, the British International Development Secretary, Baroness Valerie Amos, made overtures to Biya. While the war resolution was ultimately withdrawn from the UN Security Council, Cameroon's position remained one of abstention. In addition to more bilateral aid, Cameroon also received increased military support in the form of surplus weaponry, joint exercises between the United States and the BIR, and cooperation with the Cameroonian Navy over maritime security. The United States also supported Cameroon during international negotiations with Nigeria over the disputed Bakassi Peninsula.[29]

Continued US aid during this period also reflected changing priorities within the Bush administration. Biya committed troops to peacekeeping operations, and also abstained from a vote in the United Nations on the Goldstone report. As noted in embassy cables from Yaoundé, both actions were part of increased security cooperation with Cameroon. Likewise, assisting Cameroon with the Bakassi dispute was perceived by the United States as a way to stabilize access to significant oil reserves, and by extension to prevent regional conflict. In one cable, the tension between the United States' security concerns and its commitments to democracy and governance became clear. Marking twenty-six years of Biya's presidency, Ambassador Janet Garvey writes that:

[] we have strategic interests at stake in Cameroon; it is a large oil-producing, mineral-rich country with the largest port in Central Africa, whose stability is key to the stability of the entire region. Post will continue to explore how the USG can secure its democracy, economic/commercial and security in the country.[30]

Nor was the lack of real progress on reform lost on the US Embassy. Earlier in 2007, Ambassador Niels Marquardt noted: "evidence suggests that the pilfering of parastatal accounts for party (and personal) purposes is the rule, not the exception."[31] In 2009, Ambassador Garvey writes:

Corruption is endemic and government decision-making is sclerotic. Cameroon has supported us on some UN and other international issues, but it tends to

---

[29] U.S. Embassy, Yaoundé. "President Biya at 26" Wikileaks Cable 08YAOUNDE1169_a (December 3, 2008). In October 2002 the International Court of Justice found in favor of Cameroonian sovereignty over the Bakassi Peninsula. Disputes over implementation continued, and the territory was only conceded in August 2008 following the 2006 Greentree Accords.

[30] U.S. Embassy, Yaoundé. "President Biya at 26" Wikileaks Cable 08YAOUNDE1169_a (December 3, 2008).

[31] U.S. Embassy, Yaoundé. "Possible Successor to President Biya" Wikileaks Cable 07YAOUNDE227_a (February 22, 2007).

abstain on UN votes important to us, with a 22 percent voting coincidence with
the United States on overall votes and 0 percent on important votes in 2008.[32]

These internal deliberations suggest a conscious effort to disregard stalled
economic reform, in favor of national security goals, even if only partially
fulfilled.

Autocratic Patronage and Limited Diplomatic Engagement

French autocratic patronage has also influenced Biya's decision making
and shielded Cameroon from pressure from other countries. Primarily
this has involved downplaying issues of governance and democratic
reform, and providing Biya with diplomatic cover that protects his international reputation. Following the 1992 legislative election, which was to
recall widely condemned by the NDI and other international observers,
French President Mitterrand infamously sent a congratulatory letter to
Biya (Gros 1995). During the Chirac years, the Franco-African summit of
2001 was held in Yaoundé, where Chirac seated himself next to Biya and
referred to him as "his good friend."[33] In 2004, to much international criticism, Chirac also sent Biya his congratulations on reelection before the
Cameroonian Supreme Court had actually certified the results, and before
any other embassy had endorsed the election (ICG 2010). Most strikingly,
after Nicolas Sarkozy's victory in the French election of May 2006, some
in the US Embassy predicted possible change in French-Cameroonian
relations. Yet, within days of Paul Biya's first visit with Sarkozy in July,
the CPDM began to publicly call for constitutional change to remove
presidential term limits. It was understood by the US Embassy in Yaoundé
that Biya had travelled to Paris to ask permission from Sarkozy to change
the constitution without condemnation. The internal French response
conveyed to US embassy staff inquiries regarding their position on term
limits was that "France sees the ongoing debate about changing the constitution as an internal affair for Cameroonians to decide. France will not
make statements or press Biya on the term limit issue."[34]

---

[32] U.S. Embassy, Yaoundé. "Rethinking our Approach to Cameroon" Wikileaks Cable
    09YAOUNDE971_a (November 13, 2009).

[33] Richard Kwang Kometa. "Presidents Biya and Chirac Meet" *Cameroon Tribune*
    (February 3, 2004).

[34] U.S. Embassy, Yaoundé. "Sarkozy-Biya Summit: A French View from Cameroon"
    Wikileaks Cable 07YAOUNDE1271_a (October 24, 2007), U.S. Embassy, Yaoundé.
    "Constitution Issue Heats Up" Wikileaks Cable 08YAOUNDE33_a (July 11, 2008), U.S.

From the American perspective, there was heavier diplomatic pressure during the 1990s than in the 2000s. After the 1992 election was criticized by the NDI, the US State Department issued a warning that accused Biya of electoral fraud to strengthen his regime, and called for an end to emergency rule and the release of opposition candidate John Fru Ndi from house arrest. As noted, these public overtures were backed by a reduction in bilateral aid, but had little impact on the regime without a shift in French support. In response, Cameroon withdrew its ambassador from Washington and called for an emergency meeting with the US Ambassador in Yaoundé, Frances Cook. Relations remained cool until 2002 and the buildup to the Iraq War. In a stark reversal of prior diplomatic relations, just days prior to the invasion of Iraq on March 20, 2003, Biya was President Bush's personal guest at the White House. This was also Biya's first official visit to Washington D.C., and at a press conference President Bush congratulated Biya on his record of reform and privatization.[35] This of course contradicts sentiments expressed by US embassy staff within Cameroon, but signals the end of any real US diplomatic pressure on Biya.

As a result US pressure on Biya remained weak throughout the rest of the 2000s. American public responses to election irregularities in 2007 were tepid, and Ambassador Niels Marquardt deliberately withheld public comment during election preparations. On the other hand, Marquardt did take the rather drastic step of blacklisting corrupt Cameroonian Minister of Finance Abah Abah.[36] In 2008, the US government was vocally critical of Biya's constitutional amendment, and the response included a widely reported speech by Ambassador Janet Garvey, and a country visit from Deputy Assistant Secretary of State for African Affairs James Swan. Yet, the language of Garvey's speech was purposefully non-confrontational, stating that:

we acknowledge every country's right to change its constitution and in our experience term limits and periodic leadership change – at least every decade – are healthy for democracy.[37]

Embassy, Yaoundé. "Is Biya Preparing to Change the Constitution for a Third Term?" Wikileaks Cable 08YAOUNDE1478 (December 19, 2008).

[35] The White House. "News Release: Leadership and Opportunity in Africa" Washington, DC (March 20, 2003).

[36] U.S. Embassy, Yaoundé. "USG Should Avoid Association with Finance Minister Polycarpe Abah Abah" Wikileaks Cable 07YAOUNDE732_a (June 7, 2007).

[37] U.S. Embassy, Yaoundé. "Ambassador Engages on Constitutional Change" Wikileaks Cable 07YAOUNDE732_a (February 20, 2008).

A year later, Ambassador Garvey noted in a cable to Washington that a meeting between Biya and President Obama might "provide an opportunity to thank Biya for his unwavering pro-American stance on many important issues (especially the Iraq War and investment in Cameroon)" and to "encourage him to move forward with political and economic liberalization."[38] In 2009, the United States gathered other diplomatic missions to boycott the inauguration of ELECAM and denied a US visa to the corrupt Defense Minister Remy Ze Meka, but there were no further public US diplomatic efforts.

Low-level diplomatic engagement also limited the ability of opposition actors to gain traction. From the SDF's point of view, French support of the Biya regime has been a fundamental factor that inhibits their success at the polls. The SDF has accused the French of fabricating incriminating evidence against their chair John Fru Ndi, and of supporting Bamileké opposition parties in North West Province to counter the SDF. Some have even speculated that the French were part of an assassination attempt on John Fru Ndi (Fonchingong 1998). The British have also kept minimal ties with the SDF. In 1993, Cameroon's membership in the Commonwealth was rejected after protest from Anglophone activists over political conditions. However, by 1995 membership was eventually granted despite no tangible improvements in governance.[39] Several members of the opposition note the absence of international support. Joshua Osih of the SDF told me: "we [the opposition] expected too much from the international community."[40] Others noted a demonstrable decline in international engagement after 1992, and since the construction of the Chad-Cameroon oil pipeline.

The inability of the US government to significantly impact Cameroon's democratic progress was not lost on its embassy staff. In 2007, Ambassador Marquardt emphasized the strong ties between Cameroon and France, and noted that without a change in that relationship it would be difficult for the United States to see progress on issues of democracy and governance. In a brief issued in November 2009, reflecting on fifty years of United States–Cameroonian relations, Ambassador Garvey once again highlighted Cameroon's contribution to the Iraq War, the Bakassi Peninsula, and the Goldstone Report, while also noting American leadership in criticizing

---

[38] U.S. Embassy, Yaoundé. "Biya Promises Progress on Corruption and Governance" Wikileaks Cable 08YAOUNDE800_a (August 11, 2008).

[39] Cameroon acceptance into the Commonwealth was likely due to Nigerian lobbying on behalf of Cameroon (Konings and Nyamnjoh 2004).

[40] Joshua Osih (MP for Wouri, SDF). Author Interview. Douala. (July 22, 2015).

corruption, electoral fraud, and the end of term limits. Yet, she starkly concludes that outside of polite conversation, "it is difficult to say that we have substantially moved the ball on the things that matter the most to us," and states plainly that Cameroon has never had a free and fair election. Garvey stresses that a more sincere American push for improved democracy in Cameroon would have to involve more senior level diplomatic engagement, greater international cooperation, sharper coercive tools like visa denials, and a move beyond piecemeal democracy assistance. This revealing internal communication shows that it was not that an international actor was incapable of providing sustained democratic patronage, but that it had decided not to for conflicting foreign policy purposes.[41]

CONCLUSION

International actors can influence electoral outcomes when autocratic regimes depend heavily on access to coercion and cooptation for their survival. This is relevant more broadly, but particularly useful to consider when contrasting the divergent trajectories of electoral authoritarianism in Cameroon and Kenya. In both cases incumbents did not have access to credible ruling parties, and therefore they were less adaptable to the multiparty environment. Over time Paul Biya and the CPDM have used repression to erect an electoral hegemony, while in Kenya KANU's coercive tactics were ineffective. Using a variety of sources, this chapter has argued that international actors make decisions about where and to what extent they pressure for democratic reform. These choices have real consequences, but I do not argue that this necessarily leads to electoral turnover as in Kenya or even a longer process of democratization. Rather, international actors can shape the immediate competitive environment by limiting access to the full range of manipulative tools and patronage resources, and through their direct diplomatic engagement with regimes and oppositions.

This concludes the major empirical discussion of the three cases. In the past three chapters I have argued that credible ruling parties provide unique sources of strength during multiparty elections, which shape the structure of competition. Credible parties can retain stronger elite support by providing a stable structure that shapes their careers and levels the playing field. These kinds of parties also have unique mobilization

---

[41] U.S. Embassy, Yaoundé. "Rethinking our Approach to Cameroon" Wikileaks Cable 09YAOUNDE971_a (November 13, 2009).

capacities. They can reach more voters through permanent grassroots structures, and depend on a wider social base that will repeatedly turn out. As a result, large electoral victories are more certain, which reduces the need for widespread manipulation. Without these parties, as noted, regimes must manipulate and coopt their way to victory, and the utility of that strategy depends on the international environment. In the next chapter I turn to the tool of typological theorizing to probe the boundaries of these arguments with more cases, and to consider some of the major alternative explanations for electoral competition.

8

Electoral Authoritarian Competition in Africa's Former Single-Party Regimes

> It was not Chissano alone who appointed his successor, proving that any given individual in the party [FRELIMO], powerful as he may be, has to take in account its institutional procedures.
>
> —Giovanni M. Carbone (2005)

> Early in the 1960s there was established in Gabon what is called Le Clans des Gabonais, a clandestine web of Gabonese officials, French intelligence agents, members of the discredited Gaullist Service d'action civique, mercenaries, and businessmen. Le Clan remains firmly established in Gabon today.
>
> —Michael C. Reed (1987)

The previous chapters used the cases of Tanzania, Cameroon, and Kenya to construct a theory of electoral authoritarian competition linked to the role of credible parties and international patrons. This chapter tests the boundaries of those arguments by examining the entire range of single-party African regimes that successfully made the transition to electoral authoritarianism. To recall, the focus on single-party regimes is meant to limit the comparison to similar contexts and to highlight the role of party institutions that developed before elections. A single-party regime is one that was governed by a ruling party for at least ten years. Likewise, only including cases of regimes that survived foundational elections allows for an examination of competition and avoids potential bias associated with the uniqueness of foundational elections. This chapter adds Côte d'Ivoire, Djibouti, Gabon, Mozambique, Senegal, Seychelles, and Togo. To compare these ten cases I employ the tool of typological theorizing.

This method is established in the qualitative research tradition and is useful for parsing through complex causal processes among a smaller range of cases (Elman 2005, George and Bennett 2005).[1] It involves scoring cases along a select number of study variables, and then arranging them into an interpretative truth table.

The typological theorizing used here is primarily inductive, which is useful for theory testing, but it does not necessarily provide deeper insights into causal processes or mechanisms.[2] The method on its own cannot account for the specific ways in which credible parties impact competition through their retention of elites and voters. For our purposes, it primarily helps validate the arguments made in the previous chapters regarding the role of parties and patrons and provides some generalizability. However, another major strength of typological theorizing is that it can pit different causal theories against each other and delineate different causal pathways. Importantly, it offers an opportunity to revisit some alternative explanations discussed in Chapter 1, namely the role of opposition capacity and economic performance. While in other settings these variables might be considered controls, in the context of typological theorizing the emphasis is on what George and Bennett refer to as "equifinality." George and Bennett compare the complexity of social phenomenon to disease pathology – sickness can arise via different causal paths and therefore may exhibit real differences in its severity and duration (George and Bennett 2005, 235). Some types might be more pervasive than others, while other types might only include a few cases. Typological theorizing can therefore be used to create better contingent generalizations.

The ten cases under study vary in terms of their electoral authoritarian competition, and can be arrayed into the distinct electoral authoritarian types discussed in Chapter 3. This, as expected, corresponds to the presence or absence of a credible ruling party and a regime's relationship with major external actors. Tolerant hegemonies are consistently associated

---

[1] An alternative to typological theorizing is qualitative case analysis or the related fuzzy set qualitative case analysis. Both methods were pioneered by Charles Ragin (Ragin 2008). However, the number of cases required usually exceeds the number of cases here. Moreover, these methods assume some sort of linearity and one-dimensionality. Given the focus on a more complex and multidimensional concept of competition, it makes the use of these tools problematic.

[2] George and Bennett differentiate between deductive and inductive typological theorizing. Deductive theorizing occurs before case studies are conducted, and in fact provides the basis for case selection. Inductive theorizing, as done here, comes after some preliminary case studies have been conducted in order to identify relevant causal factors and test their generalizability (George and Bennett 2005).

with credible ruling parties, while repressive hegemonies are linked to the absence of credible ruling parties and the absence of democratic patronage. The typological theory also provides some additional insights regarding the contingent role of economic performance and opposition capacity. The first key insight is that economic performance matters less when a regime relies on repression, but can make a difference whether a tolerant electoral authoritarian regime becomes or remains hegemonic. A second key finding is that opposition capacity does not appear to shape broader competitive contexts.

That said, typological theorizing is not without its shortcomings and it requires some critical considerations. First, as coding for variables becomes more nuanced and finer-grained, and as the number of included variables increases, so does the size of the typological space. A key decision researchers must make is how to reduce the property space so that clear inferences can still be drawn. Therefore, I limit this chapter to exploring four independent variables (ruling party credibility, international patronage, opposition capacity, and economic performance), and I use a more straightforward dichotomous coding of the independent variables. The dependent variable is the type of electoral authoritarian competition: tolerant hegemony, repressive hegemony, tolerant and non-hegemonic, repressive and non-hegemonic. Given the sixteen different combinations of independent variables and the four possible outcomes, there are sixty-four potential pathways. For presentation purposes and given the scope conditions set out in this study, I only display pathways with actual empirical cases.[3]

Second, there needs to be some account for time and the boundaries of a case. I conceive of a case as a specific, non-foundational election period, or the closest presidential and legislative elections where the former single-party was still incumbent.[4] Cases exit the sample once they experience turnover or some other event that removes them from power, such as a military coup.[5] Third, typological theorizing requires extensive data, which can be qualitative or quantitative. However, it fundamentally

---

[3] In typological theorizing you can reduce the property space by excluding logically impossible types or pathways that are overly determined. Empirical compression limits the discussion, but does not preclude the possibility that outside of these ten cases there are others that might populate those empty pathways (Elman 2005).

[4] The logic is that foundational elections are poor subjects for studying these comparative trajectories of electoral authoritarian competition since they can be fairly idiosyncratic.

[5] This impacts Côte d'Ivoire, Kenya, and Senegal. While the subsequent regime type might have still been electoral authoritarianism, the end of incumbency limits the insights into party credibility. In the case of Senegal, the transition to electoral authoritarianism occurred much earlier (1978), but only the post-1990 elections are included here.

relies on qualitative judgments regarding the scores that variables receive. When possible I use quantitative measures, for instance when assessing economic performance, but otherwise the coding depends on contextual and historical knowledge of these cases. Space limitations preclude a richer discussion of each case and the score for each variable, so instead I provide a concise narrative that touches primarily on the cases not discussed previously. The specific coding selection rules and scores can be found in Appendix B.

The chapter proceeds with a discussion of party capacity in the remainder of the former single-party cases. During that discussion I highlight sources of ruling party-credibility in terms of party size, decisional autonomy, internal democracy, and social incorporation. I then compare international patronage in terms of the extent of democracy assistance and aid conditionality. What follows is a comparison of the role of two major alternative hypotheses regarding electoral authoritarian competition: opposition capacity and economic performance. In the discussion of opposition capacity I look for indicators of party stability and consider decision making during elections in terms of whether parties formed a coalition or boycotted the election. Economic performance considers macro indicators like growth and inflation, but also measures of social well-being like the human development index (HDI). The case scores for all four independent variables are aggregated into Table 8.1, which summarizes the various types and pathways.

RULING PARTY CREDIBILITY IN AFRICAN SINGLE-PARTY REGIMES

The period of single-party rule in Africa produced ruling parties of divergent size and credibility. While Tanzania represents the clearest example of a credible ruling party, ruling parties in Mozambique, Senegal, and Seychelles approximated that ideal. In these instances regimes made deeper investments into party organization, imbued parties with decisional autonomy and internal democracy, or made wider social commitments. These investments were not even across all the cases, but distinguish these ruling parties from the much weaker examples found in Côte d'Ivoire, Djibouti, Gabon, and Togo. In these cases ruling parties were more similar to those in Cameroon or Kenya. Most of these parties did not have real infrastructure outside of the capital and were largely inactive for long periods of time. Correspondingly, the party tended to be less important for day-to-day governing in comparison with the

TABLE 8.1. *A typological theory of electoral authoritarian competition in former single-party regimes*

Case	Credible ruling party	Democratic patronage	Opposition capacity	Economic performance	Outcome
Mozambique (2004–9) Seychelles (1998–2011) Senegal (2000–1)* Tanzania (2000–)	+	–	+	+	Tolerant hegemony
Mozambique (1999–2003) Senegal (1993–9)	+	–	+	–	Tolerant non-hegemony
Mozambique (2009–) Seychelles (2012–)	+	–	–	+	Tolerant hegemony
Kenya (1997–2002)*	–	+	–	–	Repressive non-hegemony
Togo (2005–9)	–	+	+	–	Repressive non-hegemony
Cameroon (2002–) Djibouti (2008–) Gabon (1996–2000) Gabon (2009–) Togo (1998–2001) Togo (2010–)	–	–	–	+	Repressive hegemony
Cameroon (1997–2001) Côte d'Ivoire (1995–9)** Djibouti (1997–2007) Gabon (2001–8) Togo (2002–4)	–	–	–	–	Repressive hegemony

Notes: Cases are aggregated according to whether they share similar scores. Each case represents a period during which it remained a specific electoral authoritarian type and shared the same scores. For example, Cameroon was a repressive hegemony from the 1997 election to the 2002 election. This means that prior to the 1997 election Cameroon's scores for the independent variables were all negative. (*) indicates electoral authoritarian regime ended by electoral turnover; (**) indicates electoral authoritarian regime ended by conflict or coup.

presidency. Ruling parties in these cases were dominated by strong presidents and associated with narrower social incorporation.

Mozambique and FRELIMO

In Mozambique the heritage of armed anti-colonial struggle and a process of ideological radicalization toward Marxism-Leninism turned the ruling Mozambique Liberation Front (FRELIMO) into a credible party. As Carrie Manning writes, FRELIMO was never a personal party, and its internal structures mattered a great deal (2007, 199). After independence the party was elevated as the supreme decision-making body in Mozambique, and quickly embarked on a program of mass mobilization and party construction at the grassroots. FRELIMO supported "dynamizing groups," that consisted of locally elected officials tasked with raising political awareness and overseeing a transition to collective agriculture. These groups later became the foundation for a party cell system and a massive membership recruitment drive. In addition to party cells, FRELIMO created important affiliated mobilizing institutions. Women in particular, through the Mozambique Women's Movement, were active and helped persuade rural women to join communal villages. FELIMO also developed the Mozambique Youth Movement and created production councils that were organized in all major factories of the country. These councils later evolved into the Mozambique Worker's Movement (Isaacman and Isaacman 1983, 126–8).

In addition to its physical size, FRELIMO was also comparatively more internally democratic and widely incorporative. Initially, elections were held at the local level through nomination from a dynamizing group and after vetting by the local party administration. Rejections rates were approximately 10 percent. However, the district, provincial, and national assemblies were indirectly elected during the 1977 election. The second legislative election only took place in 1986, at which point provincial assemblies could elect representatives to the national legislature (Isaacman and Isaacman 1983, 129–30). Policy-wise the party took its ideological commitments to rural peasants and labor seriously. An aggressive and violent campaign was launched against vestiges of the capitalist class, religious organizations, and traditional authorities. As in Tanzania, the ruling party established communal villages, but invested more heavily in large state-owned farms. While FRELIMO maintained the reputation of a party more oriented toward the south rather than the predominately Muslim center and north, the role of ethnic mobilization was clearly lower (Isaacman and Isaacman 1983, 113, Manning 2007, 191–3).

The Seychelles and the SPPF

The construction of the ruling Seychelles People Progressive Front (SPPF) in the small island nation of Seychelles also surprisingly mimicked this pattern.[6] Essentially, the successor to Albert René's Seychelles People's United Party, the SPPF turned Seychelles into a single-party state following René's 1977 coup against incumbent James Mencham. The party quickly proclaimed itself a "socialist avant-garde" party meant to counter the fiscal and personal excesses of the Mencham era (Franda 1982, 62). The SPPF organized itself into twenty-three branches, and internal elections were held by secret ballot every year for local executive committees. Likewise, the SPPF held competitive primaries for single-party legislative elections. The party generated funding through large membership drives, the sale of party publications, and external support from the Soviet Union. It also retained women and youth wings and a strong affiliated trade union (the National Worker's Union). Despite this, the executive did remain comparatively more overbearing, which impinged on ruling party credibility. Term limits were not enforced despite a 1979 constitutional provision that limited the president to three terms (Baker 2008). However, the SPPF was not ethnically defined and its socialist policies for education and health led to significant reduction in income inequality, which helped make Seychelles one of the most developed countries in Africa.

Senegal and the PS

The case of the Socialist Party (PS) in Senegal is more ambiguous, and it is the only case that made the transition to multiparty election prior to the end of the Cold War. During the brief single-party period from 1964 to 1978, the PS had a fairly wide grassroots presence and some mass mobilizing organizations in certain regions. But the party was dominated by the powerful role afforded the executive. Senegal's first president, Leopold Senghor, was considered by Robert Jackson and Carl Rosberg a "princely" figure who utilized his status to mitigate elite conflict and

---

[6] It is worth noting that both FRELIMO and the SPPF were both overtly influenced by the Tanzanian experience. Tanzania was a home base for FRELIMO rebels and the party's secretariat during the conflict against the Portuguese, and Nyerere provided financial support to the SPPF and supported its coup against the Mencham regime.

oversee a complex system that balanced clan chiefs, Islamic leaders, and urban interests (1982, 90–1). Legislative elections in 1968 and 1973 were also plebiscitary in a countrywide constituency. While not as authoritarian as Ahidjo in Cameroon, clientelism still emanated from the presidency (Fatton 1986, Boone 1990). In this sense, the PS seemed less like a credible party and more like a typical patrimonial African regime.

However, the PS did develop some unique advantages with regard to social incorporation that increased its ability to credibly commit to a wider segment of citizens. First, ethnic or religious bias was not readily evident. This was likely due to the fact that Senghor was a Catholic and Serer in a majority-Muslim and Wolof country, and therefore had no real sectarian base. Second, at independence Sufi Brotherhoods or *marabouts* were clearly a dominant form of authority outside of major coastal cities. Senghor utilized this to substitute for party expansion into rural areas, and to reach millions of voters through a quasi-formal institution. As Leonardo Villalón notes, *marabouts* had unique organizational features and established cells with strong political potential (Villalón 1999). In exchange for political largesse the *marabout* orders would endorse Senghor and his successor Abdou Diouf. This system, while outside of the formal confines of the ruling party, linked the PS with large swaths of the rural population. However, it was also brittle, and when the *marabouts* defected from Diouf in the mid-1990s it hampered the PS's competitive capacity and was a factor that led to its defeat in 2000.

Gabon and the PDG

On the other hand the Democratic Party of Gabon (PDG) retained very little credibility building mechanisms. Founded in 1968 by Omar Bongo, the PDG had established national institutions and grassroots structures known as "sections" and "committees." By 1973 the PDG even built a fairly strong affiliated labor wing called the *Confédération Syndicale Gabonaise* (Barnes 1992, 49, Yates 1996, 118–9). But, internally the party was extremely rigid. Party congresses were held intermittently every 5–7 years, elite recruitment remained plebiscitary, and Bongo himself would devise most legislation (Jackson and Rosberg 1982, 158, Aicardi de Saint-Paul 1989, 36). Bongo utilized the large patronage resources at hand from the booming oil industry to maintain a bloated cabinet of over forty ministers. Outside of a core group of leaders, cabinet shuffles were frequent. Bongo's dominance eventually led to deep contention within the PDG, and at the 1979 Delegates Conferences Bongo finally loosened his grip and allowed PDG delegates to nominate some of the central committee and legislative slate. By 1985 Bongo had also resigned as secretary-general of the PDG.

Likewise, the PDG was essentially a preferential ethnic coalition that favored the president's own cohort. Bongo was a minority Batéké from the distant eastern province of Haute-Ogooué, and therefore perceived himself above the fray of the predominant ethnic rivalry between the Fang and Myene. Cabinets tended to reflect an ethnic balance with a Fang Prime Minister and Myene President of the National Assembly. Yet, it was also evident that public investment and other public appointments disproportionately benefitted Haute-Ogooué, and specifically Bongo's immediate family. By 1985 nearly three-quarters of industrialization took place in three regions alone and included controversial projects like the Trans-Gabonaise railway, which linked Huate-Ogoouée and the capital Libreville. At one point a quarter of cabinet ministers were Batéké, many of them Bongo's relatives. Likewise, important members of the military, including the secretive *Société Générale de Sécurité* and a 1,500-strong Presidential Guard, were often Bongo's relatives.[7]

Côte d'Ivoire and the PDCI

Many scholars initially considered the Democratic Party of Côte d'Ivoire (PDCI) a ripe vehicle for mass politics and deeper institutionalization because of the influence of the planter class and powerful agricultural syndicates. However, as Ruth Morgentahu notes in an early and perceptive study of the PDCI, party leaders felt "they had little time to spend on party organization," and that "they already had a spontaneously evolving structure along ethnic lines" (1967, 182–5). The persona of President Félix Hophouët-Boigny and a small circle of trusted advisors dominated politics. Legislative elections were plebiscitary up to 1980, succession was never institutionalized, and the party atrophied and remained relatively weak (Jackson and Rosberg 1982, 149–52, Mundt 1997, 185–7). There was evidence that policies benefited Boigny's own Baoulé ethnic group, but ethnic mobilization was less overt. Instead, the PDCI retained narrower support from urban constituencies and cash-crop farmers, in particular cocoa and coffee manufacturers. There was no sincere effort to incorporate wider rural populations (Crook 1989, 226).

---

[7] While some prominent Fang were incorporated into the regime, the PDG essentially reflected an anti-Fang coalition of southern and central groups. See, Yates (1996, 47), Decalo (1998, 121–43), and Gardinier (1997, 147).

Togo and the RPT

The character of Togo's first president Gnassingbé Eyadéma likewise dominated the Rally of Togolese People (RPT). The RPT was constructed after Eyadéma's 1963 military coup, but really only existed on paper until 1979 when emergency rule finally ended. This meant that the RPT's grassroots structures were not established, and there were only symbolic youth and women wings to the party. The RPT was highly centralized and most decision-making occurred through the presidency and his strong association with the military. Eyadéma appointed the majority of the party's politburo and central committee, and internal elections remained plebiscitary until 1985 (Decalo 1987, 87, 178–9). A cult of personality further limited the credibility of the party (Ellis 1993), and there were clear ethnic divisions between the north and south regions of Togo. Cabinet membership was fairly balanced, but other public resources were skewed toward the north and the Kabye tribes, of which Eyadéma was a member (Heilbrunn 1993, 282, Nwajiaku 1994, 432).

Djibouti and the RPP

Finally, Djibouti only became independent from the French in 1977 and the ruling People's Rally for Progress (RPP), itself an amalgam of pre-independence parties, was founded in 1979 by Hassan Gouled Aptidon. This gave the regime very little time to develop robust grassroots structures, and elections under single-party rule were centralized and heavily manipulated by Aptidon. The president retained large powers of appointment and acted as head of government, state, the armed services, and public administration. Aptidon essentially handpicked the small legislature of sixty-five members (Alwan and Mibrathu 2000). The government ostensibly reflected a balance between the two major Djiboutian ethnic groups, with the president an Issa and the appointed Prime Minister an Afar. Likewise, the cabinet and legislature tended to reflect the ethnic composition of the country, even if Aptidon appointed all their members. This, however, did not prevent perceptions of Issa domination in the military, civil service, and public spending. In late 1991 the Front for the Restoration of Unity and Democracy launched an armed insurgency in support of Afar interests (Shehim and Searing 1980, Schraeder 1993).

INTERNATIONAL PATRONAGE IN THE MULTIPARTY ERA

The end of the Cold War elevated questions of democracy and human rights on the international stage, and helped foster an industry dedicated to democracy and election assistance. Take for instance the foundational election in Mozambique, which coincided with the resolution of a brutal civil war and became one of the most internationally observed elections in history. Likewise, all of these countries were at some point intertwined with bilateral lenders and international financial institutions due to economic crisis. For many the culprit was the fall in oil and commodity prices that began in the late 1970s. For oil-dependent countries, such as Gabon, and major commodity exporters, such as Côte d'Ivoire and Togo, this turn of events exacerbated severely mismanaged economies and heavy state intervention.[8] In other countries, the global fall in commodity prices aggravated deteriorating economic conditions, made worse by civil war in cases like Djibouti and Mozambique.[9] By 1990, every country had negotiated some form of structural adjustment facility.

As the electoral authoritarian period unfolded, important differences in external actor capacity and willingness to push for political and economic reform emerged. Capacity was clearly limited in the cases of Gabon and Seychelles, where ODA remained below 4 percent of GDP throughout the period of study. In the case of Gabon this was due to recovering and substantial oil rents that constituted approximately 30–50 percent of GDP. In Seychelles, the difference was made up with Foreign Direct Investment (FDI), primarily into the country's booming tourism industry. Between 1996 and 2001, FDI in Seychelles was approximately 10 percent of GDP – a rate much higher than in other African countries. This limited external actors' access to central economic tools of democratic pressure. The other countries were much more aid dependent, and therefore potentially more susceptible to international democracy efforts. The most aid-dependent country was Mozambique, and between 1994 and 2009 ODA averaged at 32 percent of GDP. In Côte d'Ivoire, Djibouti, Senegal, and Togo ODA fluctuated but remained persistently above 10 percent of GDP (Bank 2014).

Conversely, external actors, and specifically the French, often acted as bulwarks against democratic pressure, or as what Levitsky and Way have termed Black Knights (2010). By 1990, France had numerous defense

---

[8] In Gabon oil revenue fell from 65 to 30 percent of the budget in a manner of years (Gardinier 1997). In Côte d'Ivoire receipts from cotton and coffee declined 40 percent and the World Bank reclassified the country as a Low Income country instead of a Middle-Income country (Mundt 1997). Togo's economy was also heavily dependent on the export of phosphates, which declined precipitously during the 1980s (Heilbrunn 1997).

[9] Mozambique and Senegal relied heavily on agriculture as an economic mainstay (Marshall 1990, Vengroff and Creevey 1997). By contrast, during this period Seychelles elevated itself from a subsistence-based economy to one built primarily on state-owned tourism and small fisheries (Baker 2008). Similarly, Djibouti's economy was largely nonexistent prior to independence and has since relied on state-run shipping and government employment (Brass 2008).

agreements in place and viewed several African countries as key strategic and economic partners (Martin 1995, Gregory 2000). The French provided military assistance to bolster incumbents in Togo (1986), Côte d'Ivoire (1990), and Gabon (1990). Côte d'Ivoire and Gabon were likewise important trade partners and sources of resources like oil and uranium. In both instances, there were deep personal ties between African leaders and the French political elite. Hophouët-Boigny was infamously a frequent guest in Paris, and the intertwined relationship between France and Gabon's political elite is often referred to as the *Clan des Gabonais*.[10] French autocratic patronage was important, but to a lesser degree, in Djibouti, Senegal, and Togo. For instance, Togo was a major source of French phosphate imports, and during a 1999 visit Jacques Chirac expressed his support for Eyadéma and criticized a devastating Amnesty International report on Togo's human rights practices.[11] The French were not the only international power with strong conflicting foreign policy goals in the region. Most evidently, Djibouti became the site of new American strategic interests following the September 11, 2001 attacks, and was elevated as a tactical center for military operations in Somalia, Sudan, and Yemen (Bollee 2003, Brass 2008).

This leaves just a select number of instances where capacity and political will could be marshaled in the form of democratic patronage. Yet, it is rare to find instances of persistent use of democracy programming or aid conditionality. One issue is an apparent foundational election bias. In many instances democracy-programming funding declined sharply after foundational elections. This is particularly evident in Mozambique, which garnered significant international attention prior to its foundational election in 1994 but fell off international radars soon thereafter. Similarly, democracy assistance appears to respond to conflict, but is not employed systematically. For instance, Tanzania received substantially more democracy assistance prior to the 2005 election, but this aid was in response to violence that occurred in Zanzibar during the previous election, and therefore not spent on election-related activities on mainland Tanzania. Another issue is that Francophone countries generally receive less democracy aid than other countries. There are very few periods

---

[10] This phrase specifically refers to the influence of Jacques Foccart, Charles de Gaulle's chief African advisor, and Pierre Péan's book *Affaires Africaines*. It was suggested that the "clan" handpicked Omar Bongo as the successor to Gabon's first president Léon M'ba (Yates 1996, 106–17).

[11] Norimitsu Onishi. "French President Stirs Anger During Visit to West Africa" *The New York Times* (July 24, 1999).

where Francophone countries netted democracy assistance at amounts significantly above the sample average: only in Côte d'Ivoire prior to the 1995 election, and Djibouti prior to the 2003 and 2005 election cycles.[12]

The record of aid conditionality is similarly quite weak. Donors and international lenders suspended aid over corruption and political conditions in just a number of instances: Cameroon between 1994 and 1999, Kenya between 1990 and 1993 and then again between 1997 and 1999, Tanzania between 1994 and 1995, and Togo between 1993 and 2007.[13] As in Cameroon, the French joined other countries and suspended aid to Togo in 1993, but restored a more limited amount of assistance just one year later.[14] At other times, declines in international lending were temporary or not clearly tied to political conditionality. In terms of outcomes, the data is limited and difficult to parse. Cabinet size, an imperfect proxy for the strength of patronage, increased in most of these ten cases, as did perceptions of public sector corruption. Data on the privatization of state owned enterprises is also constrained since there are no consistent accounts of the size of the public sector prior to structural adjustment negotiations. Cameroon, Côte d'Ivoire, Kenya, Mozambique, and Tanzania had comparatively more state-owned enterprises than in Senegal or Togo, but significant privatization did not occur in Cameroon, Côte d'Ivoire or Togo.[15] Consequently, there are not many cases where international actors had the wherewithal to act as democratic patrons, and consistently employed both strong democracy programming *and* aid conditionality.

The one possible example of democratic patronage outside of Kenya is found in Togo between the 2005 and 2010 election. While Togo was not the target of sustained and large-scale democratic pressure, international actors did combine economic conditionality with some democracy programming. Following the 2002 election, which was boycotted by major opposition parties, international pressure began to build. This

[12] This is calculated by looking at the total amount of democracy-oriented aid, rather than aid per capita. The logic is that the amount of money it takes to train a political party or civil society organization, or to improve an election management body, is not dependent on the size of the population (Tierney et al. 2011).

[13] Staff. "Tanzania Donors U-Turn Aid Suspension Position" *Inter Press Service* (November 24, 1994), Crawford (1997) and Kari Barber. "Togolese Hope for More EU Aid Following Elections" *Voice of America* (October 9, 2007).

[14] Staff. "France Suspends Aid to Togo" *New York Times* (February 12, 1993). French aid to Togo dropped from $91 million a year in 1990 to $10.3 million a year by 2001.

[15] Data on cabinet size is from the annual *Africa South of the Sahara*, data on perceptions of corruption is from *Transparency International*, and data on privatization of SOEs' enterprises is from the World Bank's dataset on privatization (World Bank 2009).

corresponded with increased European interaction with the continent, and specifically criticism of Togo's poor human rights record. In April 2003, the EU entered into the Cotonou Agreement with the African, Caribbean, and Pacific group of states. The agreement built on the Lomé IV trade convention of 1993, but added new language that explicitly allowed the EU to condition future aid on improved governance.[16] Togo became a major target of these new international tools. After a decade of constrained foreign aid, in 2004 President Gnassingbé Eyadéma acceded to an EU-sponsored plan that would restore aid in exchange for significant democratic improvements. However, in February 2005 Eyadéma died suddenly and the military suspended the constitution to install his son Faure as president in the April 2005 election.

This succession maneuver incurred widespread international condemnation, including new sanctions from the Economic Community of West Africa and extensive EU pressure under the guise of the Cotonou Agreement.[17] This pressure, combined with an apparent desire on the part of Faure to reset trade relations with the Europeans, appeared to work. The 2007 legislative election was held under a new electoral code, and with a reformed electoral commission that had more opposition representation. There was greater international election observation and an EU-funded voter registry (Roberts 2008). However, full international aid was restored surprisingly quickly with little follow-up on political reform. In 2011, Togo received a whopping $373 million in bilateral aid alone, nearly twice the amount it had received in 1994.[18] Togo also regained access to nearly $160 million in EU aid and significant debt relief through the Highly Indebted Poor Countries Initiative.[19] Direct democracy assistance in the form of party training and domestic election observation also largely disappeared, and the next elections did not garner the same degree of international attention.

---

[16] At the time Eyadéma was seeking a controversial third term and likely saw the restoration of more substantial international aid as necessary (Seely 2009, 168–9).

[17] See, Lydia Polgreen. "Togo President, Installed by Army, Agrees to an Election" *The New York Times* (February 9, 2005), Staff. "Togo: Decades of Poor Governance and Sanctions have Taken a Heavy Toll" *IRIN News* (February 22, 2005), Kwadwo Appiagyei-Atua. "Political Developments in Post–Eyadéma Togo: A Critical Analysis" *Human Rights Brief* 12, 3 (2005).

[18] Staff. "EU Resumes Aid to Togo after Multi-Party Polls" *Reuters* (November 29, 2007).

[19] The restoration of aid was also due to the 2007 global financial crisis, although Togo was only moderately impacted given its poorer integration with financial markets and limited export base. See Dagher et al. (2009).

OPPOSITION CAPACITY IN THE MULTIPARTY ERA

As discussed in Chapter 1 the cohesion and actions of opposition parties provide an alternative explanation for variation in electoral authoritarian competition. The often-heard complaint regarding African opposition parties is that they lack physical organizations, are nonexistent between elections and make detrimental decisions during elections, such as boycotting or avoiding coalitions. Consequently, African party systems are volatile and poorly institutionalized, which allows incumbents to dominate elections. Yet, the causal direction is not always clear. Repressive conditions and overwhelming executives limit the opportunities that oppositions have to plant deeper roots and forces upon them distinct logics of contestation. If an opposition party's main incentive is to regain access to the resources of the state rather than represent or aggregate constituents' interests, it might actually remain ineffective so it can be coopted more easily. On the other hand, stronger opposition parties that either have roots in preexisting political structures, such as unions (LeBas 2011), or take deliberate steps to strengthen their parties (Morse 2014) might incur heavier repression. Therefore, repressive conditions might be the cause and the product of weak opposition parties.

I look at two major factors that are unrelated to an opposition party's success at the polls, and instead measure their institutional strengths: *party stability* and *party decision making.*[20] With regard to party stability, I ask whether a major opposition party has experienced a split prior to an election cycle, and whether important members of the party have been coopted or taken government positions that might impinge on the party's autonomy. With regard to decision making, I look for the presence of opposition coalitions and boycotts. I consider formal alliances like the NARC coalition in Kenya, but also informal patterns of cooperation seen during Tanzania's 2000 presidential election when CHADEMA entered a tacit agreement with the CUF to not run a rival presidential candidate. Looking at boycotts, since the decision by major opposition parties not to participate in an election is so drastic, when they do occur opposition capacity is coded as zero. The logic is that if opposition parties do not contest the election, it is impossible to assess their capacity.

---

[20] One could also look at more direct measures of party institutionalization like leadership turnover, the size of membership, or the party's regional vote share. These are all fine indicators, but accounting for party splits are the actual outcomes of weak party institutionalization.

Weaker opposition parties are more persistently found in more repressive contexts. This is true of the two major cases of this book, Cameroon and Kenya. Since 1992, the major opposition parties in Cameroon have either disappeared completely or have been coopted by the regime. As noted previously, the UPC split into the UPC-N under Ndeh Ntumazah and the UPC-K under Augustin Kodock. In 2002, Henri Hogbe-Nlend formed yet another faction called the UPC-H, and all three factions have joined government. In 1992, the NUDP also split when Bello Bouba Maigari forced Samuel Eboua out as chairman and Eboua left to form the Movement for Democracy and Progress. Two years later another faction left the NUDP and formed the National Alliance for Democracy. Senior members of the NUDP, including Maigari himself, have entered into a coalition with the CPDM (Ngoh 2004, 445–8). The SDF has not been immune to party factionalization either. Clashes over John Fru Ndi's leadership have caused frequent tension.[21] Between 2002 and 2006, several elites defected from the SDF to form the Alliance of Progressive Forces, and in 2011 another faction left with Edith Kah Walla to join the Cameroon People's Party.[22]

Opposition parties in Cameroon have also frequently eschewed strategic decision making that might improve their competitive capacity. In addition to the boycotts of the 1992 legislative and 1997 presidential elections, efforts at cooperation have uniformly failed. After the *villes mortes* strikes the NUDP, UDC, and UDP abandoned joint efforts with the SDF and agreed to hold elections without a national conference under what was called the Tripartite Agreement (Takougang and Krieger 1998, 141–2). Another attempt at an opposition coalition, the Union for Change, collapsed prior to the 1992 presidential election. Similarly short-lived fates awaited the Front of Allies for Change in 1997, the Coalition for National Reconciliation and Reconstruction in 2004. In both instances the SDF withdrew its support following disagreements over the choice of who the alliance's presidential candidate should be.[23]

---

[21] In 1992, the SDF's Secretary General Siga Assanga (who was also John Fru Ndi's uncle) was expelled. In 1995, the SDF's campaign manager Bernard "Ben" Muna was also dismissed. In 1998, ten of the party's legislative representatives resigned in protest over Fru Ndi's leadership. Later that year, the party's Vice Chairman Mahamat Souleymane was dismissed for calling an unauthorized party convention (Krieger 2008, 84–5).

[22] See Staff. "Crise au SDF. Le Principal Parti d'Opposition Explose" *Afrique Express* (February 9, 2002), Alhaji Sani Georges Dougueli. "Cameroon: John Fru Ndi's Problems" *Jeune Afrique* (September 19, 2006), Guy Modeste Dzudie. "Sdf: Clash Entre Fru Ndi et le Président Provincial du Sdf-Ouest" *Le Messager* (October 31, 2007).

[23] François Soudan. "How the Opposition Committed Suicide" *Jeune Afrique-L'Intelligent* (September 26, 2004).

In Kenya the opposition was likewise institutionally weak, despite the fact that it ultimately was able to defeat KANU at the polls in 2002. The major opposition party, FORD, notoriously split into rival factions prior to the 1992 election – FORD-A under Kenneth Matiba and FORD-K under Oginga Odinga. This was the prelude to persistent fractionalization, largely along ethnic lines, that would hamper opposition parties. After the 1992 election, many Kikuyu elites left FORD-K for the DP, and in 1995 many Luo followed Raila Odinga to form the NDP. The NDP later joined the KANU government prior to the 2002 election. Disputes within FORD-A forced Martin Shikuku out of the party in 1997 to form Saba Saba Asili, while other disgruntled members left and founded the rival FORD-Asili (Hornsby 2012, 601–3). The DP was not immune to party splits, and in 1996 Charity Ngilu took significant Kamba support to the Social Democratic Party. Ngilu later left to form the National Party of Kenya. There were also a number of other smaller parties that broke away from the remnants of FORD and the DP. These include Paul Muite's *Safina* and James Orengo's United Movement for Change. On the other hand, there were no major election boycotts, but also little cooperation between parties prior to 2002.

This pattern holds in a number of other repressive cases. In Gabon the opposition showed early promise, but this faded once the Movement for National Renewal split into rival factions just prior to the foundational election: the National Woodcutter's Rally (RNB) and MORENA-Original (Gardinier 1997). This factionalism continued in 1998 when the RNB also fragmented into the rival RNB-D and RNB-RPG. Many of these new parties later joined the PDG's ruling coalition and backed Omar Bongo for president in 2005. There has likewise been no cooperation between parties, and in 2011 most of the remaining opposition boycotted the election. In Djibouti the major opposition force, joined government, leaving only the much smaller Democratic Renewal Party and National Democratic Party to contest. These parties formed a coalition called the Union for a Democratic Alternative, but also boycotted elections in 2005, 2008, and 2011. In Côte d'Ivoire the Ivorian Popular Front and the Rally of Republicans did not experience party splits, but did not cooperate and boycotted the 1995 presidential election. Only in the case of Togo is there more ambiguity across elections. The major opposition parties, the Action Committee for Renewal and the Union of Forces for Change were remarkably stable between 1990 and 2010. They did not undergo major splits or cooptation, but they did consistently boycott elections until 2005. In 2005, the opposition formed a coalition to contest the presidential election, but in 2010 they controversially joined government, which forced a major party split.[24] During the 2013 legislative election there were two rival coalitions, the Save Togo Collective and the Rainbow Alliance.

Where electoral contestation is more tolerated it is more common to find stronger opposition capacities. In Tanzania, the CUF, CHADEMA, and NCCR-M, have remained the dominant political parties since 1995, even though they have also experienced some degree of factionalism. In 1999, Augustin Mrema defected from the NCCR-M to the TLP, reportedly taking the party's office furniture with him.[25] In 1998, the CUF expelled its co-founder James Mapalala, and in 2015 its Secretary General Ibrahim Lipumba suddenly left the party.[26] In 2015, CHADEMA expelled the popular MP Zitto Kabwe, and its former presidential candidate Wilibrod Slaa left the party in protest over the nomination of Edward Lowassa.[27] However, this factionalism never amounted to major party splits, whereby new parties were formed with large segments of the former party. Opposition parties in Tanzania have likewise never joined government or boycotted an election, and have been more cooperative. In 1995 and 2000 CHADEMA entered into informal alliances with other parties and did not run a rival presidential candidate. In 2015 the major opposition parties formed a true alliance called the Coalition for the People's Constitution (*Ukawa*).

In other cases where contestation is more tolerant, opposition capacity is similarly stronger. In Mozambique, the major opposition party and the regime's former civil war rival RENAMO has persistently contested elections, and has remained the primary opposition party. This persistence is despite its manifest difficulty at transitioning from a military organization to a viable political party (Manning 1998, Carbone 2005). However, in 2009 RENAMO experienced its first major split when the Democratic Movement of Mozambique broke away.[28] In Senegal, Aboudlaye Wade's

[24] Staff. "Togo Opposition to Join Coalition Government" *BBC News* (May 27, 2010).
[25] Staff. "Undermining the Very Concept of Multi-Partyism" *Tanzanian Affairs* 63 (May 1999).
[26] Staff. "The Divided Opposition" *Tanzanian Affairs* 59 (January 1998), Jenerali Ulimwengu. "Lipumba's Sudden Resignation Dents Ukawa Solidarity Ahead of Election" *The East African* (August 8, 2015).
[27] Florence Mugarula. "Zitto: Here Is Why I Chose to Join ACT" *The Citizen* (March 23, 2015), Katare Mbashiru. "CHADEMA: We Are Moving on Without Slaa" *The Citizen*, (August 4, 2015).
[28] Barry Berak. "Party's Power in Mozambique Is Criticized as Barrier to Democracy" *New York Times* (October 26, 2009).

Senegalese Democratic Party (PDS) was the dominant opposition party from 1978 onwards. While the party did not experience a major rift, Wade did sit in government between 1991 and 1992 and again between 1995 and 1998, which somewhat limited the party's autonomy. The *Sopi* coalition of 2000, which toppled the ruling PS, consisted mainly of the PDS and other minor parties. In Seychelles, James Mancham's Seychelles Democratic Party and Wavel Ramkalawan's Seychelles National Party have been the major two opposition parties. There have not been major rifts, and the Seychelles Democratic Party backed Ramakalawn presidential bid in 2001. The two parties forged an alliance in 2006 and 2007, but then surprisingly boycotted the 2011 elections.

ECONOMIC PERFORMANCE IN THE MULTIPARTY ERA

The final alternative theory to consider is the role of economic performance. In Chapter 1, I noted two advantages that a stable economy bestows upon electoral authoritarian regimes. First, more steady economies increase the range of patronage resources available to autocrats, whether it is rents from state-owned enterprises, wealth from natural resource extraction, or finances generated through control of the private sector. Second, an improving economy also helps preserve voter loyalty by providing more employment opportunities to citizens, raising incomes, and in the African context by delivering improvements in terms of citizens' social welfare. On the other hand, economic decline and crisis might dramatically shrink these resources and shock regimes. The impact of economic decline might actually be more relevant than the impact of a growing economy (Haggard and Kaufman 1995). The consequences for electoral authoritarianism are theoretically fairly straightforward. When economies are stable, if not necessarily robust the incentives for elite and voter defection are reduced. This guarantees stronger vote share during the election, and reduces the regime's need to engage in manipulation. The question is whether this holds regardless of party capacity, or rather interacts with party capacity in interesting ways. To that effect, I look at records of real economic growth, and absolute and relative changes in the Human Development Index (HDI).

Looking at the actual record of economic growth and social welfare it is difficult to find a case in the post-Cold War era that has been a real powerhouse, which is again why the emphasis is more on crisis than on rapid and stable growth. Looking at the average GDP per capita rates and price inflation in the years prior to an election allows for a succinct account of real economic growth.[29] Outside of foundational elections there are four notable patterns. First, there are countries that have "overheated," meaning their rates of inflation have far outpaced their moderate rates of growth. This captures the experience of Cameroon (1993–7), Gabon (1994–8), Mozambique (2000–9), Seychelles (2008–11), and Tanzania (1996–2000, 2006–15). Second, there are countries that have "muddled through" and sustained fairly low growth and inflation rates, as in Cameroon (1998–2013), Djibouti (2000–11), Gabon (2007–11), Senegal (1994–2001), Tanzania (2001–5), and Togo (1994–9, 2008–13). Third, there are periods of time where countries have experienced recession or actual stagflation as in Côte d'Ivoire (1991–5), Djibouti (1994–5), Gabon (1999–2006), Kenya (1993–2002), Senegal (1990–3), Seychelles (1999–2002), and Togo (2000–7). Fourth, there are few periods of time where countries have actually experienced positive real growth. This was most clearly the case in Mozambique (1995–9) and Seychelles (1994–8, 2003–7).

The HDI index measures life expectancy, education, and income per capita, and can therefore be used as proxy for the absolute level and changes in social wellbeing. In all the countries under study the HDI has increased in the post–Cold War era, but at very dissimilar rates and with ultimately different outcomes as far as absolute levels are concerned. For instance, in the case of Togo HDI rose from 0.384 in 1993 to 0.459 in 2013. This translates into annual improvements of less than 1 percent and also keeps Togo within the category of "low developed countries." By contrast, in Mozambique the HDI grew between 1994 and 2009 from 0.2 to 0.31, or an annualized 3.4 percent increase. While Mozambique is still considered a low developed country, and is comparatively still less developed than Togo, the larger annual gains deserve some accounting for when assessing economic performance. In only a few instances have there been actual declines in HDI: prior to Cameroon's 1997 election, and Kenya's 1997 and 2002 elections. Moreover, in two cases – Gabon and Seychelles – levels of HDI were associated with medium and highly developed country statuses respectively. Therefore, in these latter two cases expected improvements in HDI from one election cycle to the next were predicted to be much lower, since they started from such higher levels of development to begin with.

Combined, real rates of growth and levels and improvements in HDI can provide an assessment of economic performance for each case and

[29] I use the average rate of both factors prior to an election to account for broader economic trends that might influence elites and voters. All data comes from (World Bank 2016).

electoral period (details are found in the Appendix B). The bar for positive economic performance is fairly low since there are no real cases of sustained and broad-based economic development among this set of cases, but also because the theoretical assumption is that economic crisis rather than rapid growth will impact regime stability and competition. Several countries are coded as negative since they combined tepid to negative real growth rates with stagnant to declining rates of human development. This was the case in Cameroon (1993–7), Côte d'Ivoire (1991–5), Djibouti (1994–2005), Gabon (1994–2006), Kenya (1993–2002), Senegal (1999–2001), and Togo (2000–7). Economic performance was coded as positive when there was at least minimal growth and/or some improvement to human development, or already a high level of human development. This was the case in Cameroon (1998–), Djibouti (2006–), Gabon (1994–8, 2007–), Mozambique (1995–), Senegal (1993–9), Seychelles (1994–), Tanzania (1996–), and Togo (1994–9, 2008–).

PUTTING THE SPACE TOGETHER: A TYPOLOGICAL THEORY

Table 8.1 summarizes the scores for party credibility, international patronage, opposition capacity, and economic performance, and arranges the cases according to whether they share the same arrays of scores and similar electoral authoritarian outcomes. To recall, countries appear as separate cases based on the unit of analysis, which is the electoral cycle, meaning the closest non-foundational legislative and presidential election. Each row therefore represents a different array of variables, or a path that leads to distinct electoral authoritarian: tolerant hegemony, repressive hegemony, tolerant but non-hegemonic regime, or repressive but non-hegemonic regime. The space indicates that legacies of party building and international relations remain paramount causal factors, even in a wider array of cases.

Ruling party credibility effectively distinguishes between tolerant and repressive competition. In all cases where the regime had a credible ruling party, which admittedly is scored as a constant here while the other factors vary, electoral authoritarian competition was tolerant and hegemonic for significant periods of time. This is in-line with theoretical expectations that single-party regimes that invested into robust and inclusive ruling parties were more likely to retain elite and social support during multiparty elections, without the need for extensive manipulation. By contrast, all the single-party regimes with weaker party credibility transitioned to repressive forms of electoral authoritarianism. With the exception of Kenya and Togo – the only repressive countries that sustained some form of democratic patronage – all of these cases remained repressive hegemonies after their foundational elections. International patronage, opposition capacity, and economic performance do not wield the same discriminatory power.

The typological space does yield some additional interesting comparative findings. The first is that in tolerant cases economic performance does appear to sustain electoral hegemony. This echoes a similar finding regarding the longer-term prospects of the Mexican PRI, which is also associated with an enduring and fairly tolerant electoral authoritarian regime (Magaloni 2006). In Mozambique the 1994 foundational election was only narrowly won, and accompanied by a large degree of international involvement. Prior to the 1999 election, the level of democracy aid fell from approximately $2.5 million a year to less than $1 million. While other international aid declined by nearly 20 percent, this was not due to conditionality but the end of reconstruction efforts following the Mozambican civil war. A major challenge for the regime was the weak state of the economy. Mozambique entered the multiparty era with some of the lowest records of economic growth and human wellbeing. While there were considerable economic improvements by 1999, this was accompanied by an extremely high rate of price inflation that translated into a real growth rate of negative 18 percent. However, by 2004 these measures had stabilized while the economy continued to make profound improvements. In 2009, after the Democratic Movement of Mozambique left RENAMO, FRELIMO won 75 percent of the presidential vote and 76 percent of the legislative seats.

In Senegal the story is reversed, and economic decline preceded the end of electoral authoritarianism and the PS's nearly two-decade electoral domination. The PS had overwhelmingly and easily won elections since 1978. However, the 1980s brought new economic challenges, which also stressed the crucial relationship between president Abdou Diouf and the Sufi Brotherhoods. Between 1988 and 1998 the *marabouts* gradually stopped issuing edicts in support of the PS, which significantly altered the social basis of the regime and reduced its credibility (Galvan 2001). Electoral authoritarian competition remained as a tolerant hegemony for most the 1990s, despite anemic growth and near zero improvements in HDI. During this period, the opposition likely hurt itself by repeatedly joining government to the chagrin of its supporters. This equilibrium was temporary, and despite improved economic conditions by 2000 the opposition had coalesced into the *Sopi* coalition, which defeated the PS.

A second new finding is that among the repressive regimes economic performance has a much weaker influence on competition. The most apparent evidence for this is the fact that during several election cycles in Cameroon, Côte d'Ivoire, Djibouti, Gabon, and Togo there was no meaningful decline in hegemony despite significant economic problems. Only in Côte d'Ivoire did economic crisis have any real impact, and is linked to the military coup that swept the PDCI from power in 1999 (Toungara 2001). However, in this case economic straits were quite severe, with real growth rates at a pitiful negative 15 percent and little improvement in the HDI. In the other cases, the economic crisis was real but less severe, and performance picked up during subsequent election cycles. For instance, by 2004 growth in Cameroon was essentially flat with minimal spikes in inflation, but the HDI did improve approximately 2–6 percent between each election cycle. Therefore, while in the longer term some economic stability might be necessary for repressive hegemonies too, it might take more prolonged or acute crisis to impact the degree of competition absent some other change.

Third, the case of Togo offers some unique comparative leverage into the role of international patronage because the independent variables have changed the most from one period to the next. Between the 1998 and 2002 election, Togo was a repressive hegemony, but with relatively stronger economic performance. Between 2002 and 2004, Togo remained a repressive hegemony, this time with weaker economic performance. However, by the 2005 election there were significant changes in both international patronage and opposition capacity. In 2005, Faure Gnassingbé won just 60.15 percent of the presidential vote, and in 2007 the RPT won 62 percent of the legislative seats, which forced a government of national unity. As noted earlier, between these elections and the next election cycle, international pressure pulled back and a number of new repressive measures were put into place. In 2009, the Togolese government removed a residency requirement from presidential candidates, which was supposed to clear the way for opposition candidate Gilchrist Olympio to contest in 2010. However, the electoral commission nonetheless disqualified Olympio over alleged health issues. In 2012, Eyadéma promised to hold a census and reform the civil service, but instead the regime adopted a new electoral code without review just five months prior to the scheduled legislative election (Freedom House 2013). Absent any penalty for misbehavior, and now sustained by stronger economic growth and a weaker opposition, Eyadéma and the ruling party made significant electoral gains in 2010 and 2013 to once again became a repressive hegemony.

The typological theory does suggest that there is possibly more interaction among these variables. For instance, the change in Mozambique
from a tolerant non-hegemony between 1994 and 2004 to a tolerant
hegemony from 2004 onwards corresponds with improvements in the
economy, but also a decline in opposition capacity. Yet, the change in
the opposition did not happen until the 2009 election, and it is difficult
to tease out whether hegemony in Mozambique is due to the success
of its economy, or how the growth in the economy made it difficult for
RENAMO to effectively contest the regime, and therefore also facilitated
the party split in 2009. In Togo, causal factors also interact in perhaps
more nuanced ways. As in Kenya, the increases in democratic patronage prior to the 2005 and 2007 elections correspond with declines in
economic performance. Therefore, it is possible that democratic patronage requires greater economic vulnerability to begin with. Moreover, the
increased international attention in Togo parallels opposition coalition
making efforts. This is again similar to Kenya, where international diplomacy helped opposition parties avoid boycotts. Even though opposition
parties in Togo were relatively more capable institutions, once democratic
patronage declined so did the strength of the opposition.

More broadly, the typological space highlights some interesting
insights regarding the role of opposition capacity. As discussed here,
opposition parties are generally weaker in repressive cases and stronger
in tolerant ones. Recall, this does not mean stronger in a narrow electoral
sense, but in reference to an opposition party's ability to institutionalize and repeatedly compete. It is therefore unsurprisingly endogenous.
Repressive environments do often lead to further detrimental decision-
making like frequent election boycotts or party splits, while more open
and tolerant electoral conditions allow political parties to lay down real
roots. Yet, the inability of institutionally sounder parties to erode regime
hegemony is at first glance counterintuitive. Parties under tolerant conditions in Mozambique, Senegal, Seychelles, and Tanzania are afforded
crucial advantages, so why do they not translate electorally? However,
their electoral shortcomings should not be surprising given a better
understanding of the regimes they are up against. Opposition parties in
tolerant hegemonies armed with credible ruling parties can only really
challenge incumbents that go through longer-term processes of decline
as in Senegal. Most indicative of this is Tanzania, where there has been
remarkable opposition consistency, cooperation, and an aversion to boycotts. Nonetheless, opposition parties in Tanzania have not pushed CCM
off of its hegemonic perch.

This is not to suggest that opposition parties are irrelevant for this discussion, but rather that they might have less to do with the competitive environment and more to do with specific outcomes. For instance, in Senegal if the PDS has not formed the *Sopi* coalition at the right moment, there very well might not have been an electoral turnover in 2000. Likewise, the opposition in Kenya was objectively weak, institutionally speaking, and did not cooperate in either the 1992 or 1997 election. Prior to 2002 there were rival alliances and a major wing of the opposition had been coopted by the regime into New KANU. Yet, without the NARC coalition the KANU regime might have more easily coopted specific parties, or won with a slim plurality. The specific opposition decision-making prior to the 2002 election made a difference for the ultimate outcome – defeating KANU – but it was not the main factor that shaped the broader competitive context. That was the weakness of KANU as a ruling party, and the comparatively robust international efforts at democracy promotion sustained throughout the electoral authoritarian period.

CONCLUSION

The tool of typological theorizing is useful for testing and expanding on theories that involve in-depth and qualitative evaluations of data. In this case, the typological space largely corroborates the arguments developed in the rest of this book. First, ruling party credibility is a major explanatory factor that differentiates types of electoral authoritarian competition. All the cases of tolerant hegemonies are associated with credible parties of some variety. By contrast, all repressive electoral authoritarian outcomes are related to the absence of these parties. Second, the addition of Togo as a case suggests that the role of democratic patronage is a clearer secondary factor that explains when repression is more likely to become a winning strategy. Third, the typological space provided new insights into the contingent role of economic performance, specifically when repression is not utilized as an electoral strategy, and into the more ambiguous role of opposition capacity in determining electoral authoritarian competition. This chapter caps a longer discussion regarding the role of credible ruling parties and international patronage in the process of electoral authoritarian contestation. In the next chapter I summarize my main arguments and derive some broader conclusions for the study of authoritarian politics, Africa, and democracy studies.

Conclusions: The Comparative Study of Electoral Authoritarianism

> But elections are not the beginning and end of democracy.
> —Julius Nyerere (*Freedom and Socialism*, 1968)

What explains variation in electoral authoritarian competition? Why is it that some regimes can dominate elections with comparatively lower levels of manipulation while others cannot? Why does manipulation sometimes produce electoral dividends, but at other times it does not? These are the fundamental questions that have motivated this book, and answering them is crucial if we are to understand how contemporary authoritarianism operates. The obvious answer to the puzzle of authoritarian resilience in the face of elections is that regimes cheat. What this book has demonstrated is that electoral authoritarian resilience cannot just be about how to efficiently tilt or rig an election in the incumbent's favor. Rather, electoral authoritarian resilience depends on how effectively autocrats shape their relationships with elites, citizens, and external actors. Authoritarian institution building matters for authoritarian survival and for maintaining competitive capacities during multiparty elections. Likewise, the international relations of contemporary autocracy – particularly in the African context – impact the utility and endurance of more severe manipulative strategies.

A major impetus for this project was to break down conceptual categories that mask important and unexplored variation. Competitiveness, which is the parlance in scholarly circles for identifying electoral authoritarian variation (Diamond 2002), is an underspecified term. There are in fact configurations of competition in terms of electoral hegemony and electoral toleration that reflect different underlying causal conditions.

Single-party regimes and authoritarian parties are also terms that obscure important differences. Ruling party credibility, which is a key factor that perpetuates authoritarianism (Magaloni 2008, Gehlbach and Keefer 2011), only emerges in specific contexts and involves the creation of unique party features in terms of organization, autonomy, internal democracy, and relationships to social constituencies. Finally, international actors can deploy or withhold a variety of practices like election monitoring, aid conditionality, and direct diplomatic engagement (Donno 2013a).

My contribution to our understanding of contemporary authoritarianism is therefore to better identify the intersecting set of factors that shape electoral competition, and by consequence also influence regime resilience and durability. Elections are double-edged swords that can simultaneously increase and decrease authoritarian uncertainty. That degree of uncertainty is shaped by the institutional context that autocracies emerge from and later foster. Credible ruling parties are difficult to forge, but provide autocrats with long-lasting institutional platforms that bind elites and citizens. These kinds of parties are the central architecture upon which tolerant hegemonies are built. Without credible parties authoritarian uncertainty is exacerbated during elections, which requires comparatively higher levels of manipulation to limit electoral openness. Autocrats can be more certain of the utility of manipulative strategies, in part, when they are immune from international sanction. These findings suggest that among Africa's former single-party regimes one pathway to electoral authoritarian resilience was via institution building while the other was via the freedom to manipulate. While both can lead to equal durations of electoral authoritarian tenure, I claim that the former is built on sturdier ground.

In this concluding chapter I recap the major approaches and arguments laid out in the previous chapters of book, before turning to a discussion of the study's limitations and potential contributions to other work. Specifically, I look at ways my arguments inform and can improve the future study of comparative authoritarianism, African politics, and democratization.

A SUMMARY OF THE ARGUMENTS AND FINDINGS

In exploring variation in the competitive outcomes of electoral authoritarian regimes I have relied on a fundamental concept that permeates the literature on authoritarian politics, not just in Africa but also across the globe – authoritarian uncertainty. Autocrats suffer from severe institutional and informational deficits, which makes their hold on power more tenuous in comparison with democracies (Wintrobe 1998, Svolik 2012, Schedler 2013). Elections add another important layer of complexity to that inherent uncertainty. My argument rests on the ability of authoritarian institution building and permissive international conditions to reduce that uncertainty, which in turn structures electoral competition. This answer might seem to downplay what to other observers are the bread and butter of authoritarian politics, namely coercion and cooptation. Complex autocratic institutions are immensely difficult to create in the first place, and autocracies endure when they can continuously distribute resources to supporters and punish detractors. Likewise, another criticism would be that international action is too fickle to effectively explain differences in electoral authoritarian resilience. What matters again are the manipulative tools autocrats can muster and the range of distributive goods at their disposal.

My approach has been to provide a context-driven and limited explanation of electoral authoritarianism, which recognizes the inherent heterogeneity of political phenomenon. This drives my interest in electoral authoritarian competition rather than simply survival, and my narrower focus on the former single-party states of Africa. The former single-party regimes of Africa offer unique sources of leverage – they entered the multiparty era at approximately the same time, with ruling parties of relatively the same age, and into an international context that made them uniquely sensitive to external pressure. Yet, they transitioned to very different forms of electoral authoritarianism. Coercion and cooptation were still important factors that perpetuated electoral authoritarianism, but we cannot fully appreciate the difference in the quality of contestation without closer attention to other factors.

Credible ruling parties lie at the center of my explanation, and Chapter 4 spent time explaining their origins and describing their institutional features in three cases across an extended span of time. The postindependence period in African politics provides a quasi-critical juncture that allowed for ruling institutions to evolve in different directions. Organizational unity and relative differences in state capacity influenced the degree to which new presidents could build credible ruling institutions. In this sense rulers faced different constraints at independence that nudged them toward a specific pathway of regime building. However, the divergent evolution of ruling parties in Tanzania, Cameroon, and Kenya cannot be completely reduced to these factors. Leadership, vision, and choice all helped determine whether the ruling party would become an effective institution or not. In empirical terms, the ruling party in Tanzania developed a large-scale organization, internal procedures that gave elites voice and leveled the playing field, and reached out to a broadly defined group of citizens. By contrast, ruling parties in Cameroon and Kenya were less impressive. Presidential authority, elite brokerage, and multiethnic coalition building were the primary means by which political power was solidified after colonialism.

These regimes survived for decades, and while these differences in ruling institutions were important they did not deserve much attention from scholars. In the context of closed authoritarianism, uncertainty was mitigated primarily through traditional tools of autocracy: coercion, cooptation, and ideology. In many ways these three tools nicely map onto the three cases. In Tanzania the ideological program of *ujamaa* not only allowed Julius Nyerere to erect a credible ruling party, but to justify what he considered to be single-party democracy. In Cameroon, while elite brokerage through patronage was important, state coercion exerted a comparatively stronger influence. The emergency powers left to Ahmadou Ahidjo by the French allowed him to curtail dissent. In Kenya Jomo Kenyatta viewed himself as the chief broker in a system of clientelism that mapped onto Kenya's ethnic divisions. In all three cases, as long as economic conditions remained fairly stable and the international context was permissive, regime shortcomings were obfuscated.

The end of the Cold War and transition to multiparty elections acts as an exogenous shock that reveals the divergence in authoritarian institution building. It is not that regimes were not complicit in the transition to elections. Economic mismanagement, increased public corruption, and political violence all created the impetus for change. Therefore, to an extent elections did reflect regime vulnerability. Yet, the fact that multiparty elections spread so rapidly throughout most of Africa means that it was not easily resisted by regimes. The change in international conditions following the end of the Cold War meant that it would be very difficult for regimes to buck the spread of multiparty norms. Modes of transition to multipartyism did differ, with Tanzania taking on a more preemptive approach while regimes in Cameroon and Kenya were much more resistant. As argued in Chapter 5, these differences in how regimes agreed to and contested foundational elections were actually early indicators that they were not equally equipped for the task. The absence of institutionalized mechanisms that could channel elite and citizen dissent made regimes in Cameroon and Kenya more sensitive to the transition, and indeed foundational elections were nearly lost in both cases. On the other hand, Tanzania's credible ruling party allowed a greater degree of continuity from the single-party era.

Credible ruling parties sustain higher levels of elite and voter loyalty through their ability to forge longer-term commitments. My findings from Chapter 5 indicate that credible ruling parties are useful deterrents against elite defection. Through interview data and historical research I demonstrated how credible ruling parties manage elite competition for office by ensuring that nomination processes are followed. This is particularly evident with regard to presidential succession, but also legislative contests. In Tanzania primaries were moments of tension, but not large-scale defection. Rather the party frequently asserted its autonomy against factions that would undermine formal procedures. By contrast, in Cameroon and Kenya primaries were moments of comparatively larger elite defection, motivated strongly by the absence of party institutionalization. The crisis over the 2002 presidential succession from Daniel arap Moi to Uhuru Kenyatta ultimately heralded the end of the Kenyan African National Union (KANU) regime. In Cameroon, repression was frequently deployed against rival presidential contenders within the Cameroon Peoples Democratic Movement (CPDM) and term limits were abolished. In comparative terms, credible ruling parties incur less elite defection at similar moments of regime vulnerability.

The findings from Chapter 6 validate the importance of physical organization and coalition building during the single-party era. Through spatial representations and participant interviews I demonstrated the importance of Chama Cha Mapinduzi (CCM)'s ten-cell network in mobilizing voters and deterring opponents in Tanzania. Opposition activists often cited CCM's powerful organization as a major hurdle. This sentiment was notably absent in Cameroon or Kenya where the state administration or informal gangs were more often mentioned as barriers to contestation. These are indirect explorations of the role of party organization, but the fact that CCM can mobilize high levels of electoral support in the vast majority of constituencies is important. These vote shares are only partially generated through manipulation, and I take opposition actors at their word. On the other hand, in Cameroon and Kenya the absence of party organization exacerbated the problem of defection. Since ties to constituencies were less institutional and more personalized, when an elite or a voting bloc abandoned the regime the consequences were drastic. KANU and the CPDM lost much of their competitive capacity in many areas of the country, which necessitated more coercive means to remain in power and regain support.

Credible ruling parties are also at an advantage because they have established and repeated interactions with a widely defined constituency.

Chapter 6 provided insights into the sub-national correlates of incumbent vote share. Using the best available data, my findings demonstrate a relationship between historical patterns of social incorporation and more contemporary vote shares, while controlling for a range of other factors. In Tanzania the legacy of *ujamaa* exerts an independent influence, and those areas that benefitted from its redistributive impulses are to this day CCM's strongholds. In Cameroon and Kenya, where presidents managed more overt multiethnic coalitions, the pull and tug of identity politics is much more pronounced. Each regime was able to retain ethnic strongholds, but had to deploy resources and repression to try and entice voting blocs back into the ruling coalition. These quantitative insights were corroborated through in-depth participant interviews, in particular with opposition elites. Two things became clear from these discussions. First, in Tanzania opposition success is not just a matter of resources, but of social appeal. Second, the logic of ethnic party building in Cameroon and Kenya permeates opposition party strategies too.

The second moving part of my theory addressed the puzzle of repressive electoral authoritarianism and argued that the posture of international actors is a key pivot. Chapter 7 established broader differences across the three cases in the deployment of several democracy promotion tools. It then delved into a discussion of international patronage in Cameroon and Kenya, where repression was the initial reaction to multipartyism. Using participant interviews, historical research, and recently available embassy documents, my findings show that international actors can influence electoral competition by combining numerous tools of democracy promotion and acting as democratic patrons. In Kenya, American willingness to pressure the Moi regime directly and through international lenders led to some important political reforms, a robust domestic election observation effort, and crucial privatization of the public sector. Likewise, opposition parties felt empowered by international support, which made repressive tactics less effective. By contrast, in Cameroon it is clear that deliberate French authoritarian patronage and American reluctance sustained a more effective manipulative environment. Biya and the CPDM could resist political and economic reform, and opposition parties had very little international support. Importantly, international patronage appeared to influence decision making over presidential term limits, which in Kenya was a precursor to further regime crisis and elite defection.

The arguments in this book are specific to the three cases of Tanzania, Cameroon, and Kenya, but I also provided some broader insights by comparing a fuller range of cases using typological theorizing in Chapter 8. Among the range of African single-party regimes that transitioned successfully to electoral authoritarianism, the role of credible ruling parties appears to be influential. All cases of credible ruling parties transitioned to more tolerant forms of electoral authoritarianism. Likewise, the typological theory validated the role of international patronage, with a new comparative insight from the case of Togo between 2005 and 2010. During that time period, international actors became much more engaged, which led to a temporary reduction in regime hegemony. Chapter 8 also demonstrated that economic conditions have a contingent effect on electoral competition, and that opposition capacity and decision-making is largely derivative of the competitive environment. Opposition parties in more tolerant settings like Mozambique or Tanzania are at a significant advantage, which means that they do not experience as many party splits or make detrimental choices, such as boycotts. However, despite these benefits they are electorally uncompetitive.

The findings from this book are in many ways partial and imperfect because of my scope conditions, the nature of the research question and setting, and the need to balance between a parsimonious account and causal accuracy. I have only spent limited time discussing the origins of credible ruling parties, and have made arguments that were created and substantiated using a small range of cases. Within that narrower range of analysis there are potential concerns with data quality and the completeness of posited causal process chains. Moreover, certain deliberate choices regarding the measurement of some variables and the exclusion of others place some limitations on the causal inferences. Specifically, my measurement of ruling party credibility is constant, which is useful theoretically but might not be completely accurate empirically. Likewise, I have argued that the role of state capacity or ethnic identity is contingent rather than independent, which again might overstate some nuance.

This book relies on observational data gathered in very challenging contexts. It is not only that I am working in electoral authoritarian settings in the developing world, but also that I am working with historical processes that evolve over long periods of time. My approach has been to be creative with available data and use multiple sources that offer some degree of triangulation: media reporting, opposition elite interviews, regime elite interviews, within-case statistics, GIS mapping, archival records, and numerous secondary sources. Likewise, I have leveraged the power of comparison when possible and tried to reject major alternative hypotheses. Nonetheless, I do not have direct tests of ruling party credibility or international patronage, only measures of observable implications. In cases like Kenya, which are completely historic, direct tests are not available and historical causal processes had to be pieced together. In Tanzania and Cameroon, which are still autocratic, access to regime elites and quality data is restricted. More could be done to directly test the influence of credible parties and international patronage on elite and voter loyalty, and consequently competition.

On a similar note, my casual process chain is incomplete – I assume that electoral competition is derivative of ruling party credibility and international patronage but do not explicitly provide evidence of that connection. Throughout the book I have worked under the assumption that regimes would prefer to win more votes than less, and would ideally like to secure those votes with less manipulation. My argument is that when a regime cannot secure elite and voter loyalty it is compelled to expend more manipulation to win. The causal process links credible ruling parties from the shock of multiparty elections, to elite and voter loyalty, to greater assurance of victory, and then to decisions regarding manipulation. The link between the latter two stages remains implicit. Regime elites are generally unwilling to discuss choices about manipulation openly. Therefore, it is possible that the degree of electoral toleration might have less to do with a cost–benefit analysis based on regime capacities, and more do with regime socialization. It could be that elites in Tanzania, because of the peaceful legacy of CCM or because of their ties to the donor community, are simply averse to repression. This does not, however, explain the high degree of electoral hegemony in Tanzania.

I have also argued that credible ruling parties emerge from unique historical circumstances and have lasting power. Obviously, more could be done to discuss these origins, especially outside of the range of single-party regimes.[1] However, the limitation here is that I think of these parties as static. In order to avoid conflating ruling party credibility with the electoral outcome, I used observations from the single-party era and then demonstrated their continued relevance during multiparty elections. I have not spent as much time analyzing how credible parties might erode over time, as they apparently did quite dramatically in Senegal, or at looking into

---

[1] One case where this might relevant is in Burkina Faso, which is coded as a tolerant hegemony between 1997 and 2013. Less work has been done on this topic, but some have noted the inclusive nature of the Congress for Democracy and Progress, which was an amalgamation of other political parties. This is fairly unique among former military regimes in Africa, where subsequent ruling parties are generally weak (Harsch 1998, Santiso and Loada 2003).

how elections might provide incentives for weaker parties to eventually develop credibility building mechanisms. Indeed, during my final weeks of fieldwork in Cameroon, amidst dismay over the state of CPDM primaries, some party elites mentioned a deliberate shift toward more competitive and open primaries. These changes over time in ruling party credibility might have some influence on the degree of electoral competition.

Relatedly, I have argued that international patronage fluctuated over time but that state capacity remained uniformly weak. The assumption was that African regimes were uniquely susceptible to international pressure because of their state weakness. This is likely an overstatement, and there were in fact moderate differences at independence in the strength of civil administrations and police and military forces.[2] My argument was that these factors could not be deployed without a permissive international environment, but they still had to exist to begin with. Likewise, it ignores changes in state capacity over time. For instance, oil wealth and international patronage – particularly military aid – in Cameroon have buttressed state-based patronage and the creation of stronger state coercive institutions. At some point these state capacities likely exist independently of international conditions. This is more pronounced in a case like Gabon, where oil is a much stronger component of the economy. While Gabon has received important support from the French for decades, it is harder to make the case that democratic patronage would have significantly tied the regime's hands.

Finally, the role of ethnic identity and demography were likewise emphasized as contingent on the processes of regime formation. In Tanzania, the distribution of hundreds of smaller ethnic groups made the creation of a credible ruling party easier. On the other hand, in Cameroon and Kenya specific ethnic groups could wield significant clout, which made ethnic brokerage via the presidency a more likely outcome. I have not discussed the role of ethnicity in independent terms (Ferree 2010, Elischer 2013), but rather as part of the process of social incorporation. Nor do my three cases encompass the full range of options. Ethnic groups might not be as

---

[2] As noted in Chapter 1, the language of weaker or stronger state capacity is often in reference to either a Weberian notion of what the state provides (Migdal 1988), or comes from the literature on autocratic resilience (Levitsky and Way 2010, Slater 2010). Within African studies there is another understanding of the state as a "lame leviathan" (Callaghy 1987, Bayart 2009). The state cannot embark on major social and political transformative projects, and cannot be mobilized as a strong arm of an authoritarian regime. Yet, when states develop some minimal features of coercion and distribution that allow them to effectively manage elite coalitions they persist. Therefore, you can have a stronger patrimonial state.

dispersed as in Tanzania or regionally concentrated as in Cameroon or Kenya. For example, I argued that a clear ethnic majority could substitute for wide social incorporation. Yet the only example within my sample is Djibouti, where the Somali constitute approximately 60 percent of the population and the Afar 35 percent. In this instance ethnic bifurcation was a factor that precipitated a civil war. The ruling People's Rally for Progress (RPP), which is predominantly Somali, did not develop other features of credible ruling parties and entered into an alliance with the former rebel Afar group, FRUD. More could be done to investigate the nuanced interplay between ethnicity and regime formation.

IMPLICATIONS FOR THE STUDY OF AUTHORITARIANISM

In earlier studies of authoritarianism the emphasis generally was on the manner in which autocratic regimes exercised power. For instance, in Juan Linz's classic work on the subject he stressed that all regimes differ in their use of ideology, toleration of pluralism, and encouragement of participation (2000). Authoritarian regimes were, according to Linz, a middle-ground regime type, with combinations of quasi-ideologies, moderate pluralism, and limited competition. In Linz's account the specific institutional environment in which autocrats operated – whether single-party, military, or personal – mattered much less than the way in which they shaped fundamental political relationships. If we fast-forward to the last few decades of research, the locus is now more heavily focused on the question of how basic institutional settings shape trajectories of authoritarian rule (Geddes 1999). As noted throughout this book, this generally involves researching the question of regime survival versus breakdown, or at times even democratization. This has generated important insights into the variety of authoritarian regimes and their comparative resilience, but also suffers from some significant shortcomings.

In many ways I have attempted to return to the question of the exercise of authoritarian power, whether by looking at the ways that elections are contested differently, or at the way parties are dissimilarly utilized. A major implication from this work is that scholars of authoritarianism need to better understand the diversity of electoral authoritarianism. The terms "tolerant hegemony" and "repressive hegemony" are easily transferred into other settings, and inform us not only about *who* governs an authoritarian regime, but *how* that regime is actually governed. As discussed in Chapter 3, the conceptualization and demarcation of boundaries between regime types is likely to continue and be contested, even as more tools and data become available. One of the advantages of in-depth case study work is that it avoids some of the conceptual stretching that often plagues statistical analysis. Yet, social scientists also eschew conceptual proliferation that limits the breadth of comparison and makes research more obtuse. I imagine that future scholarship will continue to debate the nature, number, and utility of regime types, but nonetheless encourage work that provides even more fine-grained distinctions. For instance, the question of why some electoral authoritarian regimes engage in different combinations of manipulation is important. Do differences in the specific mix of physical violence, electoral fraud, exclusion, and censorship possibly convey new information about the underlying factors that sustain authoritarianism?

Another implication has to do with the crucial role of ruling parties, which is also relevant outside of Africa. The concept of a credible party again speaks to the manner in which authoritarian power is exercised. It is important to stress that parties, while institutions that generally contribute to authoritarian longevity, are fundamentally dissimilar. But, measuring differences in ruling parties presents some challenges. Party organization needs to be observed in practice, which is difficult in authoritarian settings. This book has offered some conjecture regarding the actual breadth and depth of ruling parties, but future work could do better at developing finer tools using surveys or network analysis.[3] On the other hand, assessments of credibility are subjective and likely to differ across contexts. I have stressed party congresses, primaries, and social incorporation, but I am not certain that my list is exhaustive. Importantly, I have argued that credibility arises from the process of party construction itself, an idea that is rooted in a body of literature on elite ambition. Yet, credibility could also derive from a shared history and identity as ideologues or revolutionaries (Levitsky and Way 2012).

There is also notable pessimism in the study of authoritarianism regarding the ability of external actors to foster political change in other countries. I share that skepticism, and make the point that when ruling parties are robust, international action is less effective. Moreover, the role of international actors is particular to the African context due to the history of aid dependency. Still, part of the problem is that we think too broadly about what international actors can achieve, or focus on the

---

[3] Some work has been done in the context of authoritarian successor parties in Latin America, especially as it pertains to a former ruling regime's clientelistic linkages that were sustained via the party (Kitschelt and Singer 2015).

utility of very specific tools like foreign aid (Knack 2004, Wright 2009). We need studies that look at more moderate improvements in political conditions, and that consider international action in its totality. While the case of Kenya is fairly unique in comparative perspective, it is the exception that in many ways proves the rule. Robust combinations of assistance, conditionality, and rhetoric took advantage of economic and political vulnerability, and led to limited but still meaningful reforms that empowered opposition parties and civil society.

Ultimately, these distinctions in the exercise of authoritarian power are meant to inform a better understanding of regime vulnerability. I have argued that tolerant hegemonies are at times rooted in credible ruling parties, while repressive hegemonies are rooted in the absence of such parties but the presence of permissive international conditions. What this means is that in Tanzania the sources of regime durability run deep. For electoral outcomes to become more competitive in Tanzania two things will need to change. First, the institutional sources of cohesion that have served CCM for decades, both before and during elections, need to erode to such an extent where elite defection becomes a more viable option. Second, demographic change that erodes the party's rural base needs to reach a critical point where urban areas become the key electoral constituencies. These robust sources of power also explain why opposition parties in Tanzania have not translated their many advantages into election outcomes.

By contrast, the repressive hegemonies studied here appear to be much more brittle and sensitive to short-term fluctuations. One source of crisis would be changes in the posture of international actors. Another source of crisis is presidential succession, which in Kenya and Cameroon had important political consequences. This was also the case in other repressive hegemonies. In Togo the transition to Faure Gnassingbé corresponds with a decline in presidential vote share, but also increased international attention. In Gabon the PDG selected Omar Bongo's son Ali Bongo as the 2009 presidential candidate, which led to the defection of the sitting prime minister and interior minister.[4] In 2005 Omar Bongo won 79.1 percent of the presidential vote, while in 2009 his son Ali could only muster 41 percent. Similar findings can be found elsewhere. In Djibouti the FRUD spokesman Abatte Ebo Adou defected from the ruling coalition after the 1999 transition from Hassan Gouled Aptidon to his nephew Ismail Omar Guelleh. Former members of the PDCI in Côte d'Ivoire were

---

[4] Linel Kwatsi. "Gabon PM Quits to Run for President as Independent" *Reuters* (July 17, 2009).

infuriated over the transition from Houphouët-Boigny to Henri Konan-Bédié, and left to form the Rally of Republicans. The continued battle over term limits in many African countries is indicative of the inherent weakness of several repressive hegemonies (Cheeseman 2010).

The apparent fragility of repressive hegemonies not only has electoral consequences, but also impacts our notions of regime resilience and stability. Countries like Cameroon hold together elite coalitions through the threat of coercion, the promise of economic reward, and the dominating influence of the president. Compared to regional neighbors like Central African Republic, Cameroon appears to be a pillar of stability. Yet, the internal debate over succession clearly frightens many regime insiders, and the nature of an inevitable post-Biya politics is very unclear. This is the reality elsewhere in Africa, but also in other environments where presidential figures have loomed large for long periods of time without clear succession plans that would create consensus among political elites and the military. In Cameroon, the potential for a military coup, civil unrest, or even a broader rebellion fueled by the growing influence of terrorist groups like Boko Haram should be on any observer's radar.

IMPLICATIONS FOR THE STUDY OF AFRICAN POLITICS

In their seminal work on African democracy, Michael Bratton and Nicolas van de Walle argued that neo-patrimonialism was a heritage that distinguished Africa, and would define the continent's future democratic credentials (1997). Taken further, Patrick Chabal and Jean-Pascal Daloz argued that the "instrumentalization of disorder" was a byproduct of the patrimonial nature of the African state (Chabal and Daloz 1999). And indeed the state of democracy in sub-Saharan Africa is tenuous. Turnover has remained elusive, and political instability continues to plague several countries. In those cases where opposition parties have toppled incumbents, subsequent regimes have often simply continued authoritarian practices. This begs the question, is Africa doomed to the logics of "Big Man" politics?

My answer is not to deny the continued influence of neo-patrimonialism, but to place it in some context. The assumption that overwhelmingly strong presidents dominate all African states with little regard for formal institutions is clearly untrue.[5] This book suggests that ruling parties,

---

[5] I have not mentioned it in too much depth here, but there has also been an important turn toward studying the independent role of legislatures in consolidating democracy in Africa (Barkan 2009a).

just like legislatures, opposition parties, judiciaries, and state institutions, can act as important limits on executive authority. The Tanzanian case offers an example for how a ruling party was afforded significant decision-making power and actually institutionalized some practices so that one could credibly observe its formal functions. Part of the current challenge for CCM is to reconcile its factions that want to see the party assert its independent authority with those who strive to undermine it to create personal networks of influence. This is a reality that applies elsewhere in Africa, even in those cases where ruling parties are observably less important. Political institutions in Africa contest for authority alongside informal practices and shape actor incentives in important ways. Therefore, institutions are not meaningless, but neither can they be assumed to be universally influential.

I have also suggested that the sources of institutionalization are not entirely derivative of slow-moving structural conditions. There is an inherent tension between structural imperatives and the inclinations and leadership styles of Africa's independence-era figures. Ethnicity, as argued elsewhere, was not static but dynamic and clearly constrained leaders. But this was not the only factor that shaped decision making. In Kenya, more immediate material incentives and Kenyatta's inherent conservatism made real party institutionalization less likely. Kenya's weaker ruling party was not inevitable, but a deliberate choice to cope with several conflicting interests – the needs of the landless, ethnic elites, and Kenya's upper class. Nor does the absence of ethnic mobilization necessarily lead to stronger ruling parties. Tanzania is the case in point, where the reduction of ethnic salience and creation of a robust party took massive and risky effort on the part of TANU and Julius Nyerere. A different leader, faced with similar circumstances, might have come to very different conclusions regarding what tools of political authority needed to be developed. The ruling party in Tanzania was forged, often through tremendous coercion, and guided by one of the more articulate political ideologies on the continent.

This has clear implications for the study of political institutions in Africa. First, while it is difficult to move from logics of neo-patrimonialism it is not impossible. As these cases indicate, during multiparty elections many of the dynamics of the single-party era persisted. Most clearly, ethnic politics in Tanzania remained subdued compared to Kenya and Cameroon. But, critical junctures force leaders to make choices about how to cope with diverse structural pulls and tugs. Leadership, therefore, remains an important and understudied factor in African politics, and in comparative politics more broadly. Second, it is also clear that while institutions that emerge from critical junctures have staying power, they do change and not always for the better. In Tanzania there are signs that as elections become more competitive, factors like ethnicity, religious identity, and personalized clientelism are becoming more pervasive, and could potentially erode the institutionalization of the ruling party (Heilman and Kaiser 2002). This is especially true since the 2015 election, where it remains to be seen whether president John Magufuli can fulfill his promises of institutional reform while satisfying other elite needs.[6]

IMPLICATIONS FOR THE STUDY OF DEMOCRACY AND DEMOCRATIZATION

This book also informs debates over democracy and democratization, and specifically provides insights regarding the ability of elections to become a mode of democratization. The debate over whether repeated elections, even if unfair, lock in democratic dividends and have spillover effects on the protection of civil liberties is ongoing. The notion of democratization by elections is intuitively appealing, particularly given the growing sense of democratic pessimism that pervades academic and policy circles (Platner 2015). Many of the original insights into this thesis originated in Africa, but the findings have been contested empirically in Africa and other regions (McCoy and Hartlyn 2009, Bogaards 2013, Kaya and Bernhard 2013). One critique is that electoral authoritarianism, not electoral democracy, is now more prevalent in Africa (Lynch and Crawford 2011). As noted in Chapter 3, repressive hegemony is the modal electoral authoritarian regime type during the past twenty years.

Yet, there is a more fundamental issue with regard to the definition of democratization. If elections become increasingly participatory or more peaceful, does this indicate a process of democratization? Or, can the democratic qualities of elections improve while a regime makes no meaningful movement toward democracy? This book suggests that the latter is often the case. In contexts of overwhelming executive authority, heavy manipulation, and pervasive clientelism, an increase in participation might simply reflect a "beat them or join them" attitude from opposition parties, not democratization. In other words, in systems where logics of neo-patrimonialism are more strongly entrenched, i.e. repressive hegemonies, opposition becomes a meaningless act. And in fact, one of

---

[6] Edwin Mjwahuzi. "CCM's John Magufuli Declared Tanzania's Fifth President" *The East African* (October 30, 2015).

the findings from the literature on democratization by elections is that incumbent vote shares have grown even as opposition parties participate more and accept results more often. In repressive hegemonies we have to interpret improvements in the quality of elections very carefully.

Likewise, the more open conditions in tolerant hegemonies should also not be confused with democratization. In tolerant hegemonies opposition parties by definition face less restrictive conditions, which means that they generally participate more in elections and do not engage in post-election violence. But rather than signify democratization, this in fact implies a fairly robust and durable form of authoritarianism that is confident in its ability to contest elections. It is not a regime that is necessarily pressured or socialized into greater reform, per the literature on democratization by elections. There is an obvious irony to the fact that the regimes that appear to be the most democratic are potentially the most stable autocracies. What this requires is more careful observation of broader political conditions rather than just the democratic qualities of the election itself. Moreover, improvements in some indicators of election quality might be contravened by declines in other indicators. For instance, while opposition parties have not boycotted elections in Tanzania, losers routinely reject the results.[7] Similarly, in 2011 the opposition boycotted elections for the first time in Seychelles. This does not mean the democratization by elections thesis is irrelevant, only that it needs to be carefully applied.

Scholars of democratization are also interested in whether the nature of autocracy prior to an electoral transition influences the stability of the party system to follow.[8] While this study does not engage directly with this question, the post-transition trajectory of Kenya sheds some important light. The weakness of KANU as a political institution had two distinct consequences. First, opposition parties in the 1990s in many ways imitated the type of institution that KANU was. They were notoriously elite-based, poorly institutionalized, and often ethnically oriented. The famous NARC coalition dissolved in 2005 following irreconcilable differences between Raila Odinga and Mwai Kibaki. Second, once KANU lost power it disintegrated as a political institution, sending remnants

---

[7] Florence Mugarula. "We Don't Recognize JK Government, Says CHADEMA" *The Citizen* (November 15, 2010), Henry Mwangonde. "Ukawa Demands Manual Tallying of Presidential Votes" *The Citizen* (October 29, 2015).

[8] This work on authoritarian successor parties emerged primarily from the work on post-communist successor parties (Ishiyama 1997). See also Grzymala-Busse (2002), Hicken and Kuhonta (2011), and Riedl (2014).

of the old regime across the new party system.[9] During the controversial 2007 election, KANU was part of Mwai Kibaki's Party of National Union and only won fourteen seats. By 2013, even the party founder's son Uhuru Kenyatta had left, and KANU was reduced to just six seats.

The persistent weakness of the Kenyan party system since 2002 is directly related to the outbreak of violence in 2007–8, which left over 1,000 Kenyans dead and 250,000 displaced (Cheeseman 2008, Mueller 2011). In 2007, elections were contested in an environment of fluid party identities, which pushed ethnic calculations to the front and center of coalition building. The likelihood of violence was compounded by the prevalence of informal means of violence tied to prominent individuals, localized ethnic conflicts over land, and the poor management of the election itself. This meant that the election was in many ways doomed to be close and likely violent. In 2013, much of this logic remained in place despite a new constitution and large international investments in conflict resolution and early detection. The absence of violence in 2013 can be attributed to this, but also to a new political alignment that brought together the perceived leaders of the two most antagonistic ethnic communities – the Kikuyu and Kalenjin. The Jubilee coalition of 2013 won the election, but the absence of meaningful party institutionalization means that future elections still risk violence (Cheeseman, Lynch, and Willis 2014).

On the other hand the prognosis for a case like Tanzania is more optimistic. Opposition parties in Tanzania, while not electorally powerful, have put down deeper institutional roots. The same parties have contested since 1995, and in many of the parties there has been some internal renewal of leadership without party breakdown. As in Kenya, opposition parties tend to be imitative of CCM, and aim to create grassroots cell structures and emphasize internal democracy. For instance, prior to the 2010 election CHADEMA launched "Operation Sangara," which was an effort to train local leaders to reach out to rural voters and create more sustainable party structures.[10] In a context where organizationally sound opposition parties are rare, and usually tied to preexisting structures like unions, this bodes well. Through careful engagement and effort, opposition parties can gradually develop their own sources of institutionalization.

---

[9] During my fieldwork I met with the current KANU leadership, and was amazed to find the disarray this once supposed powerful party was in. Recordkeeping was nonexistent, and the party headquarters were in a small building behind a large shopping center.

[10] Levina Kato. "CHADEMA Campaign Targets Rural Voters" *Tanzania Daily News* (September 17, 2010).

Likewise it is doubtful that CCM will go the way of KANU when it loses an election. Rather, given the institutional strength of the ruling party it is more likely that CCM will follow the path of the Mexican PRI and provide the anchor for a possibly more democratic polity and stable party system. The parallel with the PRI is informative, since in that case a long-lasting tolerant hegemony gradually lost its electoral edge, primarily due to demographic change and the rise of new business elites that were not effectively coopted by the party (Magaloni 2006). A similar scenario is possible in Tanzania, and the same sources of authoritarian durability could also be the foundation for a fairly stable two or three-party system. Tolerant hegemonies might in the end offer a mode of transition to democracy, which would be a positive development in a region where democratic progress still suffers.

The findings of this book demonstrate that authoritarian institutions and international actors play a role shaping in electoral authoritarian contestation and the nature of electoral competition. Across Africa the distribution of credible ruling parties and democratic international patronage is uneven, which has led to a variety of electoral authoritarian experiences. This variety is not only indicative of differences in authoritarian resilience, but also dissimilarities in authoritarian durability. Therefore, what might alter these electoral authoritarian equilibriums depends heavily on context, and only at times can international action make a difference. At other times, longer and slower-moving organic processes that undermine authoritarian institutions might need to occur first. Likewise, whether that political change is peaceful or disruptive, democratic or undemocratic, is also very contingent. It therefore behooves observers and scholars interested in the cause of democracy to better understand how power is exercised in electoral authoritarian regimes, and to appreciate the diversity of authoritarian institutions and politics.

Appendix A

Electoral Authoritarian Competition in Africa

Hegemony in African Electoral Authoritarian Regimes (1990–2016)

Country	Time Period	Elections Included	Presidential Vote Share	Legislative Vote Share	Hegemonic?
Angola	2008–2011	2008 (l)	na	86.8	Y
Angola	2012–	2012 (l)	na	79.6	Y
Burkina Faso	1991–1996	1991 (p) 1992 (l)	100.0	72.9	Y
Burkina Faso	1997–2001	1997 (l) 1998 (p)	87.5	90.0	Y
Burkina Faso	2002–2004	2002 (l)	87.5	51.4	Y
Burkina Faso	2005–2009	2005 (p) 2007 (l)	80.4	65.8	Y
Burkina Faso	2010–2014**	2010 (p)	80.2		Y
Burundi	2005–2009	2005 (l)		59.0	N
Burundi	2010–2014	2010 (p) 2010 (l)	91.6	80.0	Y
Burundi	2015–	2015 (p) 2015 (l)	69.4	63.6	Y
Cameroon	1992–1996	1992 (l) 1992 (p)	40.0	48.9	N
Cameroon	1997–2001	1997 (l) 1997 (p)	92.6	60.6	Y
Cameroon	2002–2006	2002 (l) 2004 (p)	70.9	82.8	Y
Cameroon	2007–2010	2007 (l)		85.0	Y
Cameroon	2011–	2011 (p) 2013 (p)	78.0	82.2	Y
Central African Republic	2005–2010	2005 (p) 2005 (l)	42.0	40.0	N
Central African Republic	2011–2012**	2011 (p) 2011 (l)	64.4	61.0	N
Chad	1996–2000	1996 (p) 1997 (l)	43.8	52.0	N
Chad	2001–2005	2001 (p) 2002 (l)	64.2	72.9	Y
Chad	2006–2010	2006 (p)	64.7		Y

Country					
Chad	2011–2015	2011 (r)	83.6	60.1	Y
Chad	2016–	2016 (p)	59.9		N
Congo-DRC	2006–2010	2006 (p) 2006 (l)	44.8	22.2	N
Congo-DRC	2011–	2011 (p) 2011 (l)	49.0	13.8	N
Congo-RoC	2002–2006	2002 (p) 2002 (l)	89.4	38.7	Y
Congo-RoC	2007–2011	2007 (l) 2009 (p)	78.6	33.6	Y
Congo-RoC	2012–2015	2012 (l)		64.0	Y
Congo-RoC	2016–	2016 (p)	60.2		Y
Côte d'Ivoire	1990–1994	1990 (p) 1990 (l)	81.7	93.1	Y
Côte d'Ivoire	1995–1999**	1995 (p) 1995 (l)	96.2	84.6	Y
Djibouti	1992–1996	1992 (l) 1993 (p)	60.8	100.0	Y
Djibouti	1997–2002	1997 (l) 1999 (p)	74.0	83.1	Y
Djibouti	2003–2007	2003 (l) 2005 (p)	89.6	100.0	Y
Djibouti	2008–2010	2008 (l)		100.0	Y
Djibouti	2011–2015	2011 (p) 2013 (p)	80.6	66.7	Y
Djibouti	2016–	2016 (p)	87.1		Y
Ethiopia	1995–1999	1995 (l)	na	88.5	Y
Ethiopia	2000–2004	2000 (l)	na	87.9	Y
Ethiopia	2005–2009	2005 (l)	na	59.8	N
Ethiopia	2010–2014	2010 (l)	na	91.2	Y
Ethiopia	2015–	2015 (l)	na	99.8	Y
Gabon	1990–1995	1990 (l) 1993 (p)	51.2	52.5	N
Gabon	1996–2000	1996 (l) 1998 (p)	66.9	70.8	Y
Gabon	2001–2004	2001 (l)		71.7	Y

(continued)

Country	Time Period	Elections Included	Presidential Vote Share	Legislative Vote Share	Hegemonic?
Gabon	2005–2008	2005 (p) 2006 (l)	79.2	68.3	Y
Gabon	2009–2015	2009 (p) 2011 (l)	41.7	90.0	Y
Gabon	2016–	2016 (p)	49.8		Y
Gambia	1996–2000	1996 (p) 1997 (l)	55.8	73.3	Y
Gambia	2001–2005	2001 (p) 2002 (l)	52.8	93.8	Y
Gambia	2006–2010	2006 (p) 2007 (l)	67.3	87.5	Y
Gambia	2011–2016*	2011 (p) 2012 (l)	71.5	89.6	Y
Ghana	1992–1995	1992 (p) 1992 (l)	58.4	95.0	Y
Ghana	1996–1999	1996 (p) 1996 (l)	57.4	67.0	Y
Ghana	2000*	2000 (p) 2000 (l)	44.5	46.0	N
Guinea	1993–1997	1993 (p) 1995 (l)	51.7	62.3	N
Guinea	1998–2001	1998 (p)	56.1		N
Guinea	2002–2007**	2002 (l) 2003 (p)	86.2	74.6	Y
Kenya	1992–1996	1992 (p) 1992 (l)	36.4	53.2	N
Kenya	1997–2001	1997 (p) 1997 (l)	40.1	51.0	N
Kenya	2002*	2002 (p) 2002 (l)	31.3	30.5	N
Mauritania	1992–1995	1992 (p) 1992 (l)	62.9	84.8	Y
Mauritania	1996–2000	1996 (l) 1997 (p)	90.9	88.6	Y
Mauritania	2001–2004**	2001 (l) 2003 (p)	67.4	79.0	Y
Mozambique	1994–1998	1994 (p) 1994 (l)	53.3	51.6	N

Mozambique	1999–2003	1999 (p) 1999 (l)	52.4	53.2	N
Mozambique	2004–2008	2004 (p) 2004 (l)	63.7	64.0	Y
Mozambique	2009–2013	2009 (p) 2009 (l)	75.0	76.5	Y
Mozambique	2014–	2014 (p) 2014 (l)	57.0	58.0	N
Niger	1999–2003	1999 (p) 1999 (l)	32.3	45.8	N
Niger	2004–2008	2004 (p) 2004 (l)	40.7	41.6	N
Niger	2009**	2009 (p) 2009 (l)	40.7	67.3	Y
Nigeria	1999–2002	1999 (p) 1999 (l)	62.8	57.2	N
Nigeria	2003–2006	2003 (p) 2003 (l)	61.9	61.94	N
Nigeria	2007–2010	2007 (p) 2007 (l)	69.6	73.06	Y
Nigeria	2011–2015*	2011 (p) 2011 (l)	58.9	34.2	N
Rwanda	2003–2007	2003 (p) 2003 (l)	95.1	62.3	Y
Rwanda	2008–2012	2008 (l)		67.9	Y
Rwanda	2013–	2010 (p) 2013 (l)	93.1	77.4	Y
Senegal	1988–1992	1998 (p) 1998 (l)	73.2	85.8	Y
Senegal	1993–1997	1993 (p) 1993 (l)	58.4	70.0	Y
Senegal	1998–1999	1998 (l)		66.4	Y
Senegal	2000–2001*	2000 (p) 2001 (l)	41.5	9.2	N
Seychelles	1993–1997	1993 (p) 1993 (l)	59.5	81.8	Y
Seychelles	1998–2000	1998 (p) 1998 (l)	66.7	88.2	Y
Seychelles	2001–2005	2001 (p) 2002 (l)	54.2	67.7	Y
Seychelles	2006–2011	2006 (p) 2007 (l)	53.7	67.7	Y
Seychelles	2012–2014	2012 (p) 2012 (l)	55.5	67.7	Y
Seychelles	2015–	2015 (p) 2016 (l)	47.7	42.4	N

(continued)

(continued)

Country	Time Period	Elections Included	Presidential Vote Share	Legislative Vote Share	Hegemonic?
Tanzania	1995–1999	1995 (p) 1995 (l)	61.8	79.7	Y
Tanzania	2000–2004	2000 (p) 2000 (l)	71.7	87.5	Y
Tanzania	2005–2009	2005 (p) 2005 (l)	80.3	85.1	Y
Tanzania	2010–2014	2010 (p) 2010 (l)	62.8	74.0	Y
Tanzania	2015–	2015 (p) 2015 (l)	58.5	68.7	Y
Togo	1993–1997	1993 (p) 1994 (l)	96.4	44.4	Y
Togo	1998–2001	1998 (p) 1999 (l)	52.1	97.5	Y
Togo	2002–2004	2002 (l) 2003 (p)	57.8	88.9	Y
Togo	2005–2009	2005 (p) 2007 (l)	60.2	61.7	N
Togo	2010–2014	2010 (p) 2013 (l)	60.9	68.1	Y
Togo	2015–	2015 (p)	58.8		Y
Uganda	1996–2000	1996 (p) 1996 (l)	74.3	56.5	Y
Uganda	2001–2005	2001 (p) 2001 (l)	69.3	100.0	Y
Uganda	2006–2010	2006 (p) 2006 (l)	59.3	67.3	Y
Uganda	2011–2015	2011 (p) 2011 (l)	68.4	71.4	Y
Uganda	2016	2016 (p) 2016 (l)	60.0	69.8	Y
Zambia	1991–1995	1991 (p) 1991 (l)	75.8	78.6	Y
Zambia	1996–2000	1996 (p) 1996 (l)	72.6	82.4	Y
Zambia	2001–2005	2001 (p) 2001 (l)	29.2	43.4	N
Zambia	2006–2007	2006 (p) 2006 (l)	42.0	45.2	N

Zambia	2008–2010	2008 (p)	40.1		N
Zambia	2011*	2011 (p) 2011 (l)	35.4	367	N
Zimbabwe	1990–1994	1990 (p) 1990 (l)	83.1	97.5	Y
Zimbabwe	1995–1999	1995 (l) 1996 (p)	90.8	98.3	Y
Zimbabwe	2000–2004	2000 (l) 2002 (p)	56.2	51.7	N
Zimbabwe	2005–2007	2005 (l)		65.0	N
Zimbabwe	2008–2012	2008 (p) 2008 (l)	43.2	47.1	N
Zimbabwe	2013–	2013 (p) 2013 (l)	61.1	75.7	Y

Notes: Time periods are constructed by referring to the nearest presidential and legislative election; * indicates electoral authoritarian regime ended by electoral turnover; ** indicates electoral authoritarian regime ended by conflict or coup.

Toleration in African Electoral Authoritarian Regimes (1990–2016)

Country	Time Period	Physical Violence	Clean Elections	Freedom of Association	Freedom of Expression	Toleration Score
Angola	2008–2011	0.47	0.28	0.57	0.41	0.22
Angola	2012–	0.47	0.28	0.61	0.40	0.23
Burkina Faso	1991–1996	0.24	0.53	0.75	0.68	0.27
Burkina Faso	1997–2001	0.29	0.53	0.89	0.79	0.32
Burkina Faso	2002–2004	0.72	0.51	0.90	0.87	0.50
Burkina Faso	2005–2009	0.73	0.52	0.90	0.87	0.51
Burkina Faso	2010–2014**	0.67	0.54	0.87	0.79	0.46
Burundi	2005–2009	0.41	0.56	0.60	0.70	0.31
Burundi	2010–2014	0.46	0.36	0.55	0.63	0.26
Burundi	2015–	0.09	0.04	0.32	0.29	0.07
Cameroon	1992–1996	0.34	0.11	0.64	0.56	0.18
Cameroon	1997–2001	0.41	0.07	0.71	0.57	0.20
Cameroon	2002–2006	0.45	0.11	0.72	0.68	0.23
Cameroon	2007–2010	0.55	0.13	0.72	0.71	0.25
Cameroon	2011–	0.56	0.18	0.72	0.69	0.27
Central African Republic	2005–2010	0.60	0.19	0.60	0.61	0.26
Central African Republic	2011–2012**	0.61	0.16	0.60	0.62	0.26
Chad	1996–2000	0.26	0.14	0.49	0.53	0.15
Chad	2001–2005	0.26	0.12	0.52	0.51	0.15
Chad	2006–2010	0.26	0.12	0.52	0.46	0.15
Chad	2011–2015	0.26	0.15	0.51	0.47	0.15

Chad	2016–	0.16	0.06	0.53	0.51	0.26
Congo-DRC	2006–2010	0.21	0.29	0.70	0.67	0.20
Congo-DRC	2011–	0.28	0.27	0.70	0.66	0.22
Congo-RoC	2002–2006	0.27	0.17	0.54	0.52	0.17
Congo-RoC	2007–2011	0.27	0.12	0.62	0.52	0.16
Congo-RoC	2012–2015	0.27	0.16	0.62	0.52	0.17
Congo-RoC	2016–	0.12	0.14	0.47	0.28	0.10
Côte d'Ivoire	1990–1994	0.56	0.19	0.70	0.53	0.25
Côte d'Ivoire	1995–1999**	0.56	0.24	0.85	0.71	0.30
Djibouti	1992–1996	0.65	0.24	0.41	0.31	0.23
Djibouti	1997–2002	0.66	0.25	0.45	0.31	0.24
Djibouti	2003–2007	0.76	0.25	0.60	0.32	0.28
Djibouti	2008–2010	0.76	0.25	0.61	0.34	0.28
Djibouti	2011–2015	0.76	0.25	0.62	0.32	0.28
Djibouti	2016–	0.55	0.27	0.53	0.24	0.22
Ethiopia	1995–1999	0.41	0.22	0.40	0.46	0.19
Ethiopia	2000–2004	0.41	0.21	0.40	0.46	0.19
Ethiopia	2005–2009	0.41	0.25	0.45	0.42	0.19
Ethiopia	2010–2014	0.40	0.24	0.44	0.31	0.18
Ethiopia	2015–	0.47	0.27	0.37	0.28	0.19
Gabon	1990–1995	0.68	0.19	0.53	0.55	0.27
Gabon	1996–2000	0.71	0.19	0.75	0.70	0.31
Gabon	2001–2004	0.71	0.19	0.76	0.71	0.32
Gabon	2005–2008	0.71	0.19	0.76	0.74	0.32
Gabon	2009–2015	0.78	0.22	0.77	0.74	0.35
Gabon	2016–	0.91	0.23	0.74	0.82	0.39

(continued)

(continued)

Country	Time Period	Physical Violence	Clean Elections	Freedom of Association	Freedom of Expression	Toleration Score
Gambia	1996–2000	0.25	0.46	0.43	0.31	0.18
Gambia	2001–2005	0.27	0.40	0.60	0.29	0.19
Gambia	2006–2010	0.25	0.44	0.63	0.31	0.20
Gambia	2011–2016*	0.26	0.39	0.61	0.31	0.19
Ghana	1992–1995	0.82	0.55	0.69	0.39	0.39
Ghana	1996–1999	0.97	0.52	0.86	0.85	0.58
Ghana	2000*	0.97	0.72	0.91	0.91	0.72
Guinea	1993–1997	0.34	0.09	0.55	0.54	0.17
Guinea	1998–2001	0.28	0.10	0.63	0.54	0.16
Guinea	2002–2007**	0.28	0.11	0.63	0.64	0.18
Kenya	1992–1996	0.13	0.19	0.66	0.54	0.15
Kenya	1997–2001	0.17	0.25	0.73	0.64	0.19
Kenya	2002*	0.37	0.36	0.80	0.75	0.28
Mauritania	1992–1995	0.41	0.26	0.43	0.58	0.21
Mauritania	1996–2000	0.42	0.21	0.53	0.62	0.22
Mauritania	2001–2004**	0.42	0.23	0.58	0.67	0.23
Mozambique	1994–1998	0.75	0.56	0.67	0.62	0.42
Mozambique	1999–2003	0.75	0.49	0.73	0.63	0.41
Mozambique	2004–2008	0.75	0.48	0.73	0.65	0.41
Mozambique	2009–2013	0.74	0.49	0.73	0.63	0.41
Mozambique	2014–	0.60	0.39	0.79	0.78	0.37
Niger	1999–2003	0.78	0.61	0.63	0.86	0.49

Niger	2004–2008	0.87	0.77	0.82	0.88	0.66
Niger	2009**	0.87	0.57	0.80	0.86	0.55
Nigeria	1999–2002	0.55	0.31	0.83	0.81	0.34
Nigeria	2003–2006	0.55	0.26	0.87	0.81	0.32
Nigeria	2007–2010	0.57	0.20	0.87	0.81	0.31
Nigeria	2011–2015*	0.55	0.34	0.83	0.81	0.35
Rwanda	2003–2007	0.41	0.37	0.19	0.29	0.18
Rwanda	2008–2012	0.45	0.36	0.24	0.29	0.19
Rwanda	2013–	0.53	0.49	0.31	0.50	0.26
Senegal	1988–1992	0.71	0.58	0.87	0.79	0.50
Senegal	1993–1997	0.71	0.70	0.89	0.81	0.56
Senegal	1998–1999	0.76	0.75	0.88	0.85	0.60
Senegal	2000–2001*	0.81	0.84	0.87	0.85	0.67
Seychelles	1993–1997	0.95	0.47	0.61	0.37	0.39
Seychelles	1998–2000	0.95	0.47	0.61	0.46	0.41
Seychelles	2001–2005	0.95	0.46	0.62	0.45	0.40
Seychelles	2006–2011	0.94	0.51	0.72	0.57	0.46
Seychelles	2012–2014	0.94	0.56	0.73	0.56	0.48
Seychelles	2015–	0.83	0.75	0.75	0.76	0.57
Tanzania	1995–1999	0.82	0.47	0.74	0.67	0.43
Tanzania	2000–2004	0.79	0.38	0.78	0.70	0.41
Tanzania	2005–2009	0.79	0.38	0.78	0.72	0.41
Tanzania	2010–2014	0.74	0.44	0.77	0.73	0.42
Tanzania	2015–	0.62	0.48	0.78	0.69	0.41
Togo	1993–1997	0.45	0.21	0.68	0.46	0.22
Togo	1998–2001	0.45	0.14	0.66	0.53	0.21

(continued)

(continued)

Country	Time Period	Physical Violence	Clean Elections	Freedom of Association	Freedom of Expression	Toleration Score
Togo	2002–2004	0.44	0.15	0.66	0.54	0.21
Togo	2005–2009	0.60	0.25	0.74	0.77	0.32
Togo	2010–2014	0.64	0.39	0.76	0.78	0.37
Togo	2015–	0.57	0.47	0.78	0.78	0.38
Uganda	1996–2000	0.43	0.42	0.31	0.69	0.24
Uganda	2001–2005	0.45	0.28	0.30	0.73	0.22
Uganda	2006–2010	0.45	0.20	0.56	0.73	0.23
Uganda	2011–2015	0.44	0.21	0.66	0.65	0.24
Zambia	1991–1995	0.53	0.49	0.42	0.46	0.27
Zambia	1996–2000	0.55	0.51	0.85	0.74	0.39
Zambia	2001–2005	0.64	0.50	0.86	0.74	0.42
Zambia	2006–2007	0.64	0.51	0.89	0.75	0.43
Zambia	2008–2010	0.64	0.52	0.88	0.75	0.44
Zambia	2011*	0.64	0.57	0.84	0.75	0.45
Zimbabwe	1990–1994	0.27	0.20	0.68	0.32	0.16
Zimbabwe	1995–1999	0.27	0.21	0.72	0.35	0.17
Zimbabwe	2000–2004	0.14	0.10	0.70	0.37	0.12
Zimbabwe	2005–2007	0.12	0.07	0.72	0.22	0.10
Zimbabwe	2008–2012	0.06	0.06	0.73	0.20	0.09
Zimbabwe	2013–	0.22	0.10	0.68	0.42	0.14

Notes: Time periods refer to the closest presidential and legislative election; Scores are the average for the year of and prior to the presidential and legislative election; * indicates electoral authoritarian regime ended by electoral turnover; ** indicates electoral authoritarian regime ended by conflict or coup.

Electoral Authoritarian Types in Africa (1990–2016)

Country	Time Period	Elections Included	Hegemonic?	Tolerant?	Electoral Authoritarian Type
Angola	2008–2011	2008 (l)	Y	N	Repressive hegemony
Angola	2012–	2012 (l)	Y	N	Repressive hegemony
Burkina Faso	1991–1996	1991 (p) 1992 (l)	Y	N	Repressive hegemony
Burkina Faso	1997–2001	1997 (l) 1998 (p)	Y	Y	Repressive hegemony
Burkina Faso	2002–2004	2002 (l)	Y	Y	Tolerant hegemony
Burkina Faso	2005–2009	2005 (p) 2007 (l)	Y	Y	Tolerant hegemony
Burkina Faso	2010–2014**	2010 (p)	Y	Y	Tolerant hegemony
Burundi	2005–2009	2005 (l)	N	N	Repressive non-hegemony
Burundi	2010–2014	2010 (p) 2010 (l)	Y	N	Repressive hegemony
Burundi	2015–	2015(p) 2015(l)	Y	N	Repressive hegemony
Cameroon	1992–1996	1992 (l) 1992 (p)	N	N	Repressive non-hegemony
Cameroon	1997–2001	1997 (l) 1997 (p)	Y	N	Repressive hegemony
Cameroon	2002–2006	2002 (l) 2004 (p)	Y	N	Repressive hegemony
Cameroon	2007–2010	2007 (l)	Y	N	Repressive hegemony
Cameroon	2011–	2011 (p) 2013 (p)	Y	N	Repressive hegemony
Central African Republic	2005–2010	2005 (p) 2005 (l)	N	N	Repressive non-hegemony
Central African Republic	2011–2012**	2011 (p) 2011 (l)	N	N	Repressive non-hegemony
Chad	1996–2000	1996 (p) 1997 (l)	N	N	Repressive non-hegemony
Chad	2001–2005	2001 (p) 2002 (l)	Y	N	Repressive hegemony
Chad	2006–2010	2006 (p)	Y	N	Repressive hegemony
Chad	2011–2015	2011 (l)	Y	N	Repressive hegemony
Chad	2016–	2016 (p)	N	N	Repressive non-hegemony

(*continued*)

(continued)

Country	Time Period	Elections Included	Hegemonic?	Tolerant?	Electoral Authoritarian Type
Congo-DRC	2006–2010	2006 (p) 2006 (l)	N	N	Repressive non-hegemony
Congo-DRC	2011–	2011 (p) 2011 (l)	N	N	Repressive non-hegemony
Congo-RoC	2002–2006	2002 (p) 2002 (l)	Y	N	Repressive hegemony
Congo-RoC	2007–2011	2007 (l) 2009 (p)	Y	N	Repressive hegemony
Congo-RoC	2012–2015	2012 (p)	Y	N	Repressive hegemony
Congo-RoC	2016–	2016(p)	Y	N	Repressive hegemony
Côte d'Ivoire	1990–1994	1990 (p) 1990 (l)	Y	N	Repressive hegemony
Côte d'Ivoire	1995–1999**	1995 (p) 1995 (l)	Y	N	Repressive hegemony
Djibouti	1992–1996	1992 (l) 1993 (p)	Y	N	Repressive hegemony
Djibouti	1997–2002	1997 (l) 1999 (p)	Y	N	Repressive hegemony
Djibouti	2003–2007	2003 (l) 2005 (p)	Y	N	Repressive hegemony
Djibouti	2008–2010	2008 (l)	Y	N	Repressive hegemony
Djibouti	2011–2015	2011 (p) 2013 (p)	Y	N	Repressive hegemony
Djibouti	2016–	2016 (p)	Y	N	Repressive hegemony
Ethiopia	1995–1999	1995 (l)	Y	N	Repressive hegemony
Ethiopia	2000–2004	2000 (l)	Y	N	Repressive hegemony
Ethiopia	2005–2009	2005 (l)	N	N	Repressive non-hegemony
Ethiopia	2010–2014	2010 (l)	Y	N	Repressive hegemony
Ethiopia	2015–	2015 (l)	Y	N	Repressive hegemony
Gabon	1990–1995	1990 (l) 1993 (p)	N	N	Repressive non-hegemony
Gabon	1996–2000	1996 (l) 1998 (p)	Y	N	Repressive hegemony

Gabon	2001–2004	2001 (l)	Y	N	Repressive hegemony
Gabon	2005–2008	2005 (p) 2006 (l)	Y	N	Repressive hegemony
Gabon	2009–2015	2009 (p) 2011 (l)	Y	Y	Repressive hegemony
Gabon	2016–	2016 (p)	Y	N	Repressive hegemony
Gambia	1996–2000	1996 (p) 1997 (l)	Y	N	Repressive hegemony
Gambia	2001–2005	2001 (p) 2002 (l)	Y	N	Repressive hegemony
Gambia	2006–2010	2006 (p) 2007 (l)	Y	N	Repressive hegemony
Gambia	2011–2016*	2011 (p) 2012 (l)	Y	N	Repressive hegemony
Ghana	1992–1995	1992 (p) 1992 (l)	Y	Y	Tolerant hegemony
Ghana	1996–1999	1996 (p) 1996 (l)	Y	Y	Tolerant hegemony
Ghana	2000*	2000 (p) 2000 (l)	N	Y	Tolerant non-hegemony
Guinea	1993–1997	1993 (p) 1995 (l)	N	N	Repressive non-hegemony
Guinea	1998–2001	1998 (p)	N	N	Repressive non-hegemony
Guinea	2002–2007**	2002 (l) 2003 (p)	Y	N	Repressive hegemony
Kenya	1992–1996	1992 (p) 1992 (l)	N	N	Repressive non-hegemony
Kenya	1997–2001	1997 (p) 1997 (l)	N	N	Repressive non-hegemony
Kenya	2002*	2002 (p) 2002 (l)	N	N	Repressive non-hegemony
Mauritania	1992–1995	1992 (p) 1992 (l)	Y	N	Repressive hegemony
Mauritania	1996–2000	1996 (l) 1997 (p)	Y	N	Repressive hegemony
Mauritania	2001–2004**	2001 (l) 2003 (p)	Y	N	Repressive hegemony
Mozambique	1994–1998	1994 (p) 1994 (l)	N	Y	Tolerant non-hegemony
Mozambique	1999–2003	1999 (p) 1999 (l)	N	Y	Tolerant non-hegemony
Mozambique	2004–2008	2004 (p) 2004 (l)	Y	Y	Tolerant hegemony
Mozambique	2009–2013	2009 (p) 2009 (l)	Y	Y	Tolerant hegemony

(continued)

(continued)

Country	Time Period	Elections Included	Hegemonic?	Tolerant?	Electoral Authoritarian Type
Mozambique	2014–	2014 (p) 2014 (l)	N	N	Repressive non-hegemony
Niger	1999–2003	1999 (p) 1999 (l)	N	Y	Tolerant non-hegemony
Niger	2004–2008	2004 (p) 2004 (l)	N	Y	Tolerant non-hegemony
Niger	2009**	2009 (p) 2009 (l)	Y	Y	Tolerant hegemony
Nigeria	1999–2002	1999 (p) 1999 (l)	N	N	Repressive non-hegemony
Nigeria	2003–2006	2003 (p) 2003 (l)	N	N	Repressive non-hegemony
Nigeria	2007–2010	2007 (p) 2007 (l)	Y	N	Repressive hegemony
Nigeria	2011–2014*	2011 (p) 2011 (l)	N	Y	Repressive hegemony
Rwanda	2003–2007	2003 (p) 2003 (l)	Y	N	Repressive hegemony
Rwanda	2008–2012	2008 (l)	Y	N	Repressive hegemony
Rwanda	2013–	2010 (p) 2013 (l)	Y	N	Repressive hegemony
Senegal	1988–1992	1988 (p) 1988 (l)	Y	Y	Tolerant hegemony
Senegal	1993–1997	1993 (p) 1993 (l)	Y	Y	Tolerant hegemony
Senegal	1998–1999	1998 (l)	Y	Y	Tolerant hegemony
Senegal	2000–2001*	2000 (p) 2001 (l)	N	Y	Tolerant hegemony
Seychelles	1993–1997	1993 (p) 1993 (l)	Y	Y	Tolerant hegemony
Seychelles	1998–2000	1998 (p) 1998 (l)	Y	Y	Tolerant hegemony
Seychelles	2001–2005	2001 (p) 2002 (l)	Y	Y	Tolerant hegemony
Seychelles	2006–2011	2006 (p) 2007 (l)	Y	Y	Tolerant hegemony
Seychelles	2012–2014	2012 (p) 2012 (l)	Y	Y	Tolerant hegemony
Seychelles	2015–	2015 (p) 2016 (l)	N	Y	Tolerant non-hegemony

Tanzania	1995–1999	1995 (p) 1995 (l)	Y	Y	Tolerant hegemony
Tanzania	2000–2004	2000 (p) 2000 (l)	Y	Y	Tolerant hegemony
Tanzania	2005–2009	2005 (p) 2005 (l)	Y	Y	Tolerant hegemony
Tanzania	2010–2014	2010 (p) 2010 (l)	Y	Y	Tolerant hegemony
Tanzania	2015–	2015 (p) 2015 (l)	Y	Y	Tolerant hegemony
Togo	1993–1997	1993 (p) 1994 (l)	Y	N	Repressive hegemony
Togo	1998–2001	1998 (p) 1999 (l)	Y	N	Repressive hegemony
Togo	2002–2004	2002 (l) 2003 (p)	Y	N	Repressive hegemony
Togo	2005–2009	2005 (p) 2007 (l)	N	Y	Repressive non-hegemony
Togo	2010–2014	2010 (p) 2013 (l)	Y	Y	Repressive hegemony
Togo	2015–	2015 (p)	Y	Y	Tolerant hegemony
Uganda	1996–2000	1996 (p) 1996 (l)	Y	N	Repressive hegemony
Uganda	2001–2005	2001 (p) 2001 (l)	Y	N	Repressive hegemony
Uganda	2006–2010	2006 (p) 2006 (l)	Y	N	Repressive hegemony
Uganda	2011–2015	2011 (p) 2011 (l)	Y	N	Repressive hegemony
Uganda	2016–	2016 (p) 2016 (p)	Y	N	Repressive hegemony
Zambia	1991–1995	1991 (p) 1991 (l)	Y	Y	Repressive hegemony
Zambia	1996–2000	1996 (p) 1996 (l)	Y	Y	Tolerant hegemony
Zambia	2001–2005	2001 (p) 2001 (l)	N	Y	Tolerant non-hegemony
Zambia	2006–2007	2006 (p) 2006 (l)	N	Y	Tolerant non-hegemony
Zambia	2008–2010	2008 (p)	N	Y	Tolerant non-hegemony
Zambia	2011*	2011 (p) 2011 (l)	N	Y	Tolerant non-hegemony
Zimbabwe	1990–1994	1990 (p) 1990 (l)	Y	N	Repressive hegemony
Zimbabwe	1995–1999	1995 (l) 1996 (p)	Y	N	Repressive hegemony

(*continued*)

(*continued*)

Country	Time Period	Elections Included	Hegemonic?	Tolerant?	Electoral Authoritarian Type
Zimbabwe	2000–2004	2000 (l) 2002 (p)	N	N	Repressive non-hegemony
Zimbabwe	2005–2007	2005 (l)	N	N	Repressive non-hegemony
Zimbabwe	2008–2012	2008 (p) 2008 (l)	N	N	Repressive non-hegemony
Zimbabwe	2013–	2013 (p) 2013 (l)	Y	N	Repressive hegemony

Notes: Time periods refer to the closest presidential and legislative election; Scores are the average for the year of and prior to the presidential and legislative election; * indicates electoral authoritarian regime ended by electoral turnover; ** indicates electoral authoritarian regime ended by conflict or coup.

Appendix B

Typological Theory Coding and Scores

The typological space relies on various secondary sources that cover the single-party era and discuss the country's international relations and major opposition parties. A single-party regime is defined as a civilian-led, party-based, closed authoritarian regime that has been in existence for at least ten years. Quantitative information on democracy assistance was available from AidData, on aid conditionality from the World Bank and IMF, and on economic growth and human development index (HDI) from the World Bank. Each dimension is scored from 0 to 2 (with 0 reflecting a low score and 2 a high score), and aggregated to score the final variable dichotomously.

RULING PARTY CREDIBILITY (>3 = CREDIBLE RULING PARTY)

Physical Infrastructure: Does the party have staffed physical offices at the national and grassroots level?

Decisional Autonomy: Does the party have the ability to make decisions that govern its own internal procedures?

Internal Competition: Is nomination for office held through a competitive primary that ensures fair competition?

Social Incorporation: Are voting constituencies conceived of broadly or narrowly?

Ruling Party Credibility in African Single Party Regimes

Case	Physical Infrastructure	Decisional Autonomy	Internal Competition	Social Incorporation	Credible Ruling Party?
Cameroon	1	0	0	0	No
Côte d'Ivoire	1	0	0	1	No
Djibouti	0	0	0	2	No
Gabon	1	1	1	0	No
Kenya	1 (2)	0	1 (0)	0	No
Mozambique	2	2	1	1	Yes
Senegal	1	1	1	1	Yes
Seychelles	2	1	1	2	Yes
Tanzania	2	2	2	2	Yes
Togo	1	1	1	0	No

Notes: Kenya's score changes under Daniel arap Moi.

INTERNATIONAL PATRONAGE (>2 = DEMOCRATIC PATRONAGE)

Democracy Assistance: Was substantial democracy assistance provided (in constant $US)?

Aid Conditionality: Was aid persistently rescinded due to violations of bilateral and multilateral reform agreements?

OPPOSITION CAPACITY (>2 = CAPABLE OPPOSITION PARTY)

Party Stability and Autonomy: Have the major opposition parties remained consistent and avoided major splits or regime cooptation?

Opposition Decision Making: Have the major opposition parties persistently participated in elections and/or avoided cooptation (automatically scored as 0 if major parties boycott the election)?

ECONOMIC PERFORMANCE (>1 = CONSISTENT ECONOMIC PERFORMANCE)

Real Growth Rates: Have growth rates increased and kept up with levels of consumer price inflation?

Level and Improvement in HDI: Have levels of Human Development increased and/or achieved high levels?

Typological Theory Scores for Individual Components, by Time Period

	Time Period	Democracy Assistance	Aid Conditionality	Opposition Stability and Autonomy	Opposition Decision Making	Real Economic Growth	Level and Improvement in HDI
Cameroon	1997–2001	0	1	0	0	0	1
Cameroon	2002–6	0	0	0	1	1	1
Cameroon	2007–10	1	0	0	1	1	1
Cameroon	2011–	0	0	0	1	1	2
Côte d'Ivoire	1995–9	2	0	2	0	0	1
Djibouti	1997–2002	0	0	0	1	0	0
Djibouti	2003–7	2	0	0	0	1	0
Djibouti	2008–10	0	0	0	0	1	2
Djibouti	2011–	0	0	0	0	1	2
Gabon	1996–2000	0	0	1	1	1	1
Gabon	2001–4	0	0	1	1	0	1
Gabon	2005–8	0	0	0	1	0	1
Gabon	2009–	0	0	1	0	1	1
Kenya	1997–2001	1	2	1	1	0	0
Kenya	2002*	2	1	0	2	0	0
Mozambique	1999–2003	1	1	2	1	0	2
Mozambique	2004–8	0	0	2	1	1	2
Mozambique	2009–14	0	0	1	1	1	2
Senegal	1993–7	0	0	2	1	0	1
Senegal	1998–9	0	1	2	1	0	0

(continued)

299

(*continued*)

	Time Period	Democracy Assistance	Aid Conditionality	Opposition Stability and Autonomy	Opposition Decision Making	Real Economic Growth	Level and Improvement in HDI
Senegal	2000–1*	0	1	2	2	1	1
Seychelles	1998–2000	0	0	2	1	2	1
Seychelles	2001–5	0	0	2	1	1	1
Seychelles	2006–11	0	0	2	2	2	1
Seychelles	2012–	0	0	2	0	1	1
Tanzania	2000–4	0	0	1	2	0	2
Tanzania	2005–9	2	0	2	1	1	2
Tanzania	2010–14	1	0	2	1	1	2
Tanzania	2015–	1	0	1	2	1	2
Togo	1998–2001	0	1	2	0	1	2
Togo	2002–4	0	1	2	0	0	1
Togo	2005–9	1	2	2	2	0	1
Togo	2010–	1	0	0	1	1	1

Notes: The time period reflects on the major span between the latest and closest presidential and legislative election, while scores reflect conditions prior to those election. Non-foundational elections are not included.

References

International Reporting

Africa Confidential
Africa Review
Afrique Express
The Associated Press
BBC News
Foreign Broadcast Information Service (FBIS)
Inter-Press Service
IRIN News
Jeune Afrqiue
Jeune Afrique Economie
Jeune Afrique L'Intelligent
The New York Times
Reuters
Voice of America
West Africa

Local Reporting

Cameroon Post (Cameroon)
Cameroon Tribune (Cameroon)
The Citizen (Tanzania)
Daily Nation (Kenya)
The East African (Kenya)
Le Libération (Gabon)
Le Messager (Cameroon)
Le Nouvelle Expression (Cameroon)
Le Yaoundé (Cameroon)
Mutations (Cameroon)

Mwananchi (Tanzania)
Post News (Cameroon)
Tanzanian Affairs (Tanzania)
Tanzania Daily News (Tanzania)
The Weekly Review (Kenya)

Datasets

African Elections Database
Afrobarometer. 2005. Round 3 Afrobarometer Survey in Tanzania. East Lansing, MI.
Beck, Thorsten, George Clarke, Alberto Groff, Philip Keefer, and Patrick Walsh. 2012. "New Tools in Comparative Political Economy: Database of Political Institutions." *World Bank Economic Review* 15 (1):165–176.
Coppedge, Michael, John Gerring, David Altman, et al. 2017. "Conceptualizing and Measuring Democracy: A New Approach." *Perspectives on Politics* 9 (2):247–267.
Europa Publications Limited. Various years. *Africa South of the Sahara*. London: Europa Publications Ltd.
Freedom House. Various years. *Freedom in the World*, New York, NY: Freedom House.
Geddes, Barbara, Joseph Wright, and Erica Franz. 2012. *Authoritarian Regimes: A New Data Set. Perspectives on Politics* 12(2):313–331.
Gibney, Mark, Linda Cornett, Reed, Wood, Peter Haschke, and Daniel Arnon. 2016. The Political Terror Scale 1976–2015. Date retrieved, from the Political Terror Scale website: www.politicalterrorscale.org.
Lewis, M. Paul, Gary F. Simons, and Charles D. Fennig, eds. 2015. *Ethnologue: Languages of the World, Eighteenth Edition*. Vol. 2015. Dallas, TX: SIL International.
Polity IV. Various years. *Political Regime Characteristics and Transitions, 1800–2013*. Center for Systemic Peace: Vienna, VA.
Tierney, Michael J., Daniel L. Nielson, Darren G. Hawkings, et al. 2011. "More Dollars than Sense: Refining Our Knowledge of Development Financing Using AidData." *World Development* 39 (11):1891–1906.
World Bank. 2009. *Financial & Private Sector Development: Privatization*. Washington, DC: The World Bank.
2016. *World Bank Development Indicators*. Washington, DC: The World Bank.

Election Observation Reports

Bakary, Tessy, and Susan L. Palmer. 1997. May 17, 1997 Legislative Elections in Cameroon: The Report of the IFES International Observer Mission. Washington, DC: International Foundation for Election Systems.
Carter Center. 2003. *Observing the 2002 Kenya Elections*. Atlanta, GA: The Carter Center.
Commonwealth Secretariat. 2003. *Kenya General Election 27 December 2002: The Report of the Commonwealth Observer Group*. London: Commonwealth Observer Group.

2010. *Report of the Commonwealth Observer Group: Tanzania General Elections 31 October 2010*. London: Commonwealth Secretariat.

2011. *Report of the Commonwealth Expert Team: Cameroon Presidential Election 9 October 2011*. London: Commonwealth Secretariat.

East African Community (EAC). 2010. *Observer Mission to the 2010 General Elections in the United Republic of Tanzania*. London: East African Community.

Electoral Institute for Sustainable Democracy in Africa (EISA). 2005. *EISA Election Observer Mission Report: Zanzibar*. Johannesberg: Electoral Institute for Sustainable Democracy in Africa.

European Union (EU). 2003. *Kenya General Elections 27 December 2002*. Brussels: European Union Election Observation Mission.

2010. *Tanzania: Final Report General Elections October 2010*. Brussels: European Union.

Institute for Education in Democracy (IED). 2003. *Enhancing the Electoral Process in Kenya: A Report on the Transition General Election, 2002*. Nairobi: Institute for Education in Democracy.

International Republican Institute (IRI). 1993. *Kenya: The December 29, 1992 Elections*. Washington, DC: International Republican Institute.

National Democratic Institute (NDI). 1993. *An Assessment of the October 11, 1992 Elections in Cameroon*. Washington, DC: National Democratic Institute for International Affairs.

2005. *Preliminary Statement of NDI's Electoral Observation Mission to Zanzibar's 2005 Elections*. Washington, DC: National Democratic Institute.

Organisation Internationale de la Francophonie. 1997. *Rapport de la Mission Exploratoire en vue des Elections Legislative 17 Mai 1997*. Paris: Organisation Internationale de la Francophonie.

2002. *Rapport des Missions de la Francophonie sue les Élections Législatives et Municipales de Juin 2002 au Cameroun*. Paris: Organisation Internationale de la Francophonie.

2004. *Rapport de la Mission D'Observation de L'Élection Présidentielle du 11 Octobre 2004 au Cameroun*. Paris: Organisation Internationale de la Francophonie.

2011. *Rapport de la Mission D'Observation de L'Élection Présidentielle du 8 Octobre 2011 au Cameroun*. Paris: Organisation Internationale de la Francophonie.

South African Development Community (SADC). 2010. *SADC Electoral Observer Mission (SEOM) to the United Republic of Tanzania*. Johannesburg: South African Development Community.

Tanzanian Election Monitoring Committee (TEMCO). 1997. *The 1995 General Elections in Tanzania*. Dar es Salaam: Tanzanian Election Monitoring Committee.

2001. *The 2000 General Elections in Tanzania: Report of the Tanzania Election Monitoring Committee*. Dar es Salaam: Tanzanian Election Monitoring Committee.

2006. *The 2005 Election in Tanzania Mainland: Report of the Tanzania Election Monitoring Committee*. Dar es Salaam: Tanzanian Election Monitoring Committee.

Transparency International (TI). 2011. *09 October 2011 Presidential Election: Final Report of the Election Observation Mission.* Yaoundé: Transparancy International Cameroon.

Primary Sources

Bureau Central des Recensements et des Etudes de Population. 2005. *Rapport De Presentation des Resultantes Definitis.* Yaoundé, Cameroun: Bureau Central des Recensements et des Etudes de Population.

Elections Cameroon. 2011. *Rapport sur l'Elections Presidentielle du 9 Octobre 2011.* Yaoundé: Elections Cameroon.

Institute of Economic Affairs. 2002. *The Little Fact Book: The Socio Economic & Political Profiles of Kenya's Districts.* Nairobi: The Institute of Economic Affairs.

International Bank for Reconstruction and Development (IBRD). 1994. *Adjustment in Africa: Reforms, Results, and the Road Ahead.* New York, NY: World Bank.

International Monetary Fund (IMF). 1991. *Annual Report.* Washington, DC: International Monetary Fund.

1996. *Kenya: Economic Reforms for 1996–1998 The Policy Framework Paper.* Washington, DC: International Monetary Fund.

2005. *Cameroon: Ex Post Assessment of Longer-Term Program Engagement.* Washington, DC: International Monetary Fund.

Ministre de l'Administration Territoriale. 1992. *Rapport sur l'Elections Presidentielle du 11 Octobre 1992.* Yaoundé: Ministre de l'Administration Territoriale.

1997. *Rapport sur les Elections Legislatives des 17,18 Mai 1997.* Yaoundé: Ministre de l'Administration Territoriale.

Ministre de L'economie de la Planification et de L'amenagement du Territoire. 2000. *Etudes Socio-Economiques Regionalies Au Cameroun (Various Provinces).* Yaoundé: Ministre de L'economie de la Planification et de L'amenagement du Territoire.

Office of the National Treasurer. *Kenyan African National Union Governing Council Meeting Notes.* KANU 1/3(252). Nairobi, Kenya (March 25, 1980).

Office the President. *Delegates to the KANU Provincial Conferences on 18th November 1978.* Nairobi, Kenya (November 10, 1978).

Republic of Kenya. 1994. *Kenya Population Census, 1989.* Nairobi: Central Bureau of Statistics, Office of the Vice President and Ministry of Planning and National Development..

2001. *The 1999 Population & Housing Census: Counting Our People for Development.* Nairobi: Central Bureau of Statistics Ministry of Finance and Planning.

Tanganyika Department of Lands & Surveys. 1956. *Atlas of Tanganyika, East Africa.* Dar es Salaam: Government Printer.

United Republic of Tanzania. 1970. *The Economic Survey Annual Plan for 1970–1971.* Dar es Salaam: Government Printer.

1972. *The Economic Survey Annual Plan for 1972–1973.* Dar es Salaam: Government Printer.

1997. *The Report of the National Electoral Commission on the 1995 Presidential and Parliamentary Elections.* Dar es Salaam: Tanzanian National Electoral Comission. Dar es Salaam.

1998. *Regional Socio-Economic Profile (Various Regions),* edited by Tanzanian Planning Commission and Regional Comissioner's Office. Dar es Salaam: Government Printer.

2001. *The Report of the National Electoral Commission on the 2000 Presidential and Parliamentary and Councilor's Elections.* Tanzanian National Electoral Commission. Dar es Salaam: Government Printer.

2002. *District Profiles (Various),* edited by Tanzanian National Bureau of Statistics. Dar es Salaam: Government Printer.

2006. *The Report of the National Electoral Commission on the 2005 Presidential and Parliamentary and Councilor's Elections.* Tanzanian National Electoral Commission. Dar es Salaam: Government Printer.

2011. *The Report of the National Electoral Commission on the 2010 Presidential and Parliamentary and Councilor's Elections.* Tanzainan National Electoral Commission. Dar es Salaam: Government Printer

2016. *The Report of the National Electoral Commission on the 2015 Presidential and Parliamentary and Councilor's Elections.* Tanzainan National Electoral Commission. Dar es Salaam: Government Printer.

U.S. Embassy, Yaoundé. "Possible Successor to President Biya." Wikileaks Cable 07YAOUNDE227_a (February 22, 2007).

"USG Should Avoid Association with Finance Minister Polycarpe Abah." Wikileaks Cable 07YAOUNDE732_a (June 7, 2007).

"While Not Pretty, Cameroon's Election Prep is Moving Ahead." Wikileaks Cable 07YAOUNDE741 (June 8, 2007).

"Cameroon Elections: Campaign Kicks into High Gear" Wikileaks Cable: 07YAOUNDE894_a (July 18, 2007).

"Election on July 22: Nuts and Bolts and USG Observation." Wikileaks Cable 07YAOUNDE902 (July 19, 2007).

"Sarkozy-Biya Summit: A French View from Cameroon." Wikileaks Cable 07YAOUNDE1271_a (October 24, 2007).

"Biya Tells Ambassador he Plans Constitutional Change." Wikileaks Cable 08YAOUNDE103_a (January 31, 2008).

"Ambassador Engages on Constitutional Change." Wikileaks Cable 08YAOUNDE732_a (February 20, 2008).

"Constitution Issue Heats Up." Wikileaks Cable 07YAOUNDE33_a (July 11, 2008).

"Biya Promises Progress on Corruption and Governance." Wikileaks Cable 08YAOUNDE800_a (August 11, 2008).

"President Biya at 26." Wikileaks Cable 08YAOUNDE1169_a (December 3, 2008).

"Is Biya Preparing to Change the Constitution for a Third Term?" Wikileaks Cable 07YAOUNDE1478 (December 19, 2008).

"Cameroon's Justice Minister Says North Will Support Biya, but not another Beti or Bami." Wikileaks Cable 09YAOUNDE256_a (March 12, 2009).

"Rethinking our Approach to Cameroon." Wikileaks Cable 09YAOUNDE971_a (November 13, 2009).

White House. "News Release: Leadership and Opportunity in Africa." Washington, DC (March 20, 2003).

Cited Author Interview Subjects

Anembom, Beatrice (Organizational Secretary, SDF). Yaoundé. (July 29, 2015).

Anonymous #CM4 (CPDM Secretariat Member). Yaoundé. (July 27, 2015).

Anonymous #CM11 (CPDM Central Committee Member). Douala. (August 3, 2015).

Anonymous #CM15 (Senior SDF Opposition Member. Yaoundé. (July 29, 2015).

Anonymous #TZ3 (Senior CCM Member). Dar es Salaam. (October 18, 2010).

Anonymous #TZ13 (Senior CCM Member). Arusha. (October 31, 2010).

Anyang N'yong'o, Peter (Foundational FORD Member). Nairobi. (August 1, 2012).

Asanganyi, Tazoacha (former Secretary General, SDF). Yaoundé. (July 22, 2015).

Bashenge, Joran (Deputy-Secretary General, CUF). Dar es Salaam. (November 15, 2010).

Braegu, Mwesigu (Campaign Chair, CHADEMA). Dar es Salaam. (November 12, 2010).

Dzongang, Albert (Former MP CPDM). Douala. (August 5, 2015).

Ekindi, Jean-Jacques (Former CPDM Section President). Douala. (August 4, 2015).

Kabwe, Zitto (CHADEMA MP, Kigoma Rural). Dar es Salaam. (November 29, 2010).

Kamba, Gaston (CPDM MP Nkam). Yaoundé. (July 23, 2015).

Kiai, Maina (Civil Society Activist). Nairobi. (July 13, 2012).

Kituyi, Mukhisa (former senior member of FORD-K). Nairobi. (July 18, 2012).

Lipumba, Ibrahim (Chairman, CUF). Dar es Salaam. (December 3, 2010).

Mbowe, Freemon (Chairman, CHADEMA). Dar es Salaam. (December 4, 2010).

Mkumbo, Kitila (Senior Technical Advisor, CHADEMA). Dar es Salaam. (October 27, 2010).

Mnyika, John (CHADEMA Interim Secretary General). Dar es Salaam. (October 25, 2010).

Mswiga, Peter Simeon (MP Iringa Urban, District Secretary General for Iringa, CHADEMA). Iringa. (November 26, 2010).

Mudavadi, Musalia (Former Finance Minister of Kenya). Nairobi. (July 25, 2012).

Muite, Paul (former Vice-Chair of FORD-K). Nairobi. (July 20, 2012).

Mwigamba, Marigu Samson (Regional Chairman for Arusha, CHADEMA). Arusha. (November 13, 2010).

Nkolo, John (Secretary General, UDP). Dar es Salaam. (November 11, 2010).

Nguini, Matthias Owona (Civil Society Activist). Yaoundé. (July 28, 2015).

Ojiambo, Julia, (Former Senior Member of KANU). Nairobi. (July 27, 2012).

Opore, John (former KANU MP for Bonchari). Nairobi. (July 20, 2012).

Osih, Joshua (MP for Wouri, SDF). Douala. (August 3, 2015).

Robert, Bappoh Lipor (Chairman, UPC). Yaoundé. (August 6, 2015).

Ruhuza, Samweli (Secretary General NCCR-M). Dar es Salaam. (November 22, 2010).

Salat, Nick (KANU Secretary General). Nairobi. (August 7, 2012).
Slaa, Wilibrod (Secretary General, CHADEMA). Dar es Salaam. (November 18, 2010).
Waka, Job (Organizational Secretary of KANU). Nairobi. (July 18, 2012).
Wetangula, Moses (former KANU MP for Sirisia). Nairobi. (July 17, 2012).

Secondary Sources

Adar, Korwa G. 1998. "The Clinton Administration and Africa: A View from Nairobi, Kenya." *Issue: A Journal of Opinion* 26 (2):70–74.
Aicardi de Saint-Paul, Marc. 1989. *Gabon: The Development of a Nation.* New York, NY: Routledge.
Ajulu, Rok. 2001. "Kenya: One Step Forward, Three Steps Back: The Succession Dilemma." *Review of African Political Economy* 28 (88):197–212.
2002. "Politicised Ethnicity, Competitive Politics and Conlict in Kenya: A Historical Perspective." *African Studies* 61 (2):251–268.
Albaugh, Erika. 2011. "An Autocrat's Toolkit: Adaptation and Manipulation in 'Democratic' Cameroon." *Democratization* 18 (2):388–414.
Alvarez, Mkie, Jose Antonio Cheibub, Fernando Limongi, and Adam Przeworski. 1996. "Classifying Political Regimes." *Studies in Comparative International Development* 31 (2):3–36.
Alwan, Daoud A., and Yohanis Mibrathu. 2000. *Historical Dictionary of Djibouti.* Lanham, MD: Scarecrow Press.
Anderson, David, Jorgen Moller, and Lasse Lykke Rorbaek. 2014. "State Capacity and Political Regime Stability." *Democratization* 21 (7):1305–1325.
Armony, Ariel C., and Hector E. Schamis. 2005. "Babel in Democratization Studies." *Journal of Democracy* 16 (4):113–128.
Arriola, Leonardo R. 2009. "Patroange and Political Stability in Africa." *Comparative Political Studies* 42 (10):1339–1362.
2012. *Multi-Ethnic Coalitions in Africa: Business Financing of Opposition Election Campaigns.* New York, NY: Cambridge University Press.
Article19. 1997. Cameroon: A Transition in Crisis.
Austen, Ralph A. 1968. *Northwest Tanzania under German and British Rule: Colonial Policy and Tribal Politics, 1889–1939.* New Haven, CT: Yale University Press.
Azarya, Victor. 1976. *Dominance and Change in North Cameroon: The Fulbe Aristocracy.* Beverly Hills, CA: Sage Publications.
Bader, Julia, Jörn Grävingholt, and Antje Kästner. 2010. "Would Autocracies Promote Autocracy? A Political Economy Perspective on Regime-Type Export in Regional Neighborhoods." *Contemporary Politics* 16 (1):81–100.
Baker, Bruce. 2008. "Seychelles: Democratising in the Shadows of the Past." *Journal of Contemporary African Studies* 26 (3):279–293.
Baldwin, Kate. 2015. *The Paradox of Traditional Chiefs in Democratic Africa.* New York, NY: Cambridge University Press.
Baregu, Mwesiga. 1994. "The Rise and Fall of the One Party State in Tanzania." In *Economic Change and Political Liberalization in Sub-Saharan Africa,* edited by Jennifer A. Widner, 158–181. Baltimore, MD: The Johns Hopkins University Press.

Barkan, Joel D. 1984a. "Legislators, Elections, and Political Linkage." In *Politics and Public Policy in Kenya and Tanzania*, edited by Joel D. Barkan, 71–101. New York, NY: Praeger.

ed. 1984b. *Politics and Public Policy in Kenya and Tanzania*. New York, NY: Praeger.

1994. "Divergence and Convergence in Kenya and Tanzania." In *Beyond Capitalism vs. Socialism in Kenya and Tanzania*, edited by Joel D. Barkan, 1–46. Boulder, CO: Lynne Rienner Publishers.

2004. "U.S. Human Rights Policy and Democratization in Kenya." In *Implementing U.S. Human Rights Policy*, edited by Debra Liang-Fenton, 51–84. Washington, DC: United States Institute of Peace.

2009a. "African Legislatures and the 'Third Wave' of Democratization." In *Legislative Power in Emerging African Democracies*, edited by Joel D. Barkan, 1–32. Boulder, CO: Lynne Rienner Publishers.

2009b. *Legislative Power in Emerging African Democracies*. Boulder, CO: Lynne Rienner Publishers.

Barkan, Joel D., and Frank Holmquist. 1989. "Peasent-State Relations and the Social Base of Self-Help in Kenya." *World Politics* 41 (3):359–380.

Barkan, Joel D., and Michael Chege. 1989. "Decentralizing the State: District Focus and the Politics of Reallocation in Kenya." *Journal of Modern African Studies* 27 (3):431–453.

Barnes, James F. 1992. *Gabon: Beyond the Colonial Legacy*. Boulder, CO: Westview Press.

Bates, Robert H. 1981. *Markets and States in Tropical Africa: The Political Basis of Agricultural Policies*. Berkeley, CA: The University of California Press.

Bayart, Jean-François. 1978a. "The Birth of the Ahidjo Regime." In *Gaullist Africa: Cameroon Under Ahmadu Ahidjo*, edited by Richard Joseph, 45–65. Enugu: Fourth Dimension Publishers.

1978b. "Clientelism, Elections, and Systems of Inequality and Domination in Cameroun: A Reconsideration of Political and Social Control." In *Elections without Choice*, edited by Guy Hermet, Richard Rose and Alain Rouquie, 67–87. New York, NY: John Wiley.

2009. *The State in Africa: the Politics of the Belly*. 2nd ed. Cambridge: Polity.

Bellin, Eva. 2000. "Contingent Democrats: Industrialists, Labor, and Democratization in Late-Developing Countries." *World Politics* 52 (2):175–205.

2012. "Reconsidering the Robustness of Authoritarianism in the Middle East: Lessons from the Arab Spring." *Comparative Politics* 44 (2):127–149.

Bennett, Andrew. 2008. "Process Tracing: A Bayesian Perspective." In *The Oxford Handbook of Political Methodology*, edited by Janet M. Box-Steffensmeier, Henry E. Brady and David Collier, 702–721. New York, NY: Oxford University Press.

Bennett, Andrew, and Jeffrey T. Checkel, eds. 2015. *Process Tracing: From Metaphor to Analytic Tool*. New York, NY: Cambridge University Press.

Bennett, George. 1966. "Kenya's 'Little General Election'." *The World Today* 22 (8):336–343.

Berman, Bruce. 1990. *Control and Crisis in Colonial Kenya: The Dialectic of Domination*. London: James Currey.

Berry, Jeffrey M. 2002. "Validity and Reliability Issues in Elite Interviewing." *PS: Political Science and Politics* 35 (4):679–682.

Bienen, Henry. 1970. *Tanzania: Party Transformation and Economic Development.* Princeton, NJ: Princeton University Press.

1974. *Kenya: The Politics of Participation and Control.* Princeton, NJ: Princeton University Press.

1978. *Armies and Parties in Africa.* New York, NY: Africana Pub. Co.

Blaydes, Lisa. 2011. *Elections and Distributive Politics.* New York, NY: Cambridge University Press.

Bogaards, Matthijs. 2004. "Counting Parties and Identifying Dominant Party Systems in Africa." *European Journal of Political Research* 43:173–197.

2009. "How to Classify Hybrid Regimes: Defective Democracy and Electoral Authoritarianism." *Democratization* 16 (2):399–423.

2013. "Reexamining African Elections." *Journal of Democracy* 24 (4):151–160.

Bollee, Amedee. 2003. "Djibouti: From French Outpost to US Base." *Review of African Political Economy* 30 (97):48184.

Boone, Catherine. 1990. "State Power and Economic Crisis in Senegal." *Comparative Politics* 22 (3):341–357.

1994. "States and Ruling Classes in Postcolonial Africa: The Enduring Contradictions of Power." In *State Power and Social Forces: Domination and Transformation in the Third World*, edited by Joel S. Migdal, Atul Kohli and Vivienne Shue, 108–140. New York, NY: Cambridge University Press.

Brady, Henry E., and David Collier. 2010. *Rethinking Social Inquiry: Diverse Tools, Shared Standards.* New York, NY: Rowman & Littlefield Publishers.

Branch, Daniel. 2011. *Between Hope and Despair: 1963–2011.* New Haven, CT: Yale University Press.

Branch, Daniel, and Nicholas Cheeseman. 2006. "The Politics of Control in Kenya: Understanding the Bureaucratic-Executive State, 1952–78." *Review of African Political Economy* 33 (107):11–31.

Brass, Jennifer N. 2008. "Djibouti's Unusual Resource Curse." *The Journal of Modern African Studies* 46 (4):523–545.

Bratton, Michael. 1998. "Second Elections in Africa." *Journal of Democracy* 9 (3):51–66.

2007. "Formal versus Informal Institutions in Africa." *Journal of Democracy* 18 (3):96–110.

Bratton, Michael, and Eric C. C. Chang. 2006. "State Building and Democraitzation in Sub-Saharan Africa: Forwards, Backwards, or Together?" *Comparative Political Studies* 39 (9):1059–1083.

Bratton, Michael, and Mwangi S. Kimenyi. 2008. "Voting in Kenya: Putting Ethnicity in Perspective." *Journal of Eastern African Studies* 2 (2):272–289.

Bratton, Michael, and Nicolas van de Walle. 1997. *Democratic Experiments in Africa: Regime Transitions in Comparative Perspective.* New York, NY: Cambridge University Press.

Brautigam, Deborah. 2009. *The Dragon's Gift: The Real Story of China in Africa.* New York, NY: Oxford University Press.

Brennan, James R. 2014. "Julius Rex: Nyerere through the Eyes of His Critics, 1953–2013." *Journal of Eastern African Studies* 8 (3):459–477.

Brown, Stephen. 2001. "Authoritarian Leaders and Multiparty Elections in Africa: How Foreign Donors Help to Keep Kenya's Daniel arap Moi in Power." *Third World Quarterly* 22 (5):725–739.

2004. "Theorising Kenya's Protracted Transition to Democracy." *Journal of Contemporary African Studies* 22 (3):325–342.

2005. "Foreign Aid and Democracy Promotion: Lessons from Africa." *The European Journal of Development Research* 17 (2):179–198.

Brownlee, Jason. 2007. *Authoritarianism in an Age of Democratization.* New York, NY: Cambridge University Press.

2009. "Harbinger of Democracy: Competitive Elections before the End of Authoritarianism." In *Democratization by Elections: A New Mode of Transition?*, edited by Staffan I Lindberg, 128–147. Baltimore, MD: The Johns Hopkins University Press.

2012. *Democracy Prevention: The Politics of the U.S. Egyptian Alliance.* New York, NY: Cambridge University Press.

Brumberg, Daniel. 2002. "The Trap of Liberalized Autocracy." *Journal of Democracy* 13 (4):56–68.

Bunce, Valerie, and Sharon L. Wolchik. 2011. *Defeating Authoritarian Leaders in Postcommunist Countries.* New York, NY: Cambridge University Press.

Burnell, Peter, and Oliver Schlumberger. 2010. "Promoting Democracy – Promoting Autocracy? International Politics and National Political Regimes." *Contemporary Politics* 16 (1):1–15.

Calingaert, Daniel. 2006. "Election Rigging and How to Fight it." *Journal of Democracy* 17 (3):138–151.

Callaghy, Thomas M. 1987. "The State as Lame Leviathan: The Patrimonial Administrative State in Africa." In *The African State in Transition*, edited by Zaki Ergas, 87–116. New York, NY: Palgrave Macmillan.

Campbell, Horace, and Howard Stein. 1992. *Tanzania and the IMF: The Dynamics of Liberalization.* Boulder, CO: Westview Press.

Carbone, Giovanni M. 2005. "Continuidade na renovacao? Ten Years of Multiparty Politics in Mozambique: Roots, Evolution and Stabilisation of the Frelimo-Renamo Party System." *The Journal of Modern African Studies* 43 (3):417–442.

Carothers, Thomas. 2000. *Aiding Democracy Abroad: The Learning Curve.* Washington, DC: Carnegie Endowment for International Peaces.

2002. "The End of the Transition Paradigm." *Journal of Democracy* 13 (1):5–21.

2006. *Confronting the Weakest Link: Aiding Political Parties in New Democracies.* Washington, DC: Carnegie Endowment for International Peace.

Case, William. 2006. "Manipulative Skills: How Do Rulers Control the Electoral Arena." In *Electoral Authoritarianism: The Dynamics of Unfree Competition*, edited by Andreas Schedler, 95–112. Boulder, CO: Lynne Rienner.

Chabal, Patrick, and Jean-Paul Daloz. 1999. *Africa Works: Disorder as Political Instrument.* Bloomington, IN: Indiana University Press.

Cheeseman, Nic. 2008. "The Kenyan Elections of 2007: An Introduction." *Journal of Eastern African Studies* 2 (2):168–184.

2010. "African Elections as Vehicles for Change." *Journal of Democracy* 21 (4):139–153.

2015. *Democracy in Africa: Successes, Failures, and the Struggle for Political Reform*. New York, NY: Cambridge University Press.

Cheeseman, Nic, Gabrielle Lynch, and Justin Willis. 2014. "Democracy and its Discontents: Understanding Kenya's 2013 Elections." *Journal of Eastern African Studies* 8 (1):2–24.

Chege, Michael. 1994. "The Return of Multiparty Politics." In *Beyond Capitalism vs. Socialism in Kenya and Tanzania*, edited by Joel D. Barkan, 47–74. Boulder, CO: Lynne Rienner Publishers.

Chehabi, H. E., and Juan J. Linz, eds. 1998. *Sultanistic Regimes*. Baltimore, MD: The Johns Hopkins University Press.

Clark, John F. 2006. "Armed Arbiters: When Does the Military Step into the Electoral Arena." In *Electoral Authoritarianism: The Dynamics of Unfree Competition*, edited by Andreas Schedler, 177–202. Boulder, CO: Lynne Rienner Publishers.

Coleman, James S., and Carl G. Rosberg. 1970. *Political Parties and National Integration in Tropical Africa*. Berkeley, CA: University of California Press.

Collier, David. 2011. "Understanding Process Tracing." *PS: Political Science and Politics* 44 (4):823–830.

Collier, David, and Robert Adcock. 1999. "Democracy an Dichotomies: A Pragmatic Approach to Choices about Concepts." *Annual Review of Political Science* 2:537–365.

Collier, David, and Steven Levitsky. 1997. "Democracy with Adjectives: Conceptual Innovation in Comparative Research." *World Politics* 49 (3):430–451.

Collier, Ruth B. 1982. *Regimes in Tropical Africa: Changing Forms of Supremacy, 1945–1975*. Berkeley, CA: University of California Press.

Collier, Ruth B., and David Collier. 2002. *Shaping the Political Arena: Critical Junctures, the Labor Movement, and Regime Dynamics in Latin America*. Notre Dame, IN: University of Notre Dame Press.

Conroy-Krutz, Jeffrey. 2013. "Information and Ethnic Politics in Africa." *British Journal of Political Science* 43 (2):345–373.

Cooksey, Brian, David Court, and Ben Makau. 1994. "Education for Self-Reliance and Harambee." In *Beyond Capitalism vs. Socialism in Kenya and Tanzania*, edited by Joel D. Barkan, 201–234. Boulder, CO: Lynne Rienner Publishers.

Cornell, Agnes. 2013. "Does Regime Type Matter for the Impact of Democracy Aid on Democracy?" *Democratization* 20 (4):642–667.

Costello, Matthew J. 1996. "Administration Triumphs over Politics: The Transformation of the Tanzanian State." *African Studies Review* 39 (1):123–148.

Coulson, Andrew. 1982. *Tanzania: A Political Economy*. New York, NY: Oxford University Press.

Cox, Gary W. 2009. "Authoritarian Elections and Leadership Succession." American Political Science Association Annual Meeting, Toronto.

Cox, Michael G., John Ikenberry, and Takashi Inoguchi, eds. 2000. *American Democracy Promotion: Impulses, Strategies, and Impacts*. Oxford: Oxford University Press.

Crawford, Gordon. 1997. "Foreign Aid and Political Conditionality: Issues in Effectiveness and Consistency." *Democratization* 4 (3):69–108.

Croke, Kevin. 2016. "Tools of Single Party Hegemony in Tanzania: Evidence from Surveys and Survey Experiments." *Democratization*:1–24.

Crook, Richard C. 1989. "Patrimonialism, Administrative Effects and Economic Development in Côte d'Ivoire." *African Affairs* 88 (351):202–228.

Cumming, Gordon. 2001. *Aid to Africa: French and British Policies from the Cold War to the New Millennium*. New York, NY: Routledge.

Dagher, Jihad, Marshall Mills, Lorraine Ocampos, and Samuele Rosa. 2009. *Togo: Selected Issues*. Washington, DC: International Monetary Fund.

Dahl, Robert. 1971. *Polyarchy*. New Haven, CT: Yale University Press.

Darden, Keith. 2008. "The Integrity of Corrupt States: Graft as an Informal State Institution." *Politics & Society* 36 (1):35–60.

De Mesquita, Bruce Bueno, Alastair Smith, Randolph M. Siverson, and James D. Morrow. 2005. *The Logic of Political Survival*. Cambridge, MA: MIT Press.

Decalo, Samuel. 1987. *Historical Dictionary of Togo*. Metuchen, NJ: The Scarecrow Press.

1998. *The Stable Minority: Civilian Rule in Africa, 1960–1990*. Gainesville, FL: FAP Books.

DeLancey, Mark D. 1989. *Cameroon: Dependence and Independence*. Boulder, CO: Westview Press.

DeLancey, Mark D., Rebecca Neh Mbuh, and Mark W. DeLancey. 2010. *Historical Dictionary of the Republic of Cameroon*. Lanham, MD: Scarecrow Press.

DeLancey, Virginia. 1986. "Agricultural Productivity in Cameroon." In *The Political Economy of Cameroon*, edited by Michael G. Schatzberg and William I. Zartman, 133–160. New York, NY: Praeger.

Diamond, Larry J. 2002. "Thinking about Hybrid Regimes." *Journal of Democracy* 13 (2):21–35.

Diklitch, Susan. 2002. "Failed Democratic Transition in Cameroon: A Human Rights Explanation." *Human Rights Quarterly* 24 (1):152–176.

Donno, Daniela. 2013a. *Defending Democratic Norms: International Actors and the Politics of Misconduct*. New York, NY: Oxford University Press.

2013b. "Elections and Democratization in Authoritarian Regimes." *American Journal of Political Science* 57 (3):703–716.

Dunning, Thad. 2004. "Conditioning the Effects of Aid: Cold War Politics, Donor Credibility, and Democracy in Africa." *International Organization* 58 (2):409–423.

Eifert, Benn, Edward Miguel, and Daniel Posner. 2010. "Political Competition and Ethnic Identification in Africa." *American Journal of Political Science* 54 (2):494–510.

Eko, Lyombe. 2004. "Hear All Evil, Rail Against All Evil: Le Messager and the Journalism of Resistance in Cameroon." In *The Leadership Challenge in Africa: Cameroon under Paul Biya*, edited by John Mukum Mbaku and Joseph Takougang, 123–152. Trenton, NJ: Africa World Press.

Elischer, Sebastian. 2013. *Political Parties in Africa: Ethnicity and Party Formation*. New York, NY: Cambridge University Press.

Ellis, Stephen. 1993. "Rumour and Power in Togo." *Africa* 63 (4):462–476.

Elman, Colin. 2005. "Explanatory Typologies in Qualitative Studies of International Politics." *International Organization* 59 (2):293–326.

Emmanuel, Nikolas G. 2010. "Undermining Cooperation: Donor-Patrons and the Failure of Political Conditionality." *Democratization* 17 (5):856–877.

2013. "'With a Friend like this ...': Shielding Cameroon from Democratization." *Journal of Asian and African Studies* 48 (2):145–160.

Fatton, Robert. 1986. "Clientelism and Patronage in Senegal." *African Studies Review* 29 (4):61–78.

Ferree, Karen E. 2010. "The Social Origins of Electoral Volatility in Africa." *British Journal of Political Science* 40 (4):759–779.

Finkel, Steven E., Aníbal Pérez-Liñán, and Mitchell A. Seligson. 2007. "The Effects of U.S. Foreign Assistance on Democracy Building, 1990–2003." *World Politics* 59 (3):404–439.

Fjeldstad, Odd-Helge, and Ole Therkildsen. 2008. "Mass Taxation and State-Society Relations in East Africa." In *Taxation and State Building in Developing Countries*, edited by Odd-Helge Fjeldstad and Mick Moore, 114–134. Cambridge: Cambridge University Press.

Foeken, Dick, and Tom Dietz. 2000. "Of Ethnicity, Manipulation, and Observation: the 1992 and 1997 Elections in Kenya." In *Election Observation and Democratization in Africa*, edited by Jon Abbink and Gerti Hessling, 122–149. New York, NY: Palgrave & Macmillan.

Fonchingong, Tangie Nsoh. 1998. "Multipartyism and Democratization in Cameroon." *Journal of Third World Studies* 15 (2):119–136.

Franda, Marcus F. 1982. *The Seychelles: Unquiet Islands*. Boulder, CO: Westview Press.

Frye, Timothy, Scott Gehlbach, Kyle L. Marquardt, and Ora John Reuter. 2017. "Is Putin's Popularity Real?" *Post-Soviet Affairs* 33 (1):1–15.

Galvan, Dennis. 2001. "Political Turnover and Social Change in Senegal." *Journal of Democracy* 12 (13):51–62.

Gandhi, Jennifer. 2008. *Political Institutions under Dictatorship*. New York, NY: Cambridge University Press.

Gandhi, Jennifer, and Adam Przeworski. 2007. "Authoritarian Institutions and the Survival of Autocrats." *Comparative Political Studies* 40 (11):1279–1301.

Gandhi, Jennifer, and Ellen Lust-Okar. 2009. "Elections under Authoritarianism." *Annual Review of Political Science* 12:403–422.

Gardinier, David E. 1997. "Gabon: Limited Reform and Regime Survival." In *Political Reform in Francophone Africa*, edited by John F. Clark and David E. Gardinier, 145–161. Boulder, CO: Westview Press.

Gasiorwoski, Mark J. 1995. "Economic Crisis and Political Regime Change: An Event History Analysis." *The American Political Science Review* 89 (4):882–892.

Geddes, Barbara. 1999. "Authoritarian Breakdown: Empirical Test of a Game Theoretic Argument." Annual Meeting of the American Political Science Association, Atlanta, GA.

2006. "Why Parties and Elections in Authoritarian Regimes." American Political Science Association Annual Meeting, Seattle, WA.

Gehlbach, Scott, and Philip Keefer. 2011. "Investment without Democracy: Ruling-Party Institutionalization and Credible Commitment in Autocracies." *Journal of Comparative Economics* 39 (2):123–139.

George, Alexander L., and Andrew Bennett. 2005. *Case Studies and Theory Development in the Social Sciences*. Cambridge, MA: MIT Press.

Gerring, John. 2012. *Social Science Methodology: A Unified Framework*. New York, NY: Cambridge University Press.

Gerring, John, and Jason Seawright. 2008. "Case Selection Techniques in Case Study Research: A Menu of Qualitative and Quantitative Options." *Political Research Quarterly* 61 (2):294–308.

Gertzel, Cherry. 1970. *The Politics of Independent Kenya 1963–68*. Evanston, IL: Northwestern University Press.

Giliomee, Hermann, and Charles Simkins. 1999. *The Awkward Embrace: One-Party Domination and Democracy in Industrialising Countries*. Amsterdam: Overseas Publishing Company.

Glickman, Harvey, ed. 1992. *Political Leaders of Contemporary Africa South of the Sahara: A Biographical Dictionary*. Westport, CT: Greenword Publishing Group.

Goertz, Gary. 2006. *Social Science Concepts: A User's Guide*. Princeton, NJ: Princeton University Press.

Goertz, Gary, and James Mahoney. 2012. *A Tale of Two Cultures: Qualitative and Quantitative Research in the Social Sciences*. Princeton, NJ: Princeton University Press.

Graham, Shirley. 1975. *Julius K. Nyerere: Teacher of Africa*. New York, NY: Julian Messner.

Greene, Kenneth F. 2007. *Why Dominant Parties Lose Mexico's Democratization in Comparative Perspective*. New York, NY: Cambridge University Press.

2010. "The Political Economy of Authoritarian Single-Party Dominance." *Comparative Political Studies* 43 (7):807–834.

Gregory, Shaun. 2000. "The French Military in Africa: Past and Present." *African Affairs* 99 (396):435–448.

Gros, Jean-Germain. 1995. "The Hard Lessons of Cameroon." *Journal of Democracy* 6 (3):112–127.

Gryzmala-Busse, Anna. 2002. *Redeeming the Communist Past: The Regeneration of Communist Parties in East Central Europe*. New York, NY: Cambridge University Press.

2008. "Beyond Clientelism: Incumbent State Captures and State Formation." *Comparative Political Studies* 41 (4/5):638–673.

Gunther, Richard, and Larry Diamond. 2003. "Species of Political Parties: A New Typology." *Party Politics* 9 (2):167–199.

Hadenius, Axel, and Jan Teorell. 2007. "Pathways from Authoritarianism." *Journal of Democracy* 18 (1):143–157.

Hafner-Burton, Emilie M. 2008. "Sticks and Stones: Naming and Shaming the Human Rights Enforcement Problem." *International Organization* 62 (4):689–716.

Hafner-Burton, Emilie M., Susan D. Hyde, and Ryan S. Jablonski. 2014. "When Do Governments Resort to Election Violence?" *British Journal of Political Science* 44 (1):149–179.

Haggard, Stephan, and Robert R. Kaufman. 1995. *The Political Economy of Democratic Transitions*. Princeton, NJ: Princeton University Press.

Hanson, Jonathan K., and Rachel Sigman. 2013. "Leviathan's Latent Dimensions: Measuring State Capacity for Comparative Political Research." American Political Science Association Annual Meeting. Chicago, IL.

Harbeson, John. 1973. *Nation-Building in Kenya: The Role of Land Reform.* Evanston, IL: Northwestern University Press.

Harsch, Ernest. 1998. "Burkina Faso in the Winds of Liberalisation." *Review of African Political Economy* 25 (78):625–641.

Hartlyn, Jonathan, and Jennifer L. McCoy. 2006. "Observer Paradoxes: How to Assess Electoral Manipulation." In *Electoral Authoritarianism: The Dynamics of Unfree Competition*, edited by Andreas Schedler, 58–78. Boulder, CO: Lynne Rienner.

Hatch, John. 1976. *Two African Statesmen: Kaunda of Zambia and Nyerere of Tanzania.* London: Secker and Warburg.

Hazan, Reuven Y., and Gideon Rahat. 2010. *Democracy within Parties: Candidate Selection Methods and their Political Consequences.* New York, NY: Oxford University Press.

Heilbrunn, John R. 1993. "Social Origins of National Conferences in Benin and Togo." *Journal of Modern African Studies* 31 (2):277–299.

  1997. "Togo: The National Conference and Stalled Reform." In *Political Reform in Francophone Africa*, edited by John F. Clark and Janet Garvey, 225–245. Boulder, CO: Westview Press.

Heilman, Bruce E., and Paul J. Kaiser. 2002. "Religion, Identity and Politics in Tanzania." *Third World Quarterly* 23 (4):691–709.

Hempstone, Smith. 1997. *Rogue Ambassador: An African Memoir.* Sewanee, TN: University of the South Press.

Herbst, Jeffrey. 2000. *States and State Power in Africa: Comparative Lessons in Authority and Control.* Princeton, NJ: Princeton University Press.

Hermet, Guy, Alain Rouquie, and Richard Rose, eds. 1978. *Elections without Choice.* New York, NY: Wiley.

Hicken, Allen, and Erik Martinez Kuhonta. 2011. "Shadows from the Past: Party System Institutionalization in Asia." *Comparative Political Studies* 44 (5):572–597.

Hodgkin, Thomas Lionel. 1961. *African Political Parties: An Introductory Guide.* Harmondsworth: Penguin.

Hoffman, Barak D., and James D. Long. 2013. "Parties, Ethnicity, and Voting in African Elections." *Comparative Politics* 45 (2):127–146.

Hornsby, Charles. 2012. *Kenya: A History since Independence.* New York, NY: I. B. Tauris.

Howard, Marc M., and Philip G. Roessler. 2006. "Liberalizing Electoral Outcomes in Competitive Authoritarian Regimes." *American Journal of Political Science* 50 (2):365–381.

Human Rights Watch (HRW). 2002. *Kenya's Unfinished Democracy: A Human Rights Agenda for the New Government.* Washington, DC: Human Rights Watch.

Huntington, Samuel P. 1968. *Political Order in Changing Societies.* New Haven, CT: Yale University Press.

  1991. *The Third Wave: Democratization in the Late Twentieth Century,* Norman, OK: University of Oklahoma Press.

Huntington, Samuel P., and Clement Henry Moore. 1970. *Authoritarian Politics in Modern Society: The Dynamics of Established One-Party Systems*. New York, NY: Basic Books.

Hyde, Susan D. 2011. *The Pseudo-Democrat's Dilemma: Why Election Observation Became an International Norm*. Ithaca, NY: Cornell University Press.

Hyde, Susan D., and Nikolay Marinov. 2012. "Which Elections Can Be Lost?" *Political Analysis* 20 (2):191–201.

Hyden, Goran. 1980. *Beyond Ujamaa in Tanzania: Underdevelopment and an Uncaptured Peasantry*. Berkeley, CA: University of California Press.

  1999. "Top-Down Democratization in Tanzania." *Journal of Democracy* 10 (4):142–155.

Hyden, Goran, and Colin Leys. 1972. "Elections and Politics in Single-Party Systems: The Case of Kenya and Tanzania." *British Journal of Political Science* 2 (4):389–420.

Iliffe, John. 1969. "The Age of Improvement and Differentiation (1907–45)." In *A History of Tanzania*, edited by Isaria N. Kimambo and Anrew J. Temu, 123–161. Nairobi: East African Publishing House.

  1973. *Modern Tanzanians: A Volume of Biographies*. Nairobi: East African Publishing House.

Ingle, Clyde R. 1972. *From Village to State in Tanzania: The Politics of Rural Development*. Ithaca, NY: Cornell University Press.

International Crisis Group (ICG). 2010. *Cameroon: The Dangers of a Fracturing Regime*. Brussels: International Crisis Group.

Isaacman, Allen F., and Barbara Isaacman. 1983. *Mozambique: From Colonialism to Revolution, 1900–1982*. Boulder, CO: Westview Press.

Ishiyama, John T. 1997. "The Sickle or the Rose? Previous Regime Types and the Evolution of the Ex-Communist Parties in Post-Communist Politics." *Comparative Political Studies* 30 (3):299–330.

Ishiyama, John T., and John Hames Quinn. 2006. "African Phoenix? Explaining the Performance of the Formerly Dominant Parties in Africa." *Party Politics* 12 (3):317–340.

Jackson, Robert, and Carl Rosberg. 1982. *Personal Rule in Black Africa: Prince, Autocrat, Prophet, Tyrant*. Berkeley, CA: University of California Press.

Jarvik, Laurence. 2007. "NGOs: A New Class in International Relations." *Orbis* 51 (2):217–238.

Johnson, Willard R. 1970. *The Cameroon Federation: Political Integration in a Fragmented Society*. Princeton, NJ: Princeton University Press.

Joseph, Richard. 1977. *Radical Nationalism in Cameroun: Social Origins of the UPC Rebellion*. Oxford: Oxford University Press.

  ed. 1978. *Gaullist Africa: Cameroon under Ahmadu Ahidjo*. Enugu: Fourth Dimension Publishing.

Kaiser, Paul J. 1996. "Structural Adjustment and the Fragile Nation: The Demise of Social Unity in Tanzania." *The Journal of Modern African Studies* 34 (2):227–237.

Kalyvas, Stathis N. 1999. "The Decay and Breakdown of Communist One-Party Systems." *Annual Review of Political Science* 2:323–343.

Kamga, Gerard Emmanuel Kamdem. 2015. "The Origin and Development of Emergency Regimes in Cameroon." *Fundamina: A Journal of Legal History* 21 (2):289–312.

Kanyinga, Karuti. 2003. "Limitations of Political Liberalization: Parties and Electoral Politics in Kenya, 1992–2002." In *The Politics of Transition in Kenya: From KANU to NARC*, edited by Walter O. Oyugi, Peter Wanyande and C. Odhiambo-Mbai, 96–127. Nairobi: Heinrich Boll Foundation.

Karl, Terry Lynn. 1990. "Dilemmas of Democratization in Latin America." *Comparative Politics* 23 (1):1–21.

Kaya, Ruchan, and Michael Bernhard. 2013. "Are Elections Mechanisms of Authoritarian Stability or Democratization? Evidence from Postcommunist Eurasia." *Perspectives on Politics* 11 (3):734–752.

Keefer, Philip. 2007. "Clientelism, Credibility, and the Policy Choices of Young Democracies." *American Journal of Political Science* 51 (4):804–821.

Kelley, Judith G. 2012a. "International Influences on Elections in New Multiparty States." *Annual Review of Political Science* 15:203–220.

2012b. *Monitoring Democracy: When International Observation Works, and Why it Often Fails*. Princeton, NJ: Princeton University Press.

King, Gary, Robert O. Keohane, and Sidney Verba. 1994. *Designing Social Inquiry: Scientific Inference in Qualitative Methodology*. Princeton, NJ: Princeton University Press.

Kitschelt, Herbert. 1994. *The Transformation of European Social Democracy*. New York, NY: Cambridge University Press.

2000. "Linkages between Citizens and Politicians in Democratic Politics." *Comparative Political Studies* 33 (6/7):845–879.

Kitschelt, Herbert, and Matthew Singer. 2015. "Linkage Strategies of Authoritarian Legacy Parties under Conditions of Democratic Party Competition." Paper presented at Life After Dictatorship: Authoritarian Successor Parties Worldwide Conference, University of Notre Dame, IN.

Kitschelt, Herbert, Zdenka Mansfeldova, Radoslaw Markowski, and Gábor Tóka. 1999. *Post-Communist Party Systems: Competition, Representation, and Inter-Party Cooperation*. New York, NY: Cambridge University Press.

Knack, Stephen. 2004. "Does Foreign Aid Promote Democracy?" *International Studies Quarterly* 48 (1):251–266.

Kofele-Kale, Ndiva, ed. 1980. *An African Experiment in Nation Building: The Bilingual Cameroon Republic since Reunification*. Boulder, CO: Westview Press.

1986. "Ethnicity, Regionalism, and Political Power: A Post-Mortem of Ahidjo's Cameroon." In *The Political Economy of Cameroon*, edited by Michael G. Schatzberg and William I. Zartman, 53–82. New York, NY: Praeger.

Konings, Piet. 1996. "The Post-Colonial State and Economic and Political Reforms in Cameroon." In *Liberalization in the Developing World: Institutional and Economic Change in Latin America, Africa, and Asia*, edited by Alex Fernandez Jiberto and Andre Mommen, 244–265. New York, NY: Routledge.

2003. "Privatisation and Ethno-Regional Protest in Cameroon." *African Spectrum* 38 (1):5–26.

Konings, Piet, and Francis Nyamnjoh. 2004. "President Paul Biya and the "Anglophone Problem" in Cameroon." In *The Leadership Challenge in Africa: Cameroon under Paul Biya*, edited by John Mukum Mbaku and Joseph Takougang, 191–234. Trenton, NJ: Africa World Press.

Kramon, Eric, and Daniel N. Posner. 2013. "Who Benefits from Distributive Politics? How the Outcomes One Studies Affect the Answers One Gets." *Perspectives on Politics* 11 (2):461–474.

Krieger, Milton. 2008. *Cameroon's Social Democratic Front: Its History & Prospects as an Opposition Political Party (1990–2011)*. Bamenda: Langaa RPCIG.

Kuenzi, Michelle, and Gina Lambright. 2001. "Party System Institutionalization in 30 African Countries." *Party Politics* 7 (4):437–468.

2005. "Party Systems and Democratic Consolidation in Africa's Electoral Regimes." *Party Politics* 11 (4):423–446.

Kuran, Timur. 1997. *Private Truths, Public Lies: The Social Consequences of Preference Falsification*. Cambridge, MA: Harvard University Press.

Lange, Matthew K. 1995. "British Colonial Legacies and Political Development." *World Development* 32 (6):905–922.

Le Vine, Victor T. 1964. *The Cameroons: From Mandate to Independence*. Berkeley, CA: The University of California Press.

1971. *The Cameroon Federal Republic*. Ithaca, NY: Cornell University Press.

1986. "Leadership and Regime Changes in Perspective." In *The Political Economy of Cameroon*, edited by Michael G. Schatzberg and William I. Zartman, 20–52. New York, NY: Praeger.

LeBas, Adrienne. 2011. *From Protest to Parties: Party-Building and Democratization in Africa*. Oxford: Oxford University Press.

Lebovic, James H., and Erik Voeten. 2009. "The Cost of Shame: International Organizations and Foreign Aid in the Punishment of Human Rights Violators." *Journal of Peace Research* 46 (1):79–97.

Lehoucq, Fabrice. 2003. "Electoral Fraud: Causes, Types, and Consequences." *Annual Review of Political Science* 6:233–256.

Leo, Christopher. 1981. "Who Benefited from the Million-Acre Scheme? Toward a Class Analysis of Kenya's Transition to Independence." *Canadian Journal of African Studies* 15 (2):201–222.

Levitsky, Steven. 1998. "Institutionalization and Peronism The Concept, the Case and the Case for Unpacking the Concept." *Party Politics* 4 (1):77–92.

Levitsky, Steven, and Lucan Way. 2010. *Competitive Authoritarianism: Hybrid Regimes After the Cold War*. New York, NY: Cambridge University Press.

2012. "Beyond Patronage: Violent Struggle, Ruling Party Cohesion, and Authoritarian Durability." *Perspectives on Politics* 10 (4):869–899.

Lieberman, Evan S. 2001. "Causal Inference in Historical-Institutional Analysis." *Comparative Political Studies* 34 (9):1011–1035.

Lindberg, Staffan I. 2006a. *Democracy and Elections in Africa*. Baltimore, MD: Johns Hopkins University Press.

2006b. "Tragic Protest: Why do Opposition Parties Boycott Elections?" In *Electoral Authoritarianism: The Dynamics of Unfree Competition*, edited by Andreas Schedler, 149–163. Boulder, CO: Lynne Rienner Publishers.

ed. 2009a. *Democratization by Elections: a New Mode of Transition*. Baltimore, MD: Johns Hopkins University Press.

2009b. "The Power of Elections in Africa Revisited." In *Democratization by Elections: A New Mode of Transition*, edited by Staffan I Lindberg, 25–46. Baltimore, MD: Johns Hopkins University Press.

Linz, Juan J. 2000. *Totalitarian and Authoritarian Regimes*. Boulder, CO: Lynne Rienner.

Linz, Juan J., and Alfred C. Stepan. 1996. *Problems of Democratic Transition and Consolidation: Southern Europe, South America, and Post-Communist Europe*. Baltimore, MD: Johns Hopkins University Press.

Lofchie, Michael. 1994. "The Politics of Agricultural Policy." In *Beyond Capitalism vs. Socialism in Kenya & Tanzania*, edited by Joel D. Barkan, 129–174. Boulder, CO: Lynne Rienner Publishers.

Lust-Okar, Ellen. 2004. "Divided They Rule: The Management and Manipulation of Political Opposition." *Comparative Politics* 36 (2):159–179.

2009. "Legislative Elections in Hegemonic Authoritarian Regimes: Competitive Clientelism and Resistance to Democratization." In *Democratization by Elections: A New Mode of Transition?*, edited by Staffan I Lindberg, 226–245. Baltimore, MD: The Johns Hopkins University Press.

Lynch, Gabrielle. 2011. *I Say to You: Ethnic Politics and the Kalenjin in Kenya*. Chicago, IL: The University of Chicago Press.

Lynch, Gabrielle, and Gordon Crawford. 2011. "Democratization in Africa 1990–2010: An Assessment." *Democratization* 18 (2):275–310.

Magaloni, Beatriz. 2006. *Voting for Autocracy: Hegemonic Party Survival and Its Demise in Mexico*. New York, NY: Cambridge University Press.

2008. "Credible Power-Sharing and the Longevity of Authoritarian Rule." *Comparative Political Studies* 41 (4–5):715–741.

Mahoney, James. 2000. "Path Dependence in Historical Sociology." *Theory and Society* 29 (4):507–548.

Mahoney, James, and Dietrich Rueschemeyer, eds. 2003. *Comparative Historical Analysis in the Social Sciences*. New York, NY: Cambridge University Press.

Mainwaring, Scott, and Timothy Scully. 1995. *Building Democratic Institutions: Party Systems in Latin America*. Stanford: Stanford University Press.

Malesky, Edmund, and Paul Schuler. 2011. "The Single-Party Dictator's Dilemma: Information in Elections without Opposition." *Legislative Studies Quarterly* 36 (4):491–530.

Manion, Melanie. 2004. *Corruption by Design: Building Clean Government in Mainland China and Hong Kong*. Cambridge, MA: Harvard University Press.

Manning, Carrie. 1998. "Constructing Opposition in Mozambique: RENAMO as political party." *Journal of Southern African Studies* 24 (1):161–189.

2005. "Assessing African Party Systems after the Third Wave." *Party Politics* 11 (6):707–727.

2007. "The Mozambican Experience: FRELIMO and RENAMO." In *From Revolutionary Movements to Political Parties: Cases from Latin America and Africa*, edited by Kalowatie Deonandan, David Close and Gary Prevost, 181–210. New York, NY: Palgrave Macmillan.

Maro, Paul S., and Wilfred F. Mlay. 1979. "Decentralization and the Organization of Space in Tanzania." *Africa: Journal of the International African Institute* 49 (3):291–301.

Marshall, Judith. 1990. "Structural Adjustment and Social Policy in Mozambique." *Review of African Political Economy* 17 (47):28–43.

Martin, Guy. 1995. "Continuity and Change in Franco-African Relations." *The Journal of Modern African Studies* 33 (1):1–20.

Mascarenhas, Adolpho. 1979. "After Villagization – What?" In *Towards Socialism in Tanzania*, edited by Bismark U. Mwansasu and Cranford Pratt, 145–168. Toronto: University of Toronto Press.

Mattes, Robert, and Michael Bratton. 2007. "Learning about Democracy in Africa: Awareness, Performance, and Experience." *American Journal of Political Science* 51 (1):192–217.

McCoy, Jennifer L., and Jonathan Hartlyn. 2009. "The Relative Powerlessness of Elections in Latin America." In *Democratization by Elections: A New Mode of Transition*, edited by Staffan I. Lindberg, 47–76. Baltimore, MD: The Johns Hopkins University Press.

McHenry, Dean E. 1994. *Limited Choices: The Political Struggle for Socialism in Tanzania*. Boulder, CO: Lynne Rienner.

Migdal, Joel S. 1988. *Strong Societies and Weak States: State-Society Relations and State Capabilities in the Third World*. Princeton, NJ: Princeton University Press.

Migot-Adholla, S. E. 1984. "Rural Development Policy and Equality." In *Politics and Public Policy in Kenya and Tanzania*, edited by Joel D. Barkan, 199–232. New York, NY: Praeger.

Mikecz, Robert. 2012. "Interviewing Elites: Addressing Methodological Issues." *Qualitative Inquiry* 18 (6):482–493.

Miller, Norman N. 1970. "The Rural African Party: Political Participation in Tanzania." *The American Political Science Review* 64 (2):549–571.

Miti, Katabaro. 1980. "Party and Politics in Tanzania." *Utafiti* 5 (2):187–198.

Mmuya, Max, and Amon Chaligha. 1994. *Political Parties and Democracy in Tanzania*. Dar es Salaam: University of Dar Es Salaam Press.

Molony, Thomas. 2014. *Nyerere: The Early Years*. Suffolk: James Currey.

Moore, Barrington Jr. 1966. *Social Origins of Dictatorship and Democracy: Lord and Peasant in the Making of the Modern World*. Boston, MA: Beacon Press.

Morgenthau, Ruth Schachter. 1967. *Political Parties in French-Speaking West Africa*. Oxford: Clarendon Press.

Morse, Yonatan L. 2012. "The Era of Electoral Authoritarianism." *World Politics* 64 (01):161–198.

——— 2014. "Party Matters: The Institutional Origins of Competitive Hegemony in Tanzania." *Democratization* 21 (4):655–667.

Mozaffar, Shaheen, and James R. Scarrit. 2005. "The Puzzle of African Party Systems." *Party Politics* 11 (4):399–421.

Mueller, Susanne. 1984. "Government and Opposition in Kenya, 1966–9." *The Journal of Modern African Studies* 22 (3):399–427.

——— 2011. "Dying to Win: Elections, Political Violence, and Institutional Decay in Kenya." *Journal of Contemporary African Studies* 29 (1):99–117.

Mukandala, Rwekaza S. 2000. "Grassroots Institutions of Governance." In *Governance and Development at the Grassroots in Tanzania*, edited by Rwekaza S. Mukandala and Charles Gasarasi, 6–43. Dar es Salaam: Research and Education for Democracy in Tanzania.

Munck, Gerardo. 2006. "Drawing Boundaries: How to Craft Intermediate Regime Categories." In *Electoral Authoritarianism: The Dynamics of Unfree Competition*, edited by Andreas Schedler, 35–57. Boulder, CO: Lynne Rienner.

Munck, Gerardo, and Jay Verkuilen. 2002. "Conceptualizing and Measuring Democracy: Evaluating Alternative Indices." *Comparative Political Studies* 35 (1):5–34.

Mundt, Robert J. 1997. "Côte d'Ivoire: Continuity and Change in a Semi-Democracy." In *Political Reform in Francophone Africa*, edited by John F. Clark and David E. Gardinier, 182–203. Boulder, CO: Westview Publishers.

Mwakikagile, Godfrey. 2006. *Nyerere and Africa: End of an Era*. London: New Africa Press.

Mwansasu, Bismarck U. 1979. "The Changing role of the Tanganyika African National Union." In *Towards Socialism in Tanzania*, edited by B. U. Mwansasu, 169–192. Toronto: University of Toronto Press.

Mwase, Ngila, and Mary Raphael. 2001. "The 1995 Presidential Elections in Tanzania." *The Round Table: The Commonwealth Journal of International Affairs* 359 (1):245–269.

Ndegwa, Stephen. 1998. "The Incomplete Transition: The Constitutional and Electoral Context in Kenya." *Africa Today* 45 (2):193–211.

2003. "Kenya: Third Time Lucky?" *Journal of Democracy* 14 (3):145–158.

Ndongko, Wilfred A. 1986. "The Political Economy of Development in Cameroon: Relations between the State, Indigenous Business, and Foreign Investors." In *The Political Economy of Cameroon*, edited by Michael G. Schatzberg and William I. Zartman, 33–110. New York, NY: Praeger.

Ngoh, Victor Julius. 2004. "Biya and the Transition to Democracy." In *The Leadership Challenge in Africa: Cameroon under Paul Biya*, edited by John Mukum Mbaku and Joseph Takougang, 427–452. Trenton, NJ: African World Press.

Norris, Pippa, Ferran Martinez i Coma, Allesandro Nai, and Max Gromping. 2016. The Expert Survey of Perceptions of Electoral Integrity, Release 4.5.

Nwajiaku, Kathryn. 1994. "The National Conferences in Benin and Togo Revisited." *The Journal of Modern African Studies* 32 (3):429–447.

Nyamnjoh, Francis, and Michael Rowlands. 1998. "Elite Association and the Politics of Belonging in Cameroon." *Africa* 68 (3):320–337.

O'Donnell, Guillermo, Philippe Schmitter, and Laurence Whitehead, eds. 1986. *Transitions from Authoritarian Rule: Comparative Perspectives*. Baltimore, MD: The Johns Hopkins University Press.

Okumu, John, and Frank Holmquist. 1984. "Party and Party-State Relations." *Politics and Public Policy in Kenya and Tanzania*, edited by Joel D. Barkan, 45–69. New York, NY: Praeger.

Ottaway, Marina. 2003. *Democracy Challenged: The Rise of Semi-Authoritarianism*. Washington, DC: Carnegie Endowment for International Peace.

Page, Scott E. 2006. "Path Dependence." *Quarterly Journal of Political Science* 1 (1):87–115.

Panebianco, Angelo. 1988. *Political Parties: Organization and Power*. New York, NY: Cambridge University Press.

Parsons, Timothy H. 2003. *The 1964 Army Mutinies and the Making of Modern East Africa*. Westport, CT: Praeger.

Pempel, T. J., ed. 1990. *Uncommon Democracies: The One Party Dominant Regimes*. Ithaca, NY: Cornell University Press.

Pepinsky, Thomas. 2014. "The Institutional Turn in Comparative Authoritarianism." *British Journal of Political Science* 44 (3): 631–653.

Pierson, Paul. 2004. *Politics in Time: History, Institutions, and Social Analysis*. Princeton, NJ: Princeton University Press.

Platner, Marc F. 2015. "Is Democracy in Decline?" *Journal of Democracy* 28 (1):5–10.

Posner, Daniel. 2004. "Measuring Ethnic Fractionalization in Africa." *American Journal of Political Science* 48 (4):849–863.

2005. *Institutions and Ethnic Politics in Africa*. New York, NY: Cambridge University Press.

Posner, Daniel, and Daniel J. Young. 2007. "The Institutionalization of Political Power in Africa." *Journal of Democracy* 18 (3):126–140.

Posusney, Marsha Pripstein. 2004. "Enduring Authoritarianism: Middle East Lessons for Comparative Theory." *Comparative Politics* 36 (2):127–138.

Putnam, Robert D. 1994. *Making Democracy Work: Civic Traditions in Modern Italy*. Princeton, NJ: Princeton University Press.

Ragin, Charles. 2008. *Rethinking Social Inquiry: Fuzzy Sets and Beyond*. Chicago, IL: The University of Chicago Press.

Rakner, Lise, and Nicolas van de Walle. 2009. "Opposition Parties and Incumbent Presidents: The New Dynamics of Electoral Competition in Africa." In *Democratization by Elections: A New Mode of Transition*, edited by Staffan I Lindberg, 202–225. Baltimore, MD: The Johns Hopkins University Press.

Randall, Vicky, and Lars Svåsand. 2002a. "Party Institutionalization in New Democracies." *Party Politics* 8 (1):5–29.

2002b. "Political Parties and Democratic Consolidation in Africa." *Democratization* 9 (3):30–52.

Reed, Michael C. 1987. "Gabon: A Neo-Colonial Enclave of Enduring French Interest." *Journal of Modern African Studies* 25 (2):283–320.

Resnick, Danielle. 2012. "Opposition Parties and the Urban Poor in African Democracies." *Comparative Political Studies* 45 (11):1351–1378.

Riedl, Rachel B. 2014. *Authoritarian Origins of Democratic Party Systems in Africa*. New York, NY: Cambridge University Press.

Roberts, Tyson. 2008. "The Legislative Election in Togo, October 2007." *Electoral Studies* 27 (3):558–561.

Roessler, Philip G. 2005. "Donor-Induced Democratization and the Privatization of State Violence in Kenya and Rwanda." *Comparative Politics* 37 (2):207–227.

Roessler, Philip G., and Marc M. Howard. 2009. "Post-Cold War Political Regimes: When Do Elections Matter?" In *Democratization by Elections,* edited by Staffan I. Lindberg, 101–127. Baltimore, MD: Johns Hopkins University Press.

Rose, Richard, and Doh Chull Shin. 2001. "Democratization Backwards: The Problem of Third Wave Democracies." *British Journal of Political Science* 31 (2):331–354.

Rueschemeyer, Dietrich, Evelyne Huber Stephens, and John D. Stephens. 1992. *Capitalist Development and Democracy*. Chicago, IL: University of Chicago Press.

Samoff, Joel. 1974. *Tanzania: Local Politics and the Structure of Power*. Madison, WI: University of Wisconsin Press.

1987. "Single Party Competitive Elections in Tanzania." In *Elections in Independent Africa*, edited by Fred M. Hayward, 148–186. Boulder, CO: Westview Press.

Sanger, Clyde, and John Nottingham. 1964. "The Kenyan General Election of 1963." *The Journal of Modern African Studies* 2 (1):1–40.

Santiso, Carlos, and Augustin Loada. 2003. "Explaining the Unexpected: Electoral Reform and Democratic Governance in Burkina Faso." *Journal of Modern African Studies* 41 (3):395–419.

Sartori, Giovanni. 1976. *Parties and Party Systems: A Framework for Analysis*. New York, NY: Cambridge University Press.

Schaffer, Frederic Charles, ed. 2007. *Elections for Sale: The Causes and Consequences of Vote Buying*. Boulder, CO: Lynne Rienner.

Schedler, Andreas, ed. 2006a. *Electoral Authoritarianism: The Dynamics of Unfree Competition*. Boulder, CO: Lynne Rienner Publishers, Inc.

2006b. "The Logic of Electoral Authoritarianism." In *Electoral Authoritarianism: The Dynamics of Unfree Competition*, edited by Andreas Schedler, 2–34. Boulder: Lynne Rienner.

2013. *The Politics of Uncertainty: Sustaining and Subverting Electoral Authoritarianism*. Oxford: Oxford University Press.

Schneider, Carsten Q., and Claudius Wagemann. 2012. *Set-Theoretic Methods for the Social Sciences: A Guide to Qualitative Comparative Analysis*. New York, NY: Cambridge University Press.

Schraeder, Peter, ed. 2002. *Exporting Democracy: Rhetoric vs. Reality*. Boulder, CO: Lynne Rienner Publishers.

Seeberg, Merete Bach. 2014. "State Capacity and the Paradox of Authoritarian Elections." *Democratization* 21 (7):1265–1285.

Seely, Jennifer C. 2009. *The Legacies of Transition Government in Africa: The Cases of Benin and Togo*. New York, NY: Palgrave Macmillan.

Shehim, Kassim, and James Searing. 1980. "Djibouti and the Question of Afar Nationalism." *African Affairs* 19 (315):209–226.

Shinn, David H., and Joshua Eisenman. 2012. *China and Africa: A Century of Engagements*. Philadelphia, PA: University of Pennsylvania.

Slater, Dan. 2010. *Ordering Power: Contentious Politics and Authoritarian Leviathans in Southeast Asia*. New York, NY: Cambridge University Press.

Smith, Benjamin. 2005. "Life of the Party." *World Politics* 57:421–451.

Smith, Edget William. 1973. *Nyerere of Tanzania*. London: Littlehampton Book Services Ltd.

Smith, Ian. 2013. "Election Boycotts and Hybrid Regime Survival." *Comparative Political Studies* 20 (10):1–23.

Snyder, Richard. 2006. "Beyond Electoral Authoritarianism: The Spectrum of Nondemocratic Regimes." In *Electoral Authoritarianism: The Dynamics of Unfree Competition*, edited by Andreas Schedler, 292–310. Boulder, CO: Lynne Rienner.

Socpa, Antoin. 2006. "Bailleurs Autochtones et Locataires Allogenes: Enjeu Foncier et Participation Politique au Cameroun." *African Studies Review* 49 (2):45–67.

Solinger, Dorothy J. 2001. "Ending One-Party Dominance: Korea, Taiwan, Mexico." *Journal of Democracy* 12 (1):30–42.

Solomon, Peter. 2007. "Courts and Judges in Authoritarian Regimes." *World Politics* 60 (1):122–145.

Steeves, Jeffrey. 2006. "Presidential Succession in Kenya: The Transition from Moi to Kibaki." *Commonwealth & Comparative Politics* 44 (2):211–233.

Stokke, Olav, ed. 1995. *Aid and Political Conditionality*. New York, NY: Frank Cass.

Stren, Richard, Mohamed Halfani, and Joyce Malombe. 1994. "Coping with Urbanization and Urban Policy." In *Beyond Capitalism vs. Socialism in Kenya and Tanzania*, edited by Joel D. Barkan, 175–200. Boulder, CO: Lynne Rienner Publishers.

Svolik, Milan W. 2012. *The Politics of Authoritarian Rule*. New York, NY: Cambridge University Press.

Takougang, Joseph. 2004a. "The Demise of Biya's New Deal in Cameroon, 1982–1992." In *The Leadership Challenge in Africa: Cameroon under Paul Biya*, edited by John Mukum Mbaku and Joseph Takougang, 95–122. Trenton, NJ: Africa World Press.

2004b. "The Nature of Politics in Cameroon." In *The Leadership Challenge in Africa: Cameroon's Political Crossroads*, edited by John Mukum Mbaku and Joseph Takougang, 67–94. Trenton, NJ: Africa World Press.

Takougang, Joseph, and Milton Krieger. 1998. *Africa State and Society in the 1990s: Cameroon's Political Crossroads*. Boulder, CO: Westview Press.

Tansey, Oisin. 2007. "Process Tracing and Elite Interviewing: A Case for Non-Probability Sampling." *PS: Political Science and Politics* 40 (4):765–772.

Temu, Andrew J. 1969. "The Rise and Triumph of Nationalism." In *A History of Tanzania*, edited by Isaria N. Kimambo and Andrew J. Temu, 189–213. Nairobi: East African Publishing House.

Temu, Andrew J., and Jean M. Due. 2000. "The Business Environment in Tanzania after Socialism: Challenges of Reforming Banks, Parastatals, Taxation and the Civil Service." *The Journal of Modern African Studies* 38 (4):683–712.

Throup, David. 2003. The Kenya General Election: December 27, 2002. *Africa Notes*. Washington, DC: Center for Strategic and International Studies.

Throup, David, and Charles Hornsby. 1998. *Multi-Party Politics in Kenya: Kenyatta and Moi and the Triumph of the System in the 1992 Election*. Bloomington, IN: Indiana University Press.

Tordoff, William. 1967. "Tanzania: Democracy and the One Party State." *Government and Opposition* 2 (4):599–614.

Toungara, Jeanne Maddox. 2001. "Ethnicity and Political Crisis in Côte d'Ivoire." *Journal of Democracy* 12 (3):63–72.

Tripp, Aili Mari. 1997. *Changing the Rules: The Politics of Liberalization and the Urban Informal Economy in Tanzania*. Berkeley, CA: University of California Press.

2000. "Political Reform in Tanzania: The Struggle for Associational Autonomy." *Comparative Politics* 32 (2):191–214.

2010. *Museveni's Uganda: Paradoxes of Power in a Hybrid Regime*. Boulder, CO: Lynne Rienner Publishers.

van de Walle, Nicolas. 1994. "Neopatrimonialism and Democracy in Africa, With an Illustration from Cameroon." In *Economic Change and Political Liberalization in Sub Saharan Africa*, edited by Jennifer A. Widner, 129–157. Baltimore, MD: The Johns Hopkins University Press.

2001. *African Economies and the Politics of Permanent Crisis, 1979–1999*. New York, NY: Cambridge University Press.

2002. "Africa's Range of Regimes." *Journal of Democracy* 13 (2):66–80.

2003. "Presidentialism and Clientelism in Africa's Emerging Party Systems." *The Journal of Modern African Studies* 41 (2):297–321.

2006. "Tipping Games: When do Opposition Parties Coalesce?" In *Electoral Authoritarianism: The Dynamics of Unfree Competition*, edited by Andreas Schedler, 105–127. Boulder, CO: Lynne Rienner.

van Donge, Jan Kees, and Athumani Liviga. 1986a. "In Defence of the Tanzanian Parliament." *Parliamentary Affairs* 39 (2):230–240.

1986b. "Tanzanian Political Culture and the Cabinet." *Journal of Modern African Studies* 24 (4):619–639.

van Evera, Stephen. 1997. *Guide to Methods for Students of Political Science*. Ithaca, NY: Cornell University Press.

Vanderhill, Rachel. 2012. *Promoting Authoritarianism Abroad*. Boulder, CO: Lynne Rienner Publishers.

Vengroff, Richard, and Lucy Creevey. 1997. "Senegal: The Evolution of a Quasi Democracy." In *Political Reform in Francophone Africa*, edited by John F. Clark and David E Gardinier, 204–222. Boulder, CO: Westview Press.

Villalón, Leonardo A. 1999. "Generational Changes, Political Stagnation, and the Evolving Dynamics of Religion and Politics in Senegal." *Africa Today* 46 (3):129–147.

Wahman, Michael. 2013. "Opposition Coalitions and Democratization by Election." *Government and Opposition* 48 (1):3–32.

Waldner, David. 1999. *State Building and Late Development*. Ithaca, NY: Cornell University Press.

2015. "What Makes Process Tracing Good? Causal Mechanisms, Causal Inference, and the Completeness Standard in Comparative Politics." In *Process Tracing: From Metaphor to Analytic Tool*, edited by Andrew Bennett and Jeffrey T. Checkel, 126–152. New York, NY: Cambridge University Press.

Wallerstein, Immanuel. 1966. "The Decline of the Party in Single-Party African States." In *Political Parties and Political Development*, edited by Joseph LaPalombara and Myron Weiner, 201–214. Princeton, NJ: Princeton University Press.

Wantchekon, Leonard. 2003. "Clientelism and Voting Behavior: Evidence from a Field Experiment in Benin." *World Politics* 55 (3):399–422.

Way, Lucan. 2002. "Pluralism by Default in Moldova." *Journal of Democracy* 13 (4):127–141.

Wedeen, Lisa. 1999. *Ambiguities of Domination: Politics, Rhetoric, and Symbols in Contemporary Syria*. Chicago, IL: University of Chicago Press.

Weghorst, Keith R., and Staffan I. Lindberg. 2013. "What Drives the Swing Voter in Africa?" *American Journal of Political Science* 57 (3):717–734.

Widner, Jennifer A. 1992. *The Rise of a Party-State in Kenya: From "Harambee!" to "Nyayo!"*. Berkeley, CA: University of California Press.

   1994. *Economic Change and Political Liberalization in Sub-Saharan Africa*. Baltimore, MD: Johns Hopkins University Press.

Wintrobe, Ronald. 1998. *The Political Economy of Dictatorship*. New York, NY: Cambridge University Press.

Wright, Joseph. 2008. "Do Authoritarian Legislatures Constrain? How Legislatures Affect Economic Growth and Investment." *American Journal of Political Science* 52 (2):322–343.

   2009. "How Foreign Aid Can Foster Democratization in Authoritarian Regimes." *American Journal of Political Science* 53 (3):552–571.

Yates, Douglas A. 1996. *The Rentier State in Africa: Oil Rent Dependency and Neocolonialism in the Republic of Gabon*. Trenton, NJ: Africa World Press.

Young, Crawford. 1994. *The African Colonial State in Comparative Perspective*. New Haven, CT: Yale University Press.

Zakaria, Fareed. 1997. "The Rise of Illiberal Democracy." *Foreign Affairs* 76 (2):22–43.

Zolberg, Aristide R. 1966. *Creating Political Order: The Party-States of West Africa*. Chicago, IL: Rand McNally.

Index

Printed in the USA
CPSIA information can be obtained
at www.ICGtesting.com
LVHW091137111223
766104LV00001B/36